FUNDAMENTALS OF MARKETING

FUNDAMENTALS OF MARKETING

By

Dr Vikas Saraf

Ph.D., M.B.A, FDP-IIM, Indore

Professor & Director,
Vidyasagar Institute of Management, Bhopal.
(Barkatullah University, Bhopal)

Former Joint Director, The Institute of Cost
& Works Accountants of India (ICWAI)

Pawan Thakur

M.C.A, M.A. (Eco.), M.Phil,

Assistant Professor, Department of Computer
Application & Information Technology,
Vidyasagar Institute of Management, Bhopal.
(Barkatullah University, Bhopal)

Secretary SCIT Group of Institutions, Bhopal

(An Imprint of Laxmi Publications (P) Ltd.)

BANGALORE • CHENNAI • COCHIN • GUWAHATI • HYDERABAD
JALANDHAR • KOLKATA • LUCKNOW • MUMBAI • RANCHI
NEW DELHI • BOSTON, USA

FUNDAMENTALS OF MARKETING

Printed and bound in India
Typeset at Excellent Graphics, Delhi
First Edition: 2014
UFM-9731-250-FUND OF MARKETING-SAR
ISBN 978-93-83828-30-2

Printed at : Repro Knowledgecast Limited, Thane
C—

PUBLISHED IN INDIA BY

UNIVERSITY SCIENCE PRESS
(An Imprint of Laxmi Publications Pvt.Ltd.)

113, GOLDEN HOUSE, DARYAGANJ,
NEW DELHI - 110002, INDIA
Telephone : 91-11-4353 2500, 4353 2501
Fax : 91-11-2325 2572, 4353 2528
www.laxmipublications.com info@laxmipublications.com

Branches

© Bangalore	080-26 75 69 30
© Chennai	044-24 34 47 26
© Cochin	0484-237 70 04, 405 13 03
© Guwahati	0361-254 36 69, 251 38 81
© Hyderabad	040-27 55 53 83, 27 55 53 93
© Jalandhar	0181-222 12 72
© Kolkata	033-22 27 43 84
© Lucknow	0522-220 99 16
© Mumbai	022-24 91 54 15, 24 92 78 69
© Ranchi	0651-220 44 64

THIS BOOK IS DEDICATED TO OUR PARENTS, MRS. SARIKA SARAF, MRS. SIKMA THAKUR, KU. VEDIKA SARAF, MASTER VIDEH SARAF AND MASTER SARTHAK THAKUR.

Contents

Chapters *Pages*

UNIT–I (1-60)

1. Marketing: Nature, Scope and Importance **3–16**

1.1 Introduction ... 3
1.2 Evolution of Marketing ... 4
1.3 Meaning and Definition of Marketing ... 5
1.4 Features of Marketing ... 6
1.5 Marketing Management ... 6
1.6 Functions of Marketing Management ... 7
1.7 Nature of Marketing ... 8
1.8 The Marketing Concept ... 9
1.9 Difference between Marketing and Selling ... 11
1.10 Marketing Myopia ... 12
1.11 Scope/Functions of Marketing ... 12
1.12 Utilities of Marketing ... 13
1.13 Types of Marketing ... 14
1.14 Importance of Marketing ... 15
1.15 Role of Marketing in an Organization ... 16

2. Marketing Environment **17–24**

2.1 Introduction ... 17
2.2 Meaning and Definition ... 17
2.3 Marketing Environment ... 18
2.4 Features of Business Environment ... 20
2.5 Environmental Scanning ... 20
2.6 Importance of Business Environment ... 23

3. Marketing Mix and Marketing Plan **25–34**

3.1 Introduction ... 25
3.2 Meaning and Definitions of Marketing Mix ... 26
3.3 Features of Marketing Mix ... 26
3.4 Components of Marketing Mix ... 27
3.5 4cs of Marketing Mix ... 30
3.6 Introduction to Marketing Planning ... 31
3.7 Meaning and Definition of Marketing Planning ... 31
3.8 Elements of Marketing Plan ... 32
3.9 Process of Marketing Plan ... 32
3.10 Importance of Marketing Plan ... 33

4. Market Segmentation, Targeting and Positioning **35–45**

4.1 Introduction ... 35
4.2 Meaning and Definition of Market Segmentation ... 36

Chapters *Pages*

4.3	Market Segmentation Objectives	...	37
4.4	Bases of Market Segmentation	...	37
4.5	Levels of Market Segmentation	...	39
4.6	Importance of Market Segmentation	...	40
4.7	Market Targeting	...	40
4.8	Meaning and Definition of Market Targeting	...	41
4.9	Selection of Target Segments	...	41
4.10	Targeting Strategies	...	42
4.11	Positioning	...	42
4.12	Meaning and Definition of Positioning	...	43
4.13	Steps to Product Positioning	...	43
4.14	Positioning Strategies	...	44
5.	**Consumer Behaviour**		**46–60**
5.1	Introduction	...	46
5.2	Meaning And Definition of Consumer Behaviour	...	47
5.3	Characteristics of Consumer Behaviour	...	47
5.4	Types of Consumer Buying Behaviour	...	48
5.5	Importance of Understanding Consumer Behaviour	...	49
5.6	Determinists of Consumer Behaviour	...	49
5.7	Process of Buying Decisions	...	51
5.8	Cognitive Dissonance	...	52
5.9	Consumer Behaviour Models	...	53

UNIT–II (61-126)

6.	**Product Concepts and Product Life Cycle**		**63–76**
6.1	Introduction	...	63
6.2	Meaning and Definition of Product	...	64
6.3	Product Classification	...	64
6.4	Product Mix	...	66
6.5	Product Line	...	67
6.6	BCG Model	...	68
6.7	Product Life Cycle Concept and Meaning	...	72
6.8	Characteristics of Product Life Cycle	...	73
6.9	Stages of Product Life Cycle	...	73
6.10	Strategies of Product Life Cycle	...	76
7.	**Product Planning, Development and Product Identification**		**77–90**
7.1	Introduction	...	77
7.2	Product Planning Concept and Meaning	...	78
7.3	Objectives/Need/Importance of New Product	...	78
7.4	Product Development	...	79
7.5	Steps Involved in New Product Development (NPD) Process	...	79
7.6	Product Identification: an Introduction	...	82
7.7	Branding	...	83

Chapters *Pages*

7.8 Trademark ... 83
7.9 Distinction between Brand and Trademark ... 83
7.10 Objectives of Branding ... 84
7.11 Essentials of Good Brand ... 85
7.12 Brand Positioning ... 86
7.13 Packaging ... 87
7.14 Levels/Classification of Packaging ... 87
7.15 Objectives of Packaging ... 88
7.16 Functions/Importance of Packaging ... 89

8. Pricing **91–100**

8.1 Introduction ... 91
8.2 Meaning of Price ... 91
8.3 Importance of Pricing ... 92
8.4 Objectives of Pricing ... 92
8.5 Factors Affecting Pricing ... 93
8.6 Methods of Pricing ... 95
8.7 Pricing of New Products ... 98
8.8 New Product Pricing Methods and Strategy ... 98

9. Marketing Communication and Marketing Research **101–120**

9.1 Introduction ... 101
9.2 Meaning and Definition ... 102
9.3 Objective of Marketing Communication ... 102
9.4 Process of Marketing Communication ... 103
9.5 Barriers in Marketing Communication ... 105
9.6 Elements of Marketing Communication Mix ... 107
9.7 Tools of Marketing Communication ... 107
9.8 Integrated Marketing Communication ... 108
9.9 Introduction to Market Research ... 109
9.10 Meaning and Definition of Marketing Research ... 109
9.11 Nature and Scope of Marketing Research ... 110
9.12 Need of Marketing Research ... 111
9.13 Characteristics of Marketing Research ... 111
9.14 The Marketing Research Process ... 112
9.15 Marketing Information System (MIS) ... 115
9.16 Types of Marketing Research ... 117
9.17 Importance of Marketing Research ... 119

10. Promotion Mix **121–126**

10.1 Introduction ... 121
10.2 Meaning and Definition ... 121
10.3 Components of Promotion Mix ... 122
10.4 Factors Governing Promotion Mix ... 124

Chapters *Pages*

UNIT–III (127-204)

11. Advertising **129–145**

11.1 Introduction ... 129
11.2 History of Advertising in India ... 130
11.3 Evolution of Advertising ... 132
11.4 Meaning and Definition ... 132
11.5 Features of Advertising ... 133
11.6 Essentials of Advertising ... 133
11.7 The 5-Ms of Advertising ... 134
11.8 Objectives/Functions of Advertising ... 135
11.9 Types of Advertising ... 137
11.10 Advertising Strategies for the Stages of the Product Life Cycle (PLC) ... 138
11.11 Benefits or Importance of Advertisement ... 139
11.12 Ethics in Advertising ... 141
11.13 Steps in Scientific Advertising Campaign ... 143
11.14 Criticisms of Advertising ... 144

12. Advertising Budget, Media and Public Relations **146–170**

12.1 Introduction ... 146
12.2 Meaning and Definition ... 147
12.3 Advertising Budgeting Methods ... 147
12.4 Advertisement Copy ... 148
12.5 Essentials of Effective Advertisement Copy ... 149
12.6 Elements of Advertising Copy ... 150
12.7 Measurement of Advertising Effectiveness ... 151
12.8 Dagmar Model ... 152
12.9 Methods of Advertising Evaluation ... 153
12.10 Advertising Agencies ... 157
12.11 Media ... 163
12.12 Public Relations (PR) ... 167
12.13 Objectives of Public Relations ... 168
12.14 Components of Public Relations ... 168
12.15 Importance of Public Relations ... 169
12.16 Developing a Marketing Public Relations Plan ... 169

13. Personal Selling and Management of Sales Force **171–187**

13.1 Introduction ... 171
13.2 Meaning and Definition ... 172
13.3 Characteristics of Personal Selling ... 172
13.4 Qualities of a Good Salesman ... 176
13.5 Advantages and Disadvantages of Personal Selling ... 177
13.6 Importance of Personal Selling ... 178
13.7 Meaning of Recruitment ... 178
13.8 Process of Recruitment ... 179
13.9 Training of Salesmen ... 180

Chapters *Pages*

13.10 Importance of Sales Training ... 181
13.11 Methods of Sales Training ... 181
13.12 Remuneration of Salesmen ... 183
13.13 Methods of Sales Remuneration ... 183
13.14 Motivation of Sales Personnel ... 185
13.15 Evaluation of Sales Force Performance ... 185
13.16 Process of Evaluating Sales Force Performance ... 186

14. Sales Forecasting, Sales Promotion and Publicity 188–204

14.1 Introduction ... 188
14.2 Meaning and Definition ... 189
14.3 Factors Affecting Sales Forecasting ... 189
14.4 Main Characteristics of Sales Forecasting ... 190
14.5 Methods/Techniques of Sales Forecasting ... 190
14.6 Significance of Sales Forecasting ... 192
14.7 Introduction of Sales Promotion ... 193
14.8 Meaning and Definition of Sales Promotion ... 193
14.9 Characteristics of Sales Promotion ... 193
14.10 Distinguish between Advertising and Sales Promotion ... 193
14.11 Objectives of Sales Promotion ... 194
14.12 Techniques of Sales Promotion ... 195
14.13 Advantages and Disadvantages of Sales Promotion ... 197
14.14 Sales Promotion Budget ... 198
14.15 Sales Promotion Programmes ... 199
14.16 Publicity ... 199
14.17 Difference between Advertisement and Publicity ... 200
14.18 Role of Publicity ... 201
14.19 Objectives of Publicity ... 201
14.20 Publicity Techniques ... 202
14.21 Importance of Publicity ... 202

UNIT–IV (205-256)

15. Physical Distribution 207–219

15.1 Introduction ... 207
15.2 Meaning of Physical Distribution ... 208
15.3 Objective of Physical Distribution ... 208
15.4 Element of Physical Distribution ... 209
15.5 Process or Component of Physical Distribution ... 210
15.6 Mode of Transportation ... 212
15.7 Distribution Cost Analysis ... 214
15.8 Customer Service in Logistics ... 215
15.9 Marketing Logistics ... 215
15.10 Trends in Logistics Development ... 215
15.11 Vertical Marketing System (VMS) ... 216
15.12 Horizontal Marketing Systems (HMS) ... 218

Chapters			Pages
	15.13 Multi-channel Distribution Systems	...	218
	15.14 Importance of Physical Distribution	...	218
16.	**Channels of Distribution**		**220–232**
	16.1 Introduction	...	220
	16.2 Meaning and Definition	...	221
	16.3 Characteristics of Distribution Channel	...	221
	16.4 Functions of Channels of Distribution	...	222
	16.5 Channel Management	...	222
	16.6 Factors Influencing the Choice of Distribution Channel	...	223
	16.7 Types of Channel	...	225
	16.8 Various Channels for the Distribution of Consumer Goods and Industrial Goods	...	226
	16.9 Wholesalers	...	227
	16.10 Characteristics of Wholesalers	...	227
	16.11 Types of Wholesalers	...	227
	16.12 Functions of Wholesalers	...	228
	16.13 Retailers	...	229
	16.14 Characteristics of Retailers	...	229
	16.15 Functions of Retailers	...	229
	16.16 Types of Retailers	...	230
17.	**Strategic Marketing Planning and Competitive Marketing Strategies**		**233–245**
	17.1 Introduction	...	233
	17.2 Meaning and Definition	...	234
	17.3 Characteristics of Strategic Planning	...	234
	17.4 Strategic Marketing Plan	...	234
	17.5 Role of Strategic Marketing Plan	...	235
	17.6 Strategic Marketing Planning Process	...	236
	17.7 Marketing Strategy Implementation	...	238
	17.8 Competitive Marketing Strategies	...	238
	17.9 Disadvantages of Porter's Five Forces Model	...	240
	17.10 Porter's Generic Competitive Strategies	...	240
	17.11 Ansoff Product Matrix (Marketing Strategies)	...	241
	17.12 Competitive Marketing Strategy Options	...	242
	17.13 Marketing Mix Strategies	...	244
18.	**Marketing Organizations and Control of Marketing Operations**		**246–256**
	18.1 Introduction	...	246
	18.2 Meaning and Definition of Marketing Organization	...	246
	18.3 Need for the Organization	...	247
	18.4 Factors Affecting Marketing Organization	...	247
	18.5 Types of Marketing Organization Structures	...	248
	18.6 Definition and Meaning of Marketing Control	...	252
	18.7 Objectives of Marketing Control	...	252

Chapters		Pages
18.8 Marketing Control Process	...	253
18.9 Techniques of Marketing Control	...	253
18.10 Marketing Audit	...	254
18.11 Characteristics of Marketing Audit	...	254
18.12 Types of Marketing Audit	...	255
18.13 Process of Marketing Audit	...	255
UNIT–V (257-312)		
19. Rural Marketing		**259–272**
19.1 Introduction	...	260
19.2 Meaning and Definition	...	260
19.3 Characteristics of Rural Marketing	...	260
19.4 Scope of Rural Marketing	...	261
19.5 Factors Contributing to Change in Rural Marketing	...	261
19.6 Importance of Rural Marketing	...	262
19.7 Changing Scenario	...	263
19.8 Distinction between Rural and Urban Marketing	...	263
19.9 Problems of Rural Marketing	...	264
19.10 Strategies in Rural Marketing	...	265
19.11 Agricultural Marketing	...	266
19.12 Classification of Agri-Product	...	266
19.13 Features of Agri-Product	...	267
19.14 Problems of Agri-Products Marketing	...	267
19.15 Types of Market	...	268
19.16 Procedure and Methods of Trading	...	269
19.17 Co-operative Marketing	...	269
19.18 Aims and Objectives of Co-Operative Marketing	...	269
19.19 Role of Co-Operative Marketing	...	270
19.20 Functions of Co-Operative Marketing	...	270
19.21 Importance of Co-Operative Marketing	...	271
19.22 Present Scenario of Co-Operative Marketing	...	272
20. Marketing of Services Banking, Transport and Insurance		**273–286**
20.1 Introduction	...	273
20.2 Meaning and Definition	...	274
20.3 Characteristics of Services	...	274
20.4 Difference between Goods and Services	...	275
20.5 Service Marketing Mix	...	276
20.6 Bank Marketing	...	276
20.7 Marketing Mix for Banking Organization	...	277
20.8 Marketing Information System	...	278
20.9 Component of Marketing Information System	...	278
20.10 Transport Marketing	...	279
20.11 Mode of Transport	...	280

Chapters *Pages*

20.12 Marketing in Indian Railways ... 280
20.13 Marketing Mix for Rail Transport ... 281
20.14 Marketing on Road Transport Corporation ... 282
20.15 Marketing Mix-road Transport Corporation ... 283
20.16 Airline Marketing Mix ... 284
20.17 Risk and Insurance Marketing ... 284
20.18 Life Insurance Corporation in India ... 284
20.19 Marketing Mix in Insurance Sector ... 285

21. E-Commerce and CRM **287–300**

21.1 Introduction ... 287
21.2 Meaning and Definition ... 288
21.3 Benefits of E-Commerce ... 288
21.4 Marketing Mix of E-Commerce ... 289
21.5 E-Commerce Models ... 290
21.6 Application of E-Commerce ... 293
21.7 Advantages of E-Commerce ... 293
21.8 Disadvantages of E-Commerce ... 293
21.9 Introduction to Customer Relationship Management (CRM) ... 293
21.10 Meaning and Definition ... 294
21.11 Need and Objective of CRM ... 294
21.12 Features of CRM ... 295
21.13 Types of CRM ... 295
21.14 Implementing CRM with Critical Success Factors (CSF) ... 297
21.15 CRM Marketing ... 298

22. New Issues in Marketing: Globalization and Green Marketing **301–312**

22.1 Meaning of Globalization ... 302
22.2 Characteristics of Globalization ... 302
22.3 Factors Affecting Globalization ... 303
22.4 Globalization of Business ... 303
22.5 Impact of Globalization ... 304
22.6 Impact of Globalization on India ... 304
22.7 Meaning of Green Marketing ... 305
22.8 Evolution and Need of Green Marketing ... 306
22.9 Need of Green Marketing ... 306
22.10 Green Products and their Characteristics ... 306
22.11 Challenges in Green Marketing ... 307
22.12 Marketing Mix of Green Marketing ... 307
22.13 Importance of Green Marketing ... 308
22.14 Consumerism ... 308
22.15 Consumer Movement in India ... 309
22.16 Consumer Protection Act, 1986 ... 309
22.17 Neuro Marketing ... 310

Index **312–316**

PREFACE

This book written in an extremely simple and lucid language with practical example and diagrams. The original purpose of a preface to Fundamentals of Marketing is to deliver a clear and concise presentation of the fundamental principles of marketing. It is praised in the market for its organization, format, clarity, brevity and flexibility. The text serves as an overview for critical issues in marketing principle. Its brief, format makes it a perfect fit for instructors who assign cases, readings, simulations or offer modules on marketing fundamentals for graduate and post graduate level students. The text also works in courses that implement a cross-functional curriculum where the students are required to purchase several texts. It is very useful book for beginners who do not have much knowledge about marketing and want to understand the fundamentals of marketing at a fair amount of depth.

Chapter 1 introduces the basic concepts of marketing, nature, scope and importance of marketing. Chapters 2 to 5 introduces marketing environment, marketing mix and marketing plan, market segmentation, targeting, positioning and consumer behaviour. Chapters 6 to 10 includes product concepts and product life cycle, product planning, development and product identification, pricing, marketing communication and marketing research. Chapters 11 to 14 discuss concepts of promotion activities like advertising, advertising budget, media and public relations, personal selling and management of sales force, sales forecasting, sales promotion and publicity. Chapters 15 to 18 we study about physical distribution, channels of distribution, strategic marketing planning and competitive marketing strategies, marketing organizations and control of marketing operations. Chapters 19 to 21 introduces rural marketing, marketing of services, banking, transport and insurance, e-commerce and CRM. Chapter 22 closes our discussion with new issues in marketing: globalization, green marketing, consumerism and neuro-marketing.

This book is a result of very strong passion—the passion for acquiring and sharing knowledge and also the passion to demystify, so that we all can learn and enjoy. To what extend this goal has been achieved, only time will tell. Readers are most welcome to write back their suggestions / criticism which will definitely be acknowledged in forthcoming edition.

— Authors

UNIT–I

1. Marketing: Nature, Scope and Importance
2. Marketing Environment
3. Marketing Mix and Marketing Plan
4. Market Segmentation, Targeting and Positioning
5. Consumer Behaviour

Marketing: Nature, Scope and Importance

POINTS TO REMEMBER

At the end of this chapter, we will be able to understand:

- Introduction
- Evolution of Marketing
- Meaning and Definition of Marketing
- Features of Marketing
- Marketing Management
- Functions of Marketing Management
- Nature of Marketing
- The Marketing Concept
- Difference between Marketing and Selling
- Marketing Myopia
- Scope/Functions of Marketing
- Utilities of Marketing
- Types of Marketing
- Importance of Marketing
- Role of Marketing in an Organization

1.1 INTRODUCTION

Marketing management is a broad scope of the study of marketing focusing on the practical application of the techniques and marketing activities of a certain company or business. This business discipline encompasses marketing planning and strategy, orientations, and processes needed in attaining company goals by providing values to clients. Since it has a wide coverage involving all factors required to satisfy customers, marketing management must be all-pervasive and a part of every employee's scope of work, from subordinates to those in the higher management.

If we look at this definition in more detail, Marketing is a management responsibility and should not be solely left to junior members of staff. Marketing requires co-ordination, planning, implementation of campaigns and a competent manager(s) with the appropriate skills to ensure success.

Marketing objectives, goals and targets have to be monitored and met, competitor strategies analyzed, anticipated and exceeded. Through effective use of market and marketing research an organization should be able to identify the needs and wants of the customer and try to deliver benefits that will enhance or add to the customers lifestyle, while at the same time ensuring that the satisfaction of these needs results in a healthy turnover for the organization.

Within this exchange transaction customers will only exchange what they value (money) if they feel that their needs are being fully satisfied; clearly the greater the benefit provided the higher transactional value an organization can charge.

1.2 EVOLUTION OF MARKETING

There are following different stages in the development of marketing:

1. **State of Self-Sufficiency:** In this stage small families as production units aimed at self-sufficiency and they met all their needs for food, clothing and shelter.
2. **Stage of Primitive Communism:** In this stage the custom was that one who had more than others was to share his surplus with all others till every one had equal quantity. In a few societies, the person had no personal right to his acquisition. It had to be divided among the people in his village.

   In the above-mentioned two stages there was no exchange and hence, no marketing.
3. **Bartering Stage:** In this stage a family or village could not meet all its needs and therefore, had to take the surplus of what it produced in excess of its needs and entered into a bartering relationship with others. Thus, trade commenced due to the production of surplus. This necessitated a search of such people who had surpluses and who desired to exchange them for what the "searchers" had and then negotiations between the two parties started.
4. **Money Economy Stage:** The emergence of money, a common medium of exchange, quickened the pace of trade. It gave a durable base for operation of local markets. In this stage, every product is being valued in terms of money.
5. **Stage of Capitalism:** In the stage of early capitalism where production began not only for meeting their own and family needs but also for making profit. This paved the way for production centres and employment of people to facilitate the distribution of goods produced. The knowledge of marketing helps in understanding consumer needs, optimum utilization of all resources, providing the most suitable product to consumer leading to better standard of living and economic growth.
6. **Mass Production Stage:** It was a result of development in population and improvement in transportation and communication. Large cities get formed, there is increased use of capital equipment in jobs, availability and flow of funds through banks and a professional management, which encourages the growth of large-scale enterprises.
7. **Affluent Society Stage:** In this stage some sections of people have surpluses of money over their basic needs. Goods and services, which meet their psychological, cultural, social desires and wants, are needed. A study has to be made about these wants of different segments of people. This makes it necessary to collect market information and conduct market research, so that the goods produced will meet the requirements of the consumers. Marketing included earlier searching and negotiation in the stages of barter and local markets. Later at the stage of early capitalism, it included distribution to centres of consumption in other towns or areas. Mass production stage saw the growing importance

of branding, packaging and advertising. In an affluent society steps are taken to interpret a consumer's desires and producing goods that will satisfy these desires.

The marketing functions increase according to the stages of development through which a country passes. The orientation of trade, which is traditional in the beginning, becomes international when the economy becomes fully commercial. Thus, marketing has been growing to include a number of marketers, processes or practices.

1.3 MEANING AND DEFINITION OF MARKETING

The term 'marketing' has changed and evolved over a period of time. Today marketing is based around providing continual benefits to the customer, these benefits will be provided and a transactional exchange will take place.

Marketing has been viewed traditionally as a business activity. Business organizations exist to satisfy human needs, especially material needs. Consequently, one way to define marketing is from the business perspective. For instance, marketing has been defined as the "delivery of a higher standard of living."

Marketing includes all activities right from transferring goods from producer to consumers. Its main aim is to sell and satisfy the consumers. Today, **market's king is consumer**. From Mahatma Gandhi to P&G to LG, they have all laid emphasis on consumer-oriented thought process. In fact, the going slogan at P&G is **"Consumer is Boss!"** So, marketing provides us good techniques to handle customers. Marketing's best technique is marketing mix. Marketing mix has 4-Ps:

1. **Product** which is made by producer must be made on the basis of quality.
2. **Price** is fixed by market but marketer should take low price than market for increasing sale.
3. **Promotion** is done by advertising; it must be used at proper time for target audience.
4. **Place** is related to distribution activities; marketer should reach by proper channel of distribution.

"'The management process responsible for identifying, anticipating and satisfying customer requirements profitably". ***Chartered Institute of Marketing***

"Marketing as the performance of business activities that directs the flow of goods and services from producer to consumer or user". ***American Marketing Association***

"Satisfying needs and wants through an exchange process". ***Philip Kotler***

"A total system of business activities designed to plan, price, promote and distribute want satisfying goods and services to the present and potential customers". ***William J. Stanton***

"The management task of strategically planning, directing and controlling the application of enterprise effort to profit making programmes which provide customer satisfaction—a task which involves the integration of all business activities into a unified system of action". ***Marting L. Bell's***

The above definitions provide us an idea on the nature of marketing. The features in the above definitions are that marketing, (*a*) Is an exchange process.

(*b*) Covers a variety of functions to be carried out in an integrated manner.

(*c*) Is directed to satisfy the needs/desires/wants of the consumer.

1.4 FEATURES OF MARKETING

The objective of marketing is not the maximization of profitable sales volume, but profits through the satisfaction of customers. The consumer is the pivot point and all marketing activities operate around this central point. It is, therefore, essential that the entrepreneurs identify the customers, establish a rapport with them, identify their needs and deliver the goods and services that would meet their requirements. Marketing has the following features:

1. **Consumers:** Consumers are the kings of market and all salesmen who want to sell goods to consumers, should create good relationship with consumers and also solve their problems for enhancing the product branding in market.
2. **Organizational Capability:** Before marketing, it is very necessary that a company should see its organizational capability which is available to fulfill the order of sale. If not, then create the limit of marketing.
3. **Competitors:** It is also the nature of marketing that you will see competitors in the market. Never ignore them and create advance strategy to fight and defeat your competitors. Sometimes, new competitors may be your friends for increasing sale because every new competitor is helpful to make a physical market for you where consumer can come and buy.
4. **Co-ordination:** It is also the nature of marketing that it is connected with other activities. It is the duty of the marketing manager to do co-ordination with other departments.
5. **Performance:** Marketing should be based on performance. We have to pay for all costs on the basis of past selling. If any branch's sale value is high, we should promote that branch by increasing the salary of that branch's salesmen and advertising cost.

1.5 MARKETING MANAGEMENT

Marketing management takes place when at least one party to a potential exchange thinks about the means of achieving desired responses from other parties.

> *"Marketing Management is the analysis, planning, implementation and control of programmes designed to bring about the desired exchanges with target audiences for the purpose of personal and mutual gain. It relies heavily on adoption and coordination of the product, price, promotion and place for achieving response".*
>
> ***Philip Kotler***

> *"Marketing (Management) is the process of planning and executing the conception, pricing, promotion, and distribution of ideas, goods, and services to create exchanges that satisfy individual and organizational goals".*
>
> ***American Marketing Association***

Marketing management has the task of influencing the level, timing, and composition of demand in a way that helps the organization to achieve its objectives. Marketing management is essentially a demand management. Marketing managers manage demand by carrying out marketing research, planning, implementation and control.

In summary, Marketing in action is Marketing Management. Marketing Management has the responsibility to perform many functions in the field of marketing such as planning, organizing, directing, motivating, coordinating and controlling. All these functions aim to achieve the marketing goals.

1.6 FUNCTIONS OF MARKETING MANAGEMENT

Marketing management takes place when at least one party to a potential exchange thinks about the means of achieving desired responses from other parties. Thus, we see marketing management as the art and science of choosing target markets and getting, keeping, and growing customers through creating, delivering and communicating superior customer value. In the marketing process, companies work to understand consumers, create customer value **and** build strong customer relationships. A brief summary of functions of marketing management is shown in Fig. 1.1:

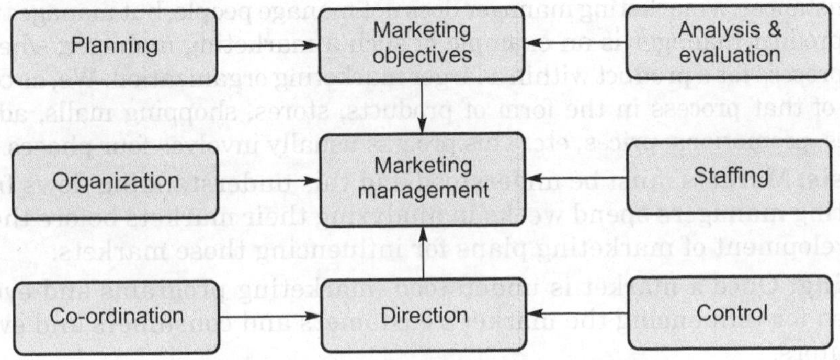

Fig. 1.1. Functions of marketing management.

1. **Marketing Objectives:** Marketing management determines the marketing objectives. The marketing objectives may be short-term or long-term and need a clear approach. They have to be in coherence with the aims and objectives of the organization.
2. **Planning:** After objectively determining the marketing objectives, the important function of the marketing management is to plan how to achieve those objectives. This includes sales forecast, marketing programmes formulation, and marketing strategies.
3. **Organization:** A plan once formulated needs implementation. Organizing functions of marketing management involves the collection and co-ordination of required means to implement a plan and to achieve pre determined objectives. The organization involves structure of marketing organization, duties, responsibilities and powers of various members of the marketing organization.
4. **Co-ordination:** Co-ordination refers to harmonious adjustment of the activities of the marketing organization. It involves co-ordination among various activities such as sales forecasting, product planning, product development, transportation, warehousing etc.
5. **Direction:** Direction in marketing management refers to development of new markets, leadership of employees, motivation, inspiration, guiding and supervision of the employees.
6. **Control:** Control refers to the effectiveness with which a marketing plan is implemented. It involves the determination of standards, evaluation of actual performance, and adoption of corrective measures.
7. **Staffing:** Employment of right and able employees is very crucial to the success of a market plan. The Marketing Manager co-ordinates with the Human Resource Manager of an organization to be able to hire the staff with desired capability.
8. **Analysis and evaluation:** The marketing management involves the analysis and evaluation of the productivity and performance of individual employees.

1.7 NATURE OF MARKETING

Marketing is a human activity directed at satisfying needs and wants through exchange processes. Marketing includes such activities as product development, marketing research, communication, pricing, promotion and service apart from selling.

Marketing is a view point which looks at the entire business process as a highly integrated effort to discover, create, arouse and satisfy consumer needs. Marketing is a delivery of a standard of living to society.

1. **Marketing as a Process:** Marketing is a process that marketing managers execute. In a number of instances, a marketing manager does not manage people, but manages the marketing process. A product manager is an example of such a marketing manager; s/he manages the marketing process for a product within a larger marketing organization. We, as consumers, see the results of that process in the form of products, stores, shopping malls, advertisements, sales pitches, promotions, prices, etc. This process usually involves four phases.
   - (*i*) **Analysis:** Markets must be understood and this understanding flows from analysis. Marketing managers spend weeks in analyzing their markets before they undertake the development of marketing plans for influencing those markets.
   - (*ii*) **Planning:** Once a market is understood, marketing programs and events must be designed for influencing the market's customers and consumers and even the firms' competitors.
   - (*iii*) **Execution:** The marketing events are executed in the markets, advertisements are aired, prices are set, sales calls are made, etc.
   - (*iv*) **Monitoring:** Markets are not static entities and thus must be monitored at all times. After events execute, they need to be evaluated. The planning assumptions upon which the upcoming events are based must be continually tested; if they are no longer true then the events may need modification.
2. **The D Roles of a Marketing Manager:** Marketing managers play many roles, and we can describe them with words that begin with the letter D.
   - (*i*) **Detective:** The marketer is given the task of understanding markets, and thus spends considerable time learning about consumers, competitors, customers, and conditions in the markets. This learning takes many forms: formal marketing research studies, analysis of market data, market visits, and discussions with people in the markets. The result of these studies includes insights about market conditions, and the identification of problems and opportunities in the various markets.
   - (*ii*) **Designer:** As soon as the problem or opportunity has been identified, the marketer shifts her/his attention in designing marketing programs that solve the problems and/or grab the opportunities.
   - (*iii*) **Decision maker:** Marketing is a group process that involves many different people, each of whom may be designing marketing programs and events. Thus the marketer must make decisions about which programs to execute.
   - (*iv*) **Decision influencer:** Marketers exist in corporate structures that require higher level executives to approve the marketing plans, programs, and events that come out of the marketing group's work. Thus, the marketer must influence the decisions of these senior executives.
   - (*v*) **Diplomat:** Marketers design marketing events that others must execute: the sales force must execute the sales plan; the advertising agency must execute the advertisements, etc. These units do not usually "report to" the marketing managers, and they are undertaking tasks given to them by multiple marketing managers. Thus,

each manager must play a diplomatic role while inducing these units to execute his/her program in a timely and high quality way.

3. **Managing the Marketing Mix:** Marketing managers can control or influence four aspects of the firm's output: its products, promotions, prices, and the places that all of these are offered.
   (*i*) **Product:** Product management involves the design of the physical product along with its packaging and warranties, the positioning of that product in terms of the benefits it delivers and the development of the product's brand identity.
   (*ii*) **Promotion:** It is generally not true that consumers will beat a path to your door if you have a superior product; they must be told about it and induced to buy it ... thus the need for promotion. Promotion includes personal selling, advertising, sales promotions, and public relations.
   (*iii*) **Price:** Pricing strategies and tactics must be determined for the product, and then followed to set prices for all the sizes and variants of the product. The result is usually a price schedule that includes the regular price, volume discounts, payment terms, seasonal prices, introductory prices, etc.
   (*iv*) **Place:** Marketing managers are involved in decisions about where the product is offered to the consumer in terms of the channels of distribution.
4. **Operating Within Constraints:** Marketing managers must undertake all of the above activities within various constraints, all of which start with the letter C. None of these constraints are under the direct control of the marketing managers; some can be influenced and all can be understood.
   (*i*) **Competition:** Other companies are competing for the same consumers and channels of distribution.
   (*ii*) **Channels:** Retail stores, electronic markets, communications media exist to serve the marketer. In the short-run, they must be accepted as constraints; in the long-run, the marketer can exert some control over them ... even vertically integrate into the channels.
   (*iii*) **Consumers:** Consumers have needs and wants. The marketers must understand those needs before they can design marketing programs aimed at impacting consumer wants.
   (*iv*) **Conditions:** Markets are not static but in constant evolution under the influences of the economy, changing tastes and fashions, population dynamics, etc.
   (*v*) **Company:** Company policies, procedures, practices, and cultures place constraints upon the marketing resources and programs that the marketer can deploy.
5. **Marketing in Collaboration:** The nature of marketing requires marketing managers and professionals to work together on all aspects of marketing. It is common for the marketing managers to be at the centre of a set of activities being worked on by people within the company (sales force, promotion manager, product development teams, etc.) and outside the company (ad agencies, consultants, marketing research firms, etc). Thus marketing managers must spend considerable time in consultation and collaboration with other people.

1.8 THE MARKETING CONCEPT

In the 1950s the marketing concept emerged. As a business philosophy, the marketing concept is aimed at orienting a firm completely towards its customers. As such, a customer focus should permeate every department from production to finance to human resources. All major decisions should be based on the relevant market considerations. This does not, of course, mean that other activities in the organization must be completely subordinate to marketing. What it means is that managers should not make important decisions in any area without taking marketing implications into account.

The objective of marketing is not the maximization of profitable sales volume, but profits through the satisfaction of customers. The consumer is the pivot point and all marketing activities operate around this central point. It is, therefore, essential that the entrepreneurs identify the customers, establish a rapport with them, identify their needs and deliver the goods and services that would meet their requirements. The components of marketing concept are as under:

(*i*) **Satisfaction of customers:** In the modern era, the customer is the focus of the organization. The organization should aim at producing those goods and services, which will lead to satisfaction of customers.

(*ii*) **Integrated marketing:** The functions of production, finance and marketing should be integrated to satisfy the needs and expectations of customers.

(*iii*) **Profitable sales volume:** Marketing is successful only when it is capable of maximizing profitable sales and achieves long-run customer satisfaction.

Table 1.1: Selling vs. Marketing Concept

Concepts	*Starting point*	*Focus*	*Means*	*End*
Selling Concept	Factory	Products	Selling and Promoting	Profit through Sales Volume
Marketing Concept	Market	Customer Needs and Wants	Coordinated Marketing	Profit through Customer Satisfaction

Source Philip Kotler

1.8.1 The Concept Benefits the Organization

The practice of the concept brings substantial benefits to the organization that practices it. For example, the concept enables the organization to keep abreast of changes. An organization practicing the concept keeps feeling the pulse of the market through continuous marketing audit, market research and consumer testing. It is quick to respond to changes in buyer behaviour, it rectifies any drawback in its products; it gives great importance to planning, research and innovation and its decisions are no longer based on hunch, but on reliable data relating to the consumers. It does not necessarily stick to one product line; it may diversify and come out with new and improved products or enter totally new areas of business. All these responses, in the long-run, prove extremely beneficial to the firm. The base of consumer satisfaction guarantees long-term financial success.

1.8.2 The Concept Benefits the Consumer

The consumer is infact the major beneficiary of the marketing concept. The attempts of various competing firms to satisfy the consumer put him in an enviable position. The concept prompts the producers to constantly improve their products and to launch totally new products as often as possible; it also prompts them to go in for changes in their business practices. All this results in solid benefits to the consumer—low price, better quality, improved new products and ready stocks at convenient locations. The consumer can choose, he can bargain, he can complain and his complaint will always be attended to. He can buy on credit, cash or on installments. He can even return the goods if not satisfied with it. When corporations take to the marketing concept, their business practices change in favour of the consumer.

1.8.3 The Concept Benefits the Society

When more and more corporations resort to the marketing concept, the society benefits. The concept guarantees that only products that are required by the consumers are produced and thereby it ensures that the society's economic resources are channelised in the right direction. It also makes economic planning more meaningful and more relevant to the life of the people.

1.9 DIFFERENCE BETWEEN MARKETING AND SELLING

The terms 'marketing' and 'selling' are related but not synonymous. 'Marketing' as stated earlier, lays emphasis on earning profits through customer satisfaction. In marketing, the focus is on the consumer's needs and their satisfaction. 'Selling' on the other hand focuses on product and emphasizes selling what has been produced. In fact it is a small part of the wide process of marketing wherein emphasis is initially on promotion of goods and services and eventually on increase in sales volume.

Marketing has long-term perspective of winning over consumer loyalty to the product by providing him maximum satisfaction. However, selling has short-term perspective of only increasing the sales volume.

In marketing, 'the consumer is the king', whose needs must be satisfied. In selling, the product is supreme and the entire focus is its sale. Marketing starts before production and continues even after the exchange of goods and services has taken place. It is so because provision of after-sale service is an important component of the marketing process. Selling starts after the production and ends as soon as the exchange of goods and services has taken place. The difference between selling and marketing may be as follows.

Table 1.2: Marketing vs. Selling

S. No.	*Marketing*	*Selling*
1.	Marketing focuses on the needs of the buyer.	Selling focuses on the needs of the seller.
2.	Converting customer's needs into product.	Converting product into cash.
3.	Importance is given to the customer.	Importance is given to the product.
4.	It focuses on customer satisfaction.	It focuses on corporate objectives.
5.	It aims at long-term objective as it has philosophical and strategic implications.	It aims at short-term objectives, as it is only a tactical and routine activity.
6.	Integrated approach to marketing is practiced.	Fragmented approach to selling is practiced.
7.	It forecasts the customer needs to undertake the production activity.	It aims at selling the goods which are already produced through intensive promotion at a profit.
8.	It gives top priority to profitable volume at fair and reasonable prices.	It gives priority to sales volume and maximization of profits through sales volume.
9.	The principle of caveat vendor (let the seller beware) is followed.	The principle of caveat emptor (let the buyer beware) is followed.
10.	Stresses on needs of the buyer.	Stresses on needs of the seller.

1.10 MARKETING MYOPIA

Marketing myopia is a term used in marketing as well as the title of an important marketing paper written by **Theodore Levitt**. This paper was first published in 1960 in the Harvard Business Review, a journal of which he was an editor. **Marketing Myopia refers to focusing on products rather than customers needs and wants.**

Management gurus define marketing myopia as a company's short-sighted, temporary or narrow-minded approach while marketing their product. Companies need to adapt themselves to the changing market. When a firm changes its marketing focus from customer to its product or the company itself, it is also called myopia.

Myopia literally means short-sightedness. Marketing Myopia is the inefficiency of the Top Management to broadly define its business and meet customer needs resulting to the decline of the product. Examples from the real world:

- Daewoo Motors
- Hindustan Motors
- Kinetic Honda
- Pager Industry

Theodore Levitt Myopia defines the following factors responsible for Marketing Myopia:

- The belief of the companies that as more and more of the population becomes affluent, the market expands and more and more people buy the goods.
- The belief that there are no substitutes for the industry's major products.
- Emphasis on mass production and in economies of scale *i.e.*, being product-oriented rather than being customer-oriented.
- Lack of experimentation, improvement, and manufacturing cost reduction.

1.11 SCOPE/FUNCTIONS OF MARKETING

Marketing is an ancient art and is everywhere. Formally or informally, people & organizations engage in a vast numbers of activities that could be called marketing. Good marketing has become an increasingly vital ingredient for business success. It is embedded in everything we do—from the clothes we wear, to the websites we click on, to the ads we see. Marketing deals with identifying and meeting human and social needs or it can be defined as "meeting needs profitably".

In order for the marketing bridge to work correctly providing consumers with opportunities to purchase the products and services they need, the marketing process must accomplish nine important functions. The functions are:

1. **Buying:** People have the opportunity to buy products that they want.
2. **Selling:** Producers function within a free market to sell products to consumers.
3. **Financing:** Banks and other financial institutions provide money for the production and marketing of products.
4. **Storage:** Products must be stored and protected/preserved until they are needed. This function is especially important for perishable products such as fruits and vegetables.
5. **Transportation:** Products must be physically relocated to the locations where consumers can buy them. This is a very important function. Transportation includes rail road, ship, airplane, truck, and telecommunications for non-tangible products such as market information.
6. **Processing:** Processing involves turning a raw product, like wheat, into something the consumer can use—for example, bread.

7. **Risk Taking:** Insurance companies provide coverage to protect producers and marketers from loss due to fire, theft, or natural disasters.
8. **Market Information:** Information from around the world about market conditions, weather, price movements, and political changes, can affect the marketing process. Market information is provided by all forms of telecommunication, such as television, the internet, and phone.
9. **Grading and Standardizing:** Many products are graded in order to conform to previously determined standards of quality. For example, when you purchase potatoes, you know you are buying the best potatoes in the market.
10. **Marketing in New Company:** Building a new customer base for your products and services takes time, money and planning. Begin by getting facts about your industry, local market, customers and competitors. With the right information, the next step is to develop a strategy like High Advertising Frequency, High Quality Product and Low Price that identifies the steps you adopt with your target market and convert prospects into customers.

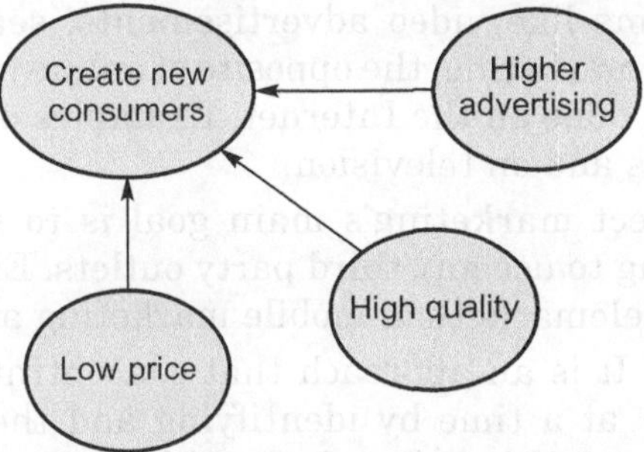

Fig. 1.2. Marketing in a new company.

11. **Marketing in an Old Company:** It is also the part of scope of marketing. In an old company, we see that there are already large number of consumers buying goods. There is no need to invest high amount on advertising but company can find its scope for improving the quality of product which will be sold to existing consumers. An old company should concentrate its mind for maintaining the stable level in market by providing quality products, continuing researching and decreasing the cost.

1.12 UTILITIES OF MARKETING

The marketing process must also add "utility" to the products consumers want. Utility is the use or satisfaction a person gets from a product. If you purchase a chain saw you anticipate that you will receive a certain amount of utility from it. You will be able to use the saw to cut fire wood, prune trees, and take care of a variety of jobs around your home. There are four types of utility.

1. **Form utility:** A product must be processed into a form that the customer wants or needs. For example, wheat is processed into bread, trees are processed into lumber, and potatoes are processed into french fries. If you ordered french fries with your lunch and the waiter brought you a raw potato, you probably wouldn't be too happy.
2. **Place utility:** Place utility involves transporting products to the location where consumers can buy them. If you live in Kerala, you certainly would not want to have to drive to J&K to buy apples. You simply drive to the local grocery store and apples are there ready to add to your shopping cart place utility.

3. **Possession Utility:** Possession utility establishes legal ownership of a product. When you purchase something you normally receive a receipt; this provides legal ownership and the right to use the product. Some products, computer software, for example, also provide a user license. A license of this kind gives you the right to use the product within certain guidelines.
4. **Time Utility:** This could be described as being in the right place at the right time when a customer is ready to purchase a product. Creating and keeping customers means having products available for when they want them, and often this requires some type of storage facility. Wheat is one example of a commodity that must be stored after it is harvested. It is stored in silos until processors are ready to convert it into food products such as bread or cereals.

1.13 TYPES OF MARKETING

Some important types of marketing are mentioned below:

1. **Internet Marketing and Offline Marketing:** Internet marketing is any marketing strategy that takes place online. Also referred to as online marketing, it encompasses a variety of marketing forms like video advertisements, search engine marketing and e-mail marketing. Offline marketing, the opposite of online marketing, includes all forms of marketing that are not done on the Internet. Examples of offline marketing are local advertising in newspapers and on television.
2. **Direct Marketing:** Direct marketing's main goal is to send a message directly to consumers, without having to use any third party outlets. Examples of direct marketing include mail marketing, telemarketing, mobile marketing and direct selling.
3. **One-to-one Marketing:** It is an approach that concentrates on providing services or products to one customer at a time by identifying and then meeting their individual needs. It then aims to repeat this many times with each customer, such that powerful lifelong relationships are forged. As such it differentiates customers rather than just products.
4. **Niche Marketing:** When a product or service is not being readily supplied to a certain portion of a market, a company can its efforts on that niche to address a need that is not currently being addressed. This targeted marketing is successful because the marketer has identified a need that is not being resolved by mainstream providers. Sometimes it is beneficial for a company to focus on a niche instead of trying to compete in a larger market.
5. **Mass Marketing:** Mass marketing is a market coverage strategy in which a firm decides to ignore market segment differences and appeal the whole market with one offer or one strategy. A mass marketing approach aims at a large, broad consumer market through one basic marketing plan. Use of this approach has declined in recent years due to the following reasons:

   1. Growth of competition.
   2. Stimulated demand by appealing to specific segments.
   3. Improved marketing research that pinpoints desires of different segments.
   4. A reduction in total production and marketing costs because of segmentation.

   A major objective of mass marketing is to maximize sales. For successful pure mass marketing, a large group of consumers must have a desire for the same product attributes or consumer demand must be so diffused that it would not be worthwhile for a firm to aim marketing plans at specific segments.

6. **Trade Show Marketing:** Companies that want to reach a large number of potential customers can participate in public or private trade shows. Trade shows and other forms of event marketing are often a large investment to participate in, but trade shows allow companies to demonstrate new products and examine what is going on in the industry.

1.14 IMPORTANCE OF MARKETING

Since marketing is consumer-oriented, it has a positive impact on the business firms. It enables the entrepreneurs to improve the quality of their goods and services. Marketing helps in improving the standard of living of the people by offering a wide variety of goods and services with freedom of choice, and by treating the customer as the most important and valuable person. The contribution of marketing in a socio-economic system can be summarized as follows:

1. **National Income:** The nation's money is composed not of money, but of the goods and services which money can buy. Any increase in efficiency of the marketing process results in lower costs of distribution and lower prices to consumers. This brings an increase in the national income.
2. **Distribution Cost:** Marketing aims at reducing the cost of distribution to the extent possible, to make it available to the consumers at reasonable price. It increases the consumption and profits of the firm. Hence, the shareholders may also get better share in profits. A part of the profit may also be utilized for further research work, for labour saving devices or for innovating new manufacturing techniques. Thus, the society is benefited in the long-run.
3. **Production and Consumption:** Marketing process links the production and consumption. It brings new varieties, quality and beneficial goods to consumers from the manufacturing centres. A wealth of merchandise can be purchased at retail stores which were not available previously. It, thus, provides the connecting link between production and consumption and avoids the scarcity of goods.
4. **Business Slumps:** Scientific marketing has a stabilizing effect on the price level. Producers produce what consumers want and consumers have a wide choice of products, there are no frequent ups and downs in prices. A sound marketing system gives protection against business slump by discovering new markets, reducing cost of distribution, making it consumer-oriented, diversifying and improving the product, extending after-sales service etc.
5. **Transmutation:** The existence of a market and the specialists engaged in performing marketing functions are helpful in creating from utility to the hidden resources to suit the requirements of consumers. Thus, the consumer needs can be satisfied by the marketer.
6. **Productive Efficiency:** The information about the use of machinery and freely after-sales services makes the farmers aware of the latest developments and helps them in improving their productive efficiency.
7. **Imbalance in Supplies:** Scientific marketing remedies the imbalance in the supply by making available the surplus stocks at deficit areas. Through better provision of transport facilities and storage, market develops the trade in perishable goods, most of which at present are wasted.
8. **Value of Goods:** Place utility is created when a product is made readily accessible to the potential consumer. Time utility is created when a product is available to customers when they want it. Possession utility is created when a customer buys the product *i.e.*, the ownership title is transferred to the buyer.

9. **Value of Service:** Marketing adds value to the services *e.g.*, business, medical, entertainment and educational services by performing the services involved.
10. **Patterns of Consumption:** Patterns of consumption are determined by the structure of marketing system, which is set up to carry the flow of goods and services from producer to consumers. The value added to the goods and services through performance of marketing activities also explains the pattern of consumption.
11. **Employment Opportunities:** Marketing is essential for full employment. In order to have continuous production, there must be continuous marketing and high level of business activity. The continuous marketing activity is required for performing various marketing functions such as buying, selling, transportation, warehousing, financing, risk bearing, etc. Each function has countless job openings. It is a continuous source of employment and provides livelihood to a number of unemployed persons.
12. **Living Standards:** Marketing helps in increasing the standard of living of the people. It is logical that a reduction in the per unit cost of distribution of goods and services to the society would result in a higher standard of living.
13. **Expansion of Home Market:** Marketing can serve to expand the home market and thus provide a more secure base for export. When a country is self sufficient and is in a position to go for exports, it results in favourable balance of trade. It is an indicator of economic development of a country.

1.15 ROLE OF MARKETING IN AN ORGANIZATION

One observes that the role of marketing in a modern organization is that of integrating the needs and wants of the customers to the other organizational functions like production, R&D, finance, personnel, etc. One look at the companies today would be sufficient to conclude that neither marketing nor any other function alone holds the key to success. All functions are equally important. However, it is marketing, which performs the role of integration.

1. **Corporate Marketing:** Provides information on competition, customer and advocates customer orientation for developing long-term corporate strategy.
2. **Strategic Marketing:** Provides competition and customer analysis for developing long-term business strategy, including competitive advantage. Develops segmenting, targeting and positioning strategies and takes product-line decisions.
3. **Marketing Management:** Evolves and implements marketing strategy in short-term to achieve business unit objectives. Co-ordinates marketing activities and allocates resources.

REVIEW QUESTIONS

1. Define marketing. State its features.
2. State the importance of marketing.
3. What are the different stages in the development of marketing?
4. Differentiate between selling and marketing.
5. How, "marketing occupies a critical role in respect of the development of developing nations" ?
6. Explain the nature and scope of marketing.
7. Briefly explain the evolution of marketing.
8. Briefly explain the various concepts of marketing.
9. Explain the contribution of marketing to the society.

CHAPTER 2

Marketing Environment

POINTS TO REMEMBER

At the end of this chapter, we will be able to understand:

- Introduction
- Meaning and Definition
- Marketing Environment
- Features of Business Environment
- Environmental Scanning
- Importance of Business Environment

2.1 INTRODUCTION

A marketing-oriented company always keeps tab on its external environment carefully to analyze opportunities and threats. This external environment influences the company's strategies at two levels *i.e.*, external macro-environment level and external micro-environment level. The macro-environment level involves political and legal, economic and natural, social and cultural and technology environment.

The micro-environment level consists of supply chain, customer and competitor. These factors are uncontrollable by the organization. Marketing environment comprises the combination of two words 'marketing' and 'environment'. Marketing means responding to the needs and demands of the consumers to provide optimum satisfaction level. Similarly environment refers to external factors influences and organizational power which is related to the aim and effective working of a firm. Thus, marketing environment refers to external or macro factors and forces which not only influence a company but also the components which affect the consumers analyzing its trend and impact on the operations and performance of the company.

2.2 MEANING AND DEFINITION

This encompasses the marketing team within an organization and includes all of the outside factors of marketing that affect the team's ability to develop and maintain successful customer relationships with their targeted customer group.

The marketing environment surrounds and impacts upon the organization. There are three key elements to the marketing environment which are the internal environment, the micro-environment and the macro-environment. Why are they important? Well marketers build both internal and external relationships. Marketers aim to deliver value to satisfied customers, so we need to assess and evaluate our internal business/corporate environment and our external environment which is subdivided into micro and macro.

"Marketing environment is that which is external to the marketing management function, largely uncontrollable, potentially relevant to marketing decision-making and changing and / or containing in nature".

Cravens et. al

"A company's marketing environment consists of the actors and forces outside marketing that affect marketing management's ability to build and maintain successful relationships with target customers".

Kotler and Armstrong

"The marketing environment of the task environment and the broad environment. The task environment includes the immediate actors involved in purchasing, distributing and promoting the offering. The broad environment consists of six components: demographic environment, economic environment, natural environment, technological environment, political legal environment, social-cultural environment".

Philip Kotler

In this manner marketing environment means external environment *i.e.*, dynamic powers, factors and which influence effectiveness and ability, marketing activities, production of goods, distribution and intermediaries on which companies marketing management and marketing department has no control.

2.3 MARKETING ENVIRONMENT

Marketing environment refers to the forces or variables of the outer and inner environment of a firm that affects the marketing management's ability to build and maintain successful relationships with the customer. The marketing environment framework consists of macro-environment and micro-environment.

Micro-environment variables are close to the firm and include the suppliers, marketing intermediaries, customer markets, competition & publics. Micro-environment also refers to the internal environment of the company and affects not only marketing but also all the departments such as management, finance, research and development, human resources, purchasing, operations and accounting.

Macro-environment deals with the demographic, economic, technological, natural, socio-cultural and politico-legal environment of the markets. The following Fig. 2.1 shows the environmental framework.

1. **Customers:** Customers are the core of the marketing environment. There are different types of customers such as end consumers, business customers, government customers, international customers and retail customers.
2. **Suppliers:** The slightest delay in receiving the supplies may result in dissatisfaction of the customers. The marketers have to watch the supply availability and other trends related to the suppliers.

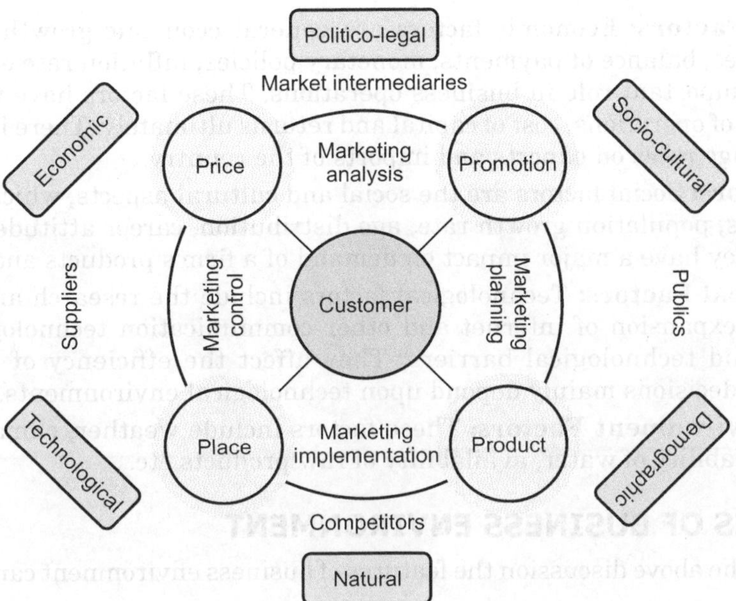

Fig. 2.1. Environmental framework.

3. **Marketing Intermediaries:** The resellers, physical distribution firms, marketing services agencies, and financial intermediaries all make marketing intermediaries. They help in promotion of the company and sales and distribution of the company's products. Stores and warehouses are the physical distribution firms that store and transport the company's product from its origin to its destination. Other intermediaries are marketing services agencies, which are responsible for conducting marketing research, advertising, and consulting. Financial intermediaries are institutions such as banks, credit companies and insurance companies.
4. **Publics:** Publics is any group that has interest or impact on a firm's ability to meet its goals. This includes the financial publics, media publics, government, publics, local publics such as NGO and citizen action organizations. While the financial publics can hinder a company's ability to obtain funds affecting the level of credit in a company, the media publics can publish articles of interest regarding the company and editorials that may influence customers' opinions. Similarly, government publics is capable of affecting the company by passing legislation and laws that put restrictions on the company's actions and citizen-action publics (*e.g.*, environmental groups and minority groups) can question the actions of a company and put them in the public spotlight.
5. **Competitors:** Competitors are the companies with similar offerings for goods and services. To remain competitive a company must consider who their biggest competitors are while considering its own size and position in the industry. The company should develop a strategic advantage over their competitors.
6. **Political-legal Factors:** Political factors include how and to what degree a government intervenes in the economy. This includes monetary and tax policies of the government, labour laws, environmental laws, various trade restrictions and tariffs. Political stability is one of the main factors. This also includes the merit goods and demerit goods as per the provisions of the local government. Legal factors deal with discrimination law, consumer law, antitrust law, employment law and health and safety law.

7. **Economic Factors:** Economic factors are general economic growth, interest rates, exchange rates, balance of payments, monetary policies, inflation rate etc. These factors play a very important role in business operations. These factors have the capability to alter the cost of operations, cost of capital and returns ultimately. There is a major impact of the exchange rates on exports and imports of the country.
8. **Social Factors:** Social factors are the social and cultural aspects, which include health consciousness, population growth rate, age distribution, career attitudes and emphasis on safety. They have a major impact on demand of a firm's products and services.
9. **Technological Factors:** Technological factors include the research and development, automation, expansion of internet and other communication technologies, technology incentives and technological barriers. They affect the efficiency of the production. Outsourcing decisions mainly depend upon technological environments.
10. **Natural Environment Factors:** These factors include weather, climate, and climate change, availability of water, availability of raw products etc.

2.4 FEATURES OF BUSINESS ENVIRONMENT

On the basis of the above discussion the features of business environment can be summarized as follows:

(*a*) Business environment is the sum total of all factors external to the business firm and that greatly influence their functioning.

(*b*) It covers factors and forces like customers, competitors, suppliers, government and social, cultural, political, technological and legal conditions.

(*c*) The business environment is dynamic in nature, which means, it keeps on changing.

(*d*) The changes in business environment are unpredictable. It is very difficult to predict the exact nature of future happenings and the changes in economic and social environment.

(*e*) Business environment differs from place to place, region to region and country to country. Political conditions in India differ from those in Pakistan. Taste and values cherished by people in India and China vary considerably.

2.5 ENVIRONMENTAL SCANNING

This is the process of gathering, analyzing and forecasting of external environments' information to identify opportunity and threats that company faces the need for environmental scanning. It helps in:

2.5.1 Analyzing the Organization's Micro-environment

Marketing department alone cannot satisfy all the needs of a customer. Therefore, it is essential to integrate the functions of suppliers, publics, company departments and intermediaries in creating the value to the customer. These forces are known as organization's micro-environment forces. Micro-environment forces which are very close to a company and have impact on value creation and customer service are shown in Fig. 2.2.

1. **The Company:** Deducing a strategic plan into a specific marketing plan requires co-ordination of other functions like finance, human resource, production and research and development.
2. **Intermediaries:** Marketing intermediaries are the firms which distribute and sell the goods of the company to the consumer.

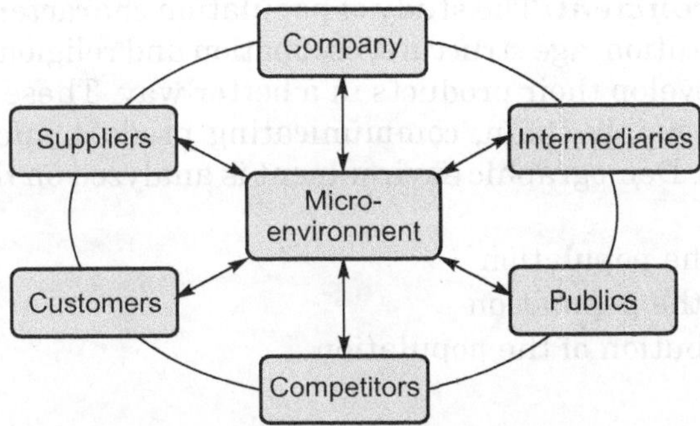

Fig. 2.2. Micro-environment forces.

3. **Publics:** These are micro-environment groups, which help a company to generate the financial resources, creating the image, examining the companies' policy and developing the attitude towards the product. We can identify six types of publics.
4. **Competitors:** A company should monitor its immediate competitor. The product should be positioned differently and able to provide better services.
5. **Suppliers:** Suppliers are the first link in the entire supply chain of the company. Hence, any problem or cost escalation in this stage will have direct effect on the company. Many companies adopted supplier relation management system to manage them well.
6. **Customers:** A company may sell their products directly to the customer or use marketing intermediaries to reach them. Direct or indirect marketing depends on what type of markets the company serves. Generally we can divide the markets into five different categories. They are:
   (*a*) Consumer market.
   (*b*) Business market
   (*c*) Reseller market
   (*d*) Government market and
   (*e*) International market.

2.5.2 Analyzing the Organization's Macro-environment

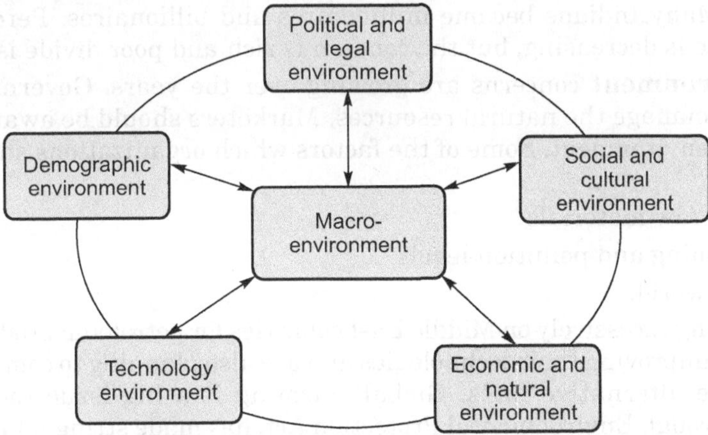

Fig. 2.3. Macro-environment of a firm.

1. **Demographic Environment:** The study of population characteristics like size, density, location, gender composition, age structure, occupation and religion. Demography statistics helps companies to develop their products in a better way. These statistics are also used in developing proper supply chain, communicating product information and changing the product attributes. Demographic environment is analyzed on the basis of the following factors.
   (*i*) Age structure of the population
   (*ii*) Marital status of the population
   (*iii*) Geographic distribution of the population
   (*iv*) Education level
   (*v*) Migration
   (*vi*) Occupation.
2. **Political and Legal Environment:** Government policies, legislations, regulations and stability will directly affect the business. Therefore, it is inevitable for the firm to closely monitor this environment. The political and legal forces are grouped into the following four categories.
   (*i*) **Monetary and fiscal policies:** These policies regulate government spending, money supply and tax legislations.
   (*ii*) **Social legislations and regulations:** Environmental protection act which specifies the emission level.
   (*iii*) **Government relationships with industries:** Government subsidies and change in tariff rate will have direct impact on the particular company.
   (*iv*) **Legislations related to marketing:** There are a list of legislations which affect marketing activities of a company.
3. **Economic and Natural Environment:** Economic environment includes the following:
   (*a*) **Interest rate:** When interest rates are high, consumers tend not to make long-term purchase like housing. If the interest rate is low people put their money in alternative financial options where they get better return.
   (*b*) **Inflation:** The higher the inflation rate, the lesser will be the purchasing power of the consumer. Hence, government always tries to control the inflation within the limit.
   (*c*) **Changes in income:** The rise in the salaries of the employees, improved performance of stock market and better industrial growth led to the change in the income pattern in India. Many Indians became millionaires and billionaires. Percentage of below poverty line is decreasing, but the concern is rich and poor divide is growing.

   Natural environment concerns are growing over the years. Governments increased regulations to manage the natural resources. Marketers should be aware of such trends in the natural environment. Some of the factors which organizations should keep a vigil on are:
   - Inadequate raw materials
   - Global warming and pollution levels
   - Regulatory world.

   We are depending excessively on Middle East countries for petroleum products. Automobile companies are improving their technologies and are also planning to come out with hybrid cars which use alternative fuels. Global warming is a big issue today. The Indian government through Environmental Protection Act, has made stringent rules on emission and environment standards. Companies, particularly in automobiles should adhere to those norms, which are expensive and time consuming.

4. **Social and Cultural Environment:**
   (*i*) **Working women and rise of metrosexual man:** The number of women who are working in India is increasing. This segment is looking towards products, which help them in bringing better work-life balance. MTR, a fast food giant in south India, started offering ready-to-eat products to this segment. These products are instant in nature where a woman dips a product in the hot water for minutes and serves.
   (*ii*) **People hard pressed for time:** This segment involves people who work long hours and have less personal time. These people are looking for products which satisfy them quickly and conveniently. For example, Easy bill, from Hero group offers one stop solution to consumers to pay their utility bills and do other financial transactions.
5. **Technology Environment:**
   (*i*) **Growth of information technology and bio-technology industries:** Information technology has revolutionized the lives of the people. It brought dramatic changes in the way organizations operate. It helped in cost reduction, automation, better communication and efficiency in the organizations. Indian banks which few years ago used to take a lot of time to process the customer requests reduced it to few hours because of information technology.
   (*ii*) **Nano technology:** The technology is waiting, which is expected to reduce the size and cost of the materials.

2.6 IMPORTANCE OF BUSINESS ENVIRONMENT

There is a close and continuous interaction between a business and its environment. This interaction helps in strengthening the business firm and using its resources more effectively. As stated above, the business environment is multifaceted, complex and dynamic in nature and has a far-reaching impact on the survival and growth of the business. To be more specific, proper understanding of the social, political, legal and economic environment helps the business in the following ways:

1. **Determining Opportunities and Threats:** The interaction between a business and its environment would identify opportunities for and threats to the business. It helps the business enterprises in meeting the challenges successfully.
2. **Giving Direction for Growth:** The interaction with the environment leads to opening up of new frontiers of growth for the business firms. It enables the business to identify the areas for growth and expansion of their activities.
3. **Continuous Learning:** Environmental analysis makes the task of managers easier in dealing with business challenges. The managers are motivated to continuously update their knowledge, understanding and skills to meet the predicted changes in the realm of business.
4. **Image Building:** Environmental understanding helps the business organizations in improving their image by showing their sensitivity to the environment within which they are working. For example, in view of the shortage of power, many companies have set up Captive Power Plants (CPP) in their factories to meet their own requirement of power.
5. **Meeting Competition:** It helps the firms to analyze the competitors' strategies and formulate their own strategies accordingly.
6. **Identifying Firm's Strength and Weakness:** Business environment helps to identify the individual strengths and weaknesses in view of the technological and global developments.

REVIEW QUESTIONS

1. Explain the need of environment scanning.
2. Bring out the difference between macro-environment and micro-environment.
3. Write a note on demographic environment in India.
4. Environment scanning is necessary to understand opportunities and threats faced by the company.
5. Micro-environment factors like marketing intermediaries, suppliers, competitors, publics and customers influence a company's strategies.
6. Population variables like age, gender, marital status and occupation help the company to assess the market and change or develop their offerings.
7. Shortage of raw material and increase in the income disparity are immediate concerns of the organizations.
8. Working women and people hard-pressed for time are changing the socio-cultural environment of the country.
9. Technology is helping companies to reduce cost, increase efficiency and save time. Explain.
10. Discuss the importance of political and legal environment study with examples.
11. Micro and macro-environment are differentiated on the basis of size, complexity and uncertainty.

CHAPTER 3

Marketing Mix and Marketing Plan

POINTS TO REMEMBER

At the end of this chapter, we will be able to understand:

Marketing Mix

- Introduction
- Meaning and Definitions of Marketing Mix
- Features of Marketing Mix
- Components of Marketing Mix
- 4Cs of Marketing Mix

Marketing Planning

- Introduction to Marketing Planning
- Meaning and Definition of Marketing Planning
- Elements of Marketing Plan
- Process of Marketing Plan
- Importance of Marketing Plan

3.1 INTRODUCTION

The basic task of marketing is the delivery of product(s) to consumers so that their needs are fulfilled and organizational objectives are also achieved. This involves several important decisions, *e.g.*, deciding about the product or products which should be offered for sale, price of the product, markets where products may be sold and the means of communication with the consumer for the sale of the product. All these decisions form part of marketing-mix. In this lesson we shall study about the concept of marketing mix, its components and the relationship among various components of marketing mix.

The concept is simple. Think about another common mix—a cake mix. All cakes contain eggs, milk, flour, and sugar. However, you can alter the final cake by altering the amounts of mix elements contained in it. So for a sweet cake add more sugar. It is the same with the marketing mix. The offer you make to your customer can be altered by varying the mix elements. So for a high profile brand, increase the focus on promotion and desensitize the weight given to price.

Marketing involves a number of activities. To begin with, an organization may decide on its target group of customers to be served. Once the target group is decided, the product is to be placed in the market by providing the appropriate product, price, distribution and promotional efforts. These are to be combined or mixed in an appropriate proportion so as to achieve the marketing goal. Such mix of product, price, distribution and promotional efforts is known as 'Marketing Mix'.

3.2 MEANING AND DEFINITIONS OF MARKETING MIX

In the general way, marketing mix means mixing of various marketing policies to achieve success in marketing. But in the broad sense, marketing mix means mixing of various sales policies by manufacturers/producers such as product, brand and trademark packaging, price distribution-medium, sales power, advertisement, sales promotion, physical distribution of products and marketing research etc., in such a way that in certain time and situation maximum profit can be earned by buyer's satisfaction.

"Marketing mix is a pack of four sets of variables namely product variables, price variables, promotion variables and place variables". **Cravens et. al**

"The marketing mix is the set of marketing tools the firm uses to pursue its marketing objectives in the target market". **Philip Kotler**

"Marketing mix is the term used to describe the combination of four inputs which constitute the core of a company's marketing system—the product, the promotional activities and the distribution system". **Stanton**

"The marketing mix refers to the apportionment of efforts, the combination, the designing, the integration of the elements of marketing into a program or mix which on the basis of an appraisal of the market force, will achieve the market objectives of an enterprise in a given time". **Prof. Neil H. Bordon**

"Marketing mix is a set of controllable, tactical tools, product, price, place and promotion that the firm blends to produce the response it wants in the target market. The marketing mix consists of everything the firm can do to influence the demand for its product". **Kotler and Armstrong**

3.3 FEATURES OF MARKETING MIX

The marketing mix has the following features:

1. **Root of Marketing Process:** Marketing mix involves many crucial decisions relating to each element of the mix. The impact of the mix would be the best when proper weightage is assigned to each element and they are integrated so that the combined effect leads to the best results.
2. **Reviewed Constantly in Order to Meet the Changing Requirements:** The marketing manager is required to constantly review the mix and conditions of the market, and make necessary changes in the marketing mix according to changes in the conditions and complexion of the market.
3. **Changes in External Environment:** Changes keep on taking place in the external environment. For many industries, customer is the most fluctuating variable of

environment. Customers' tastes and preferences change very fast. Brand loyalty and purchasing power too change over a period of time. The marketing manager has to carry out market analysis constantly to make necessary changes in the marketing mix.

4. **Changes taking place within the firm too necessitate changes in marketing mix:** Changes within the firm may take place due to technological changes, or changes in the product line, or changes in the size and scale of operation. Such changes call for correspondent changes in the marketing mix.

3.4 COMPONENTS OF MARKETING MIX

The marketing mix is one of the most famous marketing terms. The marketing mix is the tactical or operational part of a marketing plan. The marketing mix is also called the 4Ps and the 7Ps. The 4Ps are price, place, product and promotion. The services marketing mix is also called the 7Ps and includes the addition of process, people and physical evidence.

According to Philip Kotler "Marketing mix is the set of controllable variables that the firm can use to influence the buyer's response". The controllable variables in this context refer to the 4P's [product, price, place (distribution channel) and promotion]. Each firm strives to build up such a composition of 4P's, which can create the highest level of consumer satisfaction and at the same time meet its organizational objectives. Thus, this mix is assembled keeping in mind the needs of target customers, and it varies from one organization to another depending upon its available resources and marketing objectives.

Let us now have a brief idea about the four components of marketing mix. Figure 3.1 displays the components of mixing.

Fig. 3.1. Components of market mixing: the 4Ps.

(*a*) **Product:** Product refers to a physical product or a service or an idea which a consumer needs and for which he is ready to pay. Physical products include tangible goods like grocery items, garments etc. Services are intangible products which are offered and purchased by consumers. Services may involve also an innovative idea on any aspect of operation. Products are the key element of any marketing mix. The decisions concerning product may relate to:

(*i*) Product attributes

(*ii*) Branding

(*iii*) Packaging and labeling

(*iv*) Product support service

(*v*) Product mix.

Product attributes: Product attributes refer to the quality, features and design of the product. A product should serve the purpose for which it is made, in terms of utility and quality. In a competitive market, products are differentiated on the basis of certain features or design. For example, in the Whirlpool washing machine 'Agitate wash' is the distinctive feature.

> *"Product means the goods-and-services combination the company offers to the target market".*
> **Kotler and Armstrong (2010)**

Product can also take the form of a service like an air travel, telecommunication, etc. Thus, the term 'product' refers to goods and services offered by the organization for sale.

(*b*) **Price:** Price is the amount charged for a product or service. It is the second most important element in the marketing mix. Fixing the price of the product is a tricky job.

> *"Price is the amount the consumer must exchange to receive the offering".*
> **Solomon et. al (2009)**

Many factors like demand for a product, cost involved, consumer's ability to pay, prices charged by competitors for similar products, government restrictions etc., have to be kept in mind while fixing the price. In fact, pricing is a very crucial decision area as it has its effect on demand for the product and also on the profitability of the firm.

(*c*) **Place:** Goods are produced to be sold to the consumers. They must be made available to the consumers at a place where they can conveniently make the purchase. Woollens are manufactured on a large-scale in Ludhiana and you purchase them at a store from the nearby market in your town. So, it is necessary that the product is available at shops in your town. This involves a chain of individuals and institutions like distributors, wholesalers and retailers who constitute a firm's distribution network (also called a channel of distribution).

> *"Place includes company activities that make the product available to target consumers".*
> **Kotler and Armstrong (2010)**

The organization has to decide whether to sell directly to the retailer or through the distributors/wholesaler etc. It can even plan to sell it directly to consumers.

(*d*) **Promotion:** If the product is manufactured keeping the consumer needs in mind, is rightly priced and made available at outlets convenient to them but the consumer is not made aware of its price, features, availability etc., its marketing effort may not be successful.

> *"Promotion includes all of the activities marketers undertake to inform consumers about their products and to encourage potential customers to buy these products".*
> **Solomon et. al (2009)**

Therefore, promotion is an important ingredient of marketing mix as it refers to a process of informing, persuading and influencing a consumer to make choice of the product to be bought. Promotion is done through means of personal selling, advertising, publicity and sales promotion. It is done mainly with a view to provide information to prospective consumers about the availability, characteristics and uses of a product. It arouses a potential consumer's interest in the product, compare it with competitors' product and make his choice. The proliferation of print and electronic media has immensely helped the process of promotion.

The following Fig. 3.2 displays the 7Ps including the addition of process, people and physical evidence.

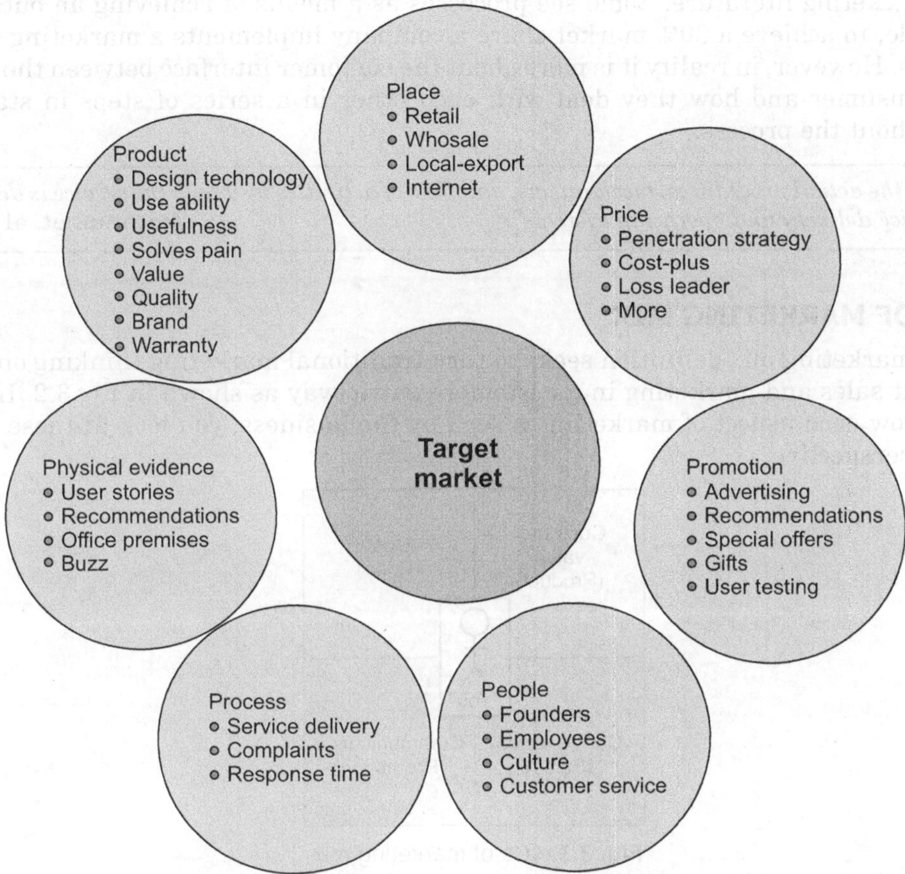

Fig. 3.2. Components of market mixing: the 7Ps.

1. **Physical evidence:** Physical evidence is the material part of a service. Strictly speaking there are no physical attributes to a service, so a consumer tends to rely on material cues.

> *"The environment in which the service is delivered, and where the firm and customer interact, and any tangible components that facilitate performance or communication of the service".*
>
> **Zeithaml et. al (2008)**

There are many examples of physical evidence, including some of the following—buildings, equipment, signs and logos, annual accounts and business reports, brochures, your website, and even your business cards.

2. **People:** People are the most important element of any service or experience. Services tend to be produced and consumed at the same moment, and aspects of the customer experience are altered to meet the individual needs of the person consuming it.

> *"All human actors who play a part in service delivery and thus influence the buyers' perceptions; namely, the firm's personnel, the customer, and other customers in the service environment".*
>
> **Zeithaml et. al (2008)**

3. **Process:** There are a number of perceptions of the concept of process within the business and marketing literature. Some see processes as a means of achieving an outcome, for example, to achieve a 30% market share a company implements a marketing planning process. However, in reality it is more about the customer interface between the business and consumer and how they deal with each other in a series of steps in stages, *i.e.*, throughout the process.

> *"Process is the actual procedures, mechanisms, and flow of activities by which the service is delivered – this service delivery and operating systems".*
>
> **Zeithaml et. al (2008)**

3.5 4Cs OF MARKETING MIX

The 4Cs marketing mix definition seeks to turn traditional marketing thinking on its head by looking at sales and marketing in a customer-centric way as shown in Fig.3.2. Instead of looking at how each aspect of marketing is seen by the business, you look at these from the customer's perspective.

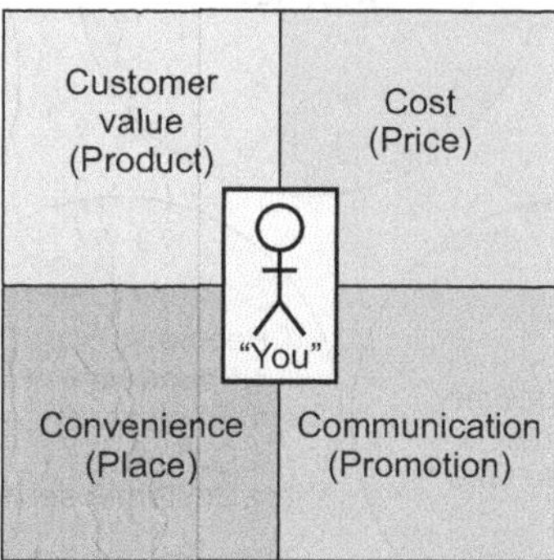

Fig. 3.3. 4Cs of marketing mix.

The point in using "4Cs" instead of "4Ps" is not an exercise in semantics. Rather, key into the thinking behind the exercise which is to get you to see things from your customers' point of view.

1. **Customer Value (Not Product):** A product is something you make which people come and buy. However, today, you can no longer succeed by making what you want and must instead find out what customers want.

   Focusing on customer value allows you to reset your perceptions around what it is you are creating and bringing to the market, be it a product, service or some other value. Everything begins and ends with your customer and you exist to serve his/her needs. Value is what your customer is concerned about, not you, your fabulous product or anything else you do. Value is how you define marketing mix "products" and what you should seek to engage your customer with. It is the value you provide that defines you in the marketplace.
2. **Cost (Not Price):** Instead of thinking of price as something you charge, think of cost as something customers pay. This simple adjustment once again opens up a whole new way of thinking about sales and marketing.

When you define marketing mix cost you tune into the customer dilemma of deciding how to spend limited money to satisfy unlimited wants. Are you providing enough capital to compete effectively? Your motivation in going to market should not be to maximize your gain but to maximize customer value. Therefore, you should ask how you can provide more for the same cost to the customer instead of asking to make more profit from a product.

3. **Convenience (Not Place):** The day is not far off when the majority of shopping will not take place in shops or through the traditional distribution channels of business. Your customers today are governed by purchase when, where and how it is convenient to them. Thinking about convenience not only allows you to open up to newer ways of connecting with customers and distributing products, but helps you shift into the mindset of providing an optimum overall experience for customers. To define marketing mix in terms of convenience reminds you that customers today are very busy and have many choices. It is no longer your right as a business owner but a privilege when customers choose you. Make it as easy as possible for them to do so.
4. **Communication (Not Promotion):** The final new market mix definition replaces the traditional notion of "promotion" with communication. This final concept of how you define marketing mix from the customer's perspective ties into creating interactive marketing communication. "Promotion" takes you back to the days of mass marketing which does not work anymore. Just like you cannot simply build a "good product" and expect people to buy it, so customers no longer believe everything you say at face value. Instead of virtuous pronouncement about how good your product or service is, customers today seek to be engaged and have meaningful interactions with you. You must therefore strive for two-way communication and building relationships.

3.6 INTRODUCTION TO MARKETING PLANNING

The central point in planning for marketing decisions is the marketing plan. Marketing plans are an essential component for all businesses. All businesses that are successful have followed a plan. Their success did not happen because of luck, it happened because the success was planned. A marketing plan helps establish, co-ordinate, and direct marketing efforts. It forces the organization to take a good, hard look at the market of your field and what is currently happening to it. Its a time to establish marketing goals and objectives, which can be later used for benchmarking yourself. Marketing plans help keep the organization on the right track by following the guidelines it sets. It is also critical when trying to borrow money. When an organization plans to allow you to borrow money or invest in your organization, they require to examine your business plan. The marketing plan is a critical part of the business plan.

3.7 MEANING AND DEFINITION OF MARKETING PLANNING

A marketing plan is a written document that summarizes what the marketer has learned about the market place and indicates how the firm plans to reach its marketing objectives. It is one of the most important outputs of the marketing process. Marketing plan and product planning is becoming more customer and competitor-oriented and is becoming a continuous process to respond to rapidly occurring and changing market conditions.

> *"Marketing plans are developed for individual products, lines, brands, channels, or customer groups. The marketing plan is one of the most important outputs of the marketing process".*
>
> **Philip Kotler**

> *"An effective marketing plan defines how and why the company is in business, what markets are good targets for its products, and how customers should be pursued. With a marketing plan in place, a company uses the plan to measure how effectively corporate goals have been met".*
>
> **Winchester**

3.8 ELEMENTS OF MARKETING PLAN

The marketing plan is often a complex and diverse document that examines many areas. For most plans the key components found in the document include:

1. **Organizational Mission:** Represents the guiding force of an organization by identifying the long-run vision for what the organization hopes to achieve. The mission comes from the top leaders of the organization and often remains unchanged for many years.
2. **Executive Summary and Table of Contents:** The marketing plan should open with a brief summary of the main goals and recommendations. A table of contents outlines the rest of the plan and all the supporting and operational details.
3. **Situation Analysis:** This section presents relevant background data on sales, costs, the market, competitors and various forces in the macro-environment. All this information is used to carry out SWOT analysis.
4. **Marketing Strategy:** Achieving objectives requires the marketer to engage in marketing decision-making which indicates where resources (*e.g.*, marketing funds) will be directed. However, before spending begins on individual marketing decisions (*e.g.*, where to advertise) the marketer needs to establish a general plan of action that summarizes what will be done to reach the stated objectives.
5. **Marketing Strategy:** Here, the product manager defines the mission and marketing and financial objectives. The manager also defines those groups and needs that the market offerings are intended to satisfy. The manager then establishes the product lines competitive positioning which will inform the game plan to accomplish the plan's objectives.
6. **Financial Projections:** Financial projections include a sales forecast, an expense forecast and a break-even analysis on the revenue side, the projections show the forecasted sales volume by month and product category. On the expense side, the projections show the expected costs of marketing.
7. **Implementation Control:** This section outlines the controls for monitoring and adjusting implementation of the plan. Typically the goals and budgets are spelled out for each month or quarter so management can review each period's result and take corrective actions as needed.

3.9 PROCESS OF MARKETING PLAN

Careful planning increases the chances of successfully accomplishing what you set out to achieve. The principles of good planning can be applied to almost any project and remain the same irrespective of the task. However, the outcome of planning, the plan, can differ according to the nature and purpose of the task. There are three stages in the process of preparing a marketing plan.

1. **Reviewing your Overall Strategy:** The first involves reviewing your overall strategy to confirm the definition of your target customer and decide on the positioning strategy you want to adopt. Positioning is generally concerned with how you differentiate your products and services from those of your competitors.

2. **Determine the Impact of your Targeting and Positioning Decisions:** The next step is to determine the impact of your targeting and positioning decisions on your strategy for the marketing mix. The marketing mix deals with such issues as **product** specification and development, **pricing** policies, delivery systems (**place**) and **promotional** activity, and is sometimes referred to as '**the 4Ps**'. By this point you will be making decisions that indicate the need for specific action to be taken which, in turn, have implications for the operational resources you will need.
3. **Review these Needs and Prepare an Action Plan:** The last step is to review these needs and prepare an action plan that states, using 'action-oriented' statements, what will be done and when preferably with allocated responsibilities for each task.

When you have formulated your marketing plan it can be helpful to produce a written document. Actually writing out the plan and including justification for intentions will help crystallize your thinking and ensure that you have covered all the important points. If you will be seeking external finance to support your marketing development, any potential patron will insist on a written plan possibly as part of an overall business plan. The core elements of a marketing plan are:

- Description of the products and/or services you intend to sell—what they do, how they work, the customer benefits they offer and how they differ from those of the competition. It may be helpful to incorporate here or possibly as a separate section, a description and analysis of your chosen market including market size, market structure, competitors and market trends.
- Definition of your target customers, including an explanation of why you believe they will buy your products/services—the benefits they seek and the reason why they are likely to choose your products in preference to those of your competitors.
- A section dealing with each element of the marketing mix stating what you will do and why.
- An assessment of the resource implications of your plan—additional people, equipment, etc.—noting why you need them and the costs involved.
- Summary action plan time-table.

3.10 IMPORTANCE OF MARKETING PLAN

A marketing plan clarifies the key marketing elements of a business and maps out directions, objectives and activities for the business and its employees. The marketing plan draws on the broader perspectives outlined in a firm's business plan. The business plan states how a company will take a product idea and transform that into a commercially viable proposition. The marketing plan focuses on issues related to the 4Ps: product, price, promotion and place.

Addressing these issues and putting them into written form can be useful for a business owner, in that it forces them to analyze their business. It can be good for employees, as the marketing plan can provide them with essential orientation and be a source of motivation.

1. **Plan for Expenses:** While there are many free and low cost ways to market your business, some marketing costs money. How much are you willing to commit to your total marketing budget? What is a realistic number for all the marketing activities you hope to accomplish?
2. **Understand your Target Market:** One of the biggest mistakes small-business owners make is that "everyone" is their target market. There's no one product or service that appeals universally. Even Coca-Cola, which targets most people and whose products are available virtually everywhere, has different marketing messages and different products they advertise to different market segments. Decide who is most likely to buy from you.

Who are they and what factors influence their decision to buy? Look at their demographics. How old are they? Are they married? What is their income level? Where do they live? What job titles do they have? Next, look at their psychographics. Why do they buy? What problems do they want solutions to? How critical is the problem? You can have multiple target markets, but keep in mind that you will need a separate marketing campaign for each market. It's better to stick with one, initially, and expand as your company grows.

3. **Determine what Media to Use:** Which marketing tactics (direct mail, word of mouth, newspaper/magazines, TV, radio, internet) you use depends on your marketing budget and your target audience. Choose one to start with, get your campaign working, and start bringing in customers. Once you have one marketing campaign in place, add another. If you try to manage too many things at one time, you dramatically limit the time, money and resources you can devote to each.
4. **Stick to a Schedule:** Too many business owners get trapped in a vicious cycle. They start marketing when business is slow. Then, either because of their marketing campaign or because someone referred them business, they end up with a client or two. All marketing halts as they focus their attention on serving their clients. As the client projects come to an end, the business owner realizes he or she is in the same boat as before—with no prospects—so he or she starts marketing again. And the cycle repeats. For your marketing to be successful, you need to stick to a schedule and keep your marketing activities going through slow and busy times.

REVIEW QUESTIONS

1. Explain the meaning and definition of market mix.
2. What are the main features of market mix?
3. Describe the different components of marketing mix.
4. Explain the 4Cs of marketing mix.
5. What is marketing planning? Explain the different types of marketing plan.
6. Describe the elements of marketing plan.
7. Explain the process of marketing plan.
8. Define the importance of marketing plan.

C H A P T E R 4

Market Segmentation, Targeting and Positioning

POINTS TO REMEMBER

At the end of this chapter, we will be able to understand:

- Introduction
- Meaning and Definition of Market Segmentation
- Market Segmentation Objectives
- Bases of Market Segmentation
- Levels of Market Segmentation
- Importance of Market Segmentation
- Market Targeting
- Meaning and Definition of Market Targeting
- Selection of Target Segments
- Targeting Strategies
- Positioning
- Meaning and Definition of Positioning
- Steps to Product Positioning
- Positioning Strategies

4.1 INTRODUCTION

In today's world of globalization, marketing has become a very important medium for running and maintaining business at national as well as international level. If you are into some business or a consultant of business, you must be aware of what marketing is and what the importance of market is. A market is basically a place where business persons exchange goods with capital or some other goods.

The chapter begins by identifying the underlying principle of market segmentation. Market segmentation is the starting step in applying the marketing strategy. In this process the marketer is meeting the expectations of the consumers. On the basis of segmentation, the company will prepare and follow different marketing programs for different segments to ensure better customer relationship.

A market consists of large number of individual customers who differ in terms of their needs, preferences and buying capacity. Therefore, it becomes necessary to divide the total market into different segments or homogeneous customer groups. Such division is called market segmentation. They may have uniformity in employment patterns, educational qualifications, socio-economic status, preferences, etc. Market segmentation enables the entrepreneur to match his marketing efforts to the requirements of the target market. Instead of wasting his efforts in trying to sell to all types of customers, a small-scale unit can focus its efforts on the segment most appropriate to its market.

4.2 MEANING AND DEFINITION OF MARKET SEGMENTATION

Market segmentation is the technique used to enable a business to better target its products at the right customers. It is about identifying the specific needs and wants of customer groups and then using those insights into providing products and services which meet customer needs.

> *"Market segmentation is the process whereby producers organize their knowledge of customer groups and select for particular attention, those whose needs and wants they are best able to supply with their products".* **Victor T.C. Middleton**

> *"Market segmentation is the process of dividing a total market into market groups consisting of people who have relatively similar product needs, tastes, and preferences. The purpose is to design a marketing mix strategy that more precisely matches the needs of individuals in a selected market segment(s)".*

Market segmentation is a method of dividing a large market into smaller groupings of consumers each having common needs or behaviour. We have two types of markets:

(*i*) **Homogeneous market:** A market in which people or organization has similar characteristics.

(*ii*) **Heterogeneous market:** A market in which people or organizations have different characteristics.

Segments are usually measured in terms of sales value or volume. As shown in Fig. 4.1 segment B is twice the size of segment C.

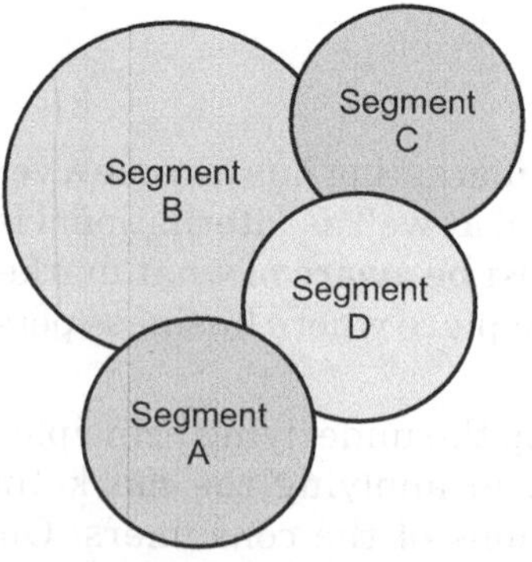

Fig. 4.1. Market segmentation.

Why do businesses need to segment their markets? Because customers differ in the:

- Benefits they want.
- Amount they are able to or willing to pay.
- Media (*e.g.*, television, newspapers, and magazines) they see.
- Quantities they buy.
- Time and place that they buy.

4.3 MARKET SEGMENTATION OBJECTIVES

In general, segmentation has the main objective to improve the competitive position of businesses. It provides better service to consumers. In addition to these main objectives are—boost sales, improve market share, to communicate, better promotion, and strengthening the image. At least there are five advantages to be gained by doing market segmentation, namely:

1. **Designing Products that are More Responsive to Market Needs:** The company puts the customer in the first place, and adjusts products to satisfy them and achieve customer satisfaction at a profit.
2. **Analyze Market:** Segmentation market is helping executives to detect anyone who attacked its product market.
3. **Assess Opportunities:** After analyzing the market, companies that master the concept of segmentation will be on the lookout for the idea to find opportunities. This opportunity is not always something that big, but in its time would be great.
4. **Mastering the Position of Superior and Competitive:** A company that controls segments well is generally well aware of their customers. Companies understand the shifts that occurred in the segment.
5. **Determining Effective Communication Strategies:** After learning about the targeted segment, the company will determine how to communicate effectively with the targeted segments.

4.4 BASES OF MARKET SEGMENTATION

There are various methods (or "bases") a business can use to segment a market. Some of the most popular are summarized in Fig. 4.2.

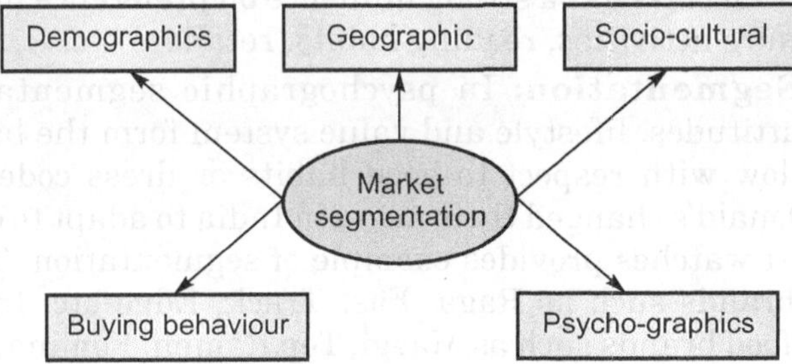

Fig. 4.2. Bases of segmentation.

The brief description of these bases are as follows:

1. **Geographic Segmentation:** Geographic segmentation calls for dividing the market into different geographical units such as nations, regions, countries, cities or neighbourhood. One of the major geographic segmentation in India is the division of rural and urban areas. The need to segment the market geographically becomes clearer

when we look at some of the characteristics of the market. In India, there are more than 5,000 towns and over 6, 37,000 villages. Nearly 88% of these villages have a population of less than 2,000 people. This variation in population is important for the marketer while formulating marketing strategy and plans.

In addition to this products penetration, income levels and availability of infrastructure like roads and electricity make the task of geographic segmentation important.

For most products, penetration levels in rural areas are lower than in urban areas. Income and lifestyle issues influence the penetration rate of products and services, for example, *haats and mandis* serve important roles in the exchange of goods and services in rural areas.

2. **Demographic Segmentation:** In demographic segmentation, the market is divided into groups on the basis of variables such as age, family size, family life cycle, gender, income, occupation, education, religion, race, generation, nationality and social class.

   (*i*) **Age and life cycle stage:** Consumer wants and abilities change with age, *e.g.*, Hindustan Unilever introduced Pears soap in pink colour especially for children. Johnson and Johnson Baby Powder and Talcum Powder are classic examples of products for infants and children. Television channels in India indicate the segmentation based on age and life cycle. There are channels like Aastha and Sanskaar which target the old generation, cartoon network, Disney are channels for children etc.

   (*ii*) **Gender:** Men and women have different behavioural orientation. Gender differentiation has been long applied to product categories such as clothing, cosmetics and magazines, *e.g.*, Axe deodorant is positioned as a masculine product. Park Avenue from Raymond is positioned as a masculine brand. Bajaj wave is a brand specifically designed for women in the scooter segment.

   (*iii*) **Income:** Income segmentation is a long standing practice in a variety of products and services and is a basic segmentation variable, *e.g.*, Nirma Washing Powder was launched as the lowest priced detergent in India primarily targeted at the middle income group. Markets for many consumers' products in India are showing rapid growth due to low unit price packaging.

   (*iv*) **Generation:** Each generation is profoundly influenced by the time in which it grows—music, movies, and politics.

   (*v*) **Social class:** Social class has a strong influence on preference in cars, clothing, home, furnishings, leisure activities, reading habits, retailers etc.

3. **Psychographic Segmentation:** In psychographic segmentation, elements like personality traits, attitudes, lifestyle and value system form the base. The strict norms that consumers follow with respect to good habits or dress codes are representative examples, *e.g.*, McDonald's changed their menu in India to adapt to consumer preference. The market for wrist watches provides example of segmentation. Titan watches have a wide range of sub-brands such as Raga, Fast Track, Edge etc. Instant noodle marks, include fast to cook food brands such as Maggi, Top Ramen. Femina, a women's magazine is targeted at modern women.

4. **Behavioural Segmentation:** Markets can be segmented on the basis of buyer behaviour as well. The primary idea in buyer behaviour is that different customer groups expect different benefits from the same product and accordingly they will be different in their motives in owning it. In buyer behaviour based segmentation also, several sub-factors form the basis, *e.g.*, purchase occasion can be one base, buyers can be segmented on the

basis of whether they are regular buyers or special occasion buyers. Degree of use can be another base, they can be segmented on the basis of whether they are light, medium or heavy users of the product or whether they are enthusiastic or indifferent or negative towards the product.

5. **Volume Segmentation:** The division of a market into segments on the basis of the varying volume of demand for the product by individuals, groups or types of customers, typically, the segment is ranked to denote heavy usage, medium usage or light usage.

4.5 LEVELS OF MARKET SEGMENTATION

There are four levels of segments:

1. **Segment Marketing:** A market segment consists of a large identifiable group within a market, with similar wants, purchasing power, geographical location, buying attitudes, or buying habits. For example, an automaker may identify four broad segments in the car market: buyers who are primarily seeking (1) basic transportation, (2) high performance, (3) luxury, or (4) safety.

   Because the needs, preferences, and behaviour of segment members are similar but not identical, Anderson and Narus urge marketers to present flexible market offerings instead of one standard offering to all members of a segment. A flexible market offering consists of the product and service elements that all segment members value, plus options (for an additional charge) that some segment members value. For example, Delta Airlines offers all economy passengers a seat, food, and soft drinks, but it charges extra for alcoholic beverages and earphones.

   Segment marketing allows a firm to create a more fine-tuned product or service offering and price it appropriately for the target audience. The choice of distribution channels and communications channels becomes much easier, and the firm may find it faces fewer competitors in certain segments.

2. **Niche Marketing:** A niche is a more narrowly defined group (typically a small market whose needs are not being well served). Marketers usually identify niches by dividing a segment into sub-segments or by defining a group seeking a distinctive mix of benefits. For example, a tobacco company might identify two sub-segments of heavy smokers: those who are trying to stop smoking, and those who don't care.

   In an attractive niche, customers have a distinct set of needs; they will pay a premium to the firm that best satisfies their needs; the niche is not likely to attract other competitors; the niche gains certain economies through specialization; and the niche has size, profit, and growth potential. Whereas segments are fairly large and normally attract several competitors, niches are fairly small and may attract only one or two rivals. Still, giants such as IBM can and do lose pieces of their market to niches.

3. **Local Marketing:** Target marketing is leading to some marketing programs that are tailored to the needs and wants of local customer groups (trading areas, neighbourhoods, even individual stores). Citibank, for instance, adjusts its banking services in each branch depending on neighbourhood demographics; Kraft helps supermarket chains identify the cheese assortment and shelf positioning that will optimize cheese sales in low-income, middle-income, and high-income stores and in different ethnic neighbourhoods.

   Those favouring local marketing see national advertising as wasteful because it fails to address local needs. On the other hand, opponents argue that local marketing drives up manufacturing and marketing costs by reducing economies of scale. Moreover, logistical problems become magnified when companies try to meet varying local requirements, and a brand's overall image might be diluted if the product and message differ in different localities.

4. **Individual Marketing:** The ultimate level of segmentation leads to "segments of one," "customized marketing," or "one-to-one marketing". For centuries, consumers were served as individuals: The tailor made the suit and the cobbler designed shoes for the individual. Much business-to-business marketing today is customized, in that a manufacturer will customize the offer, logistics, communications, and financial terms for each major account.

4.6 IMPORTANCE OF MARKET SEGMENTATION

Market segmentation allows a marketer to take a heterogeneous market and cut it up in to one or more homogeneous markets which are made up of individuals or organizations with similar needs, wants and behavioural tendencies. A market is the aggregate of consumers of a given product and consumers vary in their characteristics buying behaviour. It is feasible to disaggregate the consumers into segments in such a manner that in needs characteristics and buying behaviour, the members vary significantly among segments. Segmentation benefits the marketer as:

1. **Proper Choice of Target Market:** Segmentation helps in distinguishing one customer group from another and thereby allows him to decide which segment should form his target market.
2. **Taping of the Market, Adopting the Offer to the Target:** Segmentation also enables the marketer to crystallize the needs of the target buyers. It also helps him to generate an accurate prediction of the likely responses from each segment of the target buyers, *e.g.*, Ford Strategy. Through segmentation car manufacturers have gained useful insights on the product features to be provided to different segments of car buyers.
3. **Marketing Effort More Efficient and Economic:** Segmentation makes the marketing effort more efficient and economic. It ensures that, the marketing effort is concentrated on well defined and carefully chosen segments. After all, the resources of any firm are limited and no firm can normally afford to attack and tap the entire market.
4. **Benefits the Customer as Well:** It helps to achieve the specialization required in product, distribution, promotion and pricing for matching the customer group and developing marketing offers. Therefore, to compete more effectively, many companies go for target marketing which can establish and communicate the distinctive benefits of the company's market offering. This process is called market segmentation, *e.g.*, Global Marketing has identified 40 different customer needs and 40 different market segments in which it would be present with its vehicle.

4.7 MARKET TARGETING

Marketing concept holds that the key to achieve organizational goals consists in determining the needs and wants of target markets and delivering the desired satisfactions more effectively and efficiently than the competitiors.

It is not possible for a marketer to have similar strategies for product promotion amongst all individuals. Kids do not get attracted towards products meant for adults and vice versa. Every segment has a different need, interest and perception. No two segments can have the same ideologies or require a similar product.

Target marketing refers to a concept in marketing which helps the marketers to divide a market into small units comprising like minded people. Such segmentation helps the marketers to design specific strategies and techniques to promote a product amongst its target market. A target market refers to a group of individuals who are inclined towards similar products and respond to similar marketing techniques and promotional schemes.

4.8 MEANING AND DEFINITION OF MARKET TARGETING

Targeting is defined as a group of people or organizations for which an organization designs, implements and maintains the marketing mix. Once the bases for segmentation are selected, you have to identify the people or organization to which the product is meant for.

> *"Market targeting is made up of evaluation of market segment and selection of market segment/ segments to be in".*

Target marketing refers to a concept in marketing which helps the marketers to divide the market into small units comprising like minded people. Such segmentation helps the marketers to design specific strategies and techniques to promote a product amongst its target market. A target market refers to a group of individuals who are inclined towards similar products and respond to similar marketing techniques and promotional schemes.

4.8.1 Evaluating Market Segments

The market segments may be evaluated on the basis of the following:

1. **Segment Size and Growth:** The company must collect and analyze data on current Rupee sales, projected sales-growth, and expected profit margins for each market segment.
2. **Segment Structural Attractiveness:** Long-run attractiveness includes an assessment of current and potential competitors, the threats of substitutes, and the power of buyers and suppliers.
3. **Company Objectives and Resources:** The company's resources and core business strengths should also fit well with the market segment opportunities.

4.8.2 Selecting Market Segment(s)

1. **Undifferentiated Marketing:** This strategy uses the same marketing mix for the entire market.
2. **Differentiated Marketing:** This strategy targets several market segments and designs separate marketing mixes for each of them.
3. **Concentrated Marketing:** This strategy commits a company to pursue a large share of one or more sub-markets.
4. **Choosing a Market-coverage Strategy:** Which strategy works best depends upon the company's resources, the degree of product variability, stage in the product life cycle, market variability and the competitors' marketing strategies.

The attractiveness of target marketing is that it makes the promotion, pricing and distribution of your products and/or services easier and more cost-effective. Target marketing provides a focus to all of your marketing activities.

4.9 SELECTION OF TARGET SEGMENTS

After evaluating different segments, a company must decide which/how many segments to service/target. A company may consider any pattern(s) of target market selection. Depending upon the emerging patterns of market segmentation, homogeneous preference as in case of soft drinks sale by Pepsi and Coca-Cola, diffused preference and clustered preference, a company chooses its market segmentation strategy.

4.10 TARGETING STRATEGIES

Once a firm has identified the market segments it wishes to target, it needs to develop effective targeting strategies for these segments. Targeting strategies tend to follow certain methods to maximize their effectiveness. These are as following:

1. **Single Segment Strategy:** A single segment strategy involves the firm choosing its single preferred market segment and targeting it with a single marketing mix, aimed at serving the segment as much as possible. This is generally chosen by a smaller firm, or one which has only located one attractive market segment.
2. **Selective Specialization:** This is a multiple-segment strategy, also known as a differentiated strategy. Different marketing mixes are offered to different segments. The product itself may or may not be different—in many cases only the promotional messages or distribution channels vary.
3. **Product Specialization Strategy:** A product specialization strategy occurs when a firm possesses a particularly attractive product, and hence tailors it to a variety of feasible market segments.
4. **Market Specialization Strategy:** A market specialization strategy involves a firm which finds one market segment very attractive, and hence that segment has a variety of different products. This is often done by a firm to fill up a segment, and hence discourages any competitors from entering.
5. **Full Market Coverage:** It occurs when a firm tries to serve all segments in an entire market. This does not always imply a mass market strategy; instead a firm can offer a variety of marketing mixes to every major segment in a market. This is what many supermarket chains have attempted with their value, standard and premium ranges.

The following diagrams in Fig. 4.3 show examples of the five market selection patterns given three market segments S1, S2, and S3, and three products P1, P2, and P3.

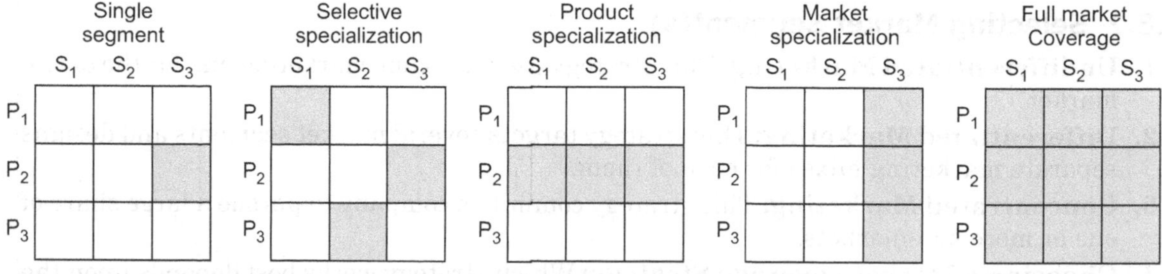

Fig. 4.3. Five market selection patterns.

A firm that is seeking to enter a market and grow should first target the most attractive segment that matches its capabilities. Once it gains a foothold, it can expand by pursuing a product specialization strategy, tailoring the product for different segments, or by pursuing a market specialization strategy and offering new products to its existing market segment.

Another strategy whose use is increasing is individual marketing, in which the marketing mix is tailored on an individual consumer basis. While in the past impractical, individual marketing is becoming more viable thanks to advances in technology.

4.11 POSITIONING

Positioning follows on logically from the segmentation and targeting stages. Customer perceptions are central to the product position especially in relation to the competition's offering.

The product or service has to satisfy key customer requirements and this has to be clearly communicated to customers.

4.12 MEANING AND DEFINITION OF POSITIONING

Positioning is the last stage in the segmentation targeting positioning cycle. Once the organization decides on its target market, it strives hard to create an image of its product in the minds of the consumers. The marketers create a first impression of the product in the minds of consumers through positioning.

> *"The process of creating an image of a product in the minds of the consumers is called positioning. Positioning helps to create first impression of brands in the minds of target audience".*

In simpler words positioning helps in creating a perception of a product or service amongst the consumers. Example: The brand "Bisleri" stands for purity. The brand "Ceat Tyre" stands for better grip.

As the companies increase the number of claims for their brand, they risk disbelief and a loss of clear positioning. In general, a company must avoid four major positioning errors.

1. **Under Positioning:** Some companies discover that buyers have only a vague idea of the brand. The brand is seen as just another entry in a crowded marketplace.
2. **Over-positioning:** Buyers may have too narrow image of the brand.
3. **Confused Positioning:** Buyers might have a confused image of the brand resulting from the company's making too many claims or changing the brand's positioning too frequently.
4. **Doubtful Positioning:** Buyers may find it hard to believe the brand claims in view of the product's features, price or manufacturer.

4.13 STEPS TO PRODUCT POSITIONING

Marketers with the positioning process try to create a unique identity of a product amongst the customers:

1. **Know your Target Audience Well:** It is important to identify the target audience and then understand their needs and preferences. The products must fulfill the demands of the individuals. Every individual has different interests, needs and preferences. No two individuals can think on the same lines.
2. **Identify the Product Features:** The marketers themselves must be well aware of the features and benefits of the products. A marketer selling Samsung phones should himself also use a Samsung handset for the customers to believe him.
3. **Unique Selling Propositions:** The marketers must themselves know what best their product can do. Every product should have unique selling propositions, at least some features which are unique. Find out how the products can be useful to the end-users? For example, why do people use "Anti-dandruff shampoo?"

   Anti-dandruff shampoos are meant to get rid of dandruff. This is how the product is positioned in the minds of the individuals. Unique Selling Propositions (USPs) of a Nokia Handset—Better battery backup.
4. **Know your Competitors:** A marketer must be aware of the competitor's offerings. Let the individuals know how your product is better than the competitors. Let the target audience know how your product is better than others.

5. **Never Compromise on Quality:** Do not drastically reduce the price of your products. A Rado watch would lose its charm if its price is equal to a Sonata or a Maxima Watch.

4.14 POSITIONING STRATEGIES

Positioning strategies has developed a unique model for analyzing a product or company positioning strategy challenge. Positioning strategies are shown in Fig. 4.4.

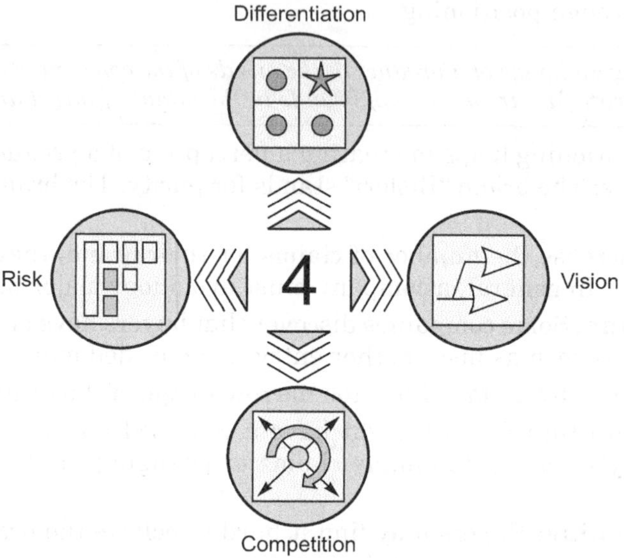

Fig. 4.4. Positioning strategies.

1. **Vision:** Vision is a term too often misapplied. To us, a market vision is always "the route to an alternative future". Visionary companies describe an unexpected future and define the benefits of change for customers. These are not the familiar benefits of the expected future. Instead, they are the new, superior benefits of the alternative future.
2. **Competition:** It is always necessary to think about other vendors currently or potentially going for the revenue we seek. It is vital to determine the positioning options that competitors have taken or soon will. For purposes of positioning, there is no point to analyze competitors beyond defining what your company can or could — do better than they do.
3. **Risk Profile:** Customers of technology companies, especially companies serving emerging categories, take a certain amount of risk. Sound positioning is the best way to reduce a prospect's perceived risk of doing business with you. One key is demonstrating how a company's product roadmap aligns with its segment penetration roadmap. That is, showing who gets what additional value and when they get it.
4. **Differentiation:** Achieving differentiation requires more than the expression of a positioning goal. A company must define for itself a space where it provides unique value. In part, that requires a willingness to accept limits. Positioning success requires discipline, both for strategically focusing company resources, as well as for foregoing opportunities that are not on-strategy. The business model implications of strategy options must be explicit.

REVIEW QUESTIONS

1. Explain the meaning and definition of market segmentation.
2. What are the major market segmentation objectives?
3. Describe the bases of segmentation marketing.
4. What do you mean by geographic segmentation and demographic segmentation?
5. What is the difference between psychographic segmentation and behavioural segmentation?
6. Explain the different levels of market segmentation.
7. Explain the importance of market segmentation.
8. What is the meaning and concept of positioning?
9. Explain the different steps to product positioning.
10. Explain the various positioning strategies.

CHAPTER 5

Consumer Behaviour

POINTS TO REMEMBER

At the end of this chapter, we will be able to understand:

- Introduction
- Meaning and Definition of Consumer Behaviour
- Characteristics of Consumer Behaviour
- Types of Consumer Buying Behaviour
- Importance of Understanding Consumer Behaviour
- Determinists of Consumer Behaviour
- Process of Buying Decisions
- Cognitive Dissonance
- Consumer Behaviour Models

5.1 INTRODUCTION

Consumers are individuals, households or businesses who use the products. Most products eventually end up in private households even though they will pass through a number of steps on their way from producer to end user. Producers and traders form vertical chains or networks, called value chains, at the end of which are the consumers. Understanding consumer behaviour is not only important for the producer but for all the other players in the chain. The value that the consumer puts on the goods or services limits what everyone else can get from the value chain.

Management is the youngest of sciences and oldest of arts and consumer behaviour in management is a very young discipline. Various scholars and academicians concentrated on it at a much later stage. It was during the 1950s, that marketing concept developed, and thus the need to study the behaviour of consumers was recognized. Marketing starts with the needs of the customer and ends with his satisfaction. When everything revolves around the customer, the study of consumer behaviour becomes a necessity. It starts with the buying of goods. Goods can be bought individually, or in groups. Goods can be bought under stress (to satisfy an immediate need), for comfort and luxury in small quantities or in bulk. For all this, exchange is required. This exchange is usually between the seller and the buyer. It can also be between consumers.

5.2 MEANING AND DEFINITION OF CONSUMER BEHAVIOUR

Consumer behaviour can be defined as the decision-making process and physical activity involved in acquiring, evaluating, using and disposing of goods and services. This definition clearly brings out that it is not just the buying of goods/services that receives attention in consumer behaviour but, the process starts much before the goods have been acquired or bought. A process of buying starts in the minds of the consumer, which leads to the finding of alternatives between products that can be acquired with their relative advantages and disadvantages. This leads to internal and external research. Then follows a process of decision-making for purchase and using the goods, and then the post purchase behaviour which is also very important, because it gives a clue to the marketers whether his product has been a successful one or not.

In another word, consumer behaviour can be defined as the behaviour of individuals in regard to acquiring, using, and disposing of products, services, ideas or experiences. Consumer behaviour also includes the acquisition and use of information. Thus, communication with consumers and receiving feedback for them is a crucial part of consumer behaviour which is of great interest to marketers.

5.2.1 Opinion Leaders and Opinion Seekers

One of those people, who deal with informal product related communication, usually provides information about a product or product category, whether it would be useful to buy, how it would be used etc. He would also offer advice as to which of several brands is the best and from where it should be bought. This person is known as the Opinion Leader and the process is known as Opinion Leadership. The people who form the audience and listen to him are called Opinion Receivers.

In other cases, prior to a purchase, people could approach an Opinion Leader and request him for information and advice about the product category and/or about brands. That is, the Opinion Leader would provide information only when asked for. In such cases, the persons (audience/or the receiver of information) are known as Opinion Seekers. Individuals who on their own seek information and advise about products and brands are called Opinion Seekers.

5.3 CHARACTERISTICS OF CONSUMER BEHAVIOUR

Consumer behaviour attempts to understand the buyer decision-making process, both individually and in groups. It studies characteristics of individual consumers such as demographics and behavioural variables in an attempt to understand what people want. It also tries to assess influences on the consumer from groups such as family, friends, reference groups, and society in general. The various variables which attempt to influence consumers are as follows:

1. **Demographics Variables:** These are current statistical characteristics of a population. These types of data are used widely in sociology, public policy, and marketing. Commonly examined demographics include gender, race, age, disabilities, mobility, home ownership, marital status, employment status, and even location. Demographic trends describe the historical changes in demographics in a population over time, for example, the average age of a population may increase or decrease over time. Both distributions and trends of values within a demographic variable are of interest. Demographics are about the population of a region and the culture of the people there.
2. **Behavioural Variables:** The behavioural variable of market segmentation groups consumers in terms of occasions, usage, loyalty and benefits sought. This is based on the

way different consumers respond to, use or know a product or service. The variable of occasion simply means the occasion on which a product or service is consumed or purchased. The behavioural variable includes:

(*i*) **Attitudes:** It represents what consumers like and dislike. An attitude is a lasting general evaluation of something—it has knowledge of that something, liking or disliking, and the strength of the feelings. They are lasting, but changeable. They help to direct behaviour—*e.g.*, do you recycle cans?

(*ii*) **Motivation:** People are motivated by many things, some positive, others not. Some motivating factors can move people only for a short-time, like hunger which will last only until you are fed. Others can drive a person onward for years. Motivation is the driving force within individuals that forces them to take action. Motivation is the activation or energization of goal-oriented behaviour.

(*iii*) **Perceptions:** Perception can be described as "how we see the world around us". All the time we are receiving messages through our five organs viz., eyes, ears, nose, mouth and skin. The different sights, sounds, smells, tastes and sensations that we feel are knows as stimuli.

(*iv*) **Personality:** The term 'personality' is the sum total of an individual's psychological traits, characteristics, motives, habits, attitudes, beliefs and outlook. Personality is the very essence of individual differences. In consumer behaviour, personality is defined as those inner psychological characteristics that both determine and reflect how a person responds to his environmental stimuli. Personality is enduring and ensures that a person's responses are consistent over time.

Personality research to predict consumer behaviour has either focused on total personality profile or a specific trait or attempted to find a correlation with product brand choice. But both these approaches assume that individuals with a given personality profile or trait are homogeneous in all other respects such as age, income, education, occupation etc.

(*v*) **Lifestyle:** A consumer's lifestyle bears the influence of his participation in social groups and of his relationships with others. An individual's lifestyle may result in certain consistency of behaviour. Knowing a person's conduct in one aspect of life may enable us to predict how he/she may behave in other areas.

(*vi*) **Knowledge:** The success or failure of products and services is ultimately determined by their acceptance in consumer markets. The consumer behaviour knowledge domain seeks to understand the psychology and behaviour of consumers—particularly consumer attitudes and buying behaviour.

5.4 TYPES OF CONSUMER BUYING BEHAVIOUR

Types of consumer buying behaviour are determined by: Level of involvement in purchase decision and importance and intensity of interest in a product in a particular situation. Buyer's level of involvement determines why he/she is motivated to seek information about certain products and brands but virtually ignores others. High involvement purchases—Honda motorbike, high priced goods, products visible to others, and the higher the risk the higher the involvement. Types of risks are :

(*a*) Personal risk

(*b*) Social risk

(*c*) Economic risk

The four types of consumer buying behaviour are:

1. **Routine Response/Programmed Behaviour:** In this type of buying behaviour, consumer buying means low involvement, frequently purchased, low cost items. Such products need very little search and decision effort; and are purchased almost automatically. Examples include soft drinks, snack foods, milk etc.
2. **Limited Decision-making:** In this type of buying behaviour, consumer buys product occasionally. When you need to obtain information about an unfamiliar brand in a familiar product category, it requires a moderate amount of time for information gathering. Examples include clothes where one knows the product class but not the brand.
3. **Extensive Decision-making:** Complex, high involvement, unfamiliar, expensive and/or infrequently bought products. High degree of economic / performance / psychological risk. Examples include: cars, homes, computers, education. Consumers spend a lot of time in seeking information and deciding. Information is from sought companies; friends and relatives, store personnel etc.
4. **Impulse Buying, no Conscious Planning:** The purchase of the same product does not always elicit the same buying behaviour. Product can shift from one category to the next. For example: Going out for dinner for one person may be extensive decision-making (for someone who does not go out often at all), but limited decision-making for someone else. The reason for the dinner, whether it is an anniversary celebration, or a meal with a couple of friends will also determine the extent of the decision-making.

5.5 IMPORTANCE OF UNDERSTANDING CONSUMER BEHAVIOUR

The success or failure in any business depends upon the behaviour of the end-user or consumer who finally uses the product or any service. It enables the manufacturer to know which products have been positively accepted in the market and which ones need changes so as to suit the consumers better. Not only is it critical to the manufacturer but also to all the intermediaries involved in transferring the product to the ultimate user. Thus, understanding the consumer behaviour helps in identifying the weak points and also reflects the positive aspects of any business. Thus, understanding consumer behaviour may be important for the following reasons:

1. **For Marketing Strategies:** It helps the marketer to take vital decisions with respect to designing of future marketing strategies and helps him to find out what kind of promotional offers or marketing campaigns need to be undertaken.
2. **Improving upon a Brand:** This involves whether the marketer should stick to the same product, extend the product portfolio, or probably launch a new product. If consumers prefer a particular brand and make the purchase and the consumption of the same as their regular habit, it is time that the marketer should think of improving upon the brand or come out with a different product. Many times, the need calls for niche marketing.
3. **Reinstate the Corporate Policies:** It also helps an organization to reinstate the corporate policies or take action to reframe the corporate mission statement.
4. **Helps to Target a Specific Audience:** The consumer behaviour also has effects on the entire social network which again helps an organization to target a specific audience or set of customers.

5.6 DETERMINISTS OF CONSUMER BEHAVIOUR

Cultural, social, personal and psychological factors influence the consumer behaviour. These are external to the company and cannot be controlled. A marketer would like to understand the impact of these factors on his organization. The explanation of these factors is as follows:

1. **Cultural Factors:** Consumer behaviour is deeply influenced by cultural factors such as: buyer culture, sub-culture, and social class.
   (*i*) **Culture:** Basically, culture is the part of every society and is the important cause of personal wants and behaviour. The influence of culture on buying behaviour varies from country to country. Therefore, marketers have to be very careful in analyzing the culture of different groups, regions or even countries.
   (*ii*) **Sub-culture:** Each culture contains different sub-cultures such as religions, nationalities, geographic regions, racial groups etc. Marketers can use these groups by segmenting the market into various small portions. For example, marketers can design products according to the needs of a particular geographic group.
   (*iii*) **Social class:** Every society possesses some form of social class which is important to the marketers because the buying behaviour of people in a given social class is similar. In this way marketing activities could be tailored according to different social classes. Here we should note that social class is not only determined by income but there are various other factors as well such as: wealth, education, occupation etc.
2. **Social Factors:** Human beings are social animals. They live and interact with other people. Therefore, there is a chance of influence by others on their opinions. Marketers like to identify such influential persons or groups of consumers. Generally such groups are classified into three major groups namely reference groups, family, roles and status.
   (*i*) **Reference groups:** Reference groups have potential in forming a person's attitude or behaviour. The impact of reference groups varies across products and brands. For example, if the product is visible such as dress, shoes, car etc., then the influence of reference groups will be high. Reference groups also include opinion leader (a person who influences others because of his special skill, knowledge or other characteristics).
   (*ii*) **Family:** Buyer behaviour is strongly influenced by the member of a family. Therefore, marketers are trying to find the roles and influence of husband, wife and children. If the buying decision of a particular product is influenced by wife then the marketers will try to target the women in their advertisement. Here we should note that buying roles change with change in consumer lifestyles.
   (*iii*) **Roles and status:** Each person possesses different roles and status in the society depending upon the groups, clubs, family, organization etc., to which he belongs. For example, a woman is working in an organization as finance manager. Now she is playing two roles, one of finance manager and the other of mother. Therefore, her buying decisions will be influenced by her status and role.
3. **Psychological Factors:** There are four important psychological factors affecting the consumer buying behaviour. These are: perception, motivation, learning, beliefs and attitudes.
   (*i*) **Motivation:** The level of motivation also affects the buying behaviour of customers. Every person has different needs such as physiological needs, biological needs, social needs etc. The nature of the needs is that, some of them are most pressing while others are least pressing. Therefore, a need becomes a motive when it is more pressing to direct the person to seek satisfaction.
   (*ii*) **Perception:** Selecting, organizing and interpreting information in a way to produce a meaningful experience of the world is called perception. There are three different perceptual processes which are selective attention, selective distortion and selective retention. In case of selective attention, marketers try to attract the customer attention. Whereas, in case of selective distortion, customers try to interpret the

information in a way that will support what the customers already believe. Similarly, in case of selective retention, marketers try to retain information that supports their beliefs.

(*iii*) **Beliefs and attitudes:** A customer possesses specific beliefs and attitudes towards various products. Since such beliefs and attitudes make up brand image and affect consumer buying behaviour therefore marketers are interested in them. Marketers can change the beliefs and attitudes of customers by launching special campaigns in this regard.

4. **Personal Factors:** Individual factors like age, occupation, lifestyle and personality influence consumer decision-making. In this section we will focus on the personality and its influence on the consumer decision-making process.

(*i*) **Age:** Age and life-cycle have potential impact on the consumer buying behaviour. It is obvious that the consumers change the purchase of goods and services with the passage of time. Family life-cycle consists of different stages such as young singles, married couples, unmarried couples etc., which help marketers to develop appropriate products for each stage.

(*ii*) **Occupation:** The occupation of a person has significant impact on his buying behaviour. For example, a marketing manager of an organization will try to purchase business suits, whereas a low level worker in the same organization will purchase rugged work clothes.

(*iii*) **Economic situation:** A consumer's economic situation has great influence on his buying behaviour. If the income and savings of a customer are high then he will purchase more expensive products. On the other hand, a person with low income and savings will purchase inexpensive products.

(*iv*) **Lifestyle:** Lifestyle of customers is another important factor affecting the consumer buying behaviour. Lifestyle refers to the way a person lives in a society and is expressed by the things in his/her surroundings. It is determined by customer interests, opinions, activities etc., and shapes his whole pattern of acting and interacting in the world.

(*v*) **Personality:** Personality characteristics are often revealed in a person's self-concept, that is the way people see themselves and the way they believe others see them. Personality changes from person to person, time to time and place to place. Therefore, it can greatly influence the buying behaviour of customers. Actually, personality is not what one wears; rather it is the totality of behaviour of a man in different circumstances. It has different characteristics such as: dominance, aggressiveness, self-confidence etc., which can be useful to determine the consumer behaviour for particular product or service.

5.7 PROCESS OF BUYING DECISIONS

After discussing the factors that influence the buying behaviour, now, we will discuss the consumer decision-making process. A consumer passes through five different stages while purchasing the product as shown in Fig. 5.1.

1. **Need Recognition:** A customer possesses two types of stimuli at this juncture. One is driven by the internal stimuli and another is external stimuli. The examples of internal stimuli are customer's desire, attitude or perception and external stimuli are advertising etc. From both stimuli a customer understands the need for the product. Here the marketer should understand which needs drew customers towards the product and should highlight those in the communication strategy.

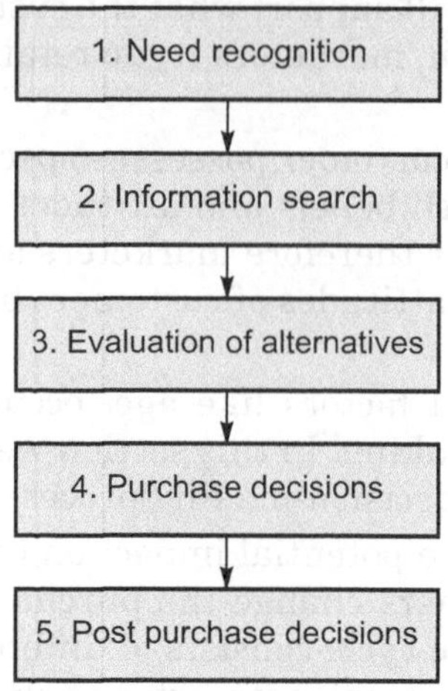

Fig. 5.1. Process of buying.

2. **Information Search:** In this stage a customer wants to find out the information about the product, place, price and point of purchase. A customer collects the information from different sources like:
   - Internal search, memory.
   - External search if you need more information. Friends and relatives (word of mouth).
   - Marketer dominated sources; comparison shopping; public sources etc.

   A successful information search leaves a buyer with possible alternatives, and the evoked set.
3. **Evaluation of Alternatives:** In this stage a customer needs to establish criteria for evaluation, features the buyer wants or does not want, rank/weight alternatives or resume search. A customer may decide that he wants to eat something spicy, Indian gets highest rank etc. The evaluation process varies from person to person. In general Indian consumers evaluate on the following parameters:

   (*a*) Price (*b*) Features
   (*c*) Availability (*d*) Quality
   (*e*) Durability
4. **Purchase Decisions:** In this stage a consumer buys the most preferred brand. He/she chooses buying alternative, includes product, package, store, method of purchase etc.
5. **Post Purchase Behaviour:** After purchasing the product the consumer will experience some level of satisfaction and dissatisfaction. The consumer will also engage in post purchase actions and product uses of interest to the marketer. The result of post purchase is satisfaction or dissatisfaction.

Sometimes, this may also lead to cognitive dissonance, *i.e.*, have you made the right decision? This can be reduced by warranties, after sales communication etc. After eating an Indian meal, you may think that really you wanted a Chinese meal instead.

5.8 COGNITIVE DISSONANCE

In 1956, Leon Festinger coined the term 'cognitive dissonance'. Cognitive dissonance is a discomfort caused by holding conflicting cognitions (*e.g.*, ideas, beliefs, values, emotional reactions) simultaneously. In a state of dissonance, people may feel surprise, guilt, anger, or embarrassment. In a theory of Cognitive Dissonance, the concept can be defined as:

> *"The psychological opposition of irreconciliable ideas (cognitions) held simultaneously by one individual, created a motivated force that would lead, under proper conditions, to the adjustment of one's belief to fit one's behaviour—instead of changing one's behaviour to fit one's belief (the sequence conventionally assumed)".* **Leon Festinger (1957)**

The theory of cognitive dissonance in social psychology proposes that people have a motivational drive to reduce dissonance by altering existing cognitions, adding new ones to create a consistent belief system, or alternatively by reducing the importance of any one of the dissonant elements. An example of this would be the conflict between wanting to smoke and knowing that smoking is unhealthy; a person may try to change his feelings about the odds that he will actually suffer the consequences, or he might add the consonant element that smoking is worth short-term benefits. A general view of cognitive dissonance is when one is biased towards a certain decision even though other factors favour an alternative.

A classical illustration of cognitive dissonance is expressed in the fable—***'The Fox and the Grapes'***. In the story, a fox sees some high-hanging grapes and wishes to eat them. When the fox is unable to think of a way to reach them, he decides that the grapes are probably not worth eating, with the justification the grapes probably are not ripe or that they are sour. This example follows a pattern: one desires something, finds it unattainable, and reduces one's dissonance by criticizing it. Jon Elster calls this pattern "adaptive preference formation".

While lab experiments have verified the presence of arousal in dissonance situations, most studies have investigated how people resolve their cognitive conflicts. A partial list of the mechanisms includes:

- Excusing own faults and failures: "I was drunk, what do you expect"?
- Selectively editing and censoring evidence; in the extreme, we can completely delete counter-evidence and create false evidence.
- Interpreting ambiguity for self-serving ends.
- Giving explanations that cast us in a good light.
- Minimizing: "It was just a fling, she meant nothing to me".
- Considering weaknesses as so common that we aren't responsible: "Everybody does it".
- Blaming: "They made me do it".
- Not exposing ourself to counter-evidence, *e.g.*, only read newspapers that support our views.
- Applying our critical judgement differently depending whether we support or oppose a view.

5.9 CONSUMER BEHAVIOUR MODELS

External and internal factors contribute to the formulation of self-concept and lifestyle, which affects the consumer decision process. During this process, experiences and acquisitions update the original external and internal influences.

This model helps marketers to understand the psychology of how consumers think, feel, reason, and select between different alternatives *e.g.*, brands, products, and retailers and how the consumer is influenced by his or her environment *e.g.*, culture, family, signs, media as shown in Fig. 5.2.

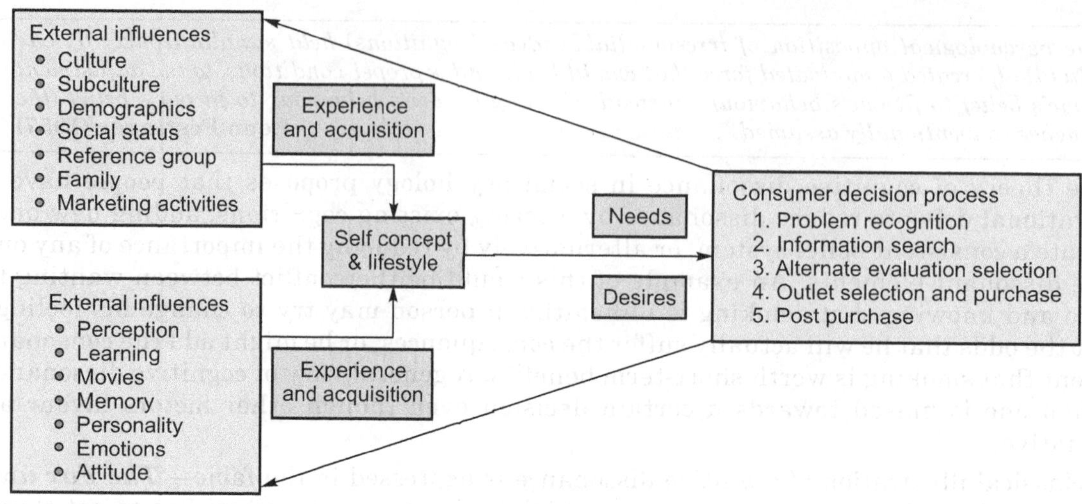

Fig. 5.2. Consumer behaviour.

5.9.1 Howard–Sheth Model

John Howard and Jagdish Sheth presented their buyer model in 1969. It's an integrated model. It assumes problem solving approach in buying and adopts input-output or system approach in buying. Howard introduced learning process in buying. Satisfaction leads to brand loyalty. Discontentment creates brand switching by the buyers. In other words, the logic of this model is that there are inputs in the form of stimuli. There are outputs beginning with attention to a given stimulus and ending the purchase. In between these inputs and outputs, there are variables affecting perception and learning. These variables are "hypothetical" as they can not be directly measured at the time of occurrence. It explains the complex decision-making process a consumer goes through. A diagram of this is shown in Fig. 5.3 below:

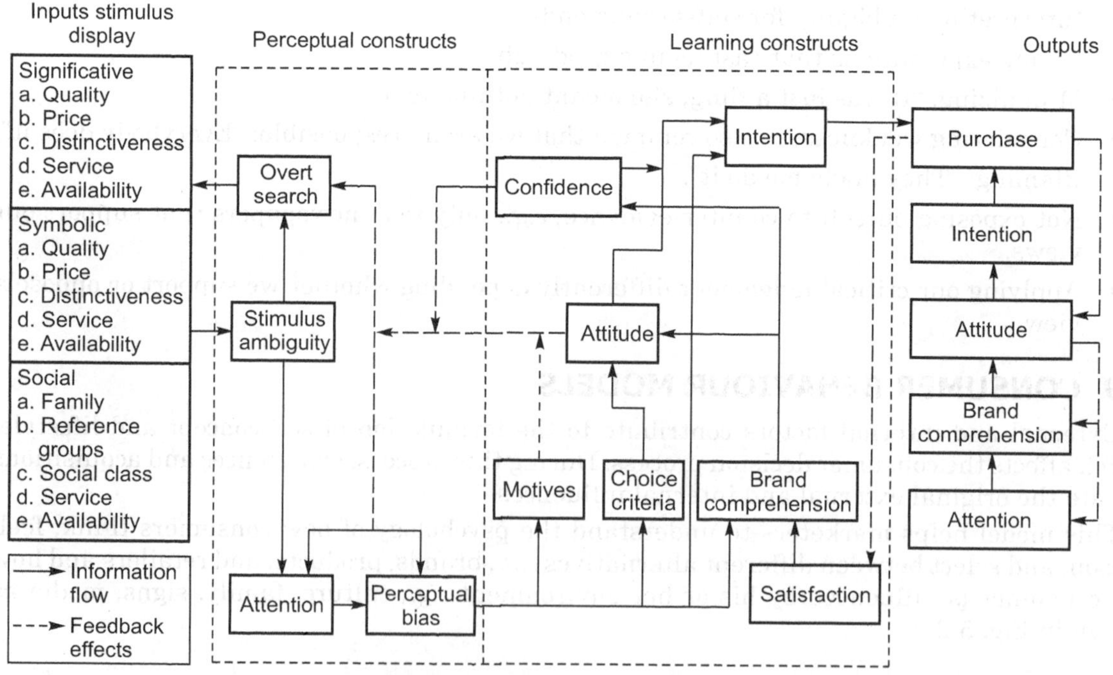

Fig. 5.3. The Howard—Sheth model.

1. **Inputs Stimulus Display:** These input variables consist of three distinct types of information sources in the consumer's environment.
   (*i*) **Significant:** Information furnishes physical brand characteristics such as quality, price, distinctive, service, availability.
   (*ii*) **Symbolic:** Verbal or visual product characteristics such as quality, price, distinctive, service, availability.
   (*iii*) **Consumer's social environment:** This is the information about the product or service offering that comes from the social environment, viz. family, groups, society and culture at large.
2. **Perceptual Constructs:** The perceptual constructs deal with how a consumer obtains and processes information received from the input variables. Once the buyer is exposed to any information, there is an attention; this attention towards the stimuli depends on the buyers' sensitivity to information in terms of his urge and receptivity towards such information. Not all information would be processed and the intake of information is subject to perceived uncertainty and lack of meaningfulness of information; this is referred to as stimulus ambiguity.
   (*i*) **Learning constructs:** The learning constructs relate to buyer learning, formation of attitudes and opinions, and the final decision. The learning constructs are seven in number, and range from a buyer's motive for a purchase to the final satisfaction from a purchase; the interplay of these constructs ultimately leads to a response output or a purchase. The motives refer to the goals that a buyer seeks to achieve through a purchase and the corresponding urge towards action or the purchase activity.
3. **Response Outputs (Output Variables):** The output variables refer to the buyer's action or response to stimulus inputs. According to Howard and Sheth, the response outputs comprise five constituents, viz., attention, comprehension, attitude, intention and purchase. These could be arranged in a hierarchy, starting from attention and ending up with purchase.
   - Attention refers to the degree or level of information that a buyer accepts when exposed to a stimulus. It reflects the magnitude of the buyer's information intake.
   - Comprehension is the amount of information that he actually processes and stores; here, it refers to brand comprehension which is buyers' knowledge about the product/service category and brand.
   - The attitude is the composite of cognition, affect and behaviour towards the offering; the attitude reflects his evaluation of the brand and the like/dislike based on the brand potential.
   - Intention refers to the buyer's intention to buy or not to buy a particular offering.
   - Purchase behaviour refers to the actual act of buying. The purchase behaviour is a cumulative result of the other four constituents.

5.9.2 Nicosia Model

Nicosia model of consumer behaviour was proposed by Nicosia (1976).This model concentrates on the buying decision for a new product. Human being is analyzed as a system with stimuli as the input and the behaviour a is the output. Nicosia model explains the consumers' buying behaviour from the marketers' perspective as shown in Fig. 5.4.

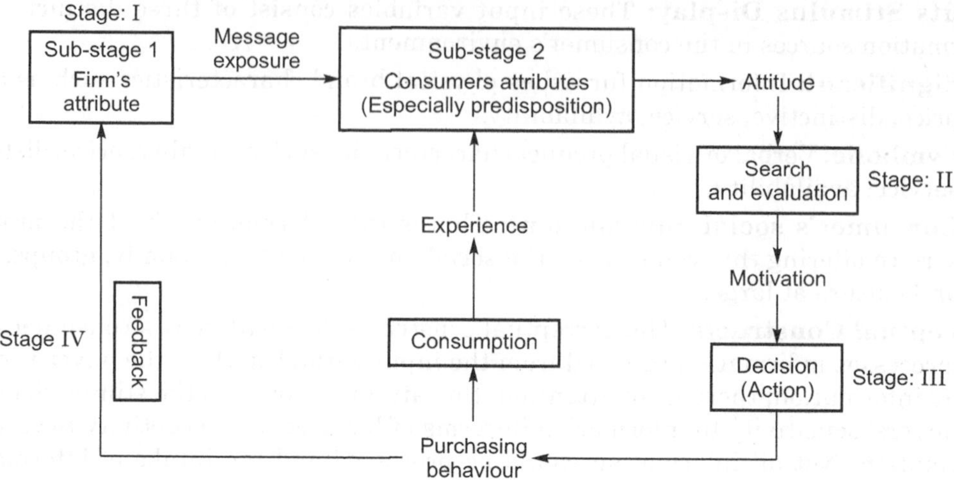

Fig. 5.4. Nicosia model.

1. **Stage I—Firm's Attributes and Consumer's Attributes:** The first stage is divided into two sub-stages: firm's attributes and the consumer's attributes. An advertising message from the firm reaches the consumer's attributes. Depending on the way the message is received by the consumer, a certain attribute may develop, and this becomes the input for stage two.
2. **Stage II—Search and Evaluation:** Stage II is the area of search and evaluation of the advertised product and other alternatives. If this process results in a motivation to buy, it becomes the input for field three.
3. **Stage III—Decision:** The result of motivation will arise by convincing the consumer to purchase the firm products from a specific retailer. Field three consists of the act of purchase.
4. **Stage IV—Feedback:** Field four consists of the use of the purchased item. This involves feedback of both the firm and the consumer after purchasing the product.
   - Firm's feedback sales data
   - Consumer's feedback—consumer's attitude based on experience and predispositions on future firm's messages.

5.9.3 The Learning Model

All theories of buyer behaviour have been basically based on a learning model namely, Stimulation-Response or more popularly known as SR model. SR learning theory is very useful to modern marketing and marketers. According to the learning model which takes its cue from the Pavlovian stimulus response theory, buyer behaviour can be influenced by manipulating the drives, stimuli and responses of the buyer. The model rests on man's ability at learning, forgetting and discriminating. The stimulus response learning theory states that there develops a bond between behaviour producing stimulus and a behaviour response (S. R. Bond) on account of the conditioning of behaviour and formation of habits. This theory may be traced to Pavlov and his experiments on salivating dogs. Pavlov's experiments brought out associations by conditioning. According to the stimulus-response, learning is dependent on drive, cue (stimulus), response and reinforcement as shown in Fig. 5.5.

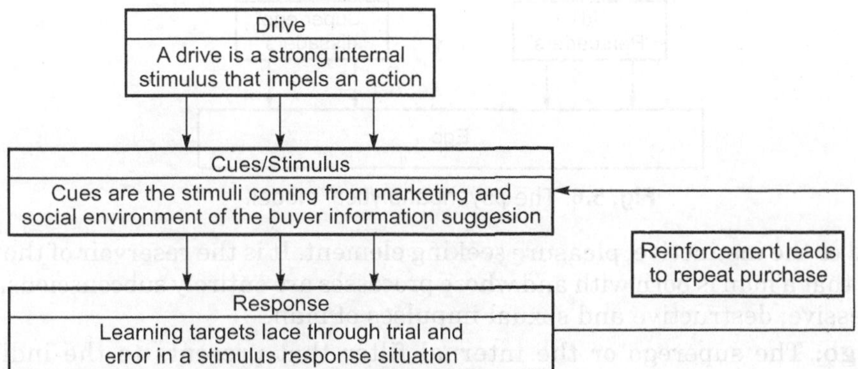

Fig. 5.5. The learning model.

(*i*) **Drive:** Drive may be defined as any strong stimulus that forces action. It arouses an individual and keeps him prepared to respond.

(*ii*) **Cue:** Cue or stimulus may be defined as any object in the environment perceived by the individual. The aim of the marketing man is to find out or create the cue of sufficient importance that it becomes the drive stimulus or elicits other responses appropriate to his objective.

(*iii*) **Response:** Response is an answer to a given drive or cue. When a man feels thirsty, he attempts to get water at any cost. Here attempt to get water is a response to the primary drive of thirst. "Response also includes attitudes, familiarity, perception and other complex phenomena". Responses may be generalized or discriminatory.

(*iv*) **Reinforcement:** Reinforcement or reward means reduction in drive and stimulus. It has been defined as "environmental events exhibiting the property of increasing the probability of occurrence of responses they accompany".

Thus, when consumption of a product or a brand of product leads to satisfaction of the initiating need there is reinforcement.

5.9.4 The Economic Model

Economics is the social science that analyzes the production, distribution, and consumption of goods and services.

According to the economic model of buyer behaviour, the buyer is a rational man and his buying decisions are totally governed by the concept of utility. If he has a certain amount of purchasing power, a set of needs to be met and a set of products to choose from, he will allocate the amount over the set of products in a very rational manner with the intention of maximizing the utility or benefits.

5.9.5 The Psycho-analytical Model

The psycho-analytical model draws from Freudian psychology. According to this model, the individual consumer has a complex set of deep seated motives which drive him towards certain buying decisions. The buyer has a private world with all his hidden fears, suppressed desires and totally subjective longings. His buying action can be influenced by appealing to these desires and longings.

The psycho-analytical theory is attributed to the work of eminent psychologist Sigmund Freud. Freud introduced personality as a motivating force in human behaviour. According to this theory, the mental framework of a human being is composed of three elements as shown in Fig. 5.6.

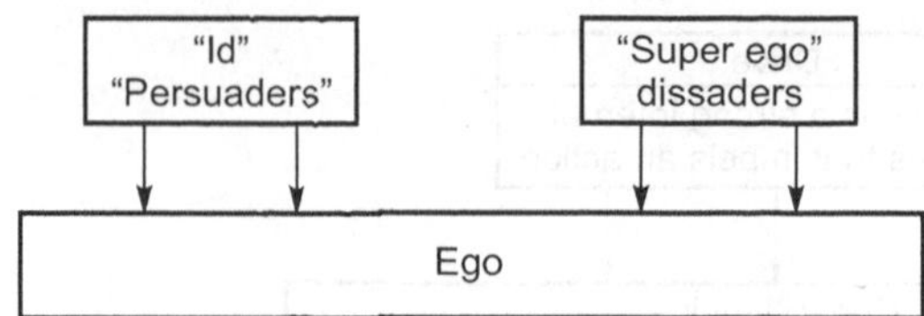

Fig. 5.6. The psychoanalytical model.

1. **Id:** The id or the instinctive, pleasure seeking element. It is the reservoir of the instinctive impulses that a man is born with and whose processes are entirely subconscious. It includes the aggressive, destructive and sexual impulses of man.
2. **Super-ego:** The superego or the internal filter that presents to the individual the behavioural expectations of society. It develops out of the id, dominates the ego and represents the inhibitions of instinct which is characteristic of man. It represents the moral and ethical elements, the conscience.
3. **Ego:** The ego or the control device that maintains a balance between the id and the superego. It is the most superficial portion of the id. It is modified by the influence of the outside world. Its processes are entirely conscious because it is concerned with the perception of the outside world. It continues to influence consumer behaviour.

5.9.6 The Sociological Model

According to the sociological model, the individual buyer behaviour is influenced by society by intimate groups as well as social classes. That is, his buying decisions are not totally determined by the concept of utility. That is his buying decisions are governed by social compulsions as shown in Fig. 5.7.

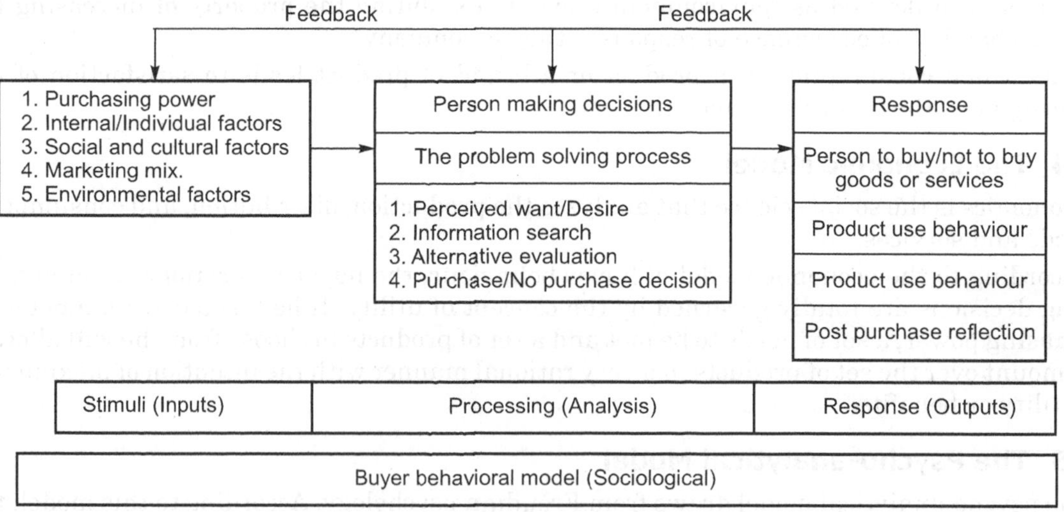

Fig. 5.7. The sociological model.

This model represents the individual buyer behaviour which is influenced by society—by intimate groups as well as social classes. That is, his buying decisions are not totally determined by the concept of utility. That is his buying decisions are governed by social compulsions. As a part of sociological model—two important variations can be considered, *viz.* Nicosia and Howard & Sheth.

The marketing scholars have tried to build buyers-behaviour models purely from the stand point view of marketing man. Here F. Nicosia model of 1966 and H. Sheth model of 1969 are of this category. These models are systems models where human being is analyzed as a system with stimuli as INPUT and behaviour as OUTPUT.

REVIEW QUESTIONS

1. Define the concepts and meaning of consumer behaviour. Explain the characteristics that affect consumer behaviour.
2. Discuss the types of consumer buyer behaviour with the help of Nicosia model.
3. Explain the consumer decision-making process.
4. Explain the consumer behaviour models.
5. What do you mean by cognitive dissonance?
6. Explain the determinists of consumer behaviour.
7. Explain the importance of consumer behaviour.
8. Discuss the buyer decision strategies for new products.
9. Write a note on buying motives.

UNIT–II

6. Product Concepts and Product Life Cycle
7. Product Planning, Development and Product Identification
8. Pricing
9. Marketing Communication and Marketing Research
10. Promotion Mix

CHAPTER 6

Product Concepts and Product Life Cycle

POINTS TO REMEMBER

At the end of this chapter, we will be able to understand:

- Introduction
- Meaning and Definition of Product
- Product Classification
- Product Mix
- Product Line
- BCG Model
- Product Life Cycle Concept and Meaning
- Characteristics of Product Life Cycle
- Stages of Product Life Cycle
- Strategies of Product Life Cycle

6.1 INTRODUCTION

Many entrepreneurs start their businesses because they have an idea for a product that is unique and they think people will buy it. The two considerations are based on interest in the product in the marketplace, called marketability, and the product not being available elsewhere.

Unfortunately, a unique idea is not always a business opportunity. The product development process helps to weed out ideas that are unique but not likely to sell in the marketplace. It also perfects an idea so that it can be profitable. The product development process translates a good idea into a product that:

- Can be produced in volume
- Has a quality level that will sell
- Will make a profit for you.

Product development takes an idea and prepares it for the marketplace, or commercializes it.

6.2 MEANING AND DEFINITION OF PRODUCT

The product concept proposes that consumers will prefer products that have better quality, performance and features as opposed to a normal product. The concept is truly applicable in some niches such as electronics and mobile handsets.

> *"A product is a bundle of utilities consisting of various product features and accompanying services".*
> **Alderson**

> *"A product is a cluster of psychological satisfactions".* **George Fisk**

> *"Product is anything that can be offered to market for attention, acquisition, or consumption including physical object, services, personalities, organizations and desires".*
> **American Marketing Association**

> *"A product is any thing that can be offered to a market to satisfy a want or a need. Product that is marketed includes physical goods, services, experiences, events, persons, places, properties, organization, information and ideas".* **Philip Kotler**

> *"A product is a complex of tangible and intangible attribute, including packaging, colour, price, manufacturer's prestige and retailers prestige and manufacturer's and retailer's services which the buyer may accept as offering satisfaction of wants and needs".* **William J. Stanton**

Thus, in marketing, a product means those goods or services which are visible or invisible, any size, quality/character or quantity, which consumers use for the satisfaction of their needs.

6.3 PRODUCT CLASSIFICATION

Product is the first of the four Ps of marketing. Product has a very special position as it constitutes the most substantive element in any marketing offer. Product can be broadly classified on the basis of (1) use, (2) durability, and (3) tangibility as shown in Fig. 6.1.

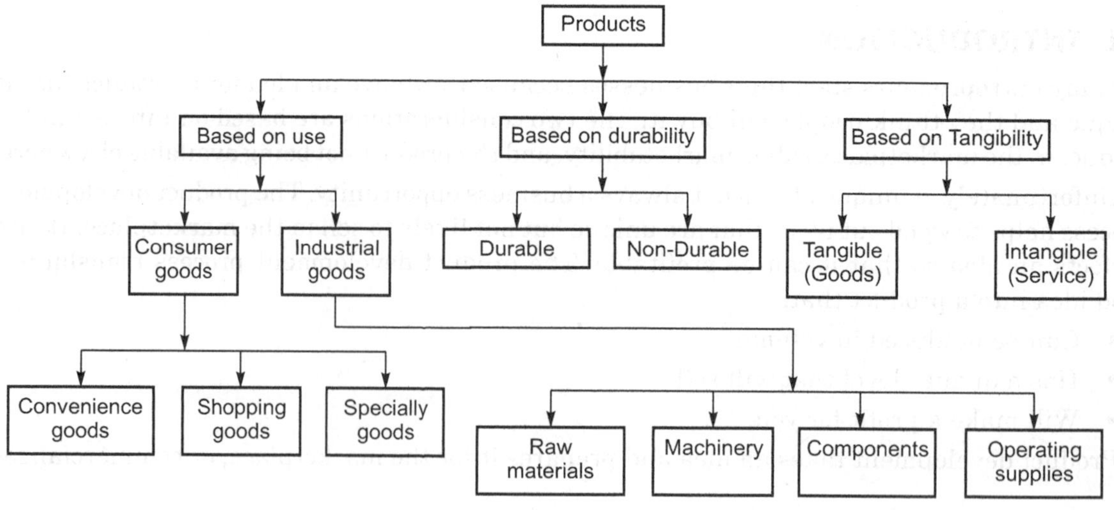

Fig. 6.1. Classification of product.

1. Based on Use: On the basis of use products can be classified as: consumer goods and industrial goods.

(A) Consumer Goods

Edward and Richard (1971) identified three classes of consumer goods namely convenience goods, shopping goods and specialty goods.

(*i*) ***Convenience goods:*** These refer to items that the consumer buys with minimum shopping effort. Essentially these are goods that are habitual with the consumers. They are bought frequently but not in large quantities because they are non-durable goods. In other words they are 'used up" goods. The buying decision of the consumers for convenience goods is ignited by habit and he knows all the retail outlets. Under this category are biscuits, newspaper, toilet soap, cigarettes etc. Consumers want to minimize the time and effort devoted to buy convenience goods, therefore the consumers are not interested in comparing the prices and quality of convenience goods with other related products in the market place. This is because the gain of such exercise is not high enough to justify the cost involved in the exercise. But in case, the price of a convenience good like bread is abnormally higher than competing brands, consumers tend to change their buying decision on the product.

(*ii*) ***Shopping goods:*** These sets of products are selected by consumers based on certain yardsticks such as suitability, quality, price and style. All products that involve shopping comparison before selection fall into this category. Such goods are, furniture, rugs, dresses, computers, shoes and household appliances. Before a consumer makes up his mind to buy shopping goods, a lot of exercise must have been carried out to know the different prices of the various stores that sell the product. Shopping goods are more durable than the convenience goods. This is why a lot of parameters must be considered before procurement. The rate of the 'use up' of shopping goods is quite slow compared to convenience goods. Shopping products are products that a consumer feels are worth the time and effort to compare with competing products.

(*iii*) ***Specialty goods:*** These refer to goods for which consumers are habitually willing to make a special purchasing effort. These categories of goods possess unique characteristics or high degree of brand identification. Examples include specific brands and types of fast foods, cars, stereo components, photographic equipment and suits. Specialty goods do not involve buyer in making comparisons. Buyers invest time only to reach the dealers of the specialty goods.

(*iv*) ***Unsought goods:*** These are goods that the consumer does not know about or know about but does not normally think of buying. Examples are insurance, cemetery plots, coffin and encyclopaedia. For consumers to be attracted to these products substantial marketing effort is required in the form of advertising and personal selling.

(B) Industrial Goods:

This classification is based on relationship of the goods to the organization's production process and cost structure. These are meant for non-personal and commercial use and include (*i*) raw materials, (*ii*) machinery, (*iii*) components, and (*iv*) operating supplies (such as lubricants, stationery etc). Industrial goods are intermediate goods and can be classified into the following three categories:

(*i*) ***Foundation goods:*** These are manufacturing machines upon which production is dependent. They are not used up in the production process but over a course of years during which a part is charged off as depreciation. Foundation goods are long-term investment.

(*ii*) ***Entering goods:*** These refer to ingredients or components of a product. These are the parts that go into the product itself.

(*iii*) ***Facilitating goods:*** These are operating supplies that are used up in the operation of the firm but do not become part of the product. They are usually budgeted as expenses and have short life. The purpose of such goods is to keep the foundation goods functioning properly and to help in the handling and supply of the entering goods. Examples are lubricating oil, saw blades, cider forms and labels.

2. **Based on Durability:** The products can be classified as: durable goods and non-durable goods.

(*i*) **Durable goods:** These are tangible goods that normally survive many uses. Goods that fall under this category include, furniture, refrigerator, clothing, rugs etc. They are not frequently purchased as non-durable goods because they are used up slowly.

(*ii*) **Non-durable goods:** Non-durable goods are tangible goods that are normally consumed in one or few uses. Examples are beer, toothpaste, sugar, soap, edible oil, salt etc. These goods are consumed fast and purchased frequently by the consumers. Many fast foods fall into this category.

3. **Based on Tangibility:** The products can be classified as: tangible goods and intangible goods.

(*a*) **Tangible goods:** Most goods, whether these are consumer goods or industrial goods and whether these are durable or non-durable, fall in this category as they have a physical form, that can be touched and seen. Thus, all items like groceries, cars, raw-materials, machinery etc., fall in the category of tangible goods.

(*b*) **Intangible goods:** Intangible goods refer to services provided to the individual consumers or to the organizational buyers (industrial, commercial, institutional, government etc.). Services are essentially intangible activities which provide want or need satisfaction. Medical treatment, postal, banking and insurance services and even electronic goods etc., all fall in this category.

6.4 PRODUCT MIX

Marketing involves a number of activities. To begin with, an organization may decide on its target group of customers to be served. Once the target group is decided, the product is to be placed in the market by providing the appropriate product, price, distribution and promotional efforts. These are to be combined or mixed in an appropriate proportion so as to achieve the marketing goal. Such mix of product, price, distribution and promotional efforts is known as 'marketing mix'.

For example, a cement plant may sell just one type of cement. Other companies, such as a large chain of retail stores may contain tens or even hundreds of thousands of products in its product mix.

A company product mix has four important dimensions (*i*) width (*ii*) length (*iii*) depth and (*iv*) consistency.

(*i*) **Width:** Product mix width refers to the number of different product lines the company carries. For example, Procter & Gamble consist of many product lines, paper, food items, household, cleaning, medicinal, cosmetics and personal care products.

(*ii*) **Length:** Product mix length refers to the total number of items the Company carries within its product lines, for example, HUL soaps:

- Lifebuoy
- Lux
- Liril
- Pears
- Dove

(iii) **Depth:** Product mix depth refers to the number of versions/variants, offered of each product in the line. Example: Lux: 3 steps / 2 formulations. Hence depth = 6, average depth for product mix/ product line can be calculated.

(iv) **Consistency:** Consistency of product mix refers to how closely related the various product lines are in end use, production requirements, distribution channels, or some other way: Example: Reliance, LG electronics.

6.4.1 Marketing Mix Variables/4Ps of Marketing

1. **Product Variables**
   (*a*) Product mix and product line
   (*b*) Design, quality, features, models, style, appearance, size and warranty of products
   (*c*) Packaging, type, materials, size, appearance and label
   (*d*) Branding and trade mark
   (*e*) Merchandising
   (*f*) Service, pre-sale and after-sale
   (*g*) New products
2. **Place Variables**
   (*a*) Channels of distribution, types of intermediaries, channel design, location of outlets, channel remuneration and dealer—principal relations.
   (*b*) Physical distribution, transportation, warehousing, inventory levels, order processing etc.
3. **Price Variables**
   (*a*) Pricing policies, levels of prices, levels of margins, discounts and rebates
   (*b*) Terms of delivery, payment terms, credit terms and installment facilities
   (*c*) Resale price maintenance.
4. **Promotion Variables**
   (*a*) Personal selling: objectives, level of effort, quality of sales force, cost level, level of motivation
   (*b*) Advertising: media mix, budgets, allocations and programmes
   (*c*) Sales promotional efforts, display, contests, trade promotions
   (*d*) Publicity and public relations.

Assembling and managing the marketing mix is the main part of the marketing task. However, no marketing man is free to assemble and operate his marketing mix in a setting of his creation; he has to necessarily operate it in the marketing environment in which he markets his products; he has to reckon the set of variables that make up the environment.

6.5 PRODUCT LINE

All the products sold by a multi-product company at times can be classified in broad categories which are called product lines. The most common example is the different product lines that are usually sold by large retail companies like Wal-Mart. Typical descriptions of product lines used in retail industry include apparel, green grocery, dry grocery, household appliances, personal care items, and so on. A company may have just one product line in its product mix. Alternatively, it can also have multiple product lines. For example, we have retailers that specialize in only one line such as watches and white goods. We also have stores that sell from the same retail outlet both these lines of product, plus many more lines.

6.5.1 Product Line Extension

Product line is a relative term. It refers to addition of items to a product line beyond the previously sold items in the line. For example, a company selling cosmetic products selling just one variety of cold cream, may decide to extend the cosmetic product line by adding two new varieties of cold cream that are meant to be used by people with extra dry and extra oily skin.

6.5.2 Product Line Analysis

It is based on:

1. **Sales and profit:** A company can classify its products based on the margins.
2. **Core products:** Basic products that have a high sales volume but with low margins as they are essentially undifferentiated commodities. For example, basic computers.
3. **Staples:** Lower sales volume, higher margins, no promotions. For example, faster CPU.
4. **Specialties:** Lower sales volume and highly promoted. For example, installation, delivery.
5. **Convenience items:** Peripherals selling in high volumes with less promotion.
6. **Market profile:** Product line managers must review how the line is positioned against competitor's lines.

6.6 BCG MODEL

A chart of four celled matrix (2 × 2 matrix) had been created by **Bruce Henderson** for the **Boston Consulting Group (BCG),** USA in 1968 to help corporations with analyzing their business units or product lines. It is the most renowned corporate portfolio analysis tool. It provides a graphic representation for an organization to examine different businesses in its portfolio on the basis of their related market share and industry growth rates. It is a two-dimensional analysis on management of Strategic Business Units (SBUs). In other words, it is a comparative analysis of business potential and the evaluation of environment.

The BCG matrix can be used during value chain selection as a tool to quickly assess the market share of the local value chain against the growth of the globalized market in which it competes. Often the necessary data can be collected easily from secondary sources. This tool though fairly low cost and easy to employ only gives a static snapshot of the value chain's performance in an end market and is not capable of describing the market dynamics or the potential for change. We had that simple BCG matrix which looked at the business growth rate and one's relative position in the market.

BCG matrix has four cells, with the horizontal axis representing relative market share and the vertical axis denoting market growth rate. The midpoint of relative market share is set at 1.0, if all the SBUs are in same industry, the average growth rate of the industry is used. While, if all the SBUs are located in different industries, then the mid-point is set at the growth rate for the economy.

Resources are allocated to the business units according to their situation on the grid. The four cells of this matrix are called stars, cash cows, question marks and dogs. Each of these cells represents a particular type of business. We had a simple and peaceful 2 x 2 matrix as shown in Fig. 6.2.

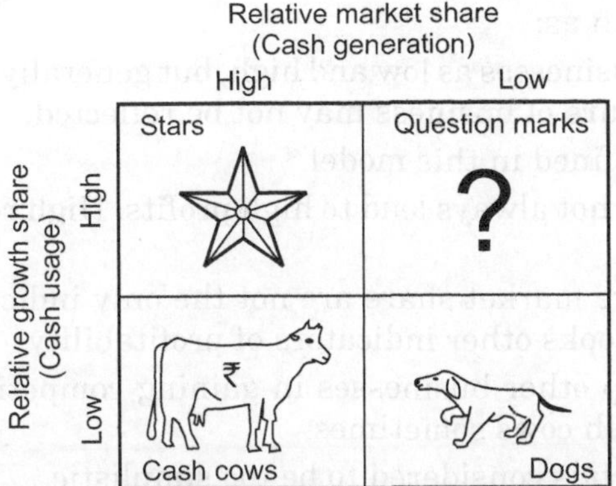

Fig. 6.2. The Boston consulting group matrix.

Each quadrant of the matrix describes the status of the value chain against its competitors and suggests its potential for competitiveness:

1. **Stars:** Stars represent business units having large market share in a fast growing industry. They may generate cash but because of a fast growing market, stars require huge investments to maintain their lead. Net cash flow is usually modest. SBUs located in this cell are attractive as they are located in a robust industry and these business units are highly competitive in the industry. If successful, a star will become a cash cow when the industry matures.
2. **Cash cows:** Cash cows represent business units having a large market share in a mature, slow growing industry. Cash cows require little investment and generate cash that can be utilized for investment in other business units. These SBUs are the corporation's key source of cash, and are specifically the core business. They are the base of an organization. These businesses usually follow stability strategies. When cash cows loose their appeal and move towards deterioration, a retrenchment policy may be pursued.
3. **Question marks:** Question marks represent business units having low relative market share and located in a high growth industry. They require huge amount of cash to maintain or gain market share. They require attention to determine if the venture can be viable. Question marks are generally new goods and services which have a good commercial prospective. There is no specific strategy which can be adopted. If the firm thinks it has dominant market share, it can adopt an expansion strategy, else retrenchment strategy can be adopted. Most businesses start as question marks as the company tries to enter a high growth market in which there is already a market-share. If ignored, question marks may become dogs, while if huge investment is made, they have the potential of becoming stars.
4. **Dogs:** Dogs represent businesses having weak market shares in low growth markets. They neither generate cash nor require huge amount of cash. Due to low market share, these business units face cost disadvantages. Generally retrenchment strategies are adopted because these firms can gain market share only at the expense of competitor's/ rival's firms. These business firms have weak market share because of high costs, poor quality, ineffective marketing, etc. Unless a dog has some other strategic aim, it should be liquidated if there are fewer prospects for it to gain market share. Number of dogs should be avoided and minimized in an organization.

6.6.1 Limitations of BCG Matrix

The BCG matrix produces a framework for allocating resources among different business units and makes it possible to compare many business units at a glance. But BCG matrix is not free from limitations, such as:

1. BCG matrix classifies businesses as low and high, but generally businesses can be medium also. Thus, the true nature of business may not be reflected.
2. Market is not clearly defined in this model.
3. High market share does not always lead to high profits. High costs are also involved with high market share.
4. Growth rate and relative market share are not the only indicators of profitability. This model ignores and overlooks other indicators of profitability.
5. At times, dogs may help other businesses in gaining competitive advantage. They can earn even more than cash cows sometimes.
6. This four-celled approach is considered to be too simplistic.

6.6.2 GE—Mckinsey Matrix

Then came the GE–Mckinsey matrix with the same kind of axis (though with slightly different terminologies) but with a twist : now you had to navigate through a 3 × 3 matrix and 9 cells instead of a benign 4 as shown in Fig. 6.3.

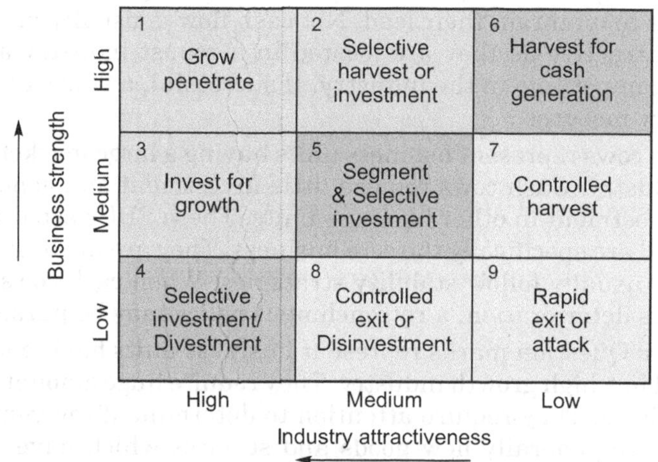

Fig. 6.3. GE–Mckinsey matrix.

1. The three cells at the top left hand side of the matrix are the most attractive cells in which to operate and require a policy of investment for growth–**these are usually coloured green.**
2. The three cells running diagonally from left to right have a medium attractiveness, **are coloured yellow** and the management of businesses within this category should be more cautious and with a greater emphasis being placed on selective investment and earning retention.
3. The three cells at the bottom right hand side are the least attractive, therefore **coloured red** and management should follow a policy of harvesting and / or divesting unless the relative strengths can be improved.

Channon and McCosh devised a set of generic investment strategies for the GE–McKinsey matrix as labelled in Fig. 6.3. A. T. Kearney (ATK) also put forward guidelines for strategies in the different boxes and where these have not been incorporated they are mentioned as follows.

(*a*) **Grow/Penetrate:** These businesses are a target for investment, they have strong business strengths, are in attractive markets and they should therefore have high returns on investment and competitive advantage. They should receive financial and managerial support to maintain their strong position and to continue contributing to long-term profitability.

- Seek dominance
- Grow
- Maximize investment

(*b*) **Invest for growth:** Businesses here are in very attractive industries but have average business strength. They should be invested in to improve their long-term competitive position.

- Evaluate potential for leadership via segmentation
- Identify weaknesses
- Build strengths

(*c*) **Selective investment or divestment:** These businesses are in very attractive markets but their business strength is weak. Investment must be aimed at improving the business strengths. These businesses will probably have to be funded by other businesses in the group as they are not self-funding. Only businesses that can improve their strengths should be retained—if not they should be divested.

- Specialize
- Seek niches
- Consider acquisitions

(*d*) **Selective harvest or investment:** Businesses in this box have good business strength in an industry that is losing its attractiveness. They should be supported if necessary but they may be self-supporting in cash flow terms. Selective harvesting is an option to extract cash flow but this should be done with caution so as to not to run down the business prematurely.

- Identify growth segments
- Invest strongly
- Maintain position elsewhere

(*e*) **Segment and selective investment:** Businesses with average business strengths and in average industries can improve their positions by creative segmentation to create profitable segments and by selective investment to support the segmentation strategy. The business needs to create superior returns by concentrating on building segment barriers to differentiate themselves.

- Identify growth segments
- Specialize
- Invest selectively

(*f*) **Controlled exit or harvest:** Businesses with weak business strengths in moderately attractive industries are candidates for a controlled exit or divestment. Attempts to gain market share by increasing business strengths could prove to be very expensive and must be done with caution.

- Specialize
- Seek niches
- Consider exit

(*g*) **Harvest for cash generation:** Strong businesses in unattractive markets should be net cash generators and could provide funds for use throughout the rest of the portfolio. Investment should be aimed at keeping these businesses in a dominant position of strength but over investment can be disastrous especially in a mature market. Be aware of competitors trying to revitalize mature industries:

- Maintain overall position
- Seek cash flow
- Invest at maintenance level

(*h*) **Controlled harvest:** They have average business strengths in an unattractive market and the strategy should be to harvest the business in a controlled way to prevent a defeat or the business could be used to upset a competitor.

- Prune lines
- Minimize investment
- Position to divest

(*i*) **Rapid exit or attack business:** These businesses have neither strengths nor an attractive industry and should be exited. Investments made should only be done to fund the exit.

- Trust leaders statesmanship
- Go after competitors cash generators
- Time exit and divest.

6.7 PRODUCT LIFE CYCLE CONCEPT AND MEANING

All products and services have certain life cycles. The life cycle refers to the period from the product's first launch into the market until its final withdrawal and it is split up in phases. During this period significant changes are made in the way that the product is behaving in the market *i.e.*, its reflection in respect of sales to the company that introduced it into the market. Since an increase in profits is the major goal of a company that introduces a product into a market, the product's life cycle management is very important. Some companies use strategic planning and others follow the basic rules of the different life cycle phases that are analyzed later.

The understanding of a product's life cycle, can help a company to understand and realize when it is time to introduce and withdraw a product from a market, its position in the market compared to competitors, and the product's success or failure.

For a company to fully understand the above and successfully manage a product's life cycle, it needs to develop strategies and methodologies, some of which are discussed later on.

> *"The product life cycle is an attempt to recognize distinct stages in the sales history of the product".*
>
> **Philip Kotler**

> *"Life cycle of market offering-stages of market acceptance through which a market offering passes in market offering's life cycle are market introduction, market growth, market saturation, market decline and market death".*
>
> **Lipson and Darling**

"A product's life cycle is very much similar to human life cycle. A product is produced, increases speedily on demand, and reaches maturity and then results in to decline". **Arch Paton**

"A product has to pass through various stages and different competitive environments from its introduction to decline. Its success of life is determined by the fact that how best it fits in such an environment and conditions". **Stanton**

Thus product life cycle means the various situations by which goods move. It may be that, life cycle of different goods may differ because few goods are perishable whereas others may be stable, *e.g.*—Fashionable clothes, which suddenly becomes outdated because of change in fashion. As against this machine, telephone, fan and other industrial products continue their life cycle for decades. In addition these are few products which take years only in completion of their introduction stage, whereas there are few which complete their introductory stage in few weeks.

6.8 CHARACTERISTICS OF PRODUCT LIFE CYCLE

The characteristics of the product life cycle are as follows:

Stages	*Introduction*	*Growth*	*Maturity*	*Decline*
1. Sales	Low sales	Rapidly increasing sales	Peak sales	Declining sales
2. Costs	High cost per customer	Average cost per customer	Low cost per customer	Low cost per customer
3. Profits	Negative	More profit	High profit	Declining profit
4. Customer	Innovators	Early adopters	Early majority + Late majority	Laggards
5. Competitor	Few	More in number	Stable number, beginning to decline	Declining numbers

6.9 STAGES OF PRODUCT LIFE CYCLE

A product passes through distinct stages during its life and is called product life cycle (PLC). The PLC is normally presented as a sales curve spanning the product's course from introduction to exit. The PLC concept says that each stage in the cycle is characterized by typical marketer behaviour and each stage leads to a distinctive marketing strategy. The product's life cycle period usually consists of four major steps or phases:

"Every product has a life cycle that is a period of time during which it appeals to the consumer".

- Introduction
- Growth
- Maturity and
- Decline

These phases can be split up into smaller ones depending on the product and must be considered when a new product is to be introduced into a market since they dictate the product's sales performance. The following Fig. 6.4 shows the life cycle of a product.

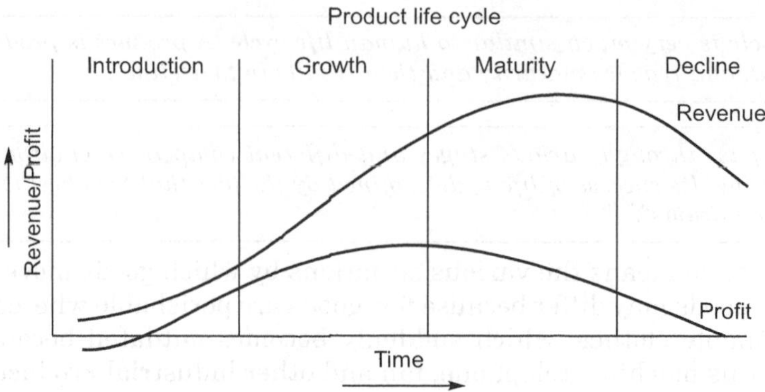

Fig. 6.4. Product life cycle.

1. **Introduction Stage:** The product is in introductory stage. At this stage, there may not be a ready market for the product. Sales are low. Profit seems a remote possibility, demand has to be created and developed and consumers have to be prompted to try out the product. One of the crucial decisions to be taken in this stage is the pricing strategy to be adopted—either market skimming or market penetration. Skimming strategy involves high price, taking advantage of early entry and the novelty of the product. Penetration pricing involves low prices with a view to having good market coverage as shown in Fig.6.5. It also aims at keeping the competition out.

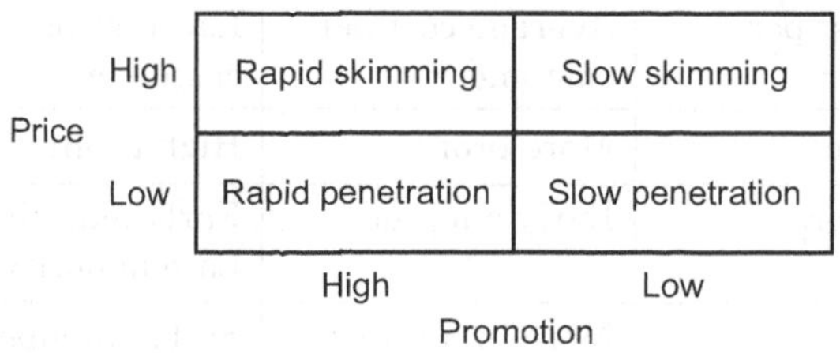

Fig. 6.5. Market skinning and penetration.

The characteristics of introductory stage of product life cycle are as follows:

1. Higher investment, lesser profits
2. Minimal competition
3. Company tries to induce acceptance and gain initial distribution
4. Company needs promotions targeted towards **customers** to increase awareness and demand for product
5. Company needs promotions targeted towards **channel** to increase confidence in the product.

2. **Growth Stage:** The product is becoming more widely known and consumed. Marketing is used to try to establish or strengthen the brand and develop an image for the product. During the market growth stage, demand for the product increases and size of market grows. The sales and profits also go up. But by the time the marketer settles down with his product, competitors may enter the scene with similar or slightly improved versions. The marketer has to stay ahead of his competitor and has to reconsider his pricing strategy. He follows competition-oriented pricing, because the total market is being shared among many firms. Marketing and distribution efficiency becomes the decisive factor at this stage. The characteristics of growth stage of product life cycle are:

1. Product is successfully launched
2. Demand increases
3. Distribution increases
4. Competition intensifies
5. Company might introduce secondary products or support services
6. Better revenue generation and ROI.

3. Maturity Stage: The product range may be extended, by adding both width and depth. Competition will increase and this has to be responded to. In the maturity stage, the demand tends to reach a saturation point and there is enough supply from competitive sources. Price competition becomes intense and exploits the brand loyalty. The marketer tries out product and packaging modification, and promotional deals and makes special offers to new market segments so that his sales volume does not shrink. Long-term and short-term marketing plans are implemented to profitably prolong the maturity stage. The characteristics of maturity stage of product life cycle are as follows:

1. Competition is high
2. Product is established and promotion expenditures are less
3. Little growth potential for the product
4. Penetration pricing, and lower profit margins
5. The major focus is towards extending the life cycle and maintaining market share
6. Converting customer's product to your own is a major challenge in maturity stage.

4. Decline Stage: In the decline stage, sales begin to fall and as a result the range sold is likely to be reduced, with the firm concentrating on core products. Advertising costs will be reduced, and attempts will be made to mop-up what is left of the potential market. Each product sold could be quite profitable as development costs have been paid back at an earlier stage in the life cycle. But overall, total profits will fall. Price is also likely to fall, but by concentrating on remaining market niches there should be some price stability. The characteristics of decline stage of product life cycle are as follows:

1. Market is saturated
2. Sales and profits decline
3. Company becomes cost conscious
4. A lot of resources are blocked in rejuvenating the dead product
5. There are only three options left with the company
6. Repositioning or rebranding of the product to extend product life cycle
7. Maintain the product as it is and reduce costs to get maximum profits till the product can produce profits
8. Take the product off the market.

Thus, PLC concept helps and is used as a tool in formulating and implementing marketing strategy.

- It facilitates pre-planning the product launch
- It facilitates prolonging the profitable phase
- It facilitates investment decisions on products
- It facilitates choice of appropriate entry strategy
- It facilitates choice of the right time to exit
- It provides useful clues for managing customers.

6.10 STRATEGIES OF PRODUCT LIFE CYCLE

The strategies of product life cycle are as follows:

Stages	*Introduction*	*Growth*	*Maturity*	*Decline*
1. Product	Offer basic product	Offer product extension, service, warranty	Diversify brands / models	Phase out weak products
2. Price	Change cost	Price to penetrate market	Price to match better competition	Cut price
3. Distribution	Build selective distribution	Build intensive distribution	Build more intensive distribution	Selective phase out of unprofitable unit
4. Advertising	Build product awareness among early adopters and dealers	Build awareness and interest in mass market	Stress on brand difference and benefits	Reduce to retain hard core loyals
5. Sales Promotion	Use heavy sales promotion to induce trial	Reduce sales promotion due to increased consumer demand	More sales promotion to encourage brand switching	Reduce to minimum level

REVIEW QUESTIONS

1. What is product? Also, classify different types of product.
2. Define product mix. Explain the marketing mix variable/four Ps of marketing.
3. Explain the product line extension and product line analysis.
4. What is BCG model? Explain the limitations of BCG matrix.
5. Explain the GE—Mckinsey matrix.
6. What is product life cycle concept and meaning? Explain the characteristics of product life cycle.
7. Explain the different stages of product life cycle.
8. What are the different strategies in different stages of product life cycle?

CHAPTER 7

Product Planning, Development and Product Identification

POINTS TO REMEMBER

At the end of this chapter, we will be able to understand:

- Introduction
- Product Planning Concept and Meaning
- Objectives/Need/Importance of New Product
- Product Development
- Steps Involved in New Product Development Process
- Product Identification: An Introduction
- Branding
- Trademark
- Distinction between Brand and Trademark
- Objectives of Branding
- Essentials of Good Brand
- Brand Positioning
- Packaging
- Levels/Classification of Packaging
- Objectives of Packaging
- Functions/Importance of Packaging

7.1 INTRODUCTION

Developing ideas for a new product and introducing them in the market from time to time is an essential and challenging job of the marketing management of a company. The existing products become old and out-dated due to the changes in the technology and the customers' needs, tastes and preferences. Therefore, a company has to replace them with new products.

New product may mean many things, *e.g.*, original products, product improvements, product modifications and new brands developed by a company through its own Research and Development (R&D) activities.

7.2 PRODUCT PLANNING CONCEPT AND MEANING

"Product planning is the ongoing process of identifying and articulating market requirements that define a product's feature set. Product planning serves as the basis for decisions about price, distribution and promotion".

Product planning is a process used to identify and develop new products. The purpose of planning is to make choices about which product ideas a company should invest in. Companies can approach product planning from a number of different perspectives. Having a system in place before planning begins is important as it helps to avoid wasted time and creates a framework for decision-making. Consultants who specialize in marketing and corporate decision-making can be involved in the development of a product planning system for a company, which will accommodate the company's approach to business while helping it avoid expensive dead ends.

> *"Product planning embraces all activities which enable producers and middlemen to determine what should continue a company's lines of products. Ideally, product planning will answer that the full complement of a firm's product are logically related, individually instifiable item, designed to strengthen the company's competitive and profit position".* **W. J. Stanton**

> *"The planning, direction and control of all stages in the life of a product from the time of its creation to the time of its removal from the company's line of product is known as product planning".*
> **Mason and Rath**

> *"Product planning determines the characteristics of products but meeting the consumers numerous desires, characteristics that add stability to products and incorporates these characteristics into the finished product".* **Johnson**

Prof. William J. Stanton states that new products can be classified into three categories.

1. Products which are really innovative and truly unique, for which there is real need for which no existing substitutes are considered satisfactory, *e.g.*, a hair restorer or a cancer cure.
2. Replacements for existing products that are significantly different from the existing products, *e.g.*, instant coffee replacing ground coffee and clothing of new fashion introduced every year, and
3. Initiative products that are new to a particular firm but not new to the market, *e.g.*, different brands of T.V. sets coming into the market now.

7.3 OBJECTIVES/NEED/IMPORTANCE OF NEW PRODUCT

New product development objectives for a new product includes:

1. Schedule of release
2. Safety and testing guidelines
3. List of features
4. Features for future release and upgrade path.

Financial and Budgetary objectives (new product development objectives) for an existing product includes:

1. Making the product better or safer
2. Making the product cheaper for the end-user

3. Making the product easier to sell
4. Upgrading the product to be state-of-the-art
5. Adding more features to the product.

7.4 PRODUCT DEVELOPMENT

Product development means addition of new goods in the product chain of company or enterprise or making changes or improvement in the goods being produced in its design, colour, shape, size and change in utility and also improvement in their packing.

> *"Product development is that progressive strategy of an institution in which new or transformed products are introduced in existing marketing segments".* **Kotler and Armstrong**

> *"Product development is that process which involves adding, dropping and modification of item specification in the product line for a given period of time, usually one year".* **Lipson and Darling**

> *"The essence of product development is transforming product concept into actual product. It is that process which combines the technical and marketing capacities and introduces new or transformed products as a replacement of decline-oriented products".* **William Lazor**

7.5 STEPS INVOLVED IN NEW PRODUCT DEVELOPMENT (NPD) PROCESS

New products are a vital part of a firm's competitive growth strategy. Leaders of successful firms know that it is not enough to develop new products on sporadic basis. What counts is a climate of products development that leads to one triumph after another. It is commonplace for major companies to have 50 per cent or more of their current sales in products introduced within the last 10 years. To develop a new product the following steps must be realized as shown in Fig. 7.1:

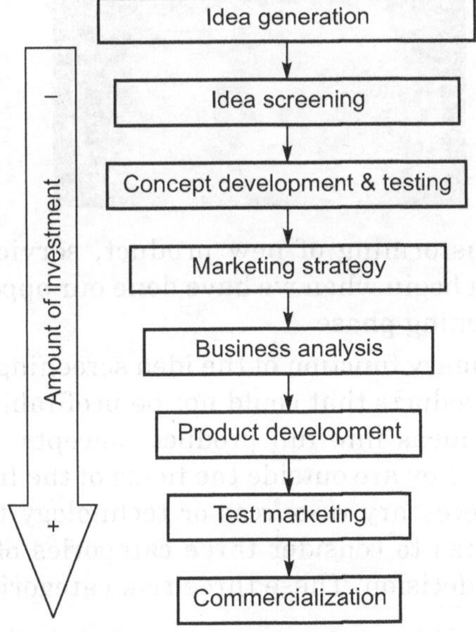

Fig. 7.1. Steps of developing a new product.

1. Idea Generation,
2. Idea Screening,
3. Concept Development and Testing,
4. Market Strategy,
5. Business Analysis,
6. Product Development,
7. Test Marketing, and
8. Commercialization.

1. **Idea Generation:** Every product starts as an idea. But all new product aides do not equal merit or potential for economic or commercial success. Some estimates indicate that as many as 60–70 ideas are necessary to yield one successful product.

   Idea generation is often called the "fuzzy front end" of the New Product Development process. Ideas for new products can be obtained from basic research using a SWOT analysis (Strengths, Weaknesses, Opportunities and Threats), market and consumer trends, company's Research and Development department, competitors, focus groups, employees, salespeople, corporate spies, trade shows, or ethnographic discovery methods (searching for user patterns and habits) may also be used to get an insight into new product lines or product features. Lots of ideas are being generated about the new product. Out of these ideas many ideas are being implemented. The ideas are used to generate many forms and their generating places are also various. Many reasons are responsible for the generation of an idea.

   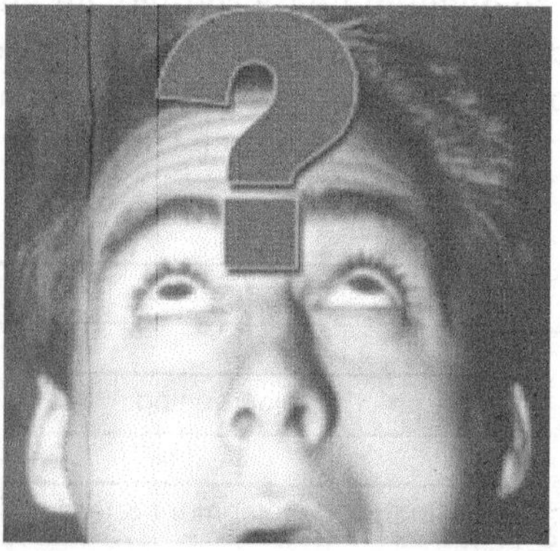

   Idea generation or brainstorming of new product, service, or store concepts—idea generation techniques can begin when we have done our opportunity analysis to support our ideas in the idea screening phase.

2. **Idea Screening:** The primary function of the idea screening process is two-fold: first, to eliminate ideas for new products that could not be profitably marketed by the firm and second, to expand viable ideas into full product concepts. New product ideas may be eliminated either because they are outside the fields of the firm's interest or because the firm does not have the necessary resources or technology to produce the product at a profit. The organization has to consider three categories of risk in the idea screening phase prior to reaching a decision. These three risk categories are:

(*i*) **Strategic risk:** Strategic risk involves the risk of not matching the role or purpose of a new product with a specific strategic need or issue of the organization.

(*ii*) **Market risk:** Market risk is the risk that a new product would not meet a market need as products are being developed, customer requirements change and new technologies evolve.

(*iii*) **Internal risk:** Internal risk is the risk that a new product won't be developed within the desired time and budget.

3. **Concept Development and Testing:** Develop the marketing and engineering details.
   1. Investigate intellectual property issues and search patent data bases.
   2. Who is the target market and who is the decision maker in the purchasing process?
   3. What product features must the product incorporate?
   4. What benefits will the product provide?
   5. How will consumers react to the product?
   6. How will the product be produced most cost effectively?
   7. Prove feasibility through virtual computer aided rendering, and rapid prototyping.
   8. What will it cost to produce the product?

   Testing the concept by asking a sample of prospective customers what they think of the idea, usually via choice modelling.
4. **Marketing Strategy:** The marketing strategy development involves three parts.

   (*a*) The first part focuses on **target market, sales, market share and profit goals**. For example, Tata's initial business plan consisted sales of 2 lakh cars per annum.

   (*b*) The second part involves **product price, distribution and marketing budget strategies.** For example, Tata's fixed ₹ 1 lakh as the car price, and finding a self-employed person who works like an agent to distribute the cars.

   (*c*) The final part contains **marketing mix strategy and profit goals.**
5. **Business Analysis (Also Called Feasibility Analysis):** It is the analysis of sales, costs and profit estimated for a new product to find out whether these align with company mission and objectives. This study involves the following:
   - Estimate likely selling price based upon competition and customer feedback
   - Estimate sales volume based upon size of market
   - Estimate profitability and break-even point.
6. **Product Development:** At this stage, the product idea has been evaluated from the standpoint of engineering, manufacturing, finance and marketing. If it has met all expectations, it is considered physical development and testing. A development report to management is prepared that spells out in fine detail:
   - Results of the studies
   - Required plan design
   - Production facilities design
   - Tooling requirements
   - Marketing test plan
   - Financial programme survey
   - Estimated release data.

7. **Test Marketing:** At this stage, the product has been a company secret. Now management goes outside the company and submits the physical product for customers' approval. Test marketing is a controlled experiment in a limited geographic area to test the new product or in some cases certain aspects of the marketing strategy, such as packaging or advertising.

   The main goal of a test market is to evaluate and adjust the general marketing strategy to be used and the appropriate marketing mix. Throughout the test market process, findings are being analyzed and forecasts of volume developed. This test involves the following:

   - The product is introduced into the realistic market.
   - The 4Ps of marketing are tested.
   - The cost of test marketing varies with the type of product.

   Upon completion of a successful test market phase, the marketing plan can be finalized and the product prepared for launch.

8. **Commercialization:** This is the launching step in which the firm commits to introduce the product into the marketplace. During this stage, heavy emphasis is placed on the organization structure and management talent needed to implement the marketing strategy. Emphasis is also given to following up on such things as bugs in the design, production costs, quality control, and inventory requirements.

7.6 PRODUCT IDENTIFICATION: AN INTRODUCTION

Companies first find the target market then segment and then customers. After these companies go about developing products, which may be product modification or it may be a completely new product. Product offerings are increasing every year as consumers are looking for more and more variety of products. Companies which are unable to churn out new products fall back on competition and suffer the consequences. Companies face danger not just from competitors but consumer needs, technology, and product life cycle. New product development has its share of challenges. Research shows that 95 per cent of new products fail in USA and in Europe the failure rate is 90 per cent.

Organizational set up has to be conducive to support new product development. Foremost companies must allocate funds for research and development, the conventional way is the per cent of sales technique. Others chose to allow employees to dedicate a certain amount of work time on new product development. Companies next have to organize the process of development. This can be done by product managers with new product development experience or by cross-functional team with members chosen from various departments having the ability of developing new products.

7.7 BRANDING

"The name of the game in branding is to make money".

A brand is a name, symbol, term, sign, design, or combination of each of these things, the purpose of which is to identify goods and services of one seller or of a group of sellers and differentiate them from competitors. A brand is also the sum of all characteristics that make a product offering unique. A company can copy a product, but it cannot replicate the brand. In a sense, the brand is the "personality" of the product, what the product means to the customer and the set of emotions evoked when the brand is encountered or used by the customer.

"The brand name is concerned with that part of the 'brand' that can be vocalized."
Lipson and Darling

"A brand is a name, term, symbol or design or a combination of them which is intended to identify the goods or services of one seller or group of sellers and to differentiate them from those of competitors". **American Marketing Association**

Brand name: It is that part which can be vocalized—the utterable examples: Samsung, Surf, Dalda, Xerox.

Brand mark: The brand mark is a design element, such as a symbol (*e.g.*, Nike swoosh-athletic shoes), logo (*e.g.*, Yahoo! graphic), a character (*e.g.*, Keebler elves) or even a sound (*e.g.*, Intel inside sound), that provides visual or auditory recognition for the product.

7.8 TRADEMARK

When a letter or a name, symbol, mark, design, picture and their combination, is registered under law then it's called trademark.

"It is a brand which is given legal protection because under the law it has been appropriated exclusively by on seller". **American Marketing Association**

"All trademarks are brands and thus include the words, letters of numbers which may be propounded; they may also include a pictorial design". **William J. Stanton**

"Trademark has been defined as any sign, mark, symbol, words which indicate the origin or ownership of an article as distinguished from the quality and which others have not the equal right to employ for the same". **Copeland**

7.9 DISTINCTION BETWEEN BRAND AND TRADEMARK

Brand and trademark are considered synonymous with each other, but the following differences can be seen from the legal point of view.

Point of Difference	*Brand*	*Trademark*
1. Meaning	When a product can be identified through the medium of trademark, word, name and design, it is called brand.	When a letter or a name, sign, picture or design or a mix of all, is registered under law it is called, Trademark.
2. Nature	All brands are not trademarks.	All trademarks are brands.
3. Objective	Objective of brand is to help the identification of product and provide it difference and speciality.	Trademark's objective is to stop products.
4. Area	Area of brand is limited because any business system can use different brands for different products.	Trademark's area is expanded, because same trademark can be used for different products.
5. Registration	Brand registration is not compulsory	Trademark registration is compulsory.
6. Legal Protection	Even if a brand is copied by other competitors, no legal action can be taken against them.	Legal action can be taken against the competitors who copy trademark.
7. Creation Existence	Brand can be created by any manufacturer.	A trademark's existence is considered only after registration.
8. Identity	Brand provides identity to a product.	Trademark provides identity to a business house.
9. Use	Brand can be used by different producers and sellers.	A trademark can be used only by that producer who has got it registered.
10. Compensation	Brand owner cannot claim any compensation from the defaulter/ cheater.	The defaulter will have to pay compensation.
11. Penalty	There is no provision of penalty or punishment on copying it.	The culprit can be punished.

7.10 OBJECTIVES OF BRANDING

1. **Brand Management begins with Having a Thorough Knowledge of the Term "Brand":** It includes developing a promise, making that promise and maintaining it. It means defining the brand, positioning the brand, and delivering the brand. Brand management is nothing but an art of creating and sustaining the brand. Branding makes customers committed to your business. A strong brand differentiates your products from the competitors. It gives a quality image to your business.
2. **Brand Management Includes Managing the Tangible and Intangible Characteristics of Brand:** In case of product brands, the tangibles include the product itself, price, packaging, etc. While in case of service brands, the tangibles include the customers' experience. The intangibles include emotional connections with the product/ service.

3. **Branding is Assembling of Various Marketing Mix Medium into a Whole so as to Give you an Identity:** It is nothing but capturing your customers' mind with your brand name. It gives an image of an experienced, huge and reliable business.

It is all about capturing the niche market for your product/service and about creating a confidence in the current and prospective customers' minds that you are the unique solution to their problem. The aim of branding is to convey:

(*a*) Brand message vividly,

(*b*) Create customer loyalty,

(*c*) Persuade the buyer for the product, and

(*d*) Establish an emotional connectivity with the customers.

Branding forms customer perceptions about the product. It should raise customer expectations about the product. The primary aim of branding is to create differentiation.

Strong brands reduce customers' perceived monetary, social and safety risks in buying goods/services. The customers can better imagine the intangible goods with the help of brand name. Strong brand organizations have a high market share. The brand should be given good support so that it can sustain itself in the long-run. It is essential to manage all brands and build brand equity over a period of time. Here comes importance and usefulness of brand management. Brand management helps in building a corporate image. A brand manager has to oversee overall brand performance. A successful brand can only be created if the brand management system is competent.

7.11 ESSENTIALS OF GOOD BRAND

Brand attributes portray a company's brand characteristics. They signify the basic nature of brand. Brand attributes are a bundle of features that highlight the physical and personality aspects of the brand. Attributes are developed through images, actions, or presumptions. Brand attributes help in creating brand identity. A strong brand must have the following attributes:

1. **Relevancy:** A strong brand must be relevant. It must meet people's expectations and should perform the way they want it to. A good job must be done to persuade consumers to buy the product; else in spite of your product being unique, customers will not buy it. Example: Encyclopaedias.
2. **Consistency:** A consistent brand signifies what the brand stands for and builds customers trust in brand. A consistent brand is where the company communicates messages in a way that does not deviate from the core brand proposition.

   Proper positioning—A strong brand should be positioned so that it makes a place for itself amongst the target audience and they prefer it to other brands. Examples of consistent brands are Tata and Reliance.
3. **Sustainable:** A strong brand makes a business competitive. A sustainable brand drives an organization towards innovation and success. Examples of sustainable brands are Maruti Suzuki and Bajaj.
4. **Credibility:** A strong brand should do what it promises. The way you communicate your brand to the audience/customers should be realistic. It should not fail to deliver what it promises. Do not exaggerate as customers want to believe in the promises you make to them. An example of a credible brand is LIC.
5. **Inspirational:** A strong brand should transcend inspire the category it is famous for. For example, Nike transcendent Jersey Polo Shirt.

6. **Uniqueness:** A strong brand should be different and unique. It should set you apart from other competitors in market. Example: Close-up tooth paste which contains mouth freshener.
7. **Appealing:** A strong brand should be attractive. Customers should be attracted by the promise you make and by the value you deliver. Example of an appealing brand could be State Bank of India.

7.12 BRAND POSITIONING

- *"A product is something that is made in a factory; a brand is something that is brought by a customer;*
- *A product can be copied by a competitor; a brand is unique;*
- *A product can be quickly outdated; a successful brand is timeless".*

Stephen King-WPP Group, London

Brand positioning is a strategic approach to establish a sustainable competitive advantage. Competitive advantage is defined as "the strategic advantage one business entity has over its rival entities within its competitive industry. Achieving competitive advantage strengthens and positions a business better within the business environment".

There are different ways of improving a business competitive advantage. It is important to understand that the objective of brand positioning is not to bring your competitors down, but to outshine them by performing better and more efficiently to cater to the needs of the industry's customers.

There are five generic competitive branding strategies useful in brand positioning. These generic competitive strategies are:

1. **A Low-cost Leadership Strategy:** It entails the process of appealing to the broad spectrum of potential buyers by being able to offer an overall low cost product or service. Examples: Bharti Wal-mart, Nokia mobiles.
2. **A Broad Differentiation Strategy:** This strategy is one in which a business seeks to differentiate its products or services from their competitors in ways that attract the broadest spectrum of customers in an established industry. Examples: Mercedes cars, Hitachi air conditioner.
3. **A Best Cost Provider Strategy:** It offers customers more value for the buck, with a lot of emphasis on the low cost of the product or service in comparison to its high quality. Great example is Maruti Suzuki cars.
4. **A Focused Strategy is on Lower Costs:** It is a brand positioning strategy that concentrates on out competing rivals, by offering customized products or services at a lower cost to a smaller portion of the established buyers. Example: Deccan Airline or many small retailers offering their own label or discounted line of products.
5. **A Focused Strategy Based on Differentiation:** Here the focus is on a narrow segment of buyers who are offered a product or service that has been customized to meet their exact tastes and demands and supersedes what competitors are offering, *i.e.*, ***"Standing out of the crowd"***. Example: A company offering cholesterol free edible oil to cardiac patients or sugar-free ice-creams to diabetic patients.

Each of these branding strategies focuses on achieving different types of market positions and demands different tactics of competition and business operation. A business' brand position should aspire to mount offensive strategies that can effectively neutralize and overcome the strengths and capabilities of established competitors. The best competitive advantage a business can attain from its brand positioning is one in which competitors find hard to compete.

The ideal brand positioning strategy will differ for each business. However, there are ways of achieving a competitive advantage by focusing brand positioning strategies on the competitor's weaknesses. Pay special attention to the portion of buyers that rivals ignore or are ill-prepared to serve. Go after the customers of competitors whose product lacks in quality. Make special sales pitches to customers of existing competitors. Try to focus on competitors with weak advertising and weak brand recognition. These offensive brand position strategies can be implemented on an individual basis or used together for a major competitive offensive strategy.

7.13 PACKAGING

Packaging means to pack or cover goods, so that it can remain safe and can be easily taken from one place to another. In other words, packaging refers to the use of container or returnable material, which includes labeling and decoration, so that it remains safe, can be sold easily and is convenient for consumer's use.

> *"Packaging may be defined as, the general group of activities in product planning which involve designing and producing the container or wrapper for a product".* **William J. Stanton**

> *"Packaging is the use of containers and wrapping materials plus decoration and labeling, to protect the product, to help and promote its sale and to make it convenient for the customers to use the product".* **Mason and Rath**

> *"Packaging may be defined as the art and/or science concerned with the development and use of materials, methods and equipment for applying a product to a container or vice-versa designed to produce the product throughout the various stages of distributions".* **R.S. Davar**

7.14 LEVELS/CLASSIFICATION OF PACKAGING

There are different levels of packaging that a consumer may be exposed to. Usually, the customer is handling the product in its primary packaging. This is the packaging that the product is seen in as it sits on the store shelf.

The primary packaging is exposed to the consumer and so will have the attributes conveying important information to the consumer. However, the overall packaging can also be sub-divided into other levels of packaging.

1. **First level of Packaging (Primary Package):** The first level of packaging is the package that the product is contained in. This level of packaging may be the one that the consumer sees, but depending on the product, the first level package may be as simple as a clear plastic bag. For example, in a cereal box, the box is displayed to the consumer; however the actual cereal is contained within a sealed plastic bag. The bag is the first level of packaging.
2. **Second Level of Packaging (Secondary Package):** A second level or secondary wrapping will occur. This happens when the packaged product is bundled in some way with several other units of the same product or the packaged product is put into a box. This secondary packaging is sometimes added to products because they need security or

tamper-resistant packaging. In this, the example would be the cereal box itself. In this case, the first level of packaging provides some protection to the food item and conveys no information to the consumer. The cereal box however, acting as the second level, provides additional protection, but it also provides information to the consumer, as well as a way for the cereal to be displayed, *i.e.*, a box will fit better on a shelf than a plastic bag full of cereal.

3. **Third Level of Packaging (Tertiary/Transportation/Transit Package):** A product may even have a third level package. Products that are sold in bulk items can often have a third level. The same cereal box sold in a bulk store may be sold in a larger box which contains two or three smaller boxes, which contains a plastic bag. Every level of packaging is very important and every aspect of it should be closely considered to convey not only its protective value to the product but as a way to communicate to the consumer.

7.15 OBJECTIVES OF PACKAGING

The function of packaging is not simply only physical protection but also marketing, barrier protection, security, information, convenience and portion control. With the advent of modern technology, the packaging machinery such as candy wrapping machines and form fill seal machines have achieved a level of perfection.

India has become a hub for the packaging industry. Packaging machines in India are of world-class level, and we can definitely say that packaging is of international standard. The main objectives of packaging are:

1. **Physical Protection:** Packaging of objects ensures that they are protected against vibration, temperature, shock, compression, etc., among other things.
2. **Barrier Protection:** Keeping the objects in the packages fresh, clean and safe for shelf life is the primary function of packaging. Packaged objects need protection from water vapour, oxygen, dust, etc. Permeability is an important factor in practice designing. Many packages contain oxygen absorbers to increase the shelf life. Sometimes, controlled atmosphere is also maintained in food packaging.
3. **Marketing:** Packaging plays an important role in marketing. Good packaging and attractive labeling is used by sellers to promote potential buyers. In package designing graphic designs are used on the surface of the package to make it attractive.
4. **Containment:** Small articles are generally grouped together in packages for the purpose of efficiency. For example, a single box of thousand pens needs less space than thousand single pens. Liquid items and flowing items need containment.
5. **Security:** Packaging plays a significant function in cutting down the security risks during shipping & transportation. Improved packaging techniques are used to discourage tampering. It helps reduce the risks of pilferage. Modern packaging techniques include anti-theft devices such as Radio Frequency Identification tags, dye-packs, and also electronic article surveillance tags that can be detected by gadgets.
6. **Impact of Information:** Packaging and labeling also tells use, transportation instructions, recycling, or disposing of the package. In some specialized fields such as medical, pharmaceutical, and chemical products, some special type of information is required by law.
7. **Convenience:** Packaging also adds to the convenience in handling, display, opening, distribution, sale, use and reuse.
8. **Portion Control:** In the medicinal and pharmaceutical field, the precise amount of contents is needed to control usage. Medicine tablets can be divided into packages that are of a more suitable size for individual use. It also helps in the control of inventory.

7.16 FUNCTIONS/IMPORTANCE OF PACKAGING

Packaging is a very important marketing strategy to glamorize your product in order to attract the consumer's attention. Sometimes packaging is so important that it costs more than the product itself in order to lure the consumers to buy it. Packaging should definitely be included in the 4 major Ps of marketing (product, place, promotion and price).

1. **To protect a Product from Damage, Air and Moisture:** The product must be protected against being dropped, crushed, and the vibration it suffers during transport. Delicate products such as fruits need to be protected by a rigid package such as a laminated container.

   The product must also be protected against the climate including high temperatures, humidity, light and gases in the air. It must also be protected against microorganisms, chemicals, soil and insects.

2. **To Keep the Product Together, to Contain it (i.e., so that it does not Spill):** Some shapes cannot be easily packaged, for example, certain vegetables. However, there are methods of getting around this problem. Suppliers of canned vegetables such as carrots have developed a particular type of plant that yields carrots that are straight and smaller than the normal variety. These fit into cans. Some products such as fruit juices and sauces need to be contained in packages that hold them together and are sealed to prevent spillage and loss.

3. **To Identify the Product:** Packaging is the main way products are advertised and identified. To the manufacturer the package clearly identifies the product inside and it is usually the package that the customer recognizes while shopping. Advertising is very important when a manufacturer launches a new or existing product. The package, through its colour scheme or logo, is what is normally identified by the customer. The package will also contain important information including ingredients and expiry date.

   A firm spends huge amount of money on packaging food and other items each year. Sixty per cent of all packaging is for food products. At the beginning of the 20th century most food was sold loose. It was weighed and measured out and placed in bags or directly into the shoppers bag to carry home. Packaging and advertising were virtually unknown. Today packaging is a massive, lucrative industry and often it is the way the packaging looks that persuades the shopper to buy the product inside it.

4. **Protection During Transport and Ease of Transport:** A package should be designed to make it easy to transport, move and lift. A regular shaped package (such as a cuboid) can be stacked without too much space between each package being wasted. This means that more packages can be transported in a container of a lorry. Unusually shaped packages can lead to space being wasted and this can be costly if thousands of the same package are being transported.

5. **Stacking and Storage:** In supermarkets and shops it must be possible to stack packages so that space is not wasted on the shelves. Lost space on shelves is looked upon as a lost opportunity to sell to a customer. Also, the package must be designed in such a way that all the important information can be seen by a potential buyer, especially the product name. It is the selection of colours and shades that determine whether the product inside is regarded as a quality, sophisticated or cheap item. Often packages are stacked on top and alongside each other to reduce wasted space. The shape and form of the package determines how efficiently they can be stacked or stored.

6. **Printed Information:** Information that is useful to consumers and companies such as supermarkets, is printed on packaging. This includes—ingredients, price, special offers,

manufacturing and expiry date, batch number, manufacturers' address, contact information, product title, barcode and more. The barcode is extremely useful to the shop selling the product. When the barcode is scanned, the computer system automatically determines if the product needs re-ordering. Also, the price of the product appears at the till.

REVIEW QUESTIONS

1. What is the meaning of product development? Explain the objectives of a new product.
2. Explain the steps involved in new product development process.
3. Explain the concepts of product identification.
4. What is brand and trademark? Distinguish between brand and trademark.
5. Explain the objectives of branding.
6. Describe the essentials of a good brand.
7. What is brand positioning and packaging.
8. Discuss the different levels/classifications of packaging.
9. What are the major objectives of packaging?
10. Explain the functions of packaging.
11. Explain the importance of packaging.

CHAPTER 8

Pricing

POINTS TO REMEMBER

At the end of this chapter, we will be able to understand:

- Introduction
- Meaning of Price
- Importance of Pricing
- Objectives of Pricing
- Factors Affecting Pricing
- Methods of Pricing
- Pricing of New Products
- New Product Pricing Methods and Strategy

8.1 INTRODUCTION

Price is all around us. We pay rent for our apartment, tuition for our education, airline, railways, buses charge us a fare, local banks charge interest for the money, you pay a fee to your doctor, advocate etc. Thus price is not just a number on a tag or an item.

Every marketer and organization, whether a profit seeking organization or non-profit organization, has to set a price for its products or services. Price is the value of a product or service expressed in monetary terms. It is the consideration which the buyer has to give to the seller for purchasing a product or utilizing a service.

We are concerned with price in different ways, in our life. We pay the bill of the provision store for the purchases made from it, rent to the landlord in whose building we live, fee to the doctor when we consult him and bus fare to the conductor when we travel by a bus. All these are the prices of different products and services we consume or utilize.

The salary of a business executive or a lecturer for a lecture in a college is the price of his services and the wage paid to a labourer is the price of the work done by him.

8.2 MEANING OF PRICE

'Pricing' is the function of determining the value of a product or service in monetary terms by its marketer before it is offered to the target consumers or customers for sale. While making the pricing decision, the management of a company has to establish the pricing objectives, identify the factors governing the price and ascertain their relative importance, determine the product/service value in monetary terms and formulate pricing policies and strategies with a view to effectively employ price as a strategic instrument in marketing the products/services of the company.

"Price is the exchange value of goods or services in terms of money".

"Price of a product or service is what the seller feels it is worth, in terms of money, to the buyer".

8.3 IMPORTANCE OF PRICING

Price is an important element of the marketing mix of a company. It is the only element in the marketing mix that produces revenue, the other elements represent costs or expenses. It can be used as a strategic marketing variable to meet competition. It is an important weapon in the marketing armoury of a company to fight with the competitors. Price is highly perceptible to consumers or customers and, therefore, significantly affects their decision to buy a product or service. It is a factor that directly determines the volume of sales.

1. **Maintain Appropriate Living Standard:** Price rise lets living standard of people fall and economic development of the country is obstructed. To maintain the proper living standard, price control is essential.
2. **Maintain Planning:** As price rises, the work of planning increases which results in obstruction in the prescribed aims and objectives of the planning. To maintain the planning process in a fine manner, prices should be controlled at all costs.
3. **Protection from Monetary Instability:** When price increase is more than investment and national income increases, monetary fluctuation defects are created. To remove them appropriate price control is required.
4. **Establishment of Balance in Demand and Supply:** In a developing economy, due to changing circumstances, balance of demand and supply disrupts by which consumer, producer and investor have to take hardships. This shows that there is a need to balance the demand and supply in a proper way.
5. **Well Adjusted for Distribution Management:** With the view point of consumers for quick supply of goods on less prices distribution management should be well adjusted. For this, it is necessary to control the consumer price.
6. **Multi-faced Development of National Resources:** The major objective of economic planning is multi-faced development of national resources. Thus, price policy should be quite independent as price regulation can adjust this motto.

8.4 OBJECTIVES OF PRICING

Pricing decisions are usually considered a part of the general strategy for achieving a broadly defined goal. Before determining the price itself, the management should decide the objectives. While setting the price, the firm may aim at one or more of the following objectives.

1. **Profit Maximization:** Since the primary motive of business is to earn maximum profit, pricing always aims at maximization of profit through maximization of sales. When a short-run policy is adopted for maximizing the profit, it will exploit the customers. The customers have a feeling of monopoly and high price. But a long-run policy to maximize the profit has no drawbacks. A short-run policy will attract competitors, who produce

similar goods at low cost. As a result, price control and government regulations will be introduced.

2. **Market Share:** For maximizing market share a firm may lower its price in relation to the competitors' product.
3. **Prevent Competition:** The pricing objective may be to meet or prevent competition. While fixing the price, the price of similar products, produced by other firms, will have to be considered.
4. **Target Return in Investment:** The firm should fix the price for the product in such a way that it will satisfy expected returns for the investment.

   When a businessman invests capital in a business, he calculates the probable return on his investment. A certain rate of return on investment is aimed. Then, the price is fixed accordingly. The price includes the predetermined average return. This is seller-oriented policy. Many well-established firms adopt the objective of pricing in terms of "return on investment." Firms want to secure a certain percentage of return on their investment or on sales.
5. **Price Stabilization:** Another objective of pricing is to stabilize the product prices over a considerable period of time. It also prevents price war amongst the competitors. When the price changes often, there arises no confidence on the product.
6. **Resource Mobilization:** A company may fix its prices in such a way that sufficient resources are made available for the firm's expansion, developmental investment etc.
7. **Speed up Cash Collection:** Some firms try to set a price which will enable rapid cash recovery as they may be financially tight or may regard future is too uncertain to justify patient cash recovery.
8. **Survival and Growth:** An important objective of pricing is survival and achieving the expected rate of growth. Profit is less important than survival.

   According to Peter Drucker, avoidance of loss and ensuring survival are more important than maximization of profit.
9. **Prestige and Goodwill:** Pricing also aims at maintaining the prestige and enhancing the goodwill of the firm.
10. **Achieving Product-quality Leadership:** Some companies aim at establishing product-quality leadership through premium price.

8.5 FACTORS AFFECTING PRICING

Factors governing prices may be divided into external factors and internal factors.

A. Internal Factors

B. External Factors

8.5.1 Internal Factors

These are the factors which are within the control of the organization. Various internal factors are as follows.

1. **Organizational factors:** Pricing decisions occur on two levels in the organization. Overall price strategy is dealt with by top executives. They determine the basic ranges that the product falls into in terms of market segments. The actual mechanics of pricing are dealt with at lower levels in the firm and focus on individual product strategies. Usually, some combination of production and marketing specialists are involved in choosing the price.

2. **Cost:** The price must cover the cost of production including materials, labour, overhead, administrative and selling expenses and a reasonable profit. The most important factor is the cost of production. In deciding to market a product, a firm may try to decide what prices are realistic, considering current demand and competition in the market.
3. **Marketing mix:** Other elements of marketing mix, product, place, promotion, pace and politics are influencing factors for pricing. Since these are interconnected, change in one element will influence the other.

   Marketing experts view price as only one of the many important elements of the marketing mix. A shift in any one of the elements has an immediate effect on the other three—production, promotion and distribution.
4. **Product differentiation:** The price of the product also depends upon the characteristics of the product. In order to attract the customers, different characteristics are added to the product, such as quality, size, colour, attractive package, alternative uses etc. Generally, customers pay more price for the product which is of the new style, fashion, better package etc.
5. **Objectives:** While fixing the price, the firm's objectives are to be taken into consideration. Objectives may be maximum sales, targeted rate of return, stability in prices, increased market share, meeting or preventing competition, projecting image etc.
6. **Product life cycle:** At various stages in the product life cycle, various strategic pricing decisions are to be adopted, *e.g.*, in the introduction stage, usually a firm charges lower price and in the growth stage it charges maximum price.
7. **Characteristics of product:** Nature of product, durability, availability of substitute etc., will also influence the pricing.

8.5.2 External Factors

External factors are those factors which are beyond the control of an organization. The following external factors would affect the pricing decisions:

1. **Demand:** The nature and condition of demand should be considered while fixing the price. Composition of the market, the nature of buyers, their psychology, purchasing power, standard of living, taste, preferences and customs have a large influence on the demand. Therefore, the management has to weigh these factors thoroughly. If the demand for a product is inelastic, it is better to fix a higher price for it. On the other hand, if demand is elastic, a lower price may be fixed.
2. **Competition:** Number of substitutes available in the market and the extent of competition and the price of competition etc., are to be considered while fixing a firm price.
3. **Distribution channels:** Distribution channels also sometimes affect the price. The consumer knows only the retail price. But there is a middleman working in the channel of distribution, he charges his profit. Thus, when the articles reach the hands of consumers, the price becomes higher. It sometimes happens that the consumers reject a product.
4. **General economic conditions:** Price is affected by the general economic conditions such as inflation, deflation, trade cycle etc. In the inflationary period the management is forced to fix higher price. In recession period, the prices are reduced to maintain the level of turnover. In boom period, prices are increased to cover the increasing cost of production and distribution.
5. **Government policy:** While taking pricing decision, a firm has to take into consideration the taxation policy, trade policies etc. of the Government.
6. **Reaction of consumers:** If a firm fixes the price of its product unreasonably high, the consumer may boycott the product.

8.6 METHODS OF PRICING

There are four types of basic pricing. They are:

1. Cost-based pricing
2. Demand-based pricing
3. Competition-based pricing
4. Value-based pricing.

8.6.1 Cost-based Pricing

The policy of setting price essentially on the basis of the total cost per unit is known as cost-oriented pricing policy.

(*i*) **Cost plus pricing:** This is the most common method used for price. Under this method, the price is fixed to cover all costs and a predetermined percentage of profit *i.e.*, the price is computed by adding a certain percentage to the cost of the product per unit. This method is also known as margin pricing or average cost pricing or full cost pricing or mark up pricing. The theory of full cost pricing has been developed by Hall and Mitch. According to them, business firms under the conditions of oligopoly and monopolistic competitive markets do not determine price and output with the help of the principle of MC (Marginal Cost) = MR (Marginal Revenue). They determine price on the basis of full average cost of production AVC (Average Variable Cost) + AFC (Average Fixed Cost) margin of normal profit.

(*ii*) **Target pricing:** This is a variant of full cost pricing. Under this method, the cost is added with the predetermined target rate of return on capital invested. In this case the company estimates future sales, future cost and calculates a targeted rate of return on capital invested. This is also called rate of return pricing.

(*iii*) **Marginal cost pricing:** Under both full cost pricing and rate of return pricing, the prices are set on the basis of total cost (variable cost + fixed cost). In this method, fixed costs are totally excluded.

(*iv*) **Break-even analysis and Target Profit Pricing:** Another cost-oriented pricing approach is break-even pricing, or a variation called target profit pricing. The firm tries to determine the price at which it will break-even or make the target profit it is seeking. Such pricing is used by General Motors, which prices its automobiles to achieve a 15 to 20 per cent profit on its investment. This pricing method is also used by public utilities, which are constrained to make a fair return on their investment.

Target pricing used the concept of a break-even chart, which shows the total cost and total revenue expected at different sales volume levels. Figure 8.1 shows a break-even chart for the toaster manufacturer discussed here. Fixed costs are 300,000 regardless of sales volume. The total revenue curve starts at zero and rises with each unit sold. The slope of the total revenue curve reflects the price of 20 per unit.

The total revenue and total cost curves cross at 30,000 units. This is the break-even volume. At $20, the company must sell at least 30,000 units to break-even; that is, for total revenue to cover total cost.

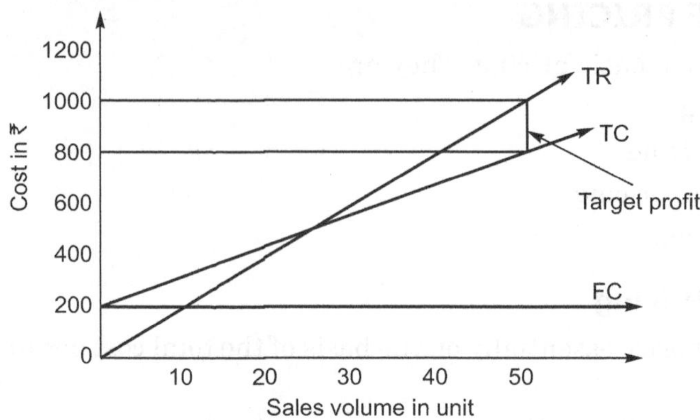

Fig. 8.1. Break-even for target pricing.

Advantages and Disadvantages of Cost-based Pricing

Advantages:

1. It is easy to apply because it's based on cost data.
2. Mark-ups can be based on industry standards, individual expert opinions, or widely accepted rules of thumb.
3. Cost-plus pricing almost guarantees that you will not sell at a loss, so a cost-plus figure generally provides a basis for the lowest price acceptable.
4. You are not required to follow the ups and downs of prices in the market.

Disadvantages:

1. Businesses that cannot identify their costs accurately may set prices at a level that does not recover actual costs.
2. Cost-plus pricing takes into account the cost and profit side of buying and selling, but it neglects demand.
3. Cost figures are generally based on an assumption of sales/production numbers.

8.6.2 Demand-based Pricing

Under this pricing policy, demand is the basic factor. Price is fixed simply adjusting it to the market conditions.

(*i*) **Differential pricing:** Under this method, the same product is sold at different prices to different customers, in different places, and at different periods. This method is called discriminatory pricing or price discrimination. Examples, Cinema, theatre, telephone bills etc.

(*ii*) **Modified break-even analysis:** This is a combination of cost-based and demand-based pricing techniques. This method reveals price-quantity mix that maximizes total profit. In other words, under this method, prices are fixed to achieve highest profit over the Break-Even Point (BEP) in consideration of the amount demanded at alternative prices.

(*iii*) **Neutral pricing:** It means offering extra value or benefits with the brand cost or price remaining competitive. Cadbury is offering 30 per cent more chocolate in its 5 Star bar at same price.

Advantages and Disadvantages of Demand-based Pricing

Advantages:

1. It is based on supply and demand. It means that public (buyers) is getting the best deal.
2. Potential for higher profits.
3. It also promotes innovation.

Disadvantages:

1. Management must be able to estimate demand at different price levels, which may be difficult to do accurately.
2. Segments must be separate enough so that those that buy at lower prices cannot sell to those who buy at higher prices.

8.6.3 Competition-based Pricing

It is the policy of fixing the prices mainly on the basis of prices fixed by competitors. This policy does not necessarily mean setting of same price. With a competition-oriented pricing policy, the firm may keep its price higher or lower than that of competitors.

(*i*) **Going rate pricing (prevailing price or follow the crowd):** Under this method, prices are maintained at par with the average level of prices in the industry, *i.e.*, under this method a firm charges the prices according to what competitors are charging. Firms accept the price prevailing in the industry in order to avoid price war. This method is also called acceptance pricing or parity pricing. This is most common with products that do not vary much from one supplier to another, like steel or toilet soap.

(*ii*) **Customary pricing:** In the case of some commodities the prices get fixed because they have prevailed over a long period of time. Examples, the price of cup of tea or coffee. In short the prices are fixed by custom. The price will change only when the cost changes significantly. It is also called conventional pricing.

(*iii*) **Sealed bid pricing:** In all business lines when the firms bid for jobs, competition-based pricing is followed. Costs and demand are not considered at all. The firm fixes its prices on how the competitors price their products. It means that if the firm is to win a contract or job, it should quote less than the competitors. A bid price is the highest price that a buyer (*i.e.*, bidder) is willing to pay for any goods. It is usually referred to simply as the bid. In bid and ask, the bid price stands in contrast to the ask price or offer, and the difference between the two is called the bid/ask spread.

Advantages and Disadvantages of Competition-based Pricing

Advantages:

1. Pricing to gain market share and attract and hold as many customers as possible.
2. Base prices on competition, if product is comparable to competitor's product.
3. Larger firms price product the same, smaller firms follow the lead of large firms.
4. Penetration pricing: price set lower than competition to lure customers away.

Disadvantages:

1. Less attention to product cost or demand risk ignoring own production costs if you focus too closely on the prices set by competitors.
2. Must constantly update market research, greater time commitment.
3. Easy for competition to mimic your pricing strategies.

8.6.4 Value-based Pricing

Under this policy the price is based on value to the customer. The following are the pricing methods based on customer value.

(*i*) **Perceived value pricing:** Another method is judging demand on the basis of value perceived by the consumers in the product. Thus perceived value pricing is concerned with setting the price on the basis of value perceived by the buyer of the product rather than the seller's cost.

(*ii*) **Value for money pricing:** This is now seen as more than a pricing method. Under this method price is based on the value which the consumers get from the product they buy. It is used as a complete marketing strategy. Videocon did it when they launched their 63 cm flat screen Bazooka when BPL's HR and Onida's KY Series models were dominating the flat sit-in TV segment. Bazooka's perceived value was ₹ 25,000/-. But driven by value for money strategy, Videocon priced Bazooka at ₹ 21,000/- only.

Advantages and Disadvantages of Value-based Pricing

Advantages:

1. It takes into account industry structure, segmentation, competitor pricing practices, and substitutes and alternatives, all of which can make pricing more coherent and complex.
2. Value-based pricing can be the only way to price new products or "breakthrough" products.
3. Pricing can be based on several customer-focused methods: expert opinion, customer surveys, price experiments (for example by using conjoint-analysis theories and techniques), and analysis of past, present and expected market data and conditions.

Disadvantages:

1. It requires more data gathering and analysis than market-based or cost-plus approaches.
2. The process for determining price is more complex than other approaches because it uses soft market data in addition to "hard" market data.
3. Most methods used to gather data for this type of pricing are relatively specialized and require expertise to convert raw data to information to knowledge (*i.e.*, needing adequate level of resources and systematic business intelligence and customer insight process in place). Thus, for small and mid-size companies it is difficult to do so (outsourcing is always a possibility).

8.7 PRICING OF NEW PRODUCTS

The introduction of a new product will pose a challenging problem for any firm. In the case of new products there is no past information for ascertaining trends and consumer reaction.

1. **Product Acceptability:** The manufacturer should ascertain whether the new product will be accepted by the consumers or whether the consumers are willing to buy the product. The willingness to buy depends upon a factor like whether it would meet their requirements.
2. **Range of Prices:** It is very essential to assess the reactions of the consumers at different prices. For this, a market research will have to be undertaken. The core question that arises is at what prices different quantities of the product are demanded.
3. **Expected Volume of Sales:** The next task is to determine the anticipated volume of sales at different prices. This depends upon demand elasticity and cross elasticity.
4. **Reaction to Price:** The assessment of the reaction of the consumers to the price is a very tricky task. The company which introduces a new product will have to monitor the activities of the rivals in order to find out the marketing strategies that they are going to adopt.

8.8 NEW PRODUCT PRICING METHODS AND STRATEGY

Pricing policy means a policy determined for normal conditions of the market. Pricing strategy is a policy determined to face a specific situation and is of temporary nature. Simply pricing policies provide guidelines to carry out the pricing strategy.

Pricing is one of the four elements of the marketing mix, along with product, place and promotion. Pricing strategy is important for companies who wish to achieve success by finding the price point where they can maximize sales and profits. Companies may use a variety of pricing strategies, depending on their own unique marketing goals and objectives. Following are the important pricing strategies.

1. **Skimming Price Strategy:** This is done with a basic idea of gaining a premium from those buyers who are always ready to pay a much higher price than others. Accordingly a product is priced at a very high level due to incurring large promotional expenses in the early stages. Thus, skimming price refers to the high initial price charged when a new product is introduced in the market. Reasons for charging this price are:
   (*a*) When the demand of new product is relatively inelastic.
   (*b*) When there is no close substitute.
   (*c*) Elasticity of demand is not known.
   (*d*) When the buyers are not able to compare the value and utility.
   (*e*) To attract the high income customers.
   (*f*) To recover early the R&D and promotional expenses.
   (*g*) When the product has distinctive qualities, luxuries etc.
2. **Penetration Price Strategy:** This is the practice of charging a low price right from the beginning to stimulate the growth of the market and to capture large share of it. Since the price is lower, the product quickly penetrates the market, and consumers with low income are able to purchase it. Reasons for adopting this policy are:
   (*a*) Product has high price elasticity in the initial stage.
   (*b*) The product is accepted by large number of customers.
   (*c*) Economies of large scale production available to firm.
   (*d*) Potential market for the product is large.
   (*e*) Cost of production is low.
   (*f*) To introduce product into the market.
   (*g*) To discourage new competitors.
   (*h*) Most of the prospective consumers are in low income class.
3. **Premium Pricing:** Premium pricing strategy establishes a price higher than the competitors. It's a strategy that can be effectively used when there is something unique about the product or when the product is first to market and the business has a distinct competitive advantage. Premium pricing can be a good strategy for companies entering the market and hoping to maximize revenue during the early stages of the product life cycle.
4. **Penetration Pricing:** A penetration pricing strategy is designed to capture market share by entering the market with a low price relative to the competition to attract buyers. The idea is that the business will be able to raise awareness and get people to try the product. Even though penetration pricing may initially create a loss for the company, the hope is that it will help to generate word-of-mouth information and create awareness amid a crowded market category.
5. **Economy Pricing:** Economy pricing is a familiar pricing strategy for organizations that include Wal-Mart, whose brand is based on this strategy. Companies take a very basic, low-cost approach to marketing nothing fancy, just the bare minimum to keep prices low and attract a specific segment of the market that is very price sensitive.
6. **Every Day Low Pricing (EDLP):** It is a pricing strategy that promises consumers the lowest available price without coupon clipping, waiting for discount promotions, or comparison shopping. It is also called value pricing. EDLP saves retailers the time and expense of periodic price markdowns, saves manufacturers the cost of distributing and processing coupons, and is believed to generate shopper loyalty. A manufacturer's

successful EDLP wholesale pricing strategy may reduce volatility in production and shipping quantities and decrease the number of time-degraded product units that consumers receive. EDLP has been championed by Wal-Mart and Procter & Gamble. In recent years, other marketers have dropped EDLP in favour of more traditional strategies, believing that consumers are more motivated by temporary markdowns and coupon savings. To be successful, EDLP requires every day low costs in line with the pricing.

7. **Psychological Pricing:** Here manufacturers fix their prices of a product in the manner that it may create an impression in the mind of consumers that the prices are low. For example, prices of Bata shoes as ₹ 99.99. This is also called odd pricing.
8. **Administered Pricing:** Here the pricing is done on the basis of managerial decisions and not on the basis of cost, demand, competition etc.
9. **Monopoly Pricing:** Monopolistic conditions exist where a product is sold exclusively by one producer or a seller. When a new product moves to the market, its price is monopoly price. There is no problem as there is no competition or no substitute. Monopoly price will maximize the profits, as there is no pricing problem.
10. **Geographical Pricing:** The distance between the seller and the buyer is considering geographic pricing.
    (*i*) **Free on Board or Freight on Board(FOB) pricing:** In FOB (original) pricing, the buyer will have to incur the cost of transit and in FOB (destination) the price influences the cost of transit charges.
    (*ii*) **Zone pricing:** Under this, the company divides the market into zones and quotes uniform prices to all buyers who buy within a zone. The prices are not uniform all over India. The price in one zone varies from that of another one. The price is quoted by adding the transport cost.
    (*iii*) **Base point pricing:** Base point policy is characterized by partial absorption of transport cost by the company. One or more cities are selected as points from which all shipping charges are calculated.
11. **Time Based Pricing:** Time-based pricing refers to a type offer or contract by a provider of a service or supplier of a commodity, in which the price depends on the time when the service is provided or the commodity is delivered. The rational background of time-based pricing is expected or observed change of the supply and demand balance during time. Time-based pricing includes fixed time of use rates for electricity and public transport. Time-based pricing is the standard method of pricing in the tourist industry. Higher prices are charged during the peak season, or during special-event periods. In the off-season, hotels may charge only the operating costs of the establishment, whereas investments and any profit are gained during the peak season.

REVIEW QUESTIONS

1. What is pricing and cost plus pricing policy?
2. What is marginal and price discrimination?
3. Explain the various methods of pricing.
4. What are the objectives of pricing policy?
5. What is the role of cost and demand factors in price determination?
6. Explain the pricing strategies of new products.
7. What is the role of consumer psychology in pricing?
8. Define pricing policy. What are the factors to be considered while making a pricing decision?

CHAPTER 9

Marketing Communication and Marketing Research

POINTS TO REMEMBER

At the end of this chapter, we will be able to understand:

Marketing Communication

- Introduction
- Meaning and Definition
- Objective of Marketing Communication
- Process of Marketing Communication
- Barriers in Marketing Communication
- Elements of Marketing Communication Mix
- Tools of Marketing Communication
- Integrated Marketing Communication
- Introduction to Market Research
- Meaning and Definition of Marketing Research
- Nature and Scope of Marketing Research
- Need of Marketing Research
- Characteristics of Marketing Research
- The Marketing Research Process
- Marketing Information System (MIS)
- Types of Marketing Research
- Importance of Marketing Research

9.1 INTRODUCTION

Marketing communication poses a special challenge to the marketing strategists for some unique reasons. First, it is the most visible clue next to the product itself of marketers' intentions and commitment to consumers. Secondly, it receives a relatively close scrutiny from the policy-makers and other consumer interest groups. Thirdly, there has been a significant change in viewing marketing communication. For a very long time, it had been seen as if promotions formed the only communication bridge between a company and its customers. This limited view of marketing communication is now being replaced with a more correct and wider proposition that marketing communication travels beyond promotion. In its linkage with buyers, it encompasses everything including product, packaging and distribution channels; and forms a vital part of overall marketing efforts towards buyers and also the other sections of society. In this chapter our endeavour is to familarize you with the emerging orientation of marketing communication and discuss the various issues related to it.

9.2 MEANING AND DEFINITION

Marketing communications are messages and related media used to communicate with a market. Marketing communications are the promotion part of the marketing mix or the four Ps: price, place, promotion, and product.

Those who practize advertising, branding, brand language, direct marketing, graphic design, marketing, packaging, promotion, sponsorship, publicity, public relations, sales, sales promotion and online marketing are termed marketing communicators, and marketing communication managers.

Marketing communication represents the collection of all elements in an organization, marketing mix that facilitates exchanges by establishing shared meaning with the organization's customers or clients.

9.3 OBJECTIVE OF MARKETING COMMUNICATION

This process is used by many marketers in their communications to entice prospects to make a purchase or take a desired action. **AIDA model** was presented by **Elmo Lewis** to explain how personal selling works. It shows a set of stair-step stages which describe the process leading a potential customer to purchase as shown in Fig.9.1.

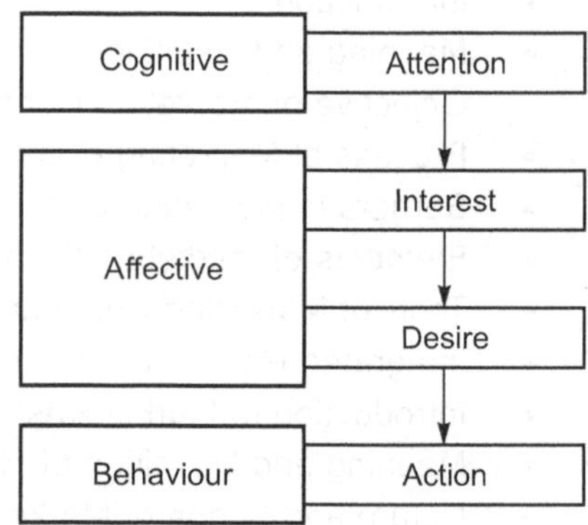

Fig. 9.1. The AIDA model.

AIDA is an acronym used in marketing that describes a common list of events that are very often undergone when a person is selling a product or service as shown in Table 9.1:

Table 9.1: Description of the AIDA Model

A	**Attention or Awareness**	Attract the attention of the customer.
I	**Interest**	Raise customer interest by demonstrating features, advantages, and benefits.
D	**Desire**	Convince customers that they want and desire the product or service and that it will satisfy their needs.
A	**Action**	Lead customers towards taking action and/or purchasing.
Nowadays some have added another letter to form AIDA(S)		
S	**Satisfaction**	Satisfy a customer so that he/she becomes a repeat customer and gives referrals to a product.

AIDA model is initiatory and simplest; the description of each element is as follows:

1. **Attention (Awareness):** The attention portion of the marketing message occurs at the beginning and is designed to give the prospects a reason to take notice. Presenting a shocking fact or statistic that identifies a problem which can be solved by the product or service is one common method of gaining attention. Other methods can include asking a thought-provoking question or using the element of surprise. The purpose is to give the prospects a reason for wanting to learn more.
2. **Interest:** Once you have gained the prospect's attention, the next step is to maintain interest in your product or service to keep the recipients engaged. Explain to the recipients how the problem you have identified in the attention step is adversely affecting their lives. A demonstration or illustration can help the recipients to further identify the problem and want to actively seek possible solutions. By personalizing the problem, you are making it hit closer to home.
3. **Desire:** In the desire stage, your objective is to show the prospects how your product or service can solve their problem. Explain the features of the product or service and the related benefits and demonstrate how the benefits fulfill the need. A common advertising process is the "before and after" technique, such as when a cleaning product makes a soiled item look brand new. If done effectively, the prospects should now have the desire to make a purchase.
4. **Action:** Now that you have created the desire to make a purchase, the final step is to persuade the prospects to take immediate action. In a one-to-one sales process, this is the time to ask for the sale. In the advertising world, techniques involve creating a sense of urgency by extending an offer for a limited time or including a bonus of special gift to those who act within a specific time-frame. Without a specific call to action, the prospect may simply forget about your offer and move on.

9.4 PROCESS OF MARKETING COMMUNICATION

The marketing communication process can be very complex but it is based on the universal model used in all forms of communication which includes a sender, the message, receivers, and a medium and, in the case of two-way communication, feedback. However, this universal model needs to be presented in the context of marketing communications in order that its relevance to marketing is understood. The purpose of a marketing communication campaign can best be described by reference to the hierarchy of communication effects represented by the following model as shown in Fig. 9.2.

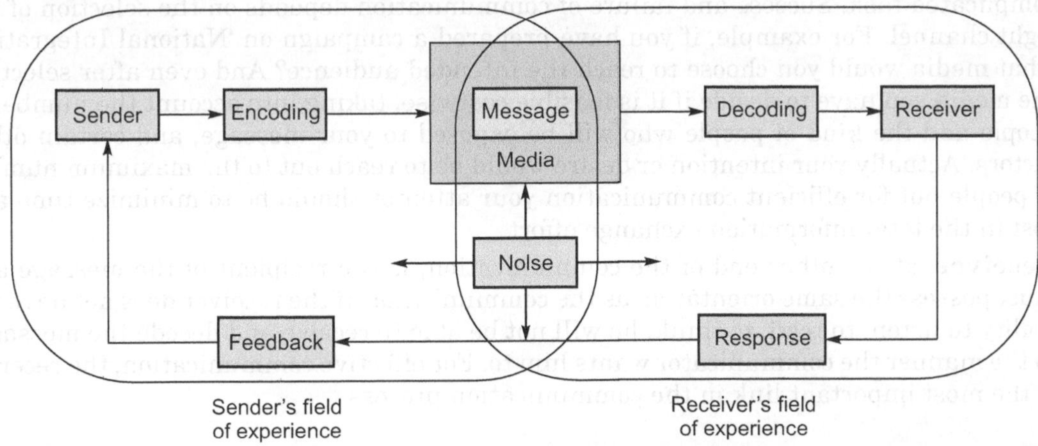

Fig. 9.2. Elements in the communication process.

1. **Communicator** (sender or encoder) is the one who initiates the communication process. He may be an editor, a reporter, a film-maker, a teacher, a writer, a speaker, a leader or anybody who takes the initiative to start a dialogue. Before one speaks or writes, the message is conceptualized first and then encoded. An effective communication depends on the communication skill, knowledge level, and attitude of the communicator and how he desires to affect his receiver. An ability to think, to organize thoughts quickly and express himself effectively are some of the attributes of a good communicator. Somebody who uses appropriate words, sentences, tone, etc., may be called a good communicator. He does not fumble, does not look for words and all that he says is accompanied by appropriate gestures and delivered at an acceptable pace. Another element, which is mentioned here, is knowledge level. We must be able to find out the knowledge level of the persons on a particular topic before we start the dialogue. Also, a person must never look down upon the people with whom he communicates. He must never think that the receivers are inferior to him. The attitudes of a person should be mature and the minimum respect due to the other person must be extended to him.
2. **Encoding** is the formulation of messages in the communicator's mind, that is, the communicator not only translates his purpose (ideas, thoughts or information) into a message but also decides on the medium to communicate his planned message. He must choose the media (speaking, writing, signaling or gesturing) that the receiver can comprehend well. For instance, an illiterate receiver will fail to understand a written message, but can understand it well if told orally. A message is what a communicator actually produces for transmission using spoken or written words, photographs, paintings, films, posters, etc. A great deal of skill and effort is required to formulate a message, the meaning of which should be understandable to the receiver. Actually the purpose of communication is to influence the receiver and get favourable responses so that appropriate decisions can be taken. The success of communication, therefore, depends on what we say and how we say it. A message can enhance or distort effective communication. For instance, in an interview your intention is to impress the interviewer, but if you give answers whose meaning is not clear, the interviewer may perceive that you are incompetent for the job.
3. **A message media or channel** is the vehicle through which a message is carried from the communicator to the receiver. The channels of communication are many—written, spoken, verbal, non-verbal, mass media like TV, radio, newspapers, books, etc. Choosing the appropriate channel, one most suitable for the message as well as the receiver, is a complicated task. Success and failure of communication depends on the selection of the right channel. For example, if you have prepared a campaign on 'National Integration' what media would you choose to reach the intended audience? And even after selecting the media you have to decide if it is feasible costwise, taking into account the number of people and the kind of people who will be exposed to your message, and certain other factors. Actually your intention or desire would be to reach out to the maximum number of people but for efficient communication your attempt should be to minimize time and cost in the total information exchange effort.
4. **Receiver**, at the other end of the communication, is the recipient of the message and must possess the same orientation as the communicator. If the receiver does not have the ability to listen, to read, to think, he will not be able to receive and decode the messages in the manner the communicator wants him to. For effective communication, the receiver is the most important link in the communication process.

5. **Decoding** is the interpretation of the message by the receiver. Actually, the receiver looks for the meaning in the message, which is common to both the receiver and the communicator.
6. **Feedback** is the response or acknowledgement of receiver to the communicator's message. The exchange is possible only if the receiver responds. Even through fluttering eyelids, raising an eyebrow, making a face, organizing a point and asking for explanation, the message is shaped and reshaped by the communicator and the receiver until the meaning becomes clear. In this way both participants in communication interact and constantly exchange roles. In face-to-face communication the receiver responds naturally, directly and immediately. This provides the communicator an opportunity to improve and make his communication effective. Feedback, thus, provides an opportunity to evaluate what is right or wrong about a particular communication. It helps to regulate the conversation among two or more individuals and also stimulates and reinforces an idea that is desired to be communicated.
7. **Noise** is an interruption that can creep in at any point of the communication process and make it ineffective. Environment is one major cause that interferes with message reception: like noises from the roadside, constant chattering of individuals outside the communication act, blaring loudspeaker, faulty transmission, etc. Noise can occur in other forms also; poor handwriting, heavy accent or soft speech, communication in a poorly lit room, etc. In fact, these are barriers to effective communication. For smooth and effective communication, it is necessary to eliminate or reduce noise as far as possible.

9.5 BARRIERS IN MARKETING COMMUNICATION

"A barrier to communication is something that keeps meanings from meeting. Meaning barriers exist between all people, making communication much more difficult than most people seem to realize as shown in Fig. 9.3. It is false to assume that if one can talk he can communicate. Because so much of our education misleads people into thinking that communication is easier than it is, they become discouraged and give up when they run into difficulty because they do not understand the nature of the problem, they do not know what to do. The wonder is not that communicating is as difficult as it is, but that it occurs as much as it does".

Fig. 9.3. Barriers in communication.

Here are the some barriers in market communication:

1. **Noise** is the term used to refer to the barriers to effective communication. The barriers will reduce productivity within a firm. There are many factors that might cause the failure of successful communication. For example, it depends on the ability of the sender, how much the sender understands of the message they are trying to send. If the sender makes the receiver misunderstand what he or she is trying to send, then this can be a barrier.
2. **Technological barriers** such as computer failure, viruses and crashes. Another barrier can be the use of jargons. Jargon is the technical language that is used to speed up communication. However, when non-specialists use jargons, this can cause the communication problems, *e.g.*, when the managers fail to identify the situations when it is important. If that happens, it will not speed up communication but actually slow down.
3. **Physical barriers** are easy to spot—doors that are closed, walls that are erected, and distance between people all work against the goal of effective communication. While most agree that people need their own personal areas in the workplace, setting up an office to remove physical barriers is the first step towards opening communication.
4. **Perceptual barriers,** in contrast, are internal. If you go into a situation thinking that the person you are talking to is not going to understand or be interested in what you have to say, you may end up sub-consciously sabotaging your effort to make your point.
5. **Emotional barriers** can be tough to overcome, but are important to put aside to engage in conversations. We are often taught to fear the words coming out of our own mouths, as in the phrase "anything you say can and will be used against you". Overcoming this fear is difficult, but necessary. The trick is to have full confidence in what you are saying and your qualifications in saying it. People often pick up on insecurity. By believing in yourself and what you have to say, you will be able to communicate clearly without becoming overly involved in your emotions.
6. **Cultural barriers** are a result of living in an ever shrinking world. Different cultures, whether they be a societal culture of a race or simply the work culture of a company, can hinder developed communication if two different cultures clash. In these cases, it is important to find a common ground to work from.
7. **Language barriers** seem pretty self-inherent, but there are often hidden language barriers that we are not always aware of. If you work in an industry that is heavy in jargon or technical language, care should be taken to avoid these words while speaking with someone from outside the industry.
8. **Gender barriers** have become less of an issue in recent years, but there is still the possibility for a man to misconstrue the words of a woman, or vice versa. Men and women tend to form their thoughts differently, and this must be taken into account while communicating. This difference has to do with how the brain of each sex is formed during gestation. In general, men are better at spatial visualization and abstract concepts such as maths, while women excel at language-based thinking and emotional identification. However, successful professionals in highly competitive fields tend to have similar thought processes regardless of their gender.
9. **Interpersonal barriers** are what ultimately keep us from reaching out to each other and opening ourselves up, not just to be heard, but to hear others. Oddly enough, this can be the most difficult area to change. Some people spend their entire lives attempting to overcome a poor self-image or a series of deeply rooted prejudices about their place in the world. They are unable to form genuine connections with people because they have too

many false perceptions blocking the way. Luckily, the cure for this is more communication. By engaging with others, we learn what our actual strengths and weaknesses are. This allows us to put forth our ideas in a clear, straightforward manner.

10. **Communication** is not a one-way street. To have others open up to you, you must open yourself.

By overcoming these barriers to communication, you can ensure that the statement you are making is not just heard, but also understood, by the person you are speaking with. In this way, you can be confident that your point has been expressed.

9.6 ELEMENTS OF MARKETING COMMUNICATION MIX

A company's total marketing communications mix consists of the specific blend of advertising, personal selling, sales promotion, and public relations tools that the company uses to pursue its advertising and marketing objectives. The five major types of promotion are:

1. **Advertising:** Any paid form of non-personal presentation and promotion of ideas, goods, or services by an identified sponsor.
2. **Personal Selling:** Personal presentation by the firm's sales force to make sales and build customer relationships.
3. **Sales Promotion:** Short-term incentives to encourage the purchase or sale of a product or service.
4. **Public Relations:** Building good relations with the company's publics by obtaining favourable publicity, building up a good "corporate image," and handling or heading off unfavourable rumours, stories, and events.
5. **Direct Marketing:** Direct communications with carefully targeted individual consumers to obtain an immediate response. The use of mail, telephone, fax, e-mail, and other non-personal tools to communicate directly with specific consumers or to solicit a direct response.

9.7 TOOLS OF MARKETING COMMUNICATION

A marketing person has many tools at his disposal for generating awareness and supporting the selling effort. While there are numerous marketing communication tools, there are also numerous mixes for these tools. Figure 9.4 displays some of the more common tools with examples of their use and some considerations. One important note is remembered that marketing communication tools do improve understanding your product or service, reinforcing your messages, supporting the sales cycle and generating awareness.

Fig. 9.4. Elements of marketing communication.

1. **Advertising:** This tool can get your messages to large audiences efficiently through such avenues as radio, TV, magazines, newspapers (ROP), Internet, billboards and other mobile technological communication devices. This method can efficiently reach a large number of consumers, although the costs may be somewhat expensive.
2. **Sales Promotion:** This tool is used through coupons, contests, samples, premiums, demonstrations, displays or incentives. It is used to accelerate short-term sales, by building brand awareness and encouraging repeat buying.
3. **Public Relations:** This integrated marketing communications tool is initiated through public appearances, news/press releases or event sponsorships, to build trust and goodwill by presenting the product, company or person in a positive light.
4. **Direct Marketing:** This tool will utilize e-mail, mail, catalogues, encourage direct responses to radio and TV, in order to reach targeted audiences to increase sales and test new products and alternate marketing tactics.
5. **Personal Selling:** Setting sales appointments and meetings, home parties, making presentations and any type of one-to-one communication, to reach your customers and strengthen your relationship with your clients, initiate this IMC (Integrated Marketing Communication) tool.
6. **Internet Marketing:** Websites provide a new way of transmitting information, entertainment, and advertising, and have generated a new dimension in marketing: electronic commerce. E-commerce is the term used to describe the act of selling goods and services over the Internet. In other words, the Internet has become more than a communication channel; it is a marketing channel itself selling goods via the Internet to individuals around the globe. For example, company and product information can be posted on the company's site for news reporters researching stories and for current and potential customers seeking information.

Websites require audiences who are active in the information-seeking process to purposely visit the site. Therefore, the quality and freshness of content is vital for the success of the website.

Thus, it is obvious that, decisions linking the overall objectives and strategies during the marketing planning phases help to evaluate and fine-tune the specific activities of integrated marketing communication. Before selecting an Integrated Marketing Communication (IMC) tool, marketing, product and brand managers must look at social, competitive, legal, regulatory, ethics, cultural and technological considerations. One thing companies want to avoid while activating the tools of integrated marketing communication is reaching inappropriate audiences and causing controversy. That could be damaging while trying to build brand awareness and encourage consumer spending with your company. When marketing managers examine the beliefs, emotions and behaviour of their targeted audience towards their brand, they can influence their beliefs to achieve product awareness, by attracting attention to their promotional campaigns.

9.8 INTEGRATED MARKETING COMMUNICATION

Integrated marketing communications is a simple concept. It ensures that all forms of communications and messages are carefully linked together.

At its most basic level, Integrated Marketing Communications, or IMC, as we'll call it, means integrating all the promotional tools, so that they work together in harmony.

Promotion is one of the Ps in the marketing mix. It has its own mix of communications tools.

All of these communications tools work better if they work together in harmony rather than in isolation. Their sum is greater than their parts—providing they speak consistently with one voice all the time. This is enhanced when integration goes beyond just the basic communications tools. There are other levels of integration such as horizontal, vertical, internal, external and data integration. Here is how they help to strengthen integrated communications.

Horizontal Integration occurs across the marketing mix and across business functions—for example, production, finance, distribution and communications should work together and be conscious that their decisions and actions send messages to customers.

Different departments such as sales, direct mail and advertising can help each other through data integration. This requires a marketing information system which collects and shares relevant data across different departments.

Vertical integration means marketing and communications objectives must support the higher level corporate objectives and corporate missions.

Whereas, internal integration requires internal marketing—keeping all staff informed and motivated about any new developments from new advertisements, to new corporate identities, new service standards, new strategic partners and so on.

External Integration, on the other hand, requires external partners such as advertising and PR agencies to work closely together to deliver a single seamless solution—a cohesive message—an integrated message.

9.9 INTRODUCTION TO MARKET RESEARCH

The key task of marketing management is to fulfill the objectives of the consumers. It is thus essential to understand what the consumers want, how they make the various choice decisions or what their sources of information and influence process are etc. As such, marketing research is the function which provides the necessary information about the consumer to the marketer. In the process, an organization can identify new opportunities in the market; evaluate and monitor marketing actions; and in general, evolve better marketing programme to serve the interests of the consumer. Thus, marketing research acts as the link between the consumer and the marketer.

9.10 MEANING AND DEFINITION OF MARKETING RESEARCH

Marketing Research has two words, viz., "Marketing" and "Research".

(*i*) **Marketing** means buying and selling activities with consumer satisfaction.

(*ii*) **Research** means a systematic and complete study of a problem. It is done by experts. It uses scientific methods.

Thus, we can say, Marketing Research is a systematic method of collecting, recording and analyzing data which is used to solve marketing problems. Its uses are shown in Fig. 9.5.

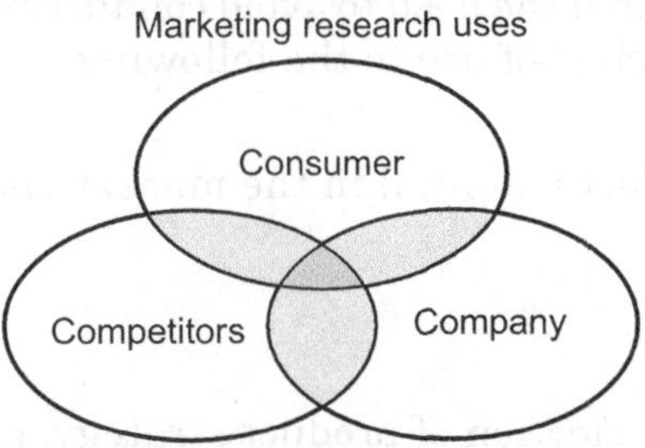

Fig. 9.5. Marketing research.

Marketing Research (MR) may be defined as systematic collection and analysis of data relating to the marketing of goods and services. Different scholars have defined it in different ways.

"Systematic problem analysis, model building and fact finding for the purpose of important, decision-making and control in the marketing of goods and services". **Philip Kotler**

"Marketing research is the application of scientific methods in the solution of marketing problems." **David Luck, Donald Taylor and Hugh Wales**

"Systematic and objective search for and analysis of information relevant to the identification and solution of any problem in the field of marketing". **Green & TD**

"Marketing research is the function that links the consumer, customer and public to the marketer through information used to identify and define marketing opportunities and problems, generate, refine and evaluate marketing actions; monitor marketing performance; and improve understanding of marketing as a process". **American Marketing Association**

Market Research vs. Marketing Research

Market Research: Researching the immediate competitive environment of the market place, including customers, competitors, suppliers, distributors and retailers.

Marketing Research: Includes Market Research Plus

- Companies and their strategies for products and markets.
- The wider environment within which the firm operates (*e.g.*, political, social, etc).

9.11 NATURE AND SCOPE OF MARKETING RESEARCH

Marketing Research (MR) plays a very significant role in identifying the needs of customers and meeting them in the best possible way. The main task of marketing research is systematic gathering and analysis of information.

Marketing research is essential for strategic market planning and decision-making. It helps a firm in identifying what the market opportunities and constraints are, in developing and implementing market strategies, and in evaluating the effectiveness of marketing plans.

Marketing research is one of the principal tools for answering questions because it links the consumer, customer, and public to the market through information used to identify and define marketing. It generates, refines, and evaluates marketing actions, monitors marketing performance, underlines the understanding of marketing as a process.

These principles relate to the timeliness and importance of data, the significance of defining objectives cautiously and clearly, and the need to avoid conducting research to support decisions already made. Marketing research is of use to the following:

(*i*) **Producers**

- To know about his product potential in the market vis-à-vis the total product
- New products
- Various brands;
- Pricing
- Market structures and selection of product strategy, etc.

(*ii*) **Business and government:** Marketing research helps businesses and government in focusing attention on the complex nature of problems faced by them. For example:

- Determination of Gross National Product; price indices, and per capita income
- Expenditure levels and budgeting
- Agricultural pricing
- The economic policies of Government
- Operational and planning problems of business and industry.

(*iii*) **Market research agencies:** Marketing research is being used extensively by professionals to help conducting various studies in Marketing research. Most prominent agencies being:

- Linta India Ltd
- India Market Research Bureau (IMRB)
- British Market Research Bureau (BMRB)
- ORG-MARG
- Hindustan Thompson Associate Ltd;
- E-SurveysPro.com.

9.12 NEED OF MARKETING RESEARCH

Market research provides important information to identify and analyze the market need, market size and competition. Market research includes social and opinion research that is the systematic gathering and interpretation of information about individuals or organizations using statistical and analytical methods and techniques of the applied social sciences to gain insight or support decision-making. Below are some prime situations where marketing research can be of value to the success of your business:

- Determining the viability of a new market for your company to enter.
- Estimating market size/share/adoption rate for investment or business planning.
- Identifying new product/service opportunities and value-added offering.
- Risk management—identifying what risks pose the greatest threat to your business.
- Understanding what customers expect from firms and how well firms are delivering.
- Root cause analysis for lost business or customer defections.
- Identifying firms' most profitable customer segments and how to protect them.
- Developing the right price points/identifying bundling opportunities.
- SWOT intelligence on competitors to plan business strategies/identify Merger and Acquisition scenarios.
- Understanding how customers perceive firms' market positioning relative to competitors.
- Determining the most effective marketing/advertising channels to support your business.

9.13 CHARACTERISTICS OF MARKETING RESEARCH

Salient features or characteristics of marketing research are as follows:

1. **Wide and Comprehensive Scope:** Marketing research has a very wide scope. It includes product research, packaging research, pricing research, market research, sales research, etc. It is used to solve marketing problems and to take marketing decisions. It is used to make marketing policies. It is also used to introduce new products in the market and to identify new markets. Marketing research is used to select channels of distribution, in advertising strategy, for sales promotion measures, etc.

2. **Systematic and Continuous Process:** Marketing research is a continuous process. One type of research is not adequate to resolve all marketing problems. Similarly, new research projects will have to be undertaken to solve new marketing problems and challenges. A marketing company faces new marketing problems from time to time and for facing them marketing research activities need to be conducted on regular basis. A marketing company has to conduct MR regularly for its survival and growth in the present dynamic marketing environment.
3. **Science and Art:** Science collects knowledge (data) while art uses this knowledge to solve problems. Marketing research first collects data. It then uses this data for solving marketing problems. Therefore, it is both, a science and an art.
4. **Data Collection and Critical Analysis:** Marketing research requires data which should be collected objectively and accurately. The data collected must be reliable. It should be analyzed in a systematic manner. This will provide comprehensive picture of the situation and possible solution.
5. **Dynamic Character:** Marketing research is dynamic in nature. Its scope is fast expanding along with the new developments in the field of marketing. In addition, development in other subjects such as economics, statistics, computer science, sociology, psychology, cultural anthropology and behavioural sciences also bring corresponding changes in the field of marketing research. This suggests that MR is a dynamic and progressive subject.
6. **Tool for Managerial Decisions:** MR acts as a tool in the hands of management for identifying and analyzing marketing problems and finding out solutions to them. It is an aid to decision-making. It suggests possible solutions for the consideration and selection by managers. MR is an aid to judgement and never a substitute for it.
7. **Benefits Company and Consumers:** Marketing research is useful to the company in many ways. It increases the sales and profits of the company. It helps the company to fight competition and boost its goodwill in the market. It reduces the marketing risks. In short, marketing research brings success to the company. It also brings the company closer to the consumers. It gives convenience and satisfaction to the consumers.
8. **Commercial Equivalent of Military Intelligence:** MR is the commercial intelligence activity. It is similar to military intelligence where systematic study is made before taking any military action. MR acts as the intelligence tool of marketing management.
9. **Applied Type of Research:** MR is applied knowledge. It is also called 'decisional' research as it provides specific alternative solution to deal with a specific marketing problem. It studies a specific marketing problem and suggests an alternative solution.
10. **Reduces Gap between Producers and Consumers:** Marketing research informs producers about the needs and wants of the consumers. The producers produce goods according to the needs and demands of the consumers. This brings satisfaction to the consumers and in return producers make good profits. So, marketing research reduces the gap between the producers and the consumers.
11. **Closely Connected with Marketing Information System:** Both the concepts are interrelated. In fact, MR is one component of MIS. Both are useful for solving marketing problems and for accurate and quick decision-making in the field of marketing.

9.14 THE MARKETING RESEARCH PROCESS

For marketing research to be systematic, it has to follow a number of steps. The following Fig. 9.6 shows the different steps of marketing research.

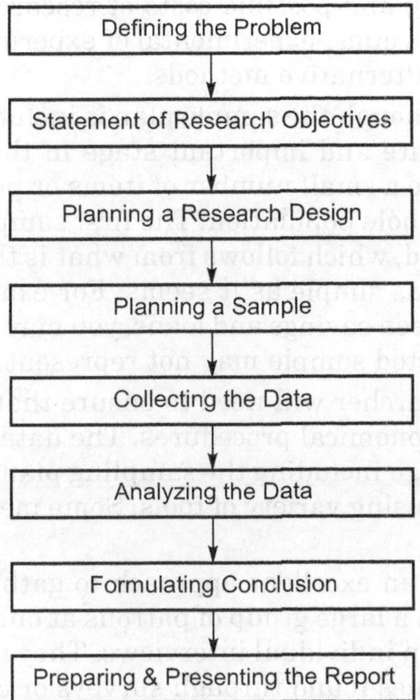

Fig. 9.6. Steps for marketing research process.

1. **Defining the Problem:** *"A problem well defined is a problem half-solved."—John Dewey.* First, the purpose of the research needs to be established. This can be done by specifying what marketing decisions need to be made and what marketing problems are to be addressed, using information from the marketing research project.
   In order to define the problem more precisely, some sort of exploratory research may also be undertaken. The methods popularly in use are survey of secondary data, expense survey or pilot studies.
2. **Research Objectives:** Next the research objectives have to be established: exactly which questions are to be answered by the research? Research objectives may be stated in qualitative or quantitative terms and expressed as research question statements or hypothesis. For example, the research objective "To find out the extent to which the sales promotion programmes affected sales" is a research objective expressed as a statement. A hypothesis on the other hand is a statement that can be refuted or supported by empirical findings. The same research objective could be stated as: "To test the hypothesis that Television Advertisements encourage children to consume food items which neither promote health nor are economically affordable by the parents". Example of another hypothesis may be "TV advertisements directly and indirectly influence parents to buy commodities which they would ordinarily not buy. Thus, it influences purchase decisions of any family".
3. **Planning the Research Design:** Once the research problem has been defined and the objectives decided, the research design must be developed. A research design is a plan specifying the procedure for collecting and analyzing the needed information. It represents a framework for the research plan of action. The objectives of the study discussed in the preceding step are included in the research design to ensure that data collected are relevant to the objectives. The researcher must, at this stage, also determine the type of sources of information needed, the data collection methods (surveys or interviews), the sampling

methodology and the timing and possible costs of research. The design chosen may be from exploratory, descriptive, quasi-experimental or experimental design categories which again include a number of alternative methods.

4. **Planning the Sample:** Although the sample plan is included in the research design, the actual sampling is a separate and important stage in the research process. Sampling involves procedures that use a small number of items or parts of the population to make conclusions regarding the whole population. The first sampling question that needs to be asked is who is to be sampled, which follows from what is the target population. Defining the population may not be as simple as it seems. For example, if you are interested in finding the association between savings and loans, you may survey the people who already have accounts and the selected sample may not represent potential customers.
5. **Data Collection:** The researcher will need to ensure that the study will be relevant to the problem and will use economical procedures. The data collection process follows the formulation of research design including the sampling plan. Data which can be secondary or primary can be collected using variety of tools. Some methods of data collection are as follows:
   (*i*) **Focus groups:** This is an excellent approach to gather in-depth attitudes, beliefs, and anecdotal data from a large group of patrons at one time. Group dynamics might generate more ideas than individual interviews. They can be effectively used to focus on details regarding issues found through surveys or other data collection methods. Participants are not required to read or write. Technique relies on oral communication.
   (*ii*) **Interviews:** It is a good approach to gather in-depth attitudes, beliefs, and anecdotal data from individual patrons. Personal contact with participants might elicit richer and more detailed responses. It provides an excellent opportunity to probe and explore questions. Its participants do not need to be able to read and write to respond.
   (*iii*) **Observation:** It is an excellent approach to discover behaviours. It provides indicators of the impact of programmes that might be more reliable than data gained by asking people.
   (*iv*) **Surveys:** Best for gathering brief written responses on attitudes, beliefs regarding library programmes. They can include both close-ended and open-ended questions. They can be administered in written form or online. Personal contact with the participants is not required. Staff and facilities requirements are minimal, since one employee can easily manage the distribution and collection of surveys, and issues such as privacy, quiet areas, etc. are typically not concerns.
6. **Data Processing and Analysis:** Once the data is collected, it needs to be processed and analyzed. The processing involves converting the raw data, by 'coding', into a form which can be analyzed. Coding is a process whereby categories for responses are established, so that numbers can be used to represent the categories. The final stages involve the analysis of data and the presentation of the results to management. The analysis needs to be undertaken so as to answer the questions originally posed.
7. **Formulating Conclusion, Preparing & Presenting the Report:** The final state in the research process is that of interpreting the information and drawing conclusions for use in managerial decisions. Often the management is not interested in details of research design and statistical analysis but in the concrete findings of the research. Researchers, therefore, must make the presentation technically accurate, understandable and useful. Frequently, the researchers are required to make both an oral and a written presentation.

9.15 MARKETING INFORMATION SYSTEM (MIS)

A Marketing Information System (MIS) consists of people, equipment, and procedures to gather, sort, analyze, evaluate, and distribute needed, timely and accurate information to marketing decision makers. MIS distributes information to managers in the right form and at the right time to help them make better marketing decisions.

Marketing Information System (MIS) is an analytical tool for marketing managers and specialists who seek to find an instrument for systematization of information, automation of routine processes and facilitation of decision-making processes.

MIS is intended to bring together disparate items of data into a coherent body of information. An MIS is, as will shortly be seen, more than raw data or information suitable for the purposes of decision-making. An MIS also provides methods for interpreting the information the MIS provides.

> *"Marketing Information System (MIS)" consists of, "people, equipment and procedures to gather, sort, analyze, evaluate and distribute needed, timely and accurate information to marketing decision makers to improve their marketing planning, implementation, and control".* **Philip Kotler**

9.15.1 Components of MIS

Figure 9.7 illustrates the major components of an MIS, the environmental factors monitored by the system and the types of marketing decision which the MIS seeks to underpin.

The explanation of this model of an MIS begins with a description of each of its four main constituent parts: the internal reporting systems, marketing intelligence system, marketing research system and marketing models. It is suggested that MIS varies in its degree of sophistication—with many in the industrialized countries being computerized and few in the developing countries being so—a fully fledged MIS should have these components, the methods (and technologies) of collection, storing, retrieving and processing data notwithstanding.

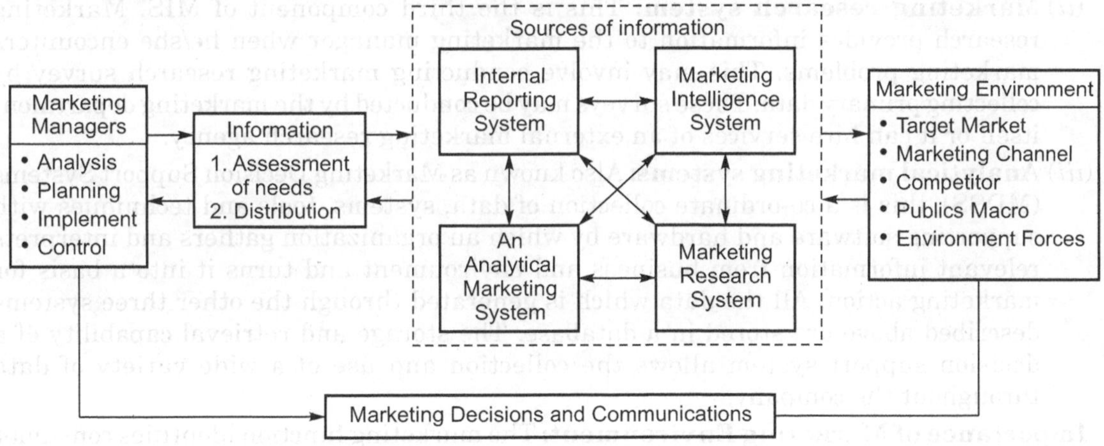

Fig. 9.7. Marketing information system.

In the course of developing the firm's marketing plan, data was collected and information about the internal and external environments was analyzed. Objectives were set, strategies determined, and evaluation metric defined. Now that all the planning has turned into implementation how do you know which part of your effort is making a difference? Is it the pricing? Channel selection? Or are the results you are seeing entirely due to the external environment? The only way to answer this type of question accurately and in a timely manner is with a Marketing Information System (MIS). At the most basic level an MIS consists of, "people, equipment and procedures to gather, sort, analyze, evaluate and distribute needed, timely and accurate information to marketing decision makers" (Kotler, 1997).

To understand the proper role of information systems one must examine what managers do and what information they need for decision-making. We must also understand how decisions are made and what kinds of decision problems can be supported by formal information systems. One can then determine whether information systems will be valuable tools and how they should be designed.

1. **Information to Marketing Managers:** All enterprises which have been in operation for any period of time have a wealth of information. However, this information often remains under-utilized because it is compartmentalized, either in the form of an individual entrepreneur or in the functional departments of larger businesses. That is, information is usually categorized according to its nature so that there are, for example, financial, production, manpower, marketing, stockholding and logistical data. Often the entrepreneur or various personnel working in the functional departments holding these pieces of data do not see how it could help decision makers in other functional areas. The internal records that are of immediate value to marketing decisions are: orders received, stockholdings and sales invoices. These are a few of the internal records that can be used by marketing managers, but even this small set of records is capable of generating a great deal of information.
2. **Sources of Information:** The information can be obtained from the following sources:
   (*i*) **Marketing intelligence system:** This is a set of procedures and sources used by managers to obtain everyday information about developments records system which supplies 'results' data. Marketing managers collect data from published sources like books, magazines and journals; by talking to customers, intermediaries and sales personnel.
   (*ii*) **Marketing research system:** This is the third component of MIS. Marketing research provides information to the marketing manager when he/she encounters marketing problems. This may involve conducting marketing research survey by collecting primary data. These surveys may be conducted by the marketing department itself or it can hire services of an external marketing research agency.
   (*iii*) **Analytical marketing systems:** Also known as Marketing Decision Support Systems (MDSS), this is a co-ordinate collection of data, systems, tools and techniques with supporting software and hardware by which an organization gathers and interprets relevant information from business and environment and turns it into a basis for marketing action. All the data which is generated through the other three systems described above are stored in a database. The storage and retrieval capability of a decision support system allows the collection and use of a wide variety of data throughout the company.
3. **Importance of Marketing Environment:** The marketing function identifies consumer needs and develops products based on such market needs. It matches the product offering with the consumer needs and ensures ready buyers for the products of a company. Marketing is a crucial activity for business firms and this function is a major user of information system facilities.
4. **Making Decisions and Communication in MIS:** Marketing information system balances the information managers would like to have against what they really need and

what is feasible to offer. Start finding out what information you would like. But managers do not always need all the information they ask for, and they may not ask for all they really need. Moreover, the MIS cannot always supply all the information that managers request. Too much information can be just as harmful as too little.

9.16 TYPES OF MARKETING RESEARCH

There are different types of marketing research and each type has its place in attempting to answer questions and meet the needs of an organization. Marketing research can be broken down in many ways as shown in Fig. 9.8.

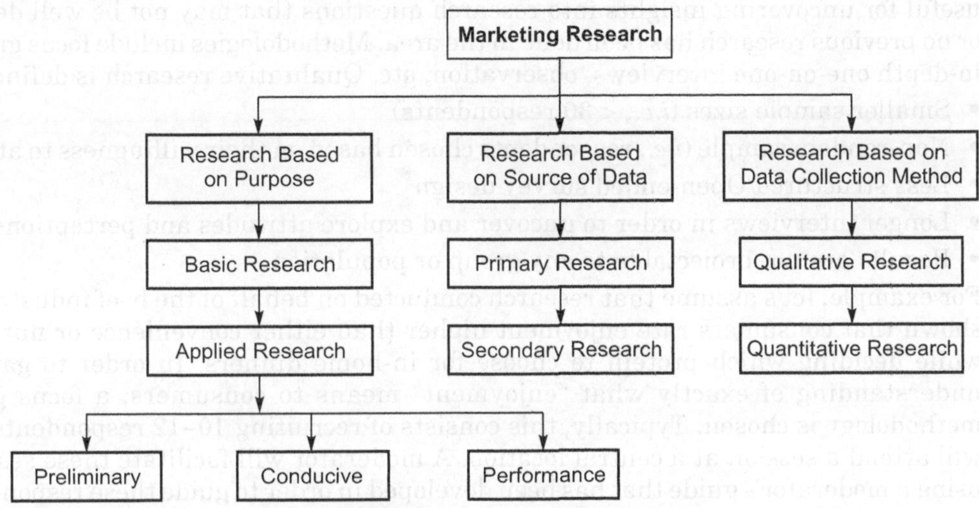

Fig. 9.8. Types of marketing research.

1. **Research Based on Purpose:** Marketing research based on purpose can be divided into two parts:

   (*i*) **Basic research or fundamental research:** Fundamental research seeks to extend the boundaries of knowledge in a given area and does not necessarily solve your immediate problems. Nevertheless, it has useful applications. It reveals information and relationships that could be useful at a later date. For example, a company conducted fundamental research about consumer preferences for certain combinations of fruits, nuts, and caramel that differ in sugar type and strength of sweetness.

   (*ii*) **Applied research:** Applied research sets out to prove a specific hypothesis of value to the clients paying for the research. For example, a cigarette company might commission research that attempts to show that fast foods are good for children's health. Many researchers have ethical misgivings about doing applied research.

2. **Research Based on Source of Data:** There are two methods of conducting marketing research on source of data: primary research and secondary research.

   (*i*) **Primary research:** In primary research, data is collected directly from the source. For example, if the objective of the research is to understand the demand of a particular product, then collecting feedback directly from the customers by talking to them is called primary research. Primary research involves the collection of crucial data via interviews, surveys or focus group sessions. It's time-consuming and expensive. However, it is suited for gathering specific data.

(*ii*) **Secondary research:** In secondary research, the analysis of information that has been collected for some other purposes is carried out. This means, that secondary research is carried out by gathering data from sources such as government publications, libraries, internet, magazines, chambers of commerce, etc. The data required may be in the form of demographic or statistical data, set of articles or some studies. Firms can analyze their target markets, evaluate competitors and assess social, political and economic factors.

3. **Research Based on Data Collection Method:** This research of marketing on the collection method is divided into two parts:

(*i*) **Qualitative research:** Qualitative research is usually exploratory in nature and is useful for uncovering insights into research questions that may not be well defined or no previous research has been done in the area. Methodologies include focus groups, in-depth one-on-one interviews, observation, etc. Qualitative research is defined by:

- Smaller sample sizes (*i.e.*, < 30 respondents)
- Non-random sample (*i.e.*, respondents chosen based on their willingness to attend)
- Less structured/Open-ended survey design
- Longer interviews in order to uncover and explore attitudes and perceptions
- Results are not projectable to any group or population.

For example, let's assume that research conducted on behalf of the beef industry has shown that consumers rate enjoyment higher than either convenience or nutrition while deciding which protein to choose for in-home dinners. In order to gain an understanding of exactly what "enjoyment" means to consumers, a focus group methodology is chosen. Typically, this consists of recruiting 10–12 respondents who will attend a session at a central location. A moderator will facilitate these sessions using a moderator's guide that has been developed in order to guide these respondents into the topics that need to be addressed. The session may last one to two hours or more and these sessions are typically video- or audio-taped. The final deliverable is the report summarizing the findings of the session with sample verbatim that give a flavour of respondents' answers to specific topics or questions.

(*ii*) **Quantitative research:** Quantitative research is used when there may already be a body of knowledge about the questions or topics of study. Methodologies include telephone, mail, internet or in-person surveys. Quantitative research is defined by:

- Larger sample sizes (*i.e.*, 100 respondents or more).
- Random sample (*i.e.*, each respondent has an equal chance of being selected).
- Structured/formalize/closed-ended survey design.
- Interviews may be as short as a few minutes or much longer.
- Results are projectable to a group or population.

Custom, or primary, research is where one client bears the total cost of the research and all of the research findings are proprietary to that client. Advantages of this type of research are the proprietary nature of the findings and the ability to customize the questionnaire in order to get the exact findings wanted. The main disadvantage of this type of research is the cost.

9.16.1 Applications of Marketing Research

MR is a special branch of marketing management. It is comparatively recent in origin. MR acts as an investigative arm of a marketing manager. It suggests possible solutions to marketing problems for the consideration and selection by a marketing manager. The applications of market research are as follows:

1. **Market trends:** Marketing research keeps business unit in touch with the latest market trends and offers guidance for facing market situation with confidence. It facilitates production as per consumer demand and preferences.
2. **Marketing policies:** Marketing research pinpoints the deficiencies as regards products, pricing, promotion, etc. It gives proper guidance regarding different aspects of marketing. They include product development, branding, packaging and advertising.
3. **Promotion techniques:** Marketing research enables a manufacturer to introduce appropriate sales promotion techniques, select the most convenient channel of distribution, suitable pricing policy for the products and provision of discounts and concessions to dealers. It facilitates sales promotion.
4. **Marketing executives:** Marketing research offers information and guidance to marketing executives while framing marketing policies. Continuous research enables a company to face adverse marketing situations boldly. It acts as an insurance against possible changes in market environment.
5. **Business expansion:** Marketing research enables a business unit to grow and expand its activities. It creates goodwill in the market and also enables a business unit to earn high profits through consumer-oriented marketing policies and programmes.
6. **Marketing opportunities:** Marketing research suggests new marketing opportunities and the manner in which they can be exploited fully. It identifies existing and emerging market opportunities.
7. **Marketing information:** Marketing research provides information on various aspects of marketing. It suggests relative strengths and weaknesses of the company. On the basis of such information, marketing executives find it easy to frame policies for the future period. It also provides information, guidance and alternative solutions to marketing problems.
8. **Distribution channels:** Marketing research can be used to study the effectiveness of existing channels of distribution and the need of making suitable changes and alternatives in the distribution system.

9.17 IMPORTANCE OF MARKETING RESEARCH

Marketing research is fast growing in its importance due to increasing competition, fast moving technological developments and changing consumer needs, expectations and attitudes. The importance of marketing research is universally accepted. The status of marketing research in business management is identical to the position of brain in a human body.

The following points suggest the importance of marketing research:

1. **Planning and Execution of Marketing Plan:** A business unit can plan and execute all activities right from manufacturing to marketing with reasonable accuracy and confidence due to the guidelines available through marketing research.
2. **Quick and Correct Decision-making:** Marketing research facilitates and enables quick and correct decision-making by marketing managers.
3. **Effective Solutions on Marketing Problems:** Marketing research provides effective solutions to marketing problems. It diagnoses the business ailments and suggests measures to remove them. Marketing researcher acts like business doctor and prescribes treatment for business elements.
4. **Huge Spending on MR:** Large companies spend crores of rupees on marketing research activities. New techniques and methods are used in the conduct of research activities in an accurate manner. This suggests the growing importance of marketing research.

REVIEW QUESTIONS

1. What is the meaning and definition of communication? Explain the objectives of marketing communication.
2. Explain the process of marketing communication.
3. Describe the barriers in marketing communication.
4. Explain the elements of marketing communication mix.
5. What are the major tools of marketing communication?
6. Explain the concepts of developing marketing communication.
7. Explain integrated marketing communication.
8. Explain the meaning and nature of marketing research.
9. What is market research? Explain the need of marketing research.
10. Explain the characteristics of marketing research.
11. Describe the different types of marketing research.
12. Explain the component of marketing research process.
13. What do you mean by Marketing Information System (MIS)?
14. Define the applications of marketing research.
15. Explain the importance of marketing research.

CHAPTER 10

Promotion Mix

POINTS TO REMEMBER

At the end of this chapter, we will be able to understand:

- Introduction
- Meaning and Definition
- Components of Promotion Mix
- Factors Governing Promotion Mix

10.1 INTRODUCTION

Promotion refers to using methods of communication with two objectives: (*i*) to inform the existing and potential consumers about a product, and (*ii*) to persuade consumers to buy the product. It is an important element of marketing mix. In the absence of communication, consumers may not be aware of the product and its potential to satisfy their needs and desires. Various tools of communication form part of promotion mix. Companies must decide which tools should be used for larger sales and in what proportion. The promotional tools should be used in combination. These decisions are known as promotion mix decisions. There are five components of promotion mix, *i.e.*, advertising, sales promotion, personal selling, publicity and public relations. Thus, promotion mix is a company's total communication programme which consists of different blends of its components and which are used to achieve the company's marketing objectives.

10.2 MEANING AND DEFINITION

Promotion is the marketing term used to describe all marketing communications activities and includes personal selling, sales promotion, public relations, direct marketing, trade fairs and exhibitions, advertising and sponsorship. Promotion needs to be precisely coordinated and integrated into the businesses global communications message, and this is called Integrated Marketing Communications (IMC). IMC integrates the message through the available channels to deliver a consistent and clear message about your company's brands, products and services. Any movement away from the single message confuses the consumer and undermines the brand.

When a business organization gives information to its consumers and motivates them to buy the products through various promotion techniques like advertising, personal selling, sale promotion, communication, public relations, branding and packaging etc., it is called promotion mix.

> *"Promotion mix is that tactical combination of advertisements, personal selling and other promotional tools, which helps in reaching to the goals of sales program".* **William J. Stanton**

> *"Promotional mix is a specific combination of advertisement, personal selling, sales promotion and public-relations through which an organization fulfills its objectives of advertisements and marketing".* **Kotler and Armstrong**

> *"Promotion mix works to so frame and influence the persons and the systems, which their inputs may convert into purchase processes, consumption-level and the outputs".* **Brink and Kelly**

In this way, promotion mix means tactical combination of those techniques or tools of promotion which help in giving information of products to the consumers, so that they can be motivated to purchase the commodity. It is thus a persuasive communication and also serves as a reminder.

10.3 COMPONENTS OF PROMOTION MIX

A firm uses different tools for its promotional activities which are as follows:

1. Advertising
2. Sales promotion
3. Personal selling
4. Publicity
5. Public relations.

These are also termed as five elements of a promotion mix as shown in Fig.10.1. Let us have a brief idea about these promotion tools.

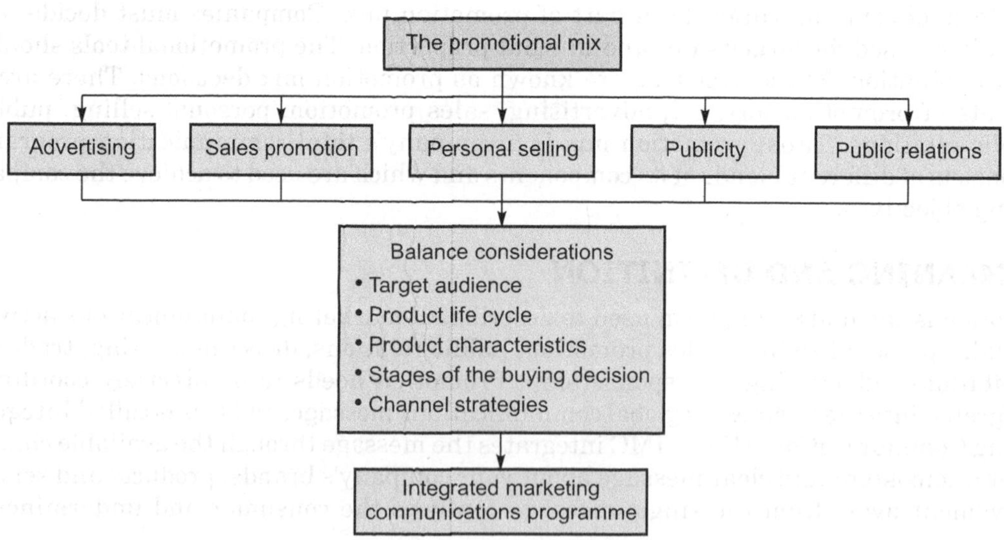

Fig. 10.1. Components of promotional mix.

10.3.1 Advertising

Advertising is the most commonly used tool for informing the present and prospective consumers about the product, its quality, features, availability, etc. It is a paid form of non-personal communication through different media about a product, idea, a service or an organization by an identified sponsor.

> *"Any paid form of non-personal presentation and promotion of ideas, goods or services by an identified sponsor".*
> **American Marketing Association**

It can be done through print media like newspaper, magazines, billboards and through electronic media like radio, television, internet etc. It is a very flexible and comparatively low cost tool of promotion.

10.3.2 Sales Promotion

Sales promotion is one level or type of marketing aimed either at the consumer or at the distribution channel (in the form of sales-incentives). It is used to introduce a new product, and clear out inventories.

> *"Media and non-media marketing pressure applied for a predetermined, limited period of time in order to stimulate trial, increase consumer demand, or improve product availability".*
> **American Marketing Association**

The tool includes contests, games, gifts, trade shows, discounts, etc. Sales promotional activities are often carried out at retail levels.

10.3.3 Personal Selling

They show certain variety of goods to you, try to explain the features of the products, if required demonstrate the functioning of the items, inform customers about the price concession available, persuade customers to buy the product and also in some cases promise customers to bring certain items of their choice in future. So not only do they inform and explain to customers about the product but also persuade customers to buy those items and want customers to buy from them in future also. On the other hand, they also gather more information about the product, see and handle it personally to judge it better.

The person who sells goods to customers in this way is called 'salesman' and the technique of selling is known as 'personal selling' or 'salesmanship'. Thus, personal selling refers to the presentation of goods before the potential buyers and persuading them to purchase it. It involves face-to-face interaction and physical verification of the goods to be purchased. The objective is not only just to sell the product to a person but also to make him/her a permanent customer.

> *"Personal selling is face-to-face interaction with one or more perspective purchasers for the purpose of making presentations, answering questions, and procuring orders".*
> **American Marketing Association**

We can also find personal selling in some shops where salesmen are employed by the shopkeeper to use this technique. For example, you can find such salesmen in jewellery stores, consumer goods stores, saree houses, etc. In case of some services, we also find personal selling used in shops. For example, we find people going to the same barber shop to cut their hair and get a massage from a specific barber. This shows that in case of personal selling the seller usually comes to know about the tasters and preferences of the customer and thus attracts him to buy the goods or services.

10.3.4 Publicity

This is a non-paid process of generating a wide range of communication to contribute a favourable attitude towards the product and the organization. You may have seen articles in newspapers about an organization, its products and policies. The other tools of publicity are press conferences, publications and news in the electronic media etc. It is published or broadcasted without charging any money from the firm.

> *"Impersonal and unpaid sponsor stimulates demand for goods, service or business organizational unit through the dissemination of commercially sensitive information in printed media or benign presentation on radio, television or from the scene".* **American Marketing Association**

Marketers often spend a lot of time and effort in getting news items placed in the media for creation of a favourable image of the company and its products.

10.3.5 Public Relations

Public relations is about reputation—the result of what you do, what you say and what others say about you. Public relations is the discipline which looks after reputation, with the aim of earning understanding and support and influencing opinion and behaviour. It is the planned and sustained effort to establish and maintain goodwill and mutual understanding between an organization and its publics.

> *"Public Relations is the art and social science of analyzing trends, predicting their consequences. Counselling organization leaders and implementing planned programmes of action which will serve both the organization's and the public interest".*
>
> **World Assembly of Public Relations Associations**

Public relations takes many forms in different organizations and comes under many titles, including public information, investor relations, public affairs, corporate communication, marketing or customer relations. To add to all the confusion, not all of these titles always relate accurately to public relations, but all of them cover at least part of what public relations is.

At its best, public relations not only tells an organization's story to its public, it also helps to shape the organization and the way it works. Through research, feedback communication and evaluation, the practitioner needs to find out the concerns and expectations of a company's public and explain them to its management.

10.4 FACTORS GOVERNING PROMOTION MIX

Each of the above components of the promotional mix has strengths and weaknesses. There are several factors that should be taken into account in deciding which, and how much of each tool to use in a promotional marketing campaign:

1. **Nature of Product:** Different types of products require different promotion mix. In case of consumer goods, advertisement is considered to be the most important because the goods are non-technical and produced on a large scale. But for industrial goods personal selling is regarded as the most important tool because the products are technical in nature, costly and persuasion is considered essential for their sale.
2. **Type of the Market:** If the number of customers is quite large and they are spread over a vast area, advertisement is more helpful because it can reach people everywhere.

However, if number of customers is not very large and they are concentrated geographically, personal selling and sales promotion may be more effective.

3. **Market Size and Concentration:** If a market size is small and the number of potential buyers is small, then personal selling may be the most cost-effective promotional tool. A good example of this would be businesses selling software systems designed for supermarket retailers. On the other hand, where markets are geographically disperse or, where there are substantial numbers of potential customers, advertising is usually the most effective.
4. **Stage of the Product Life Cycle (PLC):** The promotional mix depends upon the stage of the product in product life cycle. During introduction, heavy expenditure is incurred on advertisement followed by personal selling and sales promotion. During the growth stage, customers are aware of the benefits of a product. Hence, advertisement along with personal selling will be more effective. At the maturity stage, competition is more intense. Sales promotion becomes the most important tool to boost sales.
5. **Budget:** Funds available for promotion also decide promotion mix, *e.g.*, advertisement is a costly tool. If sufficient funds are not available this tool may not be adopted. Personal selling involves continuous spending. Thus, budget is a deciding factor for promotion mix.
6. **Resource Availability and the Cost of Each Promotional Tool:** Advertising (particularly on television and in the national newspapers can be very expensive). The overall resource budget for the promotional campaign will often determine which tools the business can afford to use.
7. **Push vs. Pull Strategy:** When the firm pushes the product to the middlemen they in turn push it to the consumers, it is known as 'push' strategy. In this case, personal selling or display should be more effective.

Pull strategy refers to the policy of a company to strive to build up consumer demand without recourse to middlemen. Generally advertising is considered more important in case of pull strategy as shown in Fig. 10.2.

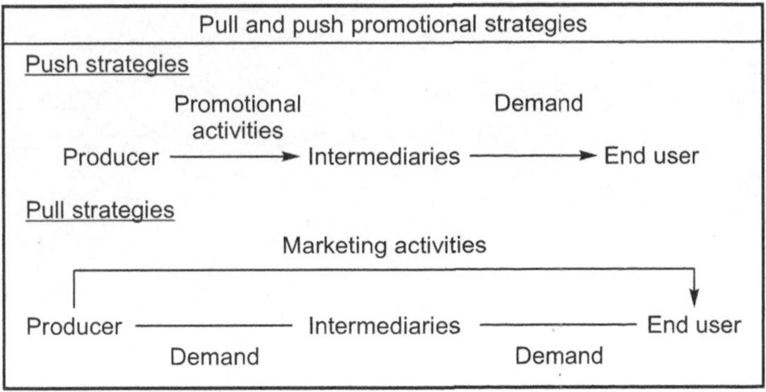

Fig. 10.2. Push and pull promotional strategy.

Thus, it may be said that all promotional tools are complementary and not competitive. The degree of emphasis on each tool will differ depending upon the influence of certain factors. A proper combination of promotional tools should be designed to attain better results.

REVIEW QUESTIONS

1. Explain the concept of promotion mix.
2. Describe the meaning and definition of promotion mix. Explain the different components of promotion mix.
3. What do you mean by advertising and sales promotion?
4. What is personal selling and publicity in promotion mix?
5. Explain public relations as a major tool of promotion mix.
6. Explain the different factors influencing promotion mix.

UNIT–III

11. Advertising

12. Advertising Budget, Media and Public Relations

13. Personal Selling and Management of Sales Force

14. Sales Forecasting, Sales Promotion and Publicity

CHAPTER 11

Advertising

POINTS TO REMEMBER

At the end of this chapter, we will be able to understand:

- Introduction
- History of Advertising in India
- Evolution of Advertising
- Meaning and Definition
- Features of Advertising
- Essentials of Advertising
- The 5-Ms of Advertising
- Objectives/Functions of Advertising
- Types of Advertising
- Advertising Strategies for the Stages of the Product Life Cycle (PLC)
- Benefits or Importance of Advertisement
- Ethics in Advertising
- Steps in Scientific Advertising Campaign
- Criticisms of Advertising

11.1 INTRODUCTION

"Doing business without advertising is like winking at a girl in the dark; you know what you are doing but nobody else". **Stewart H. Britt**

Advertising is multidimensional. It is an important tool of sales promotion. Advertising consists of all the activities involved in presenting a non-personal, oral or visual, sponsored message regarding a product, service or idea. This message is called advertisement which is disseminated through one or more media and paid for by an identified sponsor. Advertising is used for communicating business information to the present and prospective customers. It usually provides information about the advertising firm, its product qualities, place of availability of its products, etc. Advertisement is indispensable for both sellers and buyers.

In the modern age of large scale production, producers cannot think of pushing sale of their products without advertising them.

You watch television, listen to radio, and go to a cinema house to see a movie and read newspapers and magazines. While doing so, you observe a number of advertisements of several products. Some of these products are cold drinks such as Pepsi, Coca-Cola, and Limca, hot drinks such as tea and coffee (Taj, Nescafe), washing powders such as Surf, Arial and Nirma, toilet soaps such as Dove, Lux, Breeze, Hamam and Cinthol, toothpastes such as Colgate, Pepsodent, Promise, Close-up and Babool, various shampoos, cold creams, hair oils, skin care products like Dettol, refrigerators, televisions, scooters, motor cycles, cars, washing machines, computers, shoes, clothes and services such as banking, tourism, railways and insurance.

11.2 HISTORY OF ADVERTISING IN INDIA

The history of advertising in India parallels the history of the Indian Press. You would have learnt in the module on print media that the first issue of the first newspaper of the Indian subcontinent, was the 'Bengal Gazette' or the 'Calcutta General Advertiser', started by James Augustus Hicky on January 29, 1780. Did you know that it carried a few advertisements? During the early years the newspapers announced births, deaths, appointments, arrival and departure of ships and sale of furniture. By the beginning of the 19th century the pattern of advertising revealed a definite change. Even the daily newspapers announced themselves through advertisements in existing periodicals. The power of advertising increased rapidly with the growth in trade and commerce. Which newspaper does your family read? Does it have many advertisements?

By 1830, around three dozen newspapers and periodicals were being published on a regular basis from India. With the rise of new industries, advertising, even from British companies, increased. The growth of advertising in India is also linked to the Swadeshi movement (1920–1922), which gave impetus to Indian industries.

Do you remember the names of some of the freedom fighters associated with the Swadeshi movement? Mahatma Gandhi described Swadeshi as "a call to the consumer to be aware of the violence he is causing by supporting those industries that result in poverty, harm to workers and to humans and other creatures". Swadeshi movement was an attempt to take economic power from the British by the use of domestic made products. Spinning the *charkha* and wearing *khadi* became a very powerful tool to fight the British government.

Let us now find out how modern Indian advertising developed. Do you know when the Indian advertising agencies started operating? The first Indian ad agency, the Indian Advertising Agency, was launched in the very early years of the 20th century. On the other hand, B Dattaram & Co, located in Girgaum in Mumbai and launched in 1905, also claims to be the oldest existing Indian agency! This was followed by the launch of the Calcutta Advertising Agency in 1909. By the 1920s a number of Indian agencies were working from the major Indian cities, the most important being the Modern Publicity Company in Madras, Central Publicity Service in Bombay and Calcutta and the Oriental Advertising Agency in Tiruchirapalli. In 1931, the first full-fledged Indian ad agency, the National Advertising Service, was established. During the post independence era, the advertising business was well on its way to growth and expansion. The Indian Society of Advertisers was formed in 1951 and in May 1958, the Society of Advertising Practitioners was established and advertising clubs came up in Bombay and Calcutta to promote higher standards of work.

Market research and readership surveys led to further professionalization of the advertising industry. Television Rating Points, popularly known as TRP measurements, provided ad agencies with statistical data on consumer/viewer likes and dislikes and helped them create effective media plans and ad campaigns. The introduction of multi-colour printing, improved printing machines and the development of commercial art gave the ad business a further boost. The advertising agencies expanded their services and this was due to the phenomenal growth in media. Besides selling space in newspapers and magazines, they began to offer art work, organization of fairs and exhibitions and market research.

	SOME IMPORTANT YEARS IN ADVERTISING HISTORY
1780	Modern advertising history began with classified advertising. Ads appeared for the first time in print in Hickey's weekly newspaper, the *Bengal Gazette*.
1883	Horlicks becomes the first 'malted milk' to be patented.
1905	B Dattaram & Co, one of the early companies making advertisements for newspapers was launched in Mumbai.
1920	Ogilvy and Mather and Hindustan Thompson Associate agencies were formed.
1928	BOMAS Ltd. (Formerly DJ Keymer & Co Ltd.) set up.
1929	J Walter Thompson Co Pr. Ltd. formed.
1931	The first ad agency, the National Advertising Service was established.
1934	Venkatrao Sista opens Sista Advertising and Publicity Services as first full service Indian agency.
1935	Indian Publicity Bureau Pr. Ltd., Calcutta established.
1936	• Krishna Publicity Co Pr. Ltd., Kanpur begins operations. • Studio Ratan Batra Pr. Ltd., Bombay established. • Indian Broadcasting Company becomes All India Radio (AIR).
1938	Jayendra Publicity, Kolhapur started.
1939	Lever's advertising department launched Dalda—the first major example of a brand and a marketing campaign specifically developed for India.
1950	Various advertising associations were set up to safeguard the interests of various advertisers in the industry.
1951	The Indian Society of Advertisers was formed.
1967	The first commercial was aired on Vividh Bharati.
1978	The first television commercial was seen. Various companies now started advertising on television and sponsoring various shows including *Humlog* and *Yeh Jo Hai Zindagi*.
1986	Mudra Communications created India's first folk-history TV serial *Buniyaad* which was aired on Doordarshan; it became the first of the mega soaps in the country.
1991	First India-targetted satellite channel, Zee TV started its broadcast.
1995	A great boom in media with the growth of cable and satellite and increase of titles in the print medium. This decade also saw the growth of public relations and events and other new promotions that various companies and ad agencies introduced.
2000	• Ad agency Lintas merged with Lowe Group to become Lowe Lintas and Partners (LLP). • Game shows like *Kaun Banega Crorepati* has become a rage; media buying industry is bullish on KBC. • *Kyunki Saas Bhi Kabhi Bahu Thi* marks the return of family- oriented soap on TV.

2001	• Trikaya Grey becomes Grey Worldwide. • Bharti's ₹ 2.75-crore corporate TV commercial, where a baby girl is born in a football stadium, becomes the most expensive campaign of the year.
2002	• Lowe Lintas & Partners rechristened Lowe Worldwide. • For the first time in the history of Hindustan Thompson Associates, a new post of president is created. Kamal Oberoi is appointed as the first president of HTA .

11.3 EVOLUTION OF ADVERTISING

Can you imagine two people with drums walking down the streets of Mohenjodaro, the city of the Indus valley civilization you read about in your history lesson in previous classes, shouting their own and other's messages?

People would stop and listen, just as you do when you stop to read an advertisement on the road, or watch an advertisement on television! Then there used to be signs on shops or drinking houses to indicate the name of the shop or the shop owner. The highly urbanized cities of Harappa and Mohenjodaro employed signs to sell many types of art and craft items that our ancient civilizations were famous for.

In the Indian subcontinent, during Emperor Ashoka's reign, stones or pillars were used for making public announcements. There have always been advertisements of some sort or the other. The form of advertising for the transmission of information dates back to ancient Greece and Rome, when town criers, drummers and signs were used to carry information for advertising goods and services. Excavations in the ancient Roman town of Pompeii have shown evidence of some form of advertising.

One advertisement found in the Latin language reads as follows:

'A copper pot has been taken from this shop. Whoever brings it back will receive 65 cesterces. If anyone shall hand over the thief, he will receive an additional reward'.

The ancient Romans painted notices of theatre performances, games, entertainment and public events on the walls of the busy centres of the town. Roman dairies had a sign outside with a goat on it and their schools had a picture of a boy being whipped. These signs were often used because many people could not read. Which sign will you use for a school? It was much later that public notices were placed in the 'Acta Diurna', a wall newspaper that provided daily news of politics in ancient Rome in 131 BC. Lost-and-found advertising on papyrus was common in ancient Greece and ancient Rome.

Advertising soon became a powerful tool to market the products produced in the factories—from safety pins to sewing machines. Newspapers began selling space to advertisements. Soon there were more advertisements than news!

The field of advertising was revolutionized with the advent of radio and television as popular media of communication in this century. While the Press would cover only the literate population, radio and television have widely covered both literates and illiterates. Television and radio remain the most popular media in urban as well as rural areas. During the 1990s, the arrival of satellite television and internet has resulted in significant changes in the field.

11.4 MEANING AND DEFINITION

Advertising is non-personal as it is not directed to any single individual. Secondly, the sponsor *i.e.*, the manufacturer or producer is identified as his name and address is always contained in an advertisement and he also bears all the cost involved in the process. Thirdly, the producer can also promote an idea regarding quality, design, packing and pricing, etc., of any product or service.

Thus, we can say, advertising consists of all activities involved in presenting a sponsored message regarding a product, service or an idea.

> *"Any paid form of non-personal presentation and promotion of ideas, goods and services by an identified sponsor".* **American Marketing Association**

> *"Advertising is any form of paid non-personal presentation of ideas, goods or services for the purpose of inducting people to buy".* **Wheeler**

> *"Advertising is a paid form of non-personal presentation of ideas, goods or services by an identified sponsor".* **Richard Buskirk.**

> *"Advertising consists of all the activities involved in presenting to a group, a non-personal, oral or visual, openly sponsored message disseminated through one or more media and is paid for by an identified sponsor".* **William J. Stanton**

The above definitions clearly reveal the nature of advertisement. This is a powerful element of the promotion mix. Essentially, advertising means spreading of information about the characteristics of a product to the prospective customers with a view to sell the product or increase the sale volume.

11.5 FEATURES OF ADVERTISING

Looking into the meaning and definition of advertising we can sum up the following features of advertising.

1. **Non-personal Presentation of Message:** In advertising there is no face-to-face or direct contact with the customers. It is directed to the prospective buyers in general.
2. **Paid Form of Communication:** In advertising the manufacturer communicates with prospective customers through different media like newspapers, hoardings, magazines, radio, television, etc. He has to pay certain amount for using some space or time in these media.
3. **Promotion of Product, Service or an Idea:** Advertisement contains any message regarding any particular product, service or even an idea. It makes people aware of the product and induces them to buy it.
4. **Sponsor is Always Identified:** The identity of the manufacturer, the trader or the service provider who issues an advertisement is always disclosed.
5. **Communicated through Some Media:** Advertisements are always communicated through use of certain media. It is not necessary that there will be just one medium. All the media may also be used like print or electronic media.

11.6 ESSENTIALS OF ADVERTISING

Advertising initiates communication and creates opportunities for customers to see value in the products and services that are offered by a specific business. It comprises the following basic elements:

1. **Use a Benefit Headline:** A headline in a newspaper advertisement serves the same purpose as a headline in a news story: It grabs the attention of readers, it motivates them to read on, it pre-sells them on the message that follows. A headline is your first and best chance to attract interest in your advertisement, make the most of it.
2. **Use a Dominant Element:** The initial goal of your advertising is to attract attention. It is your way of flagging customers as they travel through the various media. Whether it is an eye-stopping photograph or illustration, or a hard-selling headline, use a dominant element to attract readers to your message.

   Do not overcrowd your ad with illustrations and information that might distract readers/ viewers from your message. If you sell ten styles of overcoats, pick one or two of your more eye-catching styles to feature in the ad and tell customers there are plenty more to choose from in your store. If you are having a store-wide sale, an all-type advertisement rather than one packed with illustrations, is often a more effective way to attract customers.
3. **Make your Copy Complete:** By the time customers are through viewing your ad, they should know the answers to questions like: How much does it cost? What sizes and colours are available? How will purchasing this product or ordering this service benefit me? Always include prices. Saying only that the prices are 30% off leaves them wondering about the original price. State clearly how much the advertised product or service costs and how much customers will save.
4. **Include Related Items:** Do not miss the opportunity to promote related merchandise or services. By co-ordinating items in your advertising you save time for customers. That is a favour they will appreciate and remember.
5. **Urge Readers to Buy Now:** There are several ways to build urgency into your message. For example, you can limit the time of the sale or remind them that the sale comes only once a year. You can also limit the availability of the merchandise or service with phrases like 'while stocks last' and 'one week only!'
6. **Use Colour Whenever Possible:** In a recent National Association Breweriana Advertising (NABA) study, colour ads outscored the same ads in black and white by 83%. Consider the increased power of newspaper colour as you plan your ad.
7. **Make your Name Prominent:** Make sure your business name and logo are easy to find and easy to read. Famous labels and prestige brand names are always important to include in your ads, but yours is the name you want customers to remember.
8. **Tell Customers how to Reach You:** Include your telephone number and address in every ad. Many retail advertisers even include a small map showing customers how to reach their store.
9. **Use Simple Language:** Many of your customers might not understand the trade terms that are familiar to you. So use simple and everyday language. Think of your advertisement as a conversation with customers.
10. **Deliver on Promises:** The surest way to lose customers is to make advertising claims you cannot back up. Go easy on the superlatives. If you claim your prices are unbelievable, readers are likely to agree. If every other week you advertise 'the best deal ever' readers begin to think it no more a big deal.

11.7 THE 5-Ms OF ADVERTISING

In developing a programme, marketing managers must always start by identifying the target market and the buyer's motives. Then they can make the five major decisions in developing an advertising programme, known as the 5-Ms, viz.

Mission: what are the advertising objectives?
Money: how much can be spent?
Message: what message can be sent?
Media: what media should be used?
Measurement: how should the results be evaluated? The above-mentioned can be explained by the Table 11.1 given below:

Table 11.1: Five Ms of Advertising

The 5Ms of Advertising Checklist for planning of a marketing or advertising campaign.	
Mission	What are the objectives? What is the key objective?
Money	How much is it worth to reach my objectives? How much can be spent?
Message	What message should be sent? Is the message clear and easily understood?
Media	What media vehicles are available? What media vehicles should be used?
Measurement	How should the results be measured? How should the results be evaluated and followed up?

Source: Philip Kotler

11.8 OBJECTIVES/FUNCTIONS OF ADVERTISING

The purpose of advertising is nothing but to sell something—a product, a service or an idea. The real objective of advertising is an effective communication between producers and consumers. The following are the main objectives of advertising: Informative, Persuasive and Reminder.

1. **Informative:** This is when advertising is carried out in an informative manner. The idea is to give the ad the look of an official article to give it more credibility. Also, informative ads tend to help generate a good reputation. In some circumstances a business might be required to run informative advertising as part of resolving a law suit. Tobacco companies are one of the more notable examples of this. The objectives of informative advertising include:
   (*a*) To create awareness of the organization.
   (*b*) To explain the characteristics of the organization.
   (*c*) To correct false impressions about the organization.
   (*d*) To reduce peoples' apprehensions or fears about visiting the organization.
   (*e*) To build or enhance the organization's image or position.
2. **Persuasive:** Persuasive is the influence of beliefs, attitudes, intentions, motivations, or behaviours. Persuasion is a process aimed at changing a person's or a group's attitude or behaviour toward some event, idea, object, or other person(s), by using written or spoken words to convey information, feelings, or reasoning, or a combination of them. The objectives of persuasive advertising include:

(*a*) To increase customer preference for the organization's services.

(*b*) To increase customer loyalty to the organization.

(*c*) To encourage customers to switch from using a competitive organization.

(*d*) To convince customers to book at the organization now or in the future.

(*e*) To change customers' perceptions.

3. **Reminder:** A marketing strategy typically consisting of brief messages sent with the objective of reminding a target consumer group about a product or service or of introducing a new theme into an existing marketing programme. Reminder advertising might be used by a business that has already invested considerable resources in initially promoting their product or service and still wishes to maintain its competitiveness. The objectives of reminder advertising include:

   (*a*) To remind customers about where they can book the organization's services.

   (*b*) To remind customers about facilities or services that are unique to the sponsoring organization.

   (*c*) To remind customers about when they should book or reserve the organization's services.

   (*d*) To remind customers of the existence of the organization.

4. **Other Objectives:** Some of the other objectives of advertisement are as follows:

   (*i*) **Preparing ground for new product:** New product needs introduction because potential customers have never used such product earlier and the advertisement prepares a ground for that new product.

   (*ii*) **To educate customers:** Can you remember the advertisement of *Dandi Namak* on television? In this advertisement it is said that *Dandi Namak* is good for health as it contains iodine. This message educates you that iodine is good for health and *Dandi Namak* contains iodine.

   (*iii*) **Creating demand for products:** Nowadays, goods are produced on a large scale in anticipation of future demand. It is therefore, important that sufficient demand is created for the product. Goods produced can be sold only if there exists sufficient demand for them.

   (*iv*) **To retain existing customers:** You might remember that Nirma washing powder was a very popular detergent. But, after Wheel powder came to the market the sale of Nirma suddenly decreased. Then the manufacturers of Nirma improved the product and advertised about the same in different media. After knowing this, the customers who were earlier using Nirma did not switch over to Wheel and continued using Nirma. In this manner Nirma sustained its existing demand. Thus, advertising helps the manufacturers not only to create a demand for a new product but also to retain the existing customers.

   (*v*) **Facing the competition:** Another important objective of an advertisement is to face the competition. Under competitive conditions, an advertisement helps to build up brand image and brand loyalty and when customers have developed brand loyalty, it becomes difficult for the middlemen to change it.

   (*vi*) **To increase sales:** We have learnt that advertising creates demands for new products and sustains the demand of old ones. Thus, with increase in demand, the sale of the product also increases.

   (*vii*) **Creating and enhancing goodwill of the firm:** This is another objective of advertising. Through advertising, a firm highlights the importance it attaches to consumer satisfaction. Achievements of the firm in these matters are also highlighted. This helps in creating a good image of the business in the minds of consumers, workers, investors, suppliers, government and other groups of people in society. Thus, business goodwill is created and enhanced.

(*viii*) **Informing the changes to the customers:** Whenever changes are made in the prices, channels of distribution or in the product by way of any improvement in quality, size, weight, brand, packing, etc., they must be informed to the public by the producer through advertisement.

(*ix*) **Neutralizing competitors advertising:** Advertising is unavoidable to compete with or neutralize competitors advertising. When competitors are adopting intensive advertising as their promotional strategy, it is reasonable to follow similar practices to neutralize their effects. In such cases, it is essential for the manufacturer to create a different image of his product.

(*x*) **To assist salesman:** In most advertisements the salient features of a product, its qualities and its uses are expressed in detail. This assists a salesman to sell the product quickly without spending time in explaining and convincing the customer. In short, advertising aims at benefiting the producer, educating the consumer and supplementing the salesmen. Above all it is a link between the producer and the consumers.

11.9 TYPES OF ADVERTISING

Advertisements can be categorized according to theme or content. Broadly speaking, there are five types:

1. **Product Advertising:** Have you seen how small children want to drink the same soft drink as their favourite cricketer and film star? This is the impact of product advertising and is the most common type of advertising as it is most easily identified.

   A product is something produced in large numbers by human beings, machines or by a natural process. Products advertised therefore range from fruits and vegetables to pickles and jams and bikes and cars.

   The main focus of the ad in this case is the product and not the company or manufacturer. These ads usually have a playful approach. They are low on information about the product but are high on style. Ads of soft drinks, shoes, cars, cell phones and food products belong to this category.

2. **Service Advertising:** Here the focus is not on a factory manufactured item or product but a company providing a service. This could be a bank, insurance, the railways, a call centre or travel agency. The ads usually show the company as a leading service provider in its particular field.

   Let us consider the example of the Indian Railways. In order to keep the public interested in the Railways and familiarize them with their services, advertisements are issued from time to time. You may look for these advertisements in the newspapers and the websites of Indian Railways.

   Similarly, banks are found to advertise their saving schemes and loan facilities that they offer for buying homes and vehicles.

3. **Public Service Advertising:** This is also called social service advertising or development advertising. Here the focus is on issues that impact society on a larger scale, such as family planning, national integration, polio eradication, and pollution control. The main purpose is to create public awareness through hard-hitting direct messages. These ads do not sell products and services but ideas.

Let us take the example of the polio eradication campaign. Advertisements are issued through various mass media such as newspapers, radio and television to create awareness on polio eradication. This was to motivate parents to take their children for immunization and enable them to be given polio drops.

4. **Institutional Advertising:** These ads are directed at creating a good public image of a company. The ads focus on the organization's work in areas of research, development and quality control. Often the ads concentrate on the social work done by the company by its sponsorship of educational, cultural and sports events. The purpose of these ads is to sell a positive image of the company rather than a product manufactured by the company. The TATA Steel ads in the 1980s with the tag line—'Ispat bhi hum banate hain' or 'we also make steel', is a good example of institutional advertising.
5. **Surrogate Advertising:** In cases where advertising of a particular product is banned or made illegal, product companies come up with other products with the same brand name. Advertising the legal products with the same brand name reminds the audience of their legally banned products as well. Common examples include Hayward's and Kingfisher beer brands, McDowell's No. 01 and Bagpiper whisky which is often seen to promote their brand with the help of surrogate advertising. The intention behind such advertisement is to popularize the liquor products. Different things like—Soda, mineral water, mega cricket team clubs, friends clubs etc., are shown in such advertisements.

Exhibit 11.1. Surrogate advertising—"censorship in India is an eyewash".

11.10 ADVERTISING STRATEGIES FOR THE STAGES OF THE PRODUCT LIFE CYCLE (PLC)

Advertising strategies change with the change in stages of a product life, *i.e.*, **PLC as shown in Fig. 11.1.** This focuses on changes in the way of advertising when **PLC stages** change. Every product goes through a series of stages, namely **introduction, growth, maturity, and decline.**

After a period of development it is introduced or launched into the market; it gains more and more customers as it grows; eventually the market stabilizes and the product becomes mature; then after a period of time the product is overtaken by development and the introduction of superior competitors, it goes into decline and is eventually withdrawn. However, most products fail in the introduction phase. Others have very cyclical maturity phases where decline sees the product promoted to regain customers.

Thus, in these situations, a suitable advertising and promotion campaign is required to be identified and followed.

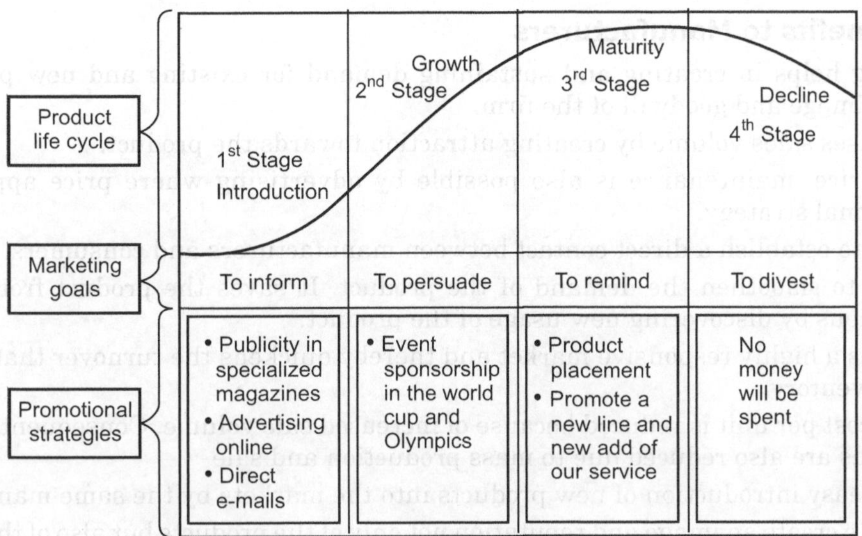

Fig. 11.1. Advertising strategies for the stages of the PLC.

1. **Advertising Strategies for Introduction Stage of PLC:** The need for immediate profit is not a pressure. The product is promoted to create awareness. If the product has no or few competitors, a skimming price strategy is employed. Limited numbers of product are available in few channels of distribution. **Advertising differentiates the product.** For example, **print ad of a printer giving details about its specifications.**
2. **Advertising Strategies for Growth Stage of PLC:** Competitors are attracted into the market with very similar offerings. Products become more profitable and companies form alliances, joint ventures and take each other over. **Advertising spend is high and focuses upon building brand.** Market share **tends to stabilize. Advertising establishes participation with the marketplace.**
3. **Advertising Strategies for Maturity Stage of PLC:** Those products that survive the earlier stages tend to spend the longest time in this phase. Sales grow at a decreasing rate and then stabilize. Producers attempt to differentiate products and brands are key to this. Price wars and intense competition occur. At this point the market reaches saturation. Producers begin to leave the market due to poor margins. **Promotion becomes more widespread and use a greater variety of media. Advertising puts price ahead of the competition.**
4. **Advertising Strategies for Decline Stage of PLC:** At this point there is a downturn in the market. For example, more innovative products are introduced or consumer tastes have changed. There is intense price-cutting and many more products are withdrawn from the market. Profits can be improved **by reducing marketing spend and cost cutting.**

11.11 BENEFITS OR IMPORTANCE OF ADVERTISEMENT

Advertising broadens the knowledge of the consumers. With the aid of advertising, consumers find and buy necessary products without much waste of time. The main benefits of advertising may be narrated as follows:

11.11.1 Benefits to Manufacturers

Advertising helps in creating and sustaining demand for existing and new products. It builds brand image and goodwill of the firm.

1. It increases sales volume by creating attraction towards the product.
2. Retail price, maintenance is also possible by advertising where price appeal is the promotional strategy.
3. It helps to establish a direct contact between manufacturers and consumers.
4. It leads to smoothen the demand of the product. It saves the product from seasonal fluctuations by discovering new usage of the product.
5. It creates a highly responsive market and thereby quickens the turnover that results in lower inventory.
6. Selling cost per unit is reduced because of increased sale volume. Consequently, product overheads are also reduced due to mass production and sale
7. It helps easy introduction of new products into the markets by the same manufacturer.
8. It helps to create an image and reputation not only of the products but also of the producer or advertiser. In this way, it creates goodwill for the manufacturer.
9. Advertising gives the employees a feeling of pride in their jobs and to be in the service of such a concern of repute. It thus inspires the executives and workers to improve their efficiency.
10. Advertising is necessary to meet the competition in the market and to survive.

11.11.2 Benefits to Wholesalers and Retailers

1. Easy sale of the products is possible since consumers are aware of the product and its quality.
2. It increases the rate of the turnover of the stock because demand is already created by advertisement.
3. It ensures more economical selling because selling overheads are reduced.
4. It enables them to have product information.
5. It supplements the selling activities.
6. The reputation created is shared by the wholesalers and retailers alike because they need not spend anything for the advertising of a well advertised product.

11.11.3 Benefits to Consumers

1. Advertising helps in eliminating the middlemen by establishing direct contacts between producers and consumers. It results in cheaper goods.
2. It helps them to know where and when the products are available. This reduces their shopping time.
3. Advertising stresses on quality and very often prices. This forms an indirect guarantee to the consumers of the quality and price. Further large scale production assumed by advertising enables the seller to sell a product at a lower cost.
4. It provides an opportunity to the customers to compare the merits and demerits of various substitute products.
5. This is perhaps the only medium through which consumers could know the varied and new uses of the product.
6. Modern advertisements are highly informative.

11.11.4 Benefits to Salesmen

A salesman acts as a friend and guide to consumers. He informs them about the new products and new uses of existing products. He helps them in choosing products, which match their needs and incomes. A salesman guides the customers in buying products that will provide maximum satisfaction. Sales are benefited by the advertisement in following ways:

1. Introducing the product becomes quite easy and convenient because the manufacturer has already advertised the goods informing the consumers about the product and its quality.
2. Advertising prepares necessary ground for a salesman to begin his work effectively. Hence sales efforts are reduced.
3. The contact established with the customer by a salesman is made permanent through effective advertising because a customer is assured of the quality and price of the product.
4. The salesman can weigh the effectiveness of advertising when he makes direct contact with the consumers.

11.11.5 Benefits to Community or Society

Advertising creates awareness among masses regarding their needs and the availability of goods to satisfy those needs. By repeated advertisement, a desire to possess the goods is aroused. Those people who do not have sufficient purchasing power, work extra hard to earn more income to purchase goods and services. Thus, advertising motivates people to earn more and buy more goods. This increases the standard of living of the people. Advertising also generates employment.

1. It helps artists by making available more job opportunities. It also supports the Press.
2. Advertising leads to a large-scale production creating more employment opportunities to the public in various jobs directly or indirectly.
3. It initiates a process of creating more wants and their satisfaction results in higher standard of living. For example, advertising has made more popular and universal the uses of such inventions as the automobiles, radios, and various household appliances.
4. Newspapers would not have become so popular and so cheap if there had been no advertisements. The cheap production of newspapers is possible only through the publication of advertisements in them. It sustains the Press.
5. It assures employment opportunities for the professional personnel and artists.
6. Advertising does provide a glimpse of a country's way of life. It is, in fact, a running commentary on the way of living and the behaviour of the people and is also an indicator of some of the future in this regard.

11.12 ETHICS IN ADVERTISING

Advertising means a mode of communication between a seller and a buyer. Thus ethics in advertising means a set of well defined principles which govern the ways of communication taking place between seller and buyer. Ethics is the most important feature of the advertising industry.

As advertising now has become a social being, it has an influence that can be persuasive and pervasive. It is important that the right message is sent across. Additionally messages sent should harbour people's thoughts, feelings and religion and avoid nudity, language and any offensive context because of the multicultural society that the world has become.

Another factor that can take the form of exaggerated claims is misleading information and concealed facts. For example, it would be unethical to claim that a car achieved 50 miles to the gallon when in reality it was only 30 miles. This led to the perception of the advertising as the most misleading tool of marketing communication.

Ethics is the most important feature of the advertising industry. Though there are many benefits of advertising but then there are some points which do not match the ethical norms of advertising.

1. **Does Not Make Fake or False Claims:** An ethical ad is the one which does not lie, does not make fake or false claims and is in the limit of decency. The main area of interest for advertisers is to increase their sales, gain more and more customers, and increase the demand for the product by presenting a well decorated, puffed and colourful ad. They claim that their product is the best, having unique qualities than the competitors, more cost-effective, and more beneficial. But most of these ads are found to be false, misleading customers and unethical. The best example of these types of ads is the one which shows evening snacks for the kids, they use colouring and gluing to make the product look glossy and attractive to the consumers who are watching the ads on television and convince them to buy the product without giving a second thought.
2. **Directly Related to the Purpose and Nature of Advertising:** Ethics in advertising is directly related to the purpose of advertising and the nature of advertising. Sometimes exaggerating the ad becomes necessary to prove the benefit of the product. For example a sanitary napkin ad which shows that when the napkin was dropped in a river by some girls, the napkin soaked water of the entire river.
3. **Ethics also Depend on what we Believe:** If the advertisers make the ads on the belief that the customers will understand, persuade them to think, and then act on their ads, then this will lead to positive results and the ad may not be called unethical.
4. **Advertising is Often Criticized for being Offensive and in the Bad Taste:** There are several grounds for criticism. For example, TV ad of unpleasant products (haemorrhoid treatment, diarrhoea products) or sexual explicitness.
5. **Pharmaceutical Advertising:** Such ads help in creating awareness, but one catchy point here is that the advertisers show what the medicine can cure but never talk about the side effects of that same thing or the risks involved in the intake of it.
6. **Alcohol:** Till today, there has not come any liquor ad which shows anyone drinking the original liquor. They use mineral water and sodas in their advertisements with their brand name. These types of ads are called surrogate ads. These types of ads are totally unethical when liquor ads are totally banned. Even if there are no advertisements for alcohol, people will continue drinking.
7. **Cigarettes and Tobacco:** These products should never be advertised as consumption of these things is directly responsible for cancer and other severe health issues. Such ads are banned in countries like India, Norway, Thailand, Finland and Singapore.
8. **Ads for Social Causes:** These types of ads are ethical and are accepted by the people. But ads like condoms and contraceptive pills should be limited, as these are sometimes unethical, and are more likely to loose morality and decency at places where there is no educational knowledge about all these products.
9. **Children:** Children are the major sellers of the ads and the product. They have the power to convince the buyers. But when advertisers are using children in their ad, they should remember not to show them alone doing work on their own like brushing teeth, playing with toys.

Looking at all these above-mentioned points, advertisers should start taking responsibility of self-regulating their ads by:

(*i*) Designing self-regulatory codes in their companies including ethical norms, truth, decency, and legal points.

(*ii*) Tracking the activities and removing ads which do not fulfill the codes.

(*iii*) Informing the consumers about the self-regulatory codes of the company.

(*iv*) Pay attention on the complaints coming from consumers about the product ads.

(*v*) Maintain transparency throughout the company and system.

11.13 STEPS IN SCIENTIFIC ADVERTISING CAMPAIGN

Here are eight steps you can follow to keep your advertising campaign on track and successful:

1. **Market Research:** Before you even start thinking about where you might want to place an ad or even what it could look like, it is important to do at least some basic research. Even if you are not in a position to bring in an expensive research firm, you can ask your current customers questions about why they come back to you, as well as take a close look at your target demographics' needs and interests.
2. **Budgeting:** Your business probably has a set advertising budget for the year but how do you divide it up between your various advertising projects? For each project you are planning, you need to be clear on just how much money you are willing to spend. You will almost certainly change exactly how you divide it between costs like copy writing and designing, but you can treat the overall amount as set in stone. Write it down and put it in your project folder.
3. **Setting Goals:** The aims you have in mind for a particular advertising project need to be written down ahead of time. While it is good to be ambitious, it's also important to decide what constitutes a successful advertising campaign for your business. Sales can be the simplest metric: if you are advertising a particular product, how many units will you need to sell to pay for that campaign?
4. **Advertising Venue:** The website, TV station, newspaper, radio station, magazines or other advertising venue you place your ad with is a crucial decision. You will need to look at not only the cost of your preferred venues but also whether they reach your target demographic. Ad buys can make up a significant portion of your budget. Deciding on where you will place your ads first tells you how much money you will have left over for actually creating your ad.
5. **Choosing Creatives:** Unless you are planning to write, shoot and design every part of your ad, you will probably need to bring in some help. Finding the right freelancers for each aspect requires checking through portfolios and rates — if you can find a business or freelancer who can handle all aspects of creating your ad, even if that means sub-contracting, it can save you a lot of time. You will also want to make sure that you find any talent you may need for your ad (voice actors for radio, models for photography and so on).
6. **Design and Wording:** While you may not have a lot of actual writing and designing to do for your ad, during the creation process you will need to review and sign off on different stages of the project. While starting with a new designer or other creative, make sure that you both know any expectations for timelines and progress checks.
7. **Placing the ad:** Once you have a finished ad in hand, it is time to actually place it with your preferred advertising venue. You may have a few contracts to sign and a check to

hand over. You will also want to make sure you actually see your ad once it is run—from a newspaper, for instance, you may like to see the tear sheets of pages containing your ad.

8. **Evaluation:** Depending on your ad, how you evaluate it can vary. If it included a coupon, for instance, you can simply count how many customers brought in the coupon. For other ads, you may be simply comparing sales before, during and after your advertising campaign. Spend as much time on analyzing how your advertising campaign worked as you can. That information can point you to more effective uses of advertising in the future.

11.14 CRITICISMS OF ADVERTISING

In fact, advertising by itself is useful and necessary. It becomes wasteful and objectionable when used by dishonest and unknowledgeable persons. Money spent on advertising yields good results when used properly. Scientific and honest advertising is in the interest of all. It pays to the advertiser provided advertising is done rightly. Many people have often criticized advertising and some people find it a social waste. The main points of criticism are as follows:

1. **Promotion of Wasteful Consumption:** Advertising creates tastes and desires for some products in such a way that many persons are forced to buy things beyond their means or requirements. Although advertising cannot force anybody to buy things, which he considers unnecessary, there is no doubt that an advertiser, does provoke human instincts through various sales appeals.
2. **Misleads the Consumer:** Advertising fails to achieve its objectives and destroys public confidence in those cases where false and exaggerated claims are made about the virtues of products. Some sellers do defraud buyers by inducing them to purchase goods of doubtful value.
3. **Creates Monopoly:** Advertising tends to develop brand monopoly by repeatedly promoting certain brand names. Brand monopolies restrict free competition to the detriment of the consumer's interests. Although the particular brand may be similar to another brand in all respects including physical construction, yet the similarity is concealed from the public by the use of an exclusive name and an illusion is created that it is superior to the competing brands.
4. **Lack of Dignity:** Advertisers sometimes adopt objectionable themes and messages that are totally devoid of ethical sense, moral value or public decency. For example, use of nude poses of fair sex and vulgar language, excitement of basic instincts, attack on the age-old values of society and similar undignified practices in some advertisements are offensive to public morality and decency.
5. **Increase in the Cost of Product:** Advertising is sometimes done in such an expensive and unbalanced manner that it increases the cost of marketing and the price of products rather than reducing the prices. This puts heavy economic burden on the consumers. However, if advertising is managed properly, it can reduce the cost and price of products by ensuring large scale production.
6. **Wastage of National Resources:** A serious criticism against advertisement is that it is used to destroy the utility of goods before the end of their normal period of usefulness.

For example, new models of automobiles with nominal improvements are advertised at such high pressure that the old models have to be discarded before they become useless. Though one cannot entirely ignore the objections, which are raised against advertising, most of the drawbacks of advertising are inherent in the competitive system of the economy.

As a tool of promotion, advertising is unparallel in its appeal. However, the importance of advertising can be fully realized only if its abuses are stopped. In order to eliminate defects of advertising, the Government has come up with a number of measures. The usual measures that are applied may be stated as follows:

(*a*) Statutory ban on all obscene advertisements, as they offend public morality.

(*b*) Restrictions on noisy advertisements through the use of loudspeakers, etc., since they become a public nuisance and create sound pollution.

(*c*) Prohibition of writings on the walls and other public places.

(*d*) Regulatory laws by the Government to guard against deceptive advertising.

(*e*) Movements and actions on the part of consumer's association formed to protect consumer's interests against unethical advertising.

REVIEW QUESTIONS

1. What is meant by advertising? Explain the medium of advertising which has an audio-visual impact.
2. What is advertising? What purposes does advertising serve?
3. Explain briefly the term advertising and state its characteristics.
4. What are the main objectives of advertising? Explain in brief.
5. "Advertising plays an important role in business and society". Discuss.
6. Explain, in brief, the essentials of good advertising.
7. What is radio advertising? Enumerate its advantages and limitations.
8. Describe any three objectives of advertising.
9. Discuss various types of advertising appeals.
10. Explain the advertising strategies for the differing stages of the Product Life Cycle (PLC).
11. Describe the benefits or importance of advertisement.
12. Define the limitations of advertising.
13. Explain the essentials of effective advertising.
14. What are the steps in a scientific advertising campaign?

CHAPTER 12

Advertising Budget, Media and Public Relations

POINTS TO REMEMBER

At the end of this chapter, we will be able to understand:

- Introduction
- Meaning and Definition
- Advertising Budgeting Methods
- Advertisement Copy
- Essentials of Effective Advertisement Copy
- Elements of Advertising Copy
- Measurement of Advertising Effectiveness
- DAGMAR Model
- Methods of Advertising Evaluation
- Advertising Agencies
- Media
- Public Relations (PR)
- Objective of Public Relations
- Components of Public Relations
- Importance of Public Relations
- Developing a Marketing Public Relations Plan

12.1 INTRODUCTION

The advertising budget of a business is typically a subset of the larger sales budget and, within that, the marketing budget. Advertising is a part of the sales and marketing effort. Money spent on advertising can also be seen as an investment in building up the business. In order to keep the advertising budget in-line with promotional and marketing goals, a business owner should start by answering several important questions:

1. **Who is the Target Consumer?** Who is interested in purchasing the product or service, and what are the specific demographics of this consumer such as age, employment, sex, attitudes, etc?

2. **What Media Type will be Most Useful in Reaching the Target Consumer?** These days, a small or mid-sized business will not only consider print, radio, and television ads, but more importantly, perhaps the Internet as a way of reaching customers.
3. **What is Required to Get the Target Consumer to Purchase the Product?** Does the product lend itself to rational or emotional appeals? Which appeals are most likely to persuade the target consumer?
4. **What is the Relationship between Advertising Expenditures and the Impact of Advertising Campaigns on Product or Service Purchases?** In other words, how much profit is likely to be earned for each rupee spent on advertising?

12.2 MEANING AND DEFINITION

An advertising budget is a method whereby the advertiser uses test markets to examine the sales level and profitability of advertising spending levels that are higher and lower than the spending level currently being used by the advertiser. The advertiser may decide to adapt to either a higher or lower spending level depending on test market results.

"Advertising budget is the amount of money which can be or has to be spent on advertising of the product to promote it, reach the target consumers and make the sales chart go on the upper side and give reasonable profits to the company".

12.3 ADVERTISING BUDGETING METHODS

There are several allocation methods used in developing an advertising budget. The most common are listed below:

1. Percentage of Sales Method
2. Objective and Task Method
3. Competitive Parity Method
4. Market Share Method
5. Unit Sales Method
6. All Available Funds Method
7. Affordable Method

It is important to notice that most of these methods are often combined in any number of ways, depending on the situation. Because of this, these methods should not be seen as rigid, but rather as building blocks that can be combined, modified, or discarded as necessary. Remember, a business must be flexible—ready to change course, goals, and philosophy when the market and the consumer demand such a change.

1. **Percentage of Sales Method:** Due to its simplicity, the percentage of sales method is most commonly used by small businesses. When using this method an advertiser takes a percentage of either past or anticipated sales and allocates that percentage of the overall budget to advertising. Critics of this method, though, charge that using past sales for figuring the advertising budget is too conservative and that it can stunt growth. However, it might be safer for a small business to use this method if the ownership feels that future returns cannot be safely anticipated. On the other hand, an established business, with well-established profit trends, will tend to use anticipated sales when figuring advertising expenditures. This method can be especially effective if the business compares its sales with those of the competition (if available) while figuring its budget.
2. **Objective and Task Method:** The importance of objectives in business, the task and objective method is considered by many to make the most sense, and is therefore used by

most large businesses. The benefit of this method is that it allows the advertiser to correlate advertising expenditures to overall marketing objectives. This correlation is important because it keeps spending focussed on primary business goals.

With this method, a business needs to first establish concrete marketing objectives, which are often articulated in the "selling proposal," and then develop complimentary advertising objectives, which are articulated in the "positioning statement". After these objectives have been established, the advertiser determines how much it will cost to meet them. Of course, fiscal realities need to be figured into this methodology as well. Some objectives (expansion of area market share by 15 per cent within a year, for instance) may only be reachable through advertising expenditures that are beyond the capacity of a small business. In such cases, small business owners must scale down their objectives so that they reflect the financial situation under which they are operating.

3. **Competitive Parity Method:** While keeping one's own objectives in mind, it is often useful for a business to compare its advertising spending with that of its competitors. The theory here is that if a business is aware of how much its competitors are spending to inform, persuade, and remind (the three general aims of advertising) the consumer of their products and services, then that business can, in order to remain competitive, either spend more, the same, or less on its own advertising. However, as Alexander Hiam and Charles D. Schewe suggested, a business should not assume that its competitors have similar or even comparable objectives. While it is important for small businesses to maintain an awareness of the competition's health and guiding philosophies, it is not always advisable to follow a competitor's course.
4. **Market Share Method:** Similar to competitive parity, the market share method bases its budgeting strategy on external market trends. With this method a business equates its market share with its advertising expenditures. Critics of this method contend that companies that use market share numbers to arrive at an advertising budget are ultimately predicating their advertising on an arbitrary guideline that does not adequately reflect future goals.
5. **Unit Sales Method:** This method takes the cost of advertising an individual item and multiplies it by the number of units the advertiser wishes to sell.
6. **All Available Funds Method:** This aggressive method involves the allocation of all available profits to advertising purposes. This can be risky for a business of any size, for it means that no money is being used to help the business grow in other ways (purchasing new technologies, expanding the work force, etc.). Yet this aggressive approach is sometimes useful when a start-up business is trying to increase consumer awareness of its products or services. However, a business using this approach needs to make sure that its advertising strategy is an effective one, and that funds which could help the business expand are not being wasted.
7. **Affordable Method:** In this method, advertisers base their budgets on what they can afford. Of course, arriving at a conclusion about what a small business can afford in the realm of advertising is often a difficult task, one that needs to incorporate overall objectives and goals, competition, presence in the market, unit sales, sales trends, operating costs, and other factors.

12.4 ADVERTISEMENT COPY

An advertising copy, or ad copy, is the text form of an advertising message aimed at catching the attention, and persuading the prospective buyer to make a purchase, all within a short span of few seconds. A copy in essence describes the advertisement (irrespective of the medium of advertising) in words. A copy employs the use of words to promote a product, business, person, or an idea.

"Advertisement copy is the act of writing copy (text) for the purpose of advertising or marketing product, business, person, opinion or idea. The addressee (reader, listener, etc.) of the copy is meant to be persuaded to buy the product advertised for, or subscribe to the viewpoint the text shares".

Thus, advertising copy means advertising text, content or graphics intended for reproduction by the company as an advertisement.

12.5 ESSENTIALS OF EFFECTIVE ADVERTISEMENT COPY

An effective advertisement copy is the one which successfully draws attention of its target audience, creates a favourable attitude towards the product and induces action. As long as the advertiser knows the project or business the company is attempting to sell, and has in mind who the key demographic is, ad copy can be written effectively. A good copy should have the following basic requisites:

1. **Brief:** Most important criteria for copywriting is the ability to craft short, crisp yet extremely interesting lines. That's one major quality that copywriters often boast vis-a-vis the content writers. Since our attention span is getting shorter day-by-day and readers prefer short, crisp advertisements it's always recommended to keep the copy short and compact.
2. **Simple and Clear:** Advertisements are means of communication and not means of confusion. So avoid the temptation of writing big, mouthful heavy words for the sake of showing your words expertise. Advertisements should be easily comprehensible, and self-explanatory. Always try to avoid ambiguous, incorrect words.
3. **Appropriate:** Copy should never be irrelevant to the target audience or the product category. Often the copywriter overlooks consumers or the product and get obsessed with the ambition of crafting award winning lines. An effective ad carries copy which matches with its consumers' insight, product features and adds style of creativity. Objective of the advertisement is not to be forgotten.
4. **Personal:** An effective ad is the one which portrays that it is just talking to you. It carries personal touch words like 'you', 'yours' instead of a general message addressing all definitely works better.
5. **Attention:** Something that grabs the visitor's attention such as the keywords or keyword phrases.
6. **Action:** The goal of ad copy is always to get some kind of action or reaction out of the visitor. Whether it is to just visit a landing page, fill out a form, or actually purchases a product, the goal of most ad copy is the same, and involves some kind of action.
7. **Promise of Benefit:** Whether it is offering information or just a particular product, the ad copy generally has some promise of benefit for the visitor if he or she clicks on the link.
8. **Honesty:** Often advertising is accused of being manipulative and deceptive. But to remain in the business for a long run companies should always put forth honest and truthful communication. Communication can be wise and playful but not deceptive. It should not leave consumers with a false or wrong idea.

An effective and nicely crafted copy is the backbone of any advertising communication.

12.6 ELEMENTS OF ADVERTISING COPY

Ads come in all shapes and sizes but they have a common goal to sell a product, a service, a brand, text, visuals, or a combination of the two are the main elements of any print ad. An effective and nicely crafted copy is the backbone of any advertising communication.

1. **The Headline:** The first and possibly the most important copy element is the headline. The headline of an advertisement will normally present a selling idea or will otherwise serve to involve the prospect in reading of the advertisement. Most advertisements have headlines of one sort or another and their primary function is to catch the eye of the reader. A headline may be set in big type or small. Headlines need not always contain special messages. Even a company or brand name could be used as a headline.

   According to David Garfinkel, author of Advertising Headlines, an effective headline is a simple formula to present a statement that begs a question.
2. **The Subhead:** Sometimes important facts may have to be conveyed to the reader and it may require more space than what should be ideally used for the headline. In order to give prominence to such formation it can be put in smaller type than the headline, known as subhead. All advertisements do not require subheads.
3. **Slogan:** It is a phrase or a sentence that describes the benefit derived from the product or one of the product's most important attributes. It consists of a single phrase by which an advertiser conveys an important idea, which will most probably lead readers or audiences to remember and think favourably of this company. Slogan is thus a short and catchy phrase that gets the attention of the audience. It is easy to remember and comes off the tongue easily.
4. **Body:** The copy is the main text of the ad. Some ads may take the most minimal approach, a line or two or a single paragraph. Other ads may be quite text-heavy with paragraphs of information, possibly arranged in columns newspaper style. While the words are the most important part of the copy, visual elements such as indentation, pull quotes, bullet lists, and creative kerning and tracking can help to organize and emphasize the message of the body of the ad.
5. **Layout:** Layout has two meanings. One means the total appearance of the advertisement, its design, and the composition of the various elements. The other meaning is the act or process of placing the elements (copy, visuals, etc.) together. A layout could be the first pencil sketch, which puts the idea on paper or could also be the final piece after finishing touches.
6. **Contact:** The contact or signature of an ad may appear anywhere in the ad although it is usually near the bottom. It consists of one or more of:
   - Logo
   - Advertiser Name
   - Address
   - Phone Number
   - Map or Driving Directions
   - Website Address
7. **Extras:** Some print ads may have additional special elements such as an attached business reply envelope, tear-out portion with a coupon, tip sheet, product sample.

12.7 MEASUREMENT OF ADVERTISING EFFECTIVENESS

Measuring advertising effectiveness is not easy. Sometimes, the results of measuring are just better guesses. Still, it is much better this way than not to address this problem at all. There are dramatic differences in the effectiveness of various forms of advertising. If you pay for advertising, then it is probably important for you to see some results. But if you waste money on inefficient advertising, you are missing better opportunities and the results may not come at all.

According to Philip Kotler and Armstrong, there are two most popular areas which need to be measured for knowing the effectiveness of advertisements and they are:

1. Communication Effect

2. Sales Effect

1. **Communication Effect:** Advertising is basically a communication process. The effectiveness of advertising can be measured by how much the communication process has been useful in motivating consumers. The communication objectives, *i.e.*, establishing brand awareness, improving recall, increasing brand recognition, bringing about an attitude change, etc., can be measured because these are realistic. Advertising effectiveness is measured by its direct and immediate impact on consumer behaviour. The communication effect research consists of three types of researches:
   (*i*) **Direct rating method:** Here, customers are directly asked to rate the advertisement and then these ratings are calculated.
   (*ii*) **Portfolio tests:** Here, the customers see the ads and listen carefully to the ads and all the contents of the ads and then they are asked to recall the ad and the contents. Then the calculations are done with the help of this data.
   (*iii*) **Laboratory tests:** Here, the apparatus to measure the heart rates, blood pressure, perspiration, etc., are used on the customer after he watches the ad, to know the physiological reactions of the body.
2. **Sales Effect:** Sales effect research totally depends on the sales of the company. The sales keep varying from time to time. There are some factors affecting sales like product availability, the price of the product, contents of the product, and sometimes the competitors. So this method is a little difficult than the communication one. The company doing sales effect research generally bothers about the sales of the product, they try to know whether or not the money they are spending on the ads is enough or excess.

   As earlier said, it is not possible to measure each and everything and the chances are at the lower end if the company has many ads running through various mediums at the same time. So the suggestion is that the advertiser or the company should use appropriate and different methods which are most suitable for the media under use.

   - The company can hold surveys and product recognition tests.
   - Questionnaire or feedback flyers can be distributed and customers could be asked to fill it up.
   - Toll free number can be highlighted on the ads so that customers can call up.
   - The response rates can be increased by telling customers what to do. For example, some ads have lines in flashy colour like "Hurry Up" or "No one can eat just one" or "be the first" etc.

These are the traditional ways. Nowadays, internet is the modern tool for measuring the effectiveness of an advertisement. There are some types such as:

(*i*) **Integrated direct marketing:** This is an internet-based tool where they have a response corner designed on the websites. Whenever the customers visit the sites, they fill up their contact details and give feedback. Thus the company supplies more information and sends newsletters and also gets the idea for further action. But then it is not that only online advertisers have this facility but then advertisers who do not work online can use coupons, discount vouchers, etc., to do this.

(*ii*) **Analysis tool:** There is an analysis tool available on Internet by using which the advertiser will know how many customers are visiting the site, who are shopping online, how many pages are viewed, etc. which in turn will help an advertiser to measure the effectiveness.

Internet is the most easy, and cost-effective way to measure the effectiveness because here no money is wasted as the ad is only viewed when the customer wants to view it whereas in normal print method or using TV, the ad sometimes goes unwatched or unattended and viewed for the sake of viewing.

12.8 DAGMAR MODEL

Russell Colley (1961) developed a model for setting advertising objectives and measuring the results. This model was entitled **'Defining Advertising Goals for Measured Advertising Results—DAGMAR'.**

DAGMAR is much more than a model for designing an advertisement, it is used to monitor and evaluate promotion campaigns. There are three parts to the DAGMAR advertising model.

- The first part is to define advertising goals so that results and therefore campaign effectiveness can be measured.
- The second part of the model comprises four stages that customers pass through before they buy a product or service. The four steps in the DAGMAR advertising model are: awareness, comprehension, conviction and action.
- The final part is to measure advertising results.

1. DAGMAR Step One: Defining Advertising Goals

It is important to understand that DAGMAR is aimed at setting advertising goals and not more general marketing goals. Elements of a good advertising goal include being a written, measurable task involving a starting point, a defined audience, and a time limit. To measure the effectiveness of advertising, a business must know the current state before advertising starts and then the new state after the campaign has finished. This means surveying the target audience to measure current awareness, comprehension and conviction. This helps to establish realistic goals for the campaign. For example, to increase product awareness from 10% to 35%.

2. DAGMAR Step Two: Awareness, Comprehension, Conviction and Action

The second part of the DAGMAR model attempts to explain the process customers go through before they buy a product. The process is as follows:

(*i*) **Awareness:** Awareness of the existence of a product or organization is necessary before the purchase behaviour can be expected. Once the awareness has been created in the target audience, it should not be neglected. If there is neglect, the audience may become distracted by competing messages and the level of awareness of focus product or organization will decline. Awareness needs to be created, developed, refined or sustained, according to the characteristics of the market and the particular situation facing an organization at any one point of time.

(*ii*) **Comprehension:** Awareness on its own may not be sufficient to stimulate a purchase. Knowledge about the product or the organization is necessary. This can be achieved by providing specific information about key brand attributes.

In attempting to persuade people to try a different brand of water, it may be necessary to compare the product with other mineral water products and provide an additional usage benefit, such as environmental claims. The ad of the Ganga mineral water, featuring Govinda, banked on the purity aspect. It related the purity of the water with that of the river Ganga.

(*iii*) **Conviction:** The next step is to establish a sense of conviction. By creating interest and preference, buyers are moved to a position where they are convinced that a particular product in the class should be tried at the next opportunity. To do this, audience's beliefs about the product have to be moulded and this is often done through messages that demonstrate the product's superiority over a rival or by talking about the rewards as a result of using the product. Many ads like Thumbs Up featured the reward of social acceptance as 'grown up'. It almost hinted that those who preferred other drinks were kids.

(*iv*) **Action:** Communication must finally encourage buyers to engage in purchase activity. Advertising can be directive and guide the buyers into certain behavioural outcomes. Use of toll free numbers, direct mail activities and reply cards and coupons. Tupperware, Aqua Guard, are famous in Indian cities as a result of personal selling efforts. For high involvement decisions, the most effective tool in the communication mix at this stage in the hierarchy is personal selling. Through the use of interpersonal skills, buyers are more likely to want to buy a product than if personal prompting is absent.

3. DAGMAR Step Three: Measure Advertising Effectiveness

In step one of the DAGMAR advertising model, goals were established for the campaign. The final step is to measure the results and effectiveness of the campaign by evaluating whether the goals were met or not. This may require another survey to measure awareness comprehension and conviction levels.

Advertising can be an important part of marketing for small business and understanding advertising models such as Awareness, Interest, Desire and Action (AIDA) and DAGMAR can help improve marketing effectiveness.

12.9 METHODS OF ADVERTISING EVALUATION

Marketers have a choice for conducting either pre-test evaluation, *i.e.*, before the campaign has been implemented or post-test evaluation, *i.e.*, after the advertisement campaign has been released or both together. As shown in Fig. 12.1 are the areas where research can be done for pre-testing as well as post-testing advertisement effectiveness.

1. **Pre-testing Techniques:** Pre-testing can be done as early as the time when only an idea is being considered for an advertisement. The testing can also be done in the later stages where a preview of advertisement is shown to a selected group of viewers to gauge their reaction before the advertisement is released on a large scale. Let us discuss the pre-testing techniques for evaluating both print and broadcast advertisements.

   (A) Pre-testing print advertisements: There are numerous popular techniques used by researchers to pre-test print advertisements.

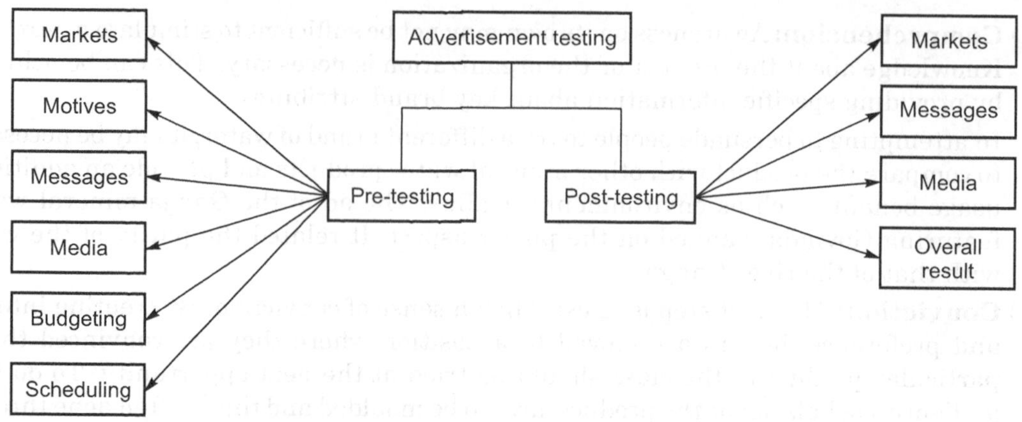

Fig. 12.1. Areas of evaluation in pre-testing and post-testing.

(*i*) ***Consumer jury:*** Consumer reaction has greater validity than the reactions of non-consumers. Consumers can provide true information on reactions to an advertising campaign. Others may underestimate or overestimate the reactions. The copy, illustrations, filming techniques, layout, etc., can be properly evaluated by the consumers concerned with the product. The consumer jury technique is adopted for print media, broadcast media and direct mail. There are common variations of the consumer jury test:

(*a*) *Order of merit test:* This test seeks to obtain a ranking given by the potential prospects to the test advertisement. The test hopes to have a consensus ultimately, about the best advertisement, even though the advertisement with the highest ranking may turn out to be the best among the worst ones.

(*b*) *Paired comparison:* The paired comparison attempts a one to one comparison between the test advertisements. The technique is easier to use than the order of merit method.

(*c*) *Portfolio test:* The technique of portfolio test seeks to mix the test advertisements with other regular advertisements. The potential consumers and audience are divided into two groups called experimental group and control group. While the experimental group is shown the large portfolio containing test advertisements with regular ones, the control group evaluates the advertisement portfolio without the test advertisements. Later a recall test is conducted to determine reactions to the test advertisements.

(*ii*) ***Mock magazine:*** It is a variation of portfolio method and uses a real magazine instead of portfolio created for testing. The method, also dubbed as too-in method, introduces test advertisements in a magazine for an experimental group to read. The magazine is like any normal one. The control group will read the same magazine but un-tempered by the introduction of test advertisements.

(*iii*) ***Direct questioning:*** The technique of direct questioning, on the other hand, seeks full answers to such questions as to what test advertisements say. What could be the purpose of advertising? etc. It seeks meaningful reactions to test advertisements.

(*iv*) ***Perceptual meaning studies:*** The Perceptual Meaning Studies (PMS) uses time-exposures to test the advertisements. It may use electronic tachistoscope presentation instrument. The respondents see the test advertisement for a predetermined time. Later, they are questioned on the recall of product, brand illustration copy and the main advertisement copy. This exercise may be repeated several times over to gain further reaction/response.

(*v*) ***Storyboard tests:*** The storyboard prepared for television advertising is tested before it is used. The storyboard pictures are transferred to a film strip and the audio section onto a tape. Vision and sound are synchronized and shown to an audience for evaluation. This test uncovers the unnecessary part. The important part of advertising is accepted for telecasting. The anteroom trailer method is used to test the commercial. The anteroom contains magazines, newspapers, distractions and television recorded programme.

(*vi*) ***Focus group:*** This technique is very familiar and quite useful in the present context as well. Focus group involves interviewing a group of people from the target audience who discusses candidly about the particular product or service. Focus group helps the advertiser and the agency as it provides direct contact with the consumers. Although focus group has its limitation it is very popular as an evaluation method.

(B) Pre-testing broadcast advertisements: Besides the ones noted above, a number of other methods are used to pre-test radio and television commercials.

(*i*) ***In-house projection tests:*** In-house projection test is also called the 'Black-Box' method, it uses a small movie projector (16 MM) to run test commercials at respondents' homes. The respondents are questioned before and after the exposure, on ad-related questions to measure change caused by the exposure. It thus, provides an early evaluation of strengths and weaknesses of the advertisement.

(*ii*) ***Trailer tests:*** Trailers are shown as commercials at shopping centers and the prospects are given discount coupons for the advertised products.

(*iii*) ***Theatre tests:*** The theatre test is the most popular method for evaluating test advertisements. The test offers captive audience for entertainment. Here, respondents selected on a random basis, may be sent a questionnaire to fill up. Later, they are sent free tickets to the programme where test advertisements are run. Once they have viewed, another set of questions would be mailed to them to find their assessment of the product, brand and advertisement theme.

(*iv*) ***Live telecast ads:*** The live telecast test commercials are shown at electronic TV or cable and subsequently respondents are interviewed on the phone.

(C) Other additional pre-testing techniques: The list of additional pre-testing techniques available at the discretion of marketers include:

(*i*) ***Sales experiments:*** Alternative TV or radio commercials are run in two or more markets and then compared.

(*ii*) ***Direct mail tests:*** The direct mail test is used through the mail. The post cards containing copy appeal, each with a reply-paid card, is sent free-of-cost to consumers, who are required to give their evaluation.

(*iii*) ***Pupil dilation test:*** In this we observe the pupil of the eye. It can widen when it sees something interesting and shrinks if the advertisement depicts violence or unpleasant things. It measures the dilation. The instrument is known as the pupilometer. The eyes of the respondents are watched to study the interest. If the pupil expands and the respondent opens his eyes widely, it shows his interest in the product. If the pupil contracts and the respondent tends to contract his eyes then he is disinterested in the scene shown.

(*iv*) ***Movement of the eye:*** The movement of the eyes is also an indicator of the interest of the respondent.

(*v*) ***Galvanic test:*** A galvanometer is used to indicate the gland activity, tension or the sweating of hands, etc., change in perspiration indicates the change in emotions. One can have different emotions by seeing a sexy object or a fight or a dramatic scene. This change in emotion is reflected on the galvanometer.

(*vi*) ***Tachistoscope:*** The method evaluates the physical perception of the subject under varying conditions of speed, exposure and illumination. It controls the subject's exposure to an advertising message with a view to find out how long it takes the respondent to reach the intended point of headline, body text and illustration.

(*vii*) ***Voice variations:*** The pitch of the voice changes with emotional responses.

2. **Post-testing techniques:** Post-testing techniques of evaluating advertisements aim to determine what awareness or attitude changes have been achieved and what impact the advertising has had on the sales results. Following are the major categories of post-testing techniques:

(*i*) ***Recall tests:*** A recall test depends on the memory of the respondents. This test is applied to measure the impression made by an advertisement on the reader's mind. It is classified into two types – aided recall and unaided recall. Some have combined the two and made it a combined recall test.

(*a*) *Aided recall:* It is used to measure the reading memory of magazine advertising impressions. It is necessary to use a large sample size for statistical reliability. The aided test measures television advertising. The interviewer may approach the respondents over the telephone or in person to find out something about their recall of the commercial. A radio advertisement may be given the aided recall test followed by an unaided question.

(*b*) *Unaided recall:* Under this method, little or no aid is given. The purpose is to measure the penetration of the advertisement. Respondents are asked whether the advertisements included a particular picture or message. The name of the product is not given to the audience. They have to recall it themselves.

(*c*) *Combined recall tests:* It includes aided as well as unaided recall tests. This test was developed by Gallup and Robinson. Respondents are asked whether they have read the magazine or newspaper, or listened to the radio or watched television. In this technique the information on age, sex, education, occupation, etc., may establish a relationship between these factors and recall. This method measures the recall of qualified readers to assess the depth of penetration achieved by the advertised message.

(*ii*) ***Recognition test:*** This is conducted to see whether the advertisement is recognized or not. This test can be conducted by mail surveys. The ad can be broken into headlines, layouts, body, copy, logo etc. and it is seen how these elements are remembered by the respondents. The recognition test can be conducted in a number of ways. The magazines are placed in the home of the respondents and they are requested to read that magazine on that day. Next day they are asked questions about the ad appearing in those magazines to assess the recall of ads.

(*iii*) ***Attitude test:*** This test measures the change in the attitude of a potential buyer towards a company, its products, or brands as a result of its advertising. It is assumed that purchases are often preceded by a favourable attitude. The tests can be done in conjunction with recall/recognition tests and may use direct questioning or some indirect story build up. There are several techniques for the measurement of attitude change after the advertising has ended. These techniques are as follows:

(*a*) *Semantic differential:* It is used to measure attitude in the field of marketing and advertising research. It uses a bi-polar (opposite) adjective statement about the subject of evaluation. The attitude is measured in the light of some objectives. The two-way scale is used for the purpose. The neutral is mid-point, while the three points on both the sides of the neutral point, on the same scale, provide the degree of favourable and unfavourable characteristics.

(*b*) *The likert scale:* The Likert scale is used to measure audience attitude to advertisements.

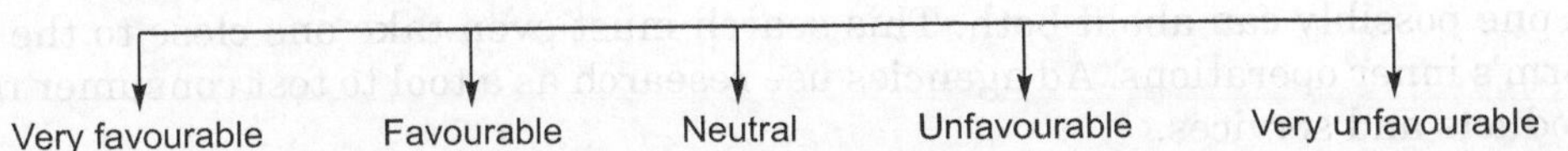

A series of statements are described to measure the attributes of the advertisement. Only the relevant statements are used for the purpose. Each statement is measured on a five-point scale.

(*c*) *Ranking techniques:* The preferences to several types of advertisements are ranked to find out the place of a particular advertisement among the several advertisements. An advertisement of one product can be measured with the advertisements of other products taken together. This is done to find out the effectiveness of the advertisement in a competitive atmosphere. The winner may be given rank 1 and loser is given rank 5. The ranking is based on awareness, interest, attitude change, attractiveness, usefulness, entertaining, respect, effectiveness, etc. A sufficient number of consumers are selected for a sample survey. The overall rank is summed up to determine the final rank of the advertisement of the brand.

(*d*) *Projective techniques:* It is used to measure attitude change. Association techniques, completion techniques, construction techniques and expressive techniques are used to measure the change in attitude.

(*iv*) ***Enquiry tests:*** Many advertisements particularly those of consumer durables, electronic products and B2B products, tour package advertisements carry a reply coupon offering a free demonstration or more details. The number of enquiries received as a result of the advertisement, indicates the effectiveness of the advertisement. It enables the advertiser to develop the cost of inquiry and help in designing its sales force decisions.

12.10 ADVERTISING AGENCIES

An advertising agency or ad agency is a service business dedicated to create, plan and handle advertising for its clients. An ad agency is independent from the client and provides an outside point of view to the effort of selling the client's products or services. An agency can also handle overall marketing and branding strategies and sales promotions for its clients.

12.10.1 Functions of Advertising Agencies

Today advertising agencies are found in virtually every major city in the world and their role in stimulating economic growth is solidly established. To understand advertising, we need to examine the functions of an ad agency. These are:

1. **Talent and Creative Productions:** The basic function of an ad agency is providing talent. The creative efforts of the art director, the detailed analysis of the research director and the political understanding of the campaign director, are just a few examples of the many abilities of the ad agency personnel have to offer. A business organization or person will contract the services of an ad agency to help market a product. This function involves processing the information collected from the client and through research and designing communication material in the form of advertisements and other publicity material. This also includes planning creative strategies, copy or script writing, visualization, designing, layout, shooting of films, editing, giving music, etc.
2. **Research:** The second function of an ad agency is research. In order to distribute the message to the public successfully, the agency must first know all that it can about the product. One of the first jobs is to research the product and the company, one must learn, what one possibly can about both. This search must even take one close to the heart of the firm's inner operations. Ad agencies use research as a tool to test consumer reactions to products and services.
3. **Distribution and Media Planning:** The third important function of an ad agency is distribution. Here you decide what type of message you will create for the company and what media will be most helpful in sending this message to the public. On the basis of the media habits of the target audience, agency people prepare a media plan. This plan includes which media to be used, which part of the media to be used, when to place the ads and for how long to place the ads, etc. Media planners keep track of the viewership, listenership and readership of all kinds of media.
4. **Monitoring Feedback:** By monitoring consumer feedback, a decision on whether to revise the message, the medium, the target audience or all of them can be made. Ad agencies are developing to reach the target audience.

As information is the backbone of all advertising, to prepare ads, one requires information about the product, its competitors, the market situation and trends, information about the audiences (their likes and dislikes and media habits) also need to be collected. Some of the most effective advertising includes advertisements written in their native language. All of these specialized campaigns are creating new demands on agencies and are requiring new talents for people who work in advertising.

12.10.2 Types of Advertising Agencies

Agencies can be classified by the range of services that they offer. Also advertising agencies range in size from one man shows to large firms that employ thousands of people. Accordingly, different types of advertising agencies are:

1. **Full-service Agencies:** As the name implies, a full service agency is one that handles all phases of advertising process for its clients: it plans, creates, produces and places advertisements for its clients. In addition, it might provide other marketing services such as sales promotion, trade shows, exhibits, newsletters and annual reports. In short a full service agency will provide four major functions—count management, creative development and production, media planning and buying and research services.

   One major point that differentiates a full service agency from another is that the personal work full time and the services provided are extensive. The services usually provided by a full service agency include collecting and analyzing market data, proposing strategy, preparing and producing the ads, placing the ads in approved media, verifying the advertisements appearance (publication, broadcasting, etc.), invoicing the client, collecting the bills and paying the media and other suppliers.

2. **Creative Boutiques:** It is an organization that specializes in the actual creation of advertisements. In general, boutiques create imaginative and interesting advertising themes and produce innovative and original advertisements. A company that uses a creative boutique would have to employ another agency to perform the planning, buying and administrative functions connected with advertising. Full service ad agency studies the product or service and determines its marketable characteristic and how it relates to the competition. At the same time the agency studies the potential market, possible distribution plans and likely advertising media. Following this, the agency makes a formal presentation to the client deadlines, its finding about the product and its recommendation for an advertising strategy. Creative boutiques are different from freelancers. Freelancers are individuals who work on their own without any formal attachment with any agency. Clients or agencies hire these from time to time. The clients also hire creative boutiques.
3. **In-house Agencies:** Such agencies are owned and supervised by advertisers or the client organizations. The organizational structure and functioning of in-house agencies are similar to full service agencies in most cases. The advertising director of the company usually heads an in-house agency. In-house agencies are organized according to the needs and requirements of the company and are staffed accordingly. Some companies solely depend on their in-house agencies for their advertising needs. Others depend both on their in-house agency and outside agencies. Some other companies allow their agencies to take outside jobs.
4. **Specialized Agencies:** There are many agencies, which take up only specialized advertising jobs. Certain fields like medicine, finance, outdoor advertising, social advertising, etc., require specialized knowledge. So there are agencies, which concentrate only on areas and employ people with the required talents. These agencies are usually small in size.
5. **Media Buying Agencies:** It is an organization that specializes in buying radio and television time and reselling it to advertisers and advertising agencies. The services sell time to the advertisers, order the spots on the various stations involved and monitor the stations to see if the ads actually run. This trend for special media buying agencies started in the 1970s. Such agencies have a lot of contacts in the media and offer very low commission on media rates. Media buying agencies complement the creative boutiques. Also large companies use their specialized negotiating talents for buying media space and time.

12.10.3 Structure of Advertising Agencies

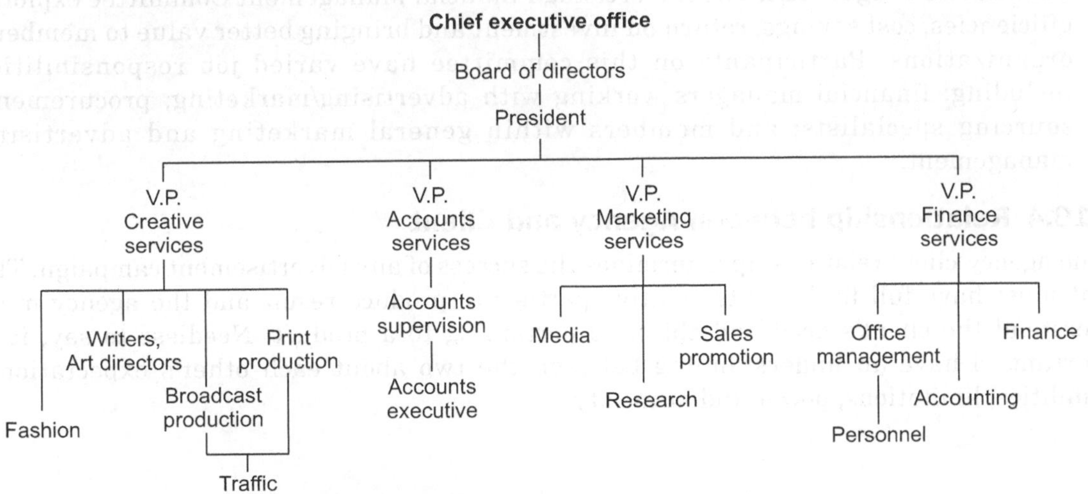

Fig. 12.2. Structure of advertising agencies.

As shown in the above Fig. 12.2, the four functional groupings are:

1. Creative Services,
2. Accounts Services,
3. Marketing Services,
4. Finance Management.

1. **Creative Services:** The creative functions are the most important of all. These people are directly involved in creating the advertising message. The principle role of account managers is to manage the overall advertising campaign for a client, which often includes delegating selective tasks to specialists. For large accounts which task account managers routinely delegate, involve generating ideas, designing concepts and creating the final advertisement, which generally becomes the responsibility of the agency's creative team. An agency's creative team consists of specialists in graphic design, film and audio production, copywriting, computer programming, and much more.
2. **Accounts Services:** Within an advertising agency the account manager or account executive is tasked with handling all major decisions related to a specific client. These responsibilities include locating and negotiating to acquire clients. Once the client has agreed to work with the agency, the account manager works closely with the client to develop an advertising strategy. For very large clients, such as large consumer products companies, an advertising agency may assign an accounts manager to work full-time with only one client and, possibly, with only one of the client's product lines. For smaller accounts an accounts manager may simultaneously manage several different, though non-competing, accounts.
3. **Marketing Services:** Marketing services include selection and evaluation of advertising media for advertising campaign, media scheduling, test marketing, marketing researches, planning and managing sales promotion programmes etc. This department is manned by media planners and buyers, research directors, marketing advisers, traffic managers and public relations people.
4. **Finance Management:** The Advertising Financial Management Committee explores efficiencies, cost savings, return on investment and bringing better value to members' organizations. Participants on this committee have varied job responsibilities including: financial managers working with advertising/marketing; procurement/ sourcing specialists; and members within general marketing and advertising management.

12.10.4 Relationship between Agency and Client

The agency-client relationship determines the success of any advertisement campaign. The client must have full faith on its creative partner to produce result and the agency must understand the client's need and objective pertaining to a product. Needless to say, it is important to have an understanding between the two about each other's expectations, capabilities, limitations, power and authority.

Table 12.1: Agencies and Client Expectations

Agencies Expectations	*Client's Expectations*
• Be enthusiastic and straightforward, • Have an ambition to be a good client, • Involve management, • Change people not agency, • Make good use of agency's resources, • Provide good feedback and recognition, • Treat the agency like a strategic thought partner, • Consider advertising vital for business success.	• Creativity and high service quality, • Quality of people assigned to accounts, • Willingness of agency to apply recommendations and critique, • Trustworthiness, • Range of services offered.

As suggested by Bovee and Arens, the agency-client relationship, like most of other business relationship goes through four stages:

1. **Pre-relationship:** The time period when the client is scouting for an agency and the agency is looking for new business. This phase constitutes the period when both discuss the possibility of a business venture.
2. **Development:** Once the account is given to an agency, the so called honeymoon period begins where both the parties are highly optimistic about developing mutually benefiting mechanisms.
3. **Maintenance:** As the word suggests it is the day to day maintenance of the working relationship of the agency and client which if successful can continue for many years or else fizzle out.
4. **Termination:** It is possible that campaigns did not work out or some other irreconciliable difference comes up, due to which the two part company, *i.e.*, decide that its time to move on. A harmonious parting keeps the option of working together, again, open.

12.10.5 Selection of an Advertising Agency

An advertising agency may be a full-service agency or part-service agency. Each has a different outlook and advertising activities. The selection of advertising agencies depends on whether a client wants a full-service agency or a part-time agency. The selection is made on the basis of compatibility of the agency team, agency stability, services, credibility and the agency's problem solving approach. When the advertising or the marketing managers go about selecting an advertising agency, they generally follow the following steps:

1. **Full-service Agency or Part-time Agency:** The full-service agency is involved completely in the advertising functions. It has a large number of expert employees. It looks upon customers as key clients. It communicates with the prospective purchasers. The distinguishing characteristics of the various agencies lie in the creative skills of the personnel of each organization and in the philosophy of advertising. Larger agencies offer better services.

   The part-time agency offers service on free of cost or project basis. These agencies perform various outside activities and co-ordinate the activities of the advertiser and media men. Clients have greater control over advertising campaigns. Advertiser's research agencies generally perform the job of part-time agencies. The selection of a particular agency depends on its size, its services, knowledge and growth.

2. **Compatibility:** The selection of an advertising agency depends on the compatibility of the agency. The needs of the company determine the fitness of the agency. The advertiser visits several agencies and chooses the best agency on the basis of its merits, demerits, accreditation, its methods of handling the accounts and using the available opportunities.
3. **Agency Team:** This includes management specialists, market researchers, copywriters, media experts, production managers and art directors. The attitude, thinking, experience and personalities of the team members have positive effects on the selection process.
4. **Agency Stability:** An agency, which has been long in existence generally, performs efficiently and effectively. The greater the investment in the agency, the more vital the contribution of the agency to the advertising activities. The personnel, finance, management and credit are examined before selecting a suitable advertising agency.
5. **Services:** The services rendered by the agency are evaluated with a view to choose the best advertising agency. Cost accounting, general agreements, project estimates, selling attitudes and other services performed by the advertising agencies are considered to evaluate their efficiency and credibility in performing advertising jobs. The greater the range of an agency's services, the more fully it can serve the clients' needs. The agency can serve the clients by its potential capacity for advertising, sales promotion, media placement, public relations, market research, sales training and distribution channels.
6. **Creativity:** Creativity is the main element in advertising. If the advertising agency is capable of great creative efforts, it is selected for the purpose. Style, clarity, impact, memorability and action—these are taken into account while evaluating creativity.
7. **Problem Solving Approach:** The agency which has a problem solving approach is considered to be superior and useful. The importance of choosing the right agency cannot be ignored. Calibre, compatibility, balanced services, responsiveness, talent, an equitable compensation—these are important factors in selecting an advertising agency. A few general parameters that the client looks for while choosing an ad agency are as follows:
   - Agencies knowledge of the advertising process
   - Agencies knowledge of the product category
   - Client's basis of experience with the ad agency
   - Client's knowledge of the abilities of the agency
   - The chemistry between the agency and the client with respect to the kind of interaction between them, the understanding of mutual needs, etc.

12.10.6 Agency Compensation

The advertising agencies are paid for creative work. The method of paying the agency has been subject of much discussion. There are, basically, three methods in practice. These are:

1. **Commission System:** The traditional method of compensating agencies is through a commission system, where the agency receives a specified commission (usually 15 per cent) from the media on any advertising time or space it purchases for its clients.

   For example, assume an agency prepares a full-page magazine ad and arranges to place the ad on the back cover of a magazine at a cost of ₹ 1,00,000/-. The agency places the order for the space and delivers the ad to the magazine. Once the ad is run, the magazine will bill the agency for ₹ 1,00,000/- less the 15 per cent (₹ 15,000/-) commission. The media will also offer a 2 per cent cash discount for early payment, which the agency may pass along to the client. The agency will bill the client ₹ 1,00, 000/-, less 2% cash discount on the net amount, or a total of ₹ 98,300/-. The ₹ 15,000/- commission represents the agency's commission for its services.

2. **Fee System:** The fee system is basically a cost-plus system which breeds inefficiencies, the commission system is a discipline on the agency to keep down costs. The fee system could lead to a price war between agencies and thus a skimping of services to clients. It could also lead to a deterioration in the standards of advertising. The fee system is complicated to administer and needs to be constantly reviewed. The settling of fees can lead to friction between agencies and their clients. With a fee system media cutbacks are no longer all savings—the agencies fee still has to be paid.
3. **Service Charges:** The services charges are added cost of materials, and services brought by the agency for the client in artwork, photography, typography, plates, etc. Generally, it is cost plus 15 per cent.

In practice, one of the above systems of compensation, or a combination of the fee-and-media commission plan, or a method by which commissions granted by the media are credited against professional fees, is used. Industrial advertising, involving the preparation of catalogues and sales materials, and retail advertising, point-of-purchase materials for advertising and direct-mail prices do not usually involve a commission.

12.11 MEDIA

Advertising is the promotion of a company's products and services carried out primarily to drive up sales of the products and services. It is also done to build a brand identity and communicate changes in old products or introduce new product/services to the customers. Advertising has become an essential element of the corporate world and hence companies allot a considerable amount of resources towards their advertising budget. There are several reasons for advertising, some of which are as follows:

- Increasing the sales of the product/service
- Creating and maintaining a brand identity or brand image
- Communicating a change in the existing product line
- Introduction of a new product or service
- Increasing the buzz-value of the brand or the company.

12.11.1 Types of Media

The media are classified into two parts as shown in Fig. 12.3.

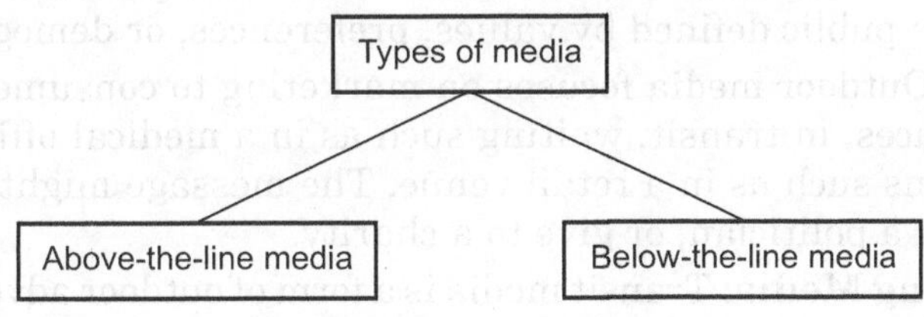

Fig. 12.3. Types of media.

1. **Above-the-line Media:** The recognized agencies get commission from these media. The examples are: Press, TV, outdoor posters, cinema and radio.
2. **Below-the–line Media:** Those who do not give commission to the ad agency. The agency adds a percentage as a handling or profit change. The example is: Direct mail, Point-of-Sale (POS), sales promotion, merchandising, exhibition and sales literature.

The following are the various types of media available to a media buyer or an advertiser:

1. **Print Media:** Print media is a very commonly used medium of advertising by businessmen. It includes advertising through newspapers, magazines, journals, etc., and is also called press advertising.
   (*i*) **Newspapers:** You must have read newspapers. In our country newspapers are published in English, Hindi and in other regional languages. These are the sources of news, opinions and current events. In addition, newspapers are also a very common medium of advertising. The advertiser communicates his message through newspapers which reach to crores of people.
   (*ii*) **Magazines:** These are publications which come out regularly but not on a daily basis. These may be published on a weekly, fortnightly, monthly, bimonthly, quarterly or even yearly basis. For example you must have come across magazines and journals like *Outlook, India Today, Business Today, Frontline, Yojana, Swagat, Femina,* etc., published regularly in English, *Aaha Zindagi, Grihasobha, Sarita, Nandan and Champak* in Hindi.
   (*iii*) **Direct advertising:** Direct advertising is a strategy aimed at reaching consumers without the need for some type of intermediary to establish the connection. The process of direct advertising calls for using various sales and marketing tools to present consumers with the opportunity to do business directly with the company. In order to accomplish this goal, direct advertising can take on several forms.
2. **Broadcast Media:** This includes radio, television and narrow cast-media.
   (*i*) **Radio:** All of us are aware of a radio and must have heard advertisements for various products in it. In radio there are short breaks during transmission of any programme which is filled by advertisements of products and services. There are also popular programmes sponsored by advertisers.
   (*ii*) **Television:** With rapid growth of information technology and electronic media, television has topped the list among the media of advertising. TV has the most effective impact as it appeals to both eye and ear. Products can be shown, their uses can be demonstrated and their utilities can be told over television. Just like radio, advertisements are shown in TV during short breaks and there are also sponsored programmes by advertisers.
   (*iii*) **Narrow-cast-media:** Narrow-casting involves aiming media messages at specific segments of the public defined by values, preferences, or demographic attributes.
3. **Outdoor Media:** Outdoor media focuses on marketing to consumers when they are on the go in public places, in transit, waiting such as in a medical office, and/or in specific commercial locations such as in a retail venue. The message might be to buy a product, take a trip, vote for a politician, or give to a charity.
4. **Transit Advertising Media:** Transit media is a form of outdoor advertising that displays advertisements in or outside of vehicles. A typical installation will display advertisements on the side of, on, or above the seats of a bus or passenger train car. Generally transit media campaigns are employed in denser urban environments to advertise to both pedestrian and on-road traffic. The medium has traditionally been limited to featured advertisements on buses and trams, but in recent years has extended to various sub-categories, such as dedicated car, van or truck advertising.
5. **Other Media:** Some of such advertising are internet, hoardings, posters, vehicular displays, gift items, etc.

(*i*) **Internet:** When we do not have website addresses we take help of search engines or portals. In almost all the search engines or portals different manufacturers or service providers advertise their products.

(*ii*) **Hoardings:** While moving on roads you must have seen large hoardings placed on iron frames or roof tops or walls. These are normally boards on which advertisements are painted or electronically designed so that they are visible during day or night. The advertisers have to pay an amount to the owners of the space, where the hoardings are placed.

(*iii*) **Posters:** Posters are printed and posted on walls, buildings, bridges, etc., to attract the attention of customers. Posters of films which are screened on cinema halls are a common sight in our country.

(*iv*) **Vehicular displays:** You must have seen advertisements on the public transport like buses, trains, etc. Unlike hoardings these vehicles give mobility to advertisements and cover a large number of people.

(*v*) **Gift items from manufacturers:** Sometimes manufacturers give diaries, calendars, purse, etc., to buyers and prospective customers. In all these items the name, address and telephone number of the manufacturer, or trader or service provider as well as descriptions of the products in which they deal in are printed. These items are normally items of daily use given freely to the customers. While using, the user remembers the products as well as the producer.

Comparison Profiles of Major Media Types

Medium	*Advantages*	*Limitations*
Newspapers	Flexibility; timeliness; good local market coverage; broad acceptability; high believability	Short life; poor reproduction quality; small pass-along audience
Television	Good mass market coverage; low cost per exposure; combines sight, sound, and motion; appealing to the senses	High absolute costs; high clutter; fleeting exposure; less audience selectivity
Direct mail	High audience selectivity; flexibility; no ad competition within the same medium; allows personalization	Relatively high cost per exposure; "junk mail" image
Radio	Good local acceptance; high geographic and demographic selectivity; low cost	Audio only, fleeting exposure; low attention (the "half-heard" medium); fragmented audiences
Magazines	High and demographic selectivity; credibility and prestige; high-quality reproduction; long-life and good pass-along readership	Long ad purchase lead time; high cost; no guarantee of position
Outdoor	Flexibility; high repeat exposure; low cost; low message competition; good positional selectivity	Little audience selectivity, creative limitations
Online	High selectivity; low cost; immediacy; interactive capabilities.	Small, demographically skewed audience; relatively low impact; audience controls exposure.

12.11.2 Media Plan

Media planning is generally the task of a media agency and entails finding the most appropriate media platforms for a client's brand or product. The job of media planning involves several areas of expertise that the media planner uses to determine what the best combination of media is to achieve the given marketing campaign objectives. In the process of planning the media planner needs to answer questions such as:

1. How many of the audience can I reach through different media?
2. On which media (and ad vehicles) should I place ads?
3. Which frequency should I select?
4. How much money should be spent in each medium?

In answering these questions the media planner then comes to an optimum media plan that enables him or her to deliver on the client's objectives. The three components of a media plan are as follows:

1. **Defining the Marketing Problem:** Do you know where your business is coming from and where the potential for increased business lies? Do you know which markets offer the greatest opportunity? Do you need to reach everybody or only a select group of consumers? How often is the product used? How much product loyalty exists?
2. **Translating the Marketing Requirements into Attainable Media Objectives:** Do you want to reach lots of people in a wide area? Then mass media, like newspaper and radio, might work for you. If your target market is a select group in a defined geographic area, then direct mail could be your best bet.
3. **Defining a Media Solution by Formulating Media Strategies:** Certain schedules work best with different media. For example, the rule of thumb is that a print ad must run three times before it gets noticed. Radio advertising is most effective when run at certain times of the day or around certain programmes, depending on what market you are trying to reach. Advertising media generally include:
   - Television
   - Radio
   - Internet
   - Newspapers
   - Magazines (consumer and trade)
   - Outdoor billboards
   - Public transportation
   - Yellow pages
   - Direct mail
   - Speciality advertising (on items such as matchbooks, pencils, calendars, telephone pads, shopping bags and so on)
   - Other media (catalogues, samples, handouts, brochures, newsletters and so on).

While comparing the cost and effectiveness of various advertising media, consider the following factors:

- **Reach:** Expressed as a percentage, reach is the number of individuals (or homes) you want to expose your product through specific media scheduled over a given period of time.
- **Frequency:** Using specific media, how many times, on an average, should the individuals in your target audience be exposed to your advertising message? It takes an average of three or more exposures to an advertising message before consumers take action.

- **Cost per thousand:** How much will it cost to reach a thousand of your prospective customers (a method used in comparing print media)? To determine a publication's cost per thousand, also known as CPM, divide the cost of the advertising by the publication's circulation in thousands.
- **Cost per point:** How much will it cost to buy one rating point for your target audience, a method used in comparing broadcast media? One rating point equals one per cent of your target audience. Divide the cost of the schedule being considered by the number of rating points it delivers.
- **Impact:** Does the medium in question offer full opportunities for appealing to the appropriate senses, such as sight and hearing, in its graphic design and production quality?
- **Selectivity:** To what degree can the message be restricted to those people who are known to be the most logical prospects?

Reach and frequency are important aspects of an advertising plan and are used to analyze alternative advertising schedules to determine which produce the best results relative to the media plan's objectives.

Calculate reach and frequency and then compare the two on the basis of how many people you will reach with each schedule and the number of times you will connect with the average person. Let's say you aired one commercial in each of four television programmes (A, B, C, D), and each programme has a 20 point rating, resulting in a total of 80 gross rating points. It is possible that some viewers will see more than one announcement—some viewers of programme A might also see programme B, C, or D, or any combination of them. For example, in a population of 100 TV homes, a total of 40 are exposed to one or more TV programs. The reach of the four programs combined is therefore 40 per cent (40 homes reached divided by the 100 TV-home populations).

12.12 PUBLIC RELATIONS (PR)

Public relations includes promotional activities that work to create a strong public image of the company. Public relations activities include helping the public to understand the company and its products. Public relations if done right can reach a large audience without the expensive cost of traditional advertising and marketing.

Public relations started as publicity, but today its scope has enlarged to an extent that it is being defined as "helping an organization and its publics adapt mutually to each other." The focus in this management function is on mutual accommodation rather than a one-sided imposition of a view point. Perhaps, it is only because of this reason the scope of PR has become so wide. Further, the use of variety of terms as substitutes or euphemisms—such as corporate communication, corporate affairs, public affairs, has caused confusion about what PR is and what it is not. Here are some additional elements that are part of a contemporary understanding of public relations.

Public relations is a management function, part of the decision-making of an organization (corporate or non-profit), which is based on research, strategic planning and evaluation.

Public relations is built on two-way communication and exists in a mutual give-and-take relationship in which both an organization and its publics initiate and respond to messages. Public relations is performance-based, rooted more in what an organization does than what it says. Thus, it fosters accountability and exists in an open and transparent as well as competitive environment.

Public relations is rooted in high ethical standards of honesty, accuracy, decency, truth, public interest and mutual good. Ideally, public relations is proactive, taking the initiative in developing the relationship and communicating with its publics. In crisis situations, public relations may be forced into a more reactive and defensive situation.

12.13 OBJECTIVES OF PUBLIC RELATIONS

In business, many organizational objectives can be accomplished through professional public relations programmes. In fact, professionalism in public relations can help in achieving a number of objectives some of which are as follows:

- Education of the publics to the use of a product or service
- Education of the publics to a point of view
- Goodwill of customers or supporters
- Investigation of the attitude of various groups towards the company
- Formulation and guidance of policies
- Fostering the viability of the society in which the organization functions
- Prestige of "favourable image" and its benefits
- Promotion of products or services
- Detecting and dealing with its publics
- Determining the organization's posture in dealing with its publics
- Goodwill of the employees or members
- Prevention of and solution to labour problems
- Fostering the goodwill of communities in which the organization has units
- Goodwill of the stockholders or constituents
- Overcoming misconceptions and prejudices
- Forestalling attacks, goodwill of suppliers, government, industry and of dealers and attraction of other dealers
- Ability to attract the best personnel.

12.14 COMPONENTS OF PUBLIC RELATIONS

The following are various components of comprehensive public relations.

1. **Community Relations:** Interaction with a geographic or cultural community in order to enhance mutual understanding, goodwill and support.
2. **Consumer Relations:** Interaction with consumer groups and media for the purpose of generating consumer understanding and support. A sub-category, customer relations, also involves interaction with individual customers.
3. **Corporate Communications:** The production and dissemination of messages by an organization through both internal media such as brochures and websites as well as through external media such as news and advertising.
4. **Employee Communication:** Interaction with employees, volunteers, members, and other internal publics in order to enhance mutual understanding, goodwill and support.
5. **Government Affairs and Lobbying:** Interaction with legislators and regulatory agencies of government to generate support for an organization and its causes. Lobbying specifically refers to interaction with legislators and regulators for the purpose of influencing their votes and/or official decisions.

6. **Litigation Public Relations:** The engagement of the news media in a bid for public understanding and support within the context of lawsuits and litigation.
7. **Marketing Communication:** Interaction with consumer and trade media, particularly associated with the introduction of new products and services.
8. **Media Relations:** Interaction with the news media in order to gain publicity or editorial support or to respond to journalistic inquiries.

12.15 IMPORTANCE OF PUBLIC RELATIONS

Public relations is a powerful tool for creating image, building awareness and consumer preference, and establishing useful liaisons with influential groups. It contributes in the following ways:

1. PR is all about building relationships to advance, promote, and benefit your reputation, department and institution.
2. PR is about communicating your message to gain allies, advocates, supporters, etc., in the community and the institution.
3. It aids in marketing the department for recruitment purposes and can lead to improved quality of student applicants.
4. It demonstrates to funding agencies that you are making a difference and actually have results.
5. It can improve the reputation of an individual department.
6. It can also serve the greater physics community by convincing the publics that "quarks, quantum dots, and nanostructures are cool".
7. It can lead to strong community and industrial partnerships, and even financial support.

12.16 DEVELOPING A MARKETING PUBLIC RELATIONS PLAN

A public relations campaign planned by marketing experts is often far more effective than advertising. Developing and creating the core of your public relations campaign involves six easy steps.

Step 1: Determine the objectives of PR: Define and write down your objectives for your publicity. How will you design the public relations campaign? Will it be designed to:

- Establish your expertise among your peers, the press, or your potential clients or customers.
- Build goodwill among your customers, suppliers, or your community.
- Create and reinforce your brand and professional corporate image.
- Inform and create good perceptions regarding your company and services.
- Assist you in introducing a new service or product to your market.
- Generate sales or leads.
- Mitigate the impact of negative publicity and/or corporate crisis.

Step 2: Define your goals in achieving this objective: It is important that your goals be specific, measurable, result-oriented and time-bound. These goals must be in-line with your overall business, marketing, and sales objectives.

Step 3: Target audience: Determine the target audience. This consists of:

- Who is it that we want to reach with this campaign?
- What do you want your key message to be?

Step 4: Scheduling: Develop a schedule for your public relations campaigns by coinciding your public relations plan with other marketing and sales efforts.

Step 5: Develop your plan of attack: What communication vehicles will you use to get your message to the public? Examples may include:

- Press releases
- Articles
- Customer success stories
- Letters to the editor
- Press conferences, interview, or media tours
- Radio, television, or press interviews
- Seminars or speaking engagements
- Event sponsorships.

Select from the list and begin researching and developing your approach.

Step 6: Review the results: Put measures in place to track the results of your PR campaign. After each campaign sit down and review the results on the following basis:

- Did you achieve the defined objectives and goals of this campaign?
- Should you consider modifying your original plan?
- If so, how and why?

REVIEW QUESTIONS

1. Define the meaning and definition of advertising. Explain the advertising budgeting methods.
2. What do you mean by advertisement copy? Explain the essentials of effective advertisement copy.
3. Explain the different elements of advertising copy.
4. Explain the measurement of advertising effectiveness.
5. Describe the DAGMAR model briefly.
6. Define the different methods of advertising evaluation.
7. What do you mean by advertising agencies? Explain the different functions of advertising agencies.
8. Explain the different types of advertising agencies.
9. What is advertising media? Explain the types of media.
10. Write down the different steps of media plan.
11. What are public relations? Explain the objectives of public relations.
12. Explain the different components of public relations.
13. Define the importance of public relations.
14. Explain the structure of advertising agencies.
15. What is the relationship between agency and client?
16. Describe the selection of an advertising agency.

CHAPTER 13

Personal Selling and Management of Sales Force

POINTS TO REMEMBER

At the end of this chapter, we will be able to understand:

- Introduction
- Meaning and Definition
- Characteristics of Personal Selling
- Qualities of a Good Salesman
- Advantages and Disadvantages of Personal Selling
- Importance of Personal Selling
- Meaning of Recruitment
- Process of Recruitment
- Training of Salesmen
- Importance of Sales Training
- Methods of Sales Training
- Remuneration of Salesmen
- Methods of Sales Remuneration
- Motivation of Sales Personnel
- Evaluation of Sales Force Performance
- Process of Evaluating Sales Force Performance

13.1 INTRODUCTION

Personal selling or salesmanship is one of the most important methods to contact the prospective buyer personally and to persuade him or her to buy the products. The objective is not only to sell the product to a buyer but to make him or her a permanent customer. Consumer satisfaction is the core of marketing. Goods and services are produced after studying the requirements of the consumers. Once these are produced, the consumers are informed and convinced that the products in question can satisfy their needs. Advertisement serves the purpose of keeping the customers informed about the products available in the market. Besides this, consumers also need to be informed about the new products likely to be introduced.

Consumers are to be convinced about the quality of the products and the benefits thereof. They need to be persuaded to buy the products. This can best be done by personally contacting the prospective buyers. It is called personal selling.

13.2 MEANING AND DEFINITION

Personal selling is the oldest and the most popular method of selling goods and services. It involves face-to-face communication between the seller and the potential buyer. It may be two types:

(*i*) **Across the Counter Selling:** In this case, the customer comes to the shop or store and the salesperson attends him. It primarily involves retail store selling. It also includes 'phone-in-orders'.

(*ii*) **Door-to-Door Selling:** In this case the salesperson goes to the residence or office of the customer. This is also known as field selling. These days salespersons also approach customers through telephone, fax and internet.

Personal selling is the process of assisting and persuading a prospective buyer to buy a product or service in a face-to-face situation. It involves direct and personal contact between the seller or his representative with the prospective buyer for persuading the latter to buy the seller's product or service. Personal selling is beneficial to both the seller and the buyer. It increases the sales and profit for the seller and helps to satisfy the wants of consumers. The real purpose of personal selling is not simply to sell the present product or service but to win a regular customer. Aggression selling or selling by pressurizing the customers is unethical and cannot pay in the long run. A good salesman should assist the customers in satisfying their needs by offering products or services that suit their capacity and provide them lasting satisfaction.

Personal selling is the process of achieving mutually profitable economic exchanges between buyer and seller, based on interpersonal contact between buyer and seller, and on the seller's persuasive communication of his product or service qualities and benefits to the buyer.

> *"Personal selling is the oral presentation in a conversation with one or more prospective purchasers for the purpose of making sales".*
> **Philip Kotler**

> *"Personal selling consists in individual personal communication in contrast to mass, relatively impersonal communication of advertising, sales promotion and the other promotional tools".*
> **W.J. Stanton**

> *"Personal selling consists of contracting prospective buyers of products personally".*
> **Richard Buskrik**

13.3 CHARACTERISTICS OF PERSONAL SELLING

Personal selling occurs where an individual salesperson sells a product, service or solution to a client. Salespeople match the benefits of their offering to the specific needs of a client. Personal selling has the following features:

1. **Feedback:** As it is a face-to-face process the feedback from the clients are directly received by the sales personnel.
2. **Persuasion:** Clients or customers can be persuaded to buy the product or the salesman can convince them to buy the product.

3. **Flexibility:** The sales presentation can be adapted according to the situations or clients.
4. **Builds Relationships:** A bond is made between the company and the customer through personal selling. For example, marketing relationship is created between two persons.
5. **Efficient Communicative Interchange:** It is a two-fold communication where the message is conveyed and the reply is also received immediately.
6. **Process:** It is a set of activities and not a single activity. The process continues infinitely.
7. **Mutual Benefit:** It is a two-way process, both buyer and seller are benefited from this.
8. **Supply of Information:** The customers are made aware of the company's product. For example, valuable information is supplied to the customers about the availability of the product, special features, uses, prices, offers, etc.
9. **Promotes Sales:** The end objective is achieved through this, *i.e.*, promotion of sales is achieved.
10. **Expensive:** Recruiting, training, and development of the sales force is an expensive procedure as in personal selling this factor is very essential.

Distinguish between Advertising and Personal Selling

Advertising and personal selling are two most important methods of creating and increasing demand for goods and services. These are widely used throughout the world to introduce the products to the prospective buyers and pushing the sales. But the two are different from each other in many ways. The points of difference between the two are as follows:

Advertising	*Personal Selling*
Advertising is non-personal and is addressed to the customers in general.	Personal selling involves direct interaction of salesmen with individuals.
Advertisement is generally found to cover a large number of people.	Personal selling is confined to a particular area.
In advertisement there is a one-way communication. The targeted persons' reactions cannot be known immediately.	In personal selling there is a two-way communication. The salesman explains his viewpoint to the potential buyer and knows about his/her reaction.
Advertisement offers a wide choice of channels, audio such as radio and audiovisual such as television.	In personal selling there is only one channel of transmission of messages, *i.e.*, personal talk of the salesman with the potential buyers.

13.3.1 Objectives of Personal Selling

Personal selling is used for the following objectives of promotion in the following ways:

1. **Building Product Awareness:** A common task of salespeople, in particular while selling in business markets, is to educate customers on new product offerings. In fact, salespeople serve a major role at industry trades shows where they discuss products with show attendees. But building awareness using personal selling is also important in consumer markets. In word-of-mouth, marketing is leading to personal selling becoming a useful mechanism for introducing consumers to new products.
2. **Creating Interest:** The fact that personal selling involves person-to-person communication is a natural method. That helps in getting customers experience about

the product for the first time. In fact, creating interest goes hand-in-hand with building product awareness as sales professionals can often accomplish both objectives during the first encounter with a potential customer.

3. **Providing Information:** When salespeople connect with customers a large part of the conversation focuses on product information. Marketing organizations provide their sales staff with large amounts of sales support including brochures, research reports, computer programs and many other forms of informational material.
4. **Stimulating Demand:** By far, the most important objective of personal selling is to encourage customers to make a purchase.
5. **Reinforcing the Brand:** Most personal selling is intended to build long-term relationships with customers. A strong relationship can only be built overtime and requires regular communication with a customer. Meeting customers on a regular basis allows salespeople to repeatedly discuss their company's products and by doing so helps strengthen customers' knowledge of what the company has to offer.

13.3.2 Process of Personal Selling

A logical sequence of six steps of the personal selling process that are to be carried out by any salesman while interacting with a prospective buyer, is shown in Fig. 13.1.

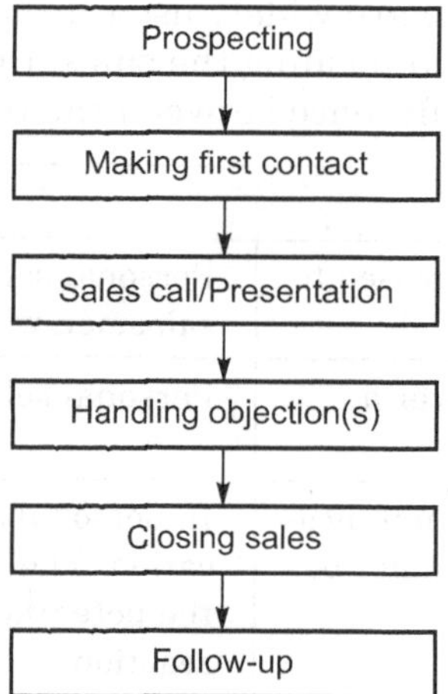

Fig. 13.1. Personal selling process.

Step 1: Prospecting: Prospecting is all about finding prospects, or potential new customers. Prospects should be qualified, which means that they need to be assessed to see if there is business potential, otherwise you could be wasting your time. The various sources of collecting data of prospects may be: referrals, friends, family members, and centres of influence, directories and trade publications, trade shows and telemarketing, direct response advertising and sales letters, websites and computerized databases, organized sector, unorganized sector, etc. In order to qualify your prospects, one needs to:

- Plan a sales approach focused upon the needs of the customer.
- Determine which products or services best meet their needs.
- In order to save time, rank the prospects and leave out those that are least likely to buy.

Step 2: Making first contact: This is the preparation that a salesperson goes through before meeting the client, for example via e-mail, telephone or letter. Preparation will make a call more focused. Make sure that you are on time.

- Before meeting the client, set some objectives for the sales call. What is the purpose of the call? What outcome is desirable before you leave?
- Make sure that you have done some homework before meeting your prospect. This will show that you are committed in the eyes of your customer.
- To save time, send some information before you visit. This will whet the prospect's appetite.
- Keep a set of samples at hand, and make sure that they are in a very good condition.
- Within the first minute or two, state the purpose of your call so that time with the client is maximized, and also to demonstrate to the client that you are not wasting his or her time.
- Humour is fine, but try to be sincere and friendly.

Step 3: The sales presentation (sales call): It is best to be enthusiastic about your product or service. If you are not excited about it, do not expect your prospect to be excited. Focus on the real benefits of the product or service to the specific needs of your client, rather than listing endless features.

- Try to be relaxed during the call, and put your client at ease.
- Let the client do at least 80% of the talking. This will give you invaluable information on your client's needs.
- Remember to ask plenty of questions. Use open questions and closed questions, *i.e.*, questions that will only give the answer 'yes' or 'no.' This way a salesperson can dictate the direction of the conversation.
- Never be too afraid to ask for the business straight away.

Step 4: Objection handling: The course of objection handling includes the prospective buyers holding, inspecting or testing the product directly. The product is demonstrated by the sales people by means of audio-visual presentations such as slide presentations or product videos. It should be the endeavour of the sales person to let the prospect do most of the talking during the presentation. Their responsibility should be restricted to address the needs of the organizational buyers as far as possible. They should have the ability to convince them by showing that they truly understand them and care about their problem(s).

Stage 5: Closing the sale: This is a very important stage. Often salespeople will leave without ever successfully closing a deal. Therefore, it is vital to learn the skills of closing.

- It makes sense to be direct and come straight to the point, that is, after the above steps; the salesperson should ask if now he/she can take an order.
- While communicating with the customer, the client's interest in buying (or disinterest) becomes apparent from the body language—for example enquiries about the discount, delivery, etc., indicate a heightened state of interest while silence, listlessness or attempts to wrap up the meeting convey disinterest. The salesperson should read these signals and act accordingly.
- By making a 'summary close', the salesperson summarizes everything that the client needs, based upon the discussions during the call, and asks for the order.
- Another way to close is the 'alternative close', in which the salesperson closes by giving the customer two options such as "Do you want product model ABC or the higher version?" Often, this can work with a dithering customer.

Stage 6: Follow-up: The selling process does not end with the closing of a sale. A good salesperson follows up to ensure that the customer is satisfied. He checks to find out if the product was delivered on time, if it is working properly or if there are any problems. This can give the right signals to the customer that the salesperson cares about the customer and not just about selling his product. In the long run, this will increase the chances that a customer will return to the same salesperson or store to buy another product and even recommend the place to his friends and relatives. As customer satisfaction is an important part of marketing, follow-up is necessary to build a long-term relationship.

13.4 QUALITIES OF A GOOD SALESMAN

There are some qualities which make a salesman more effective. The essential qualities are explained below:

1. **Impressive Personality:** A salesman should have a good appearance. He should have a good built and be well dressed. As soon as a salesman comes into contact with potential customers, the latter will be impressed by the salesman's pleasing personality.
2. **Training and Experience:** A good salesman should be an expert in his respective field. He should have knowledge about the technique of production and art of salesmanship. He must be trained in speaking regional and other languages. It is advisable for the successful result of the operation that a salesman must undergo practical training before coming to the actual job.
3. **Knowledge of the Product and the Company:** A salesman should have full knowledge of the product and the company he is representing. He should be able to explain each and every aspect of the product, *i.e.*, its qualities, how to use it, what precautions to be taken, etc. He should be able to explain the business and service record of the company. He should also have knowledge of products of rival companies so that he can put across the superiority of his own products.
4. **Psychological Approach:** A salesman should be in a position to follow the psychology of human nature. He must have the ability to understand his customer's choice. So he should talk in terms of the customer's interest and he must create a pleasant atmosphere to achieve favourable attention and interest on the part of the prospect live buyer.
5. **Integrity of Character:** A good salesman should possess the qualities of honesty and integrity. He has to gain the confidence of the customers. He should be able to understand their needs and to satisfy those needs. His employer too should have faith in him. A salesman should be loyal both to employer and consumer.
6. **Sociability:** A good salesman must keep in touch with the people of different nature in the world and not keep to himself. He should move about with a view to widen his range of acquaintances. Salesman should therefore, possess a quality of mixing freely with unknown person within a short time. He should be sociable and popular in order to win new friends.
7. **Good Behaviour:** A salesman should be co-operative and courteous. Good behaviour enables one to win the confidence of the customers. He should not feel irritated if the buyer asks many questions even if the questions are irrelevant. It is also not necessary that the person he is trying to convince buys the products. A salesman has to remain courteous in every case.
8. **Ability to Persuade:** A salesman should be good in conversation so that he can engage the person he is attending to. He should be able to convince him and create the desire in his mind to possess the commodity.
9. **Flexibility of Approach:** He should interact with customers with a flexible approach, *i.e.*, try to persuade different types of customers with different reasons.

13.5 ADVANTAGES AND DISADVANTAGES OF PERSONAL SELLING

There are several advantages and disadvantages of personal selling. However, the benefits of personal selling can outshine the disadvantages in definite stages. This is predominantly correct when rivalry is strong and corporations are marketing extremely technological goods. Personal selling in addition functions principally well when there are numerous assessment makers occupied in the trade procedure. Whatsoever the situations, opponents in your business will probably be incurring the same benefits and disadvantages of personal selling. For that reason, use personal selling in the correct conditions.

Advantages of Personal Selling

1. **Convey more information:** You can express added information with personal selling when compared to any other types of promotion, such as advertising. Personal selling is predominantly beneficial while functioning with goods of high value. You will require influencing buyers more with supplementary luxurious stuff. Most enterprises use notebook presentation, exhibitions and extremely comprehensive product information while promoting goods like medical equipment, computers, and industrial goods.
2. **More impact:** Personal selling has a superior impact on consumers than direct mail or other forms of advertising. The buyers do not require to wait long to get responses to their queries. He can find out what he requires to be acquainted with instantly. You as a retailer also obtain an enhanced experience for what a consumer demands. You can recommend specific goods if you have a widespread merchandise line or adapt your services, like discussing, to the buyer's specific requirements.
3. **Customers get personal attention:** Personal selling is a one-to-one activity where customers get personal attention. This gives an opportunity to understand the customer needs better and make an effective sale. The marketing manager can customize the sales message accordingly depending upon the needs and types of customers.
4. **Respond:** As there is a two-way communication process in personal selling, the sales team has a good opportunity to respond directly and promptly to any of the customer's queries and concerns.
5. **Educates the customers:** Personal selling helps in passing on large amounts of technical data or other complex product information to the customers. This indirectly educates the customers and updates them on latest happenings on the industry, company and new products.

Disadvantages of Personal Selling

1. **Limited reach:** One disadvantage is that your customer reach is limited through personal sales. As a result, it will require extended time period to create product awareness, particularly if you do not use other forms of advertising. Sales representatives have to cover up one region or place at a time. As a sales representative, you can only talk to twenty five potential buyers per day and put together 3–5 presentations. Contact can be principally partial in rural regions where fewer potential buyers are situated.
2. **Expensive:** Personal selling is in addition costly, particularly while bearing in mind the sales representative's salary, bonus, commission as well as travel time. Furthermore, it requires plenty of money to prepare your sales representatives, educating them on a range of goods and sales techniques. That is the reason it is paramount to study the advantages and disadvantages of personal selling against other forms of advertising.

13.6 IMPORTANCE OF PERSONAL SELLING

Personal selling is an important element of promotion mix and an effective promotional tool. As you have already noted, personal selling is a process that offers mutual benefit, both to the customer and to the seller. Personal selling offers the following compensation.

1. **Flexible Tool:** Personal selling involves individual and personal communication as compared to the mass and impersonal communication of advertising and sales promotion. Therefore, personal selling is most flexible in operation. A salesman can tailor his sales presentation to fit the needs, motives and attitudes of individual customers. He can observe the customer's reaction to a particular sales approach and thus make necessary adjustments right on the spot. Face-to-face contact with customers is the most effective means of communication and persuasion.
2. **Involves Minimum Wasted Effort:** In personal selling, a salesman can select the target market and concentrate on the prospective customers. He need not communicate with the people who are not the real prospects. Therefore, personal selling involves minimum wastage of effort.
3. **Results in Actual Sale:** Advertising and sales promotion techniques can only attract attention and arouse desire. By themselves they cannot create actual sale. Personal selling in most cases leads to actual sale. A salesman can find prospective buyers, demonstrate the product, explain its operation, and convince customers to buy it, install it at the customer's place and provide after-sales service. No other method of promotion can perform all these functions. Therefore, personal selling does the entire job of selling. Personal selling is a complete promotional technique of keeping customers satisfied.
4. **Provides Feedback:** Personal selling involves two-way flow of communication between buyer and seller. It is a useful method of understanding the needs and behaviour of customers. It provides knowledge about the tastes, habits and attitudes of the prospective customers.
5. **Complements Advertising:** In most situations, there is a need for explaining the uses and price of the product. Salesmen can persuade the prospective customers to buy a product. Advertising attracts customers but their doubts and questions about the product are answered by salesmen. In this way personal selling supports advertising. Salesmen educate the consumers about new products and about new and varied uses of existing products.
6. **Educates Customers:** Salesmanship is not simply a tool of convincing people to buy certain products. It assists customers in satisfying their wants. A salesman provides: information, education and guidance to customers. He handles their complaints and assists them in getting value for their money. He can clear their doubts on the spot.
7. **Assists the Society:** Salesmen help to increase aggregate sales and production in the country thereby increasing employment opportunities. They help to maintain equilibrium between demand and supply.

13.7 MEANING OF RECRUITMENT

Employees of an organization are essential and active factor of production. In addition to their major contribution to all the affairs of the business, they activate other factors. Without employees, the enterprise would have been a collector of material and equipment.

Recruitment is the process to discover sources of manpower to meet the requirement of staffing schedule and to employ effective measures for attracting that manpower in adequate numbers to facilitate effective selection of an efficient working force.

"Recruitment is the process of searching the candidates for employment and stimulating them to apply for jobs in the organization". **Edwin B. Flippo**

Recruitment of candidates is the function preceding this management can select the right candidate for the right job from this pool. The main objective of the recruitment process is to expedite the selection process.

13.8 PROCESS OF RECRUITMENT

The recruitment process is the major and first step towards creating the competitive strength and the strategic advantage for the organizations. Recruitment process involves a systematic procedure from sourcing the candidates to arranging and conducting the interviews and requires many resources and time. A general recruitment process is as follows:

1. **Identifying the Nature and Vacancy of Salesman:** The nature of sales job varies from company to company. The recruitment process begins with the human resource department receiving requisitions for recruitment from any department of the company. These contain:
   (*a*) Job analysis
   (*b*) Posts to be filled
   (*c*) Number of persons
   (*d*) Duties to be performed
   (*e*) Job description
   (*f*) Qualifications required
   (*g*) Job specification.
2. **Determination of Number of the Salesmen:** A company or organization should determine the number of salesmen needed.
3. **Determination of the Source of Recruitment Process:** The sources can be classified into two parts:
   (*a*) Internal sources
   (*b*) External sources.

   (*a*) Internal sources: Persons who are already working in an organization constitute the 'internal sources'. Retrenched employees, retired employees, dependents of deceased employees may also constitute the internal sources. Whenever any vacancy arises, someone from within the organization is upgraded, transferred, promoted or even demoted. Whenever any vacancy arises, somebody from within the organization may be looked into:

   - Internal promotions
   - Referrals
   - Former employees.

   Merits of Internal Sources

   (*i*) It improves the morale of employees, for they are assured of the fact that they would be preferred to outsiders when vacancies occur. The employers are in a better position to evaluate those presently employed than outside candidates. This is because the company maintains a record of the progress, experience and service of its employees.

   (*ii*) It promotes loyalty among the employees, for it gives them a sense of job security and opportunities for advancement.

(*iii*) As the persons in the employment of the company are fully aware of, and well acquainted with its policies and know its operating procedures, they require little training, and the chances are that they would stay longer in the employment of the organization than a new outsider would.

(*iv*) It is less costly than going outside to recruit.

Demerits of Internal Sources

(*i*) It often leads to inbreeding, and discourages new blood from entering an organization.

(*ii*) There are possibilities that internal sources may "dry up", and it may be difficult to find the requisite personnel from within an organization.

(*iii*) Since the learner does not know more than the lecture, no innovation worth the name can made. Therefore, on jobs which require marginal thinking, this practice is not followed.

(*iv*) As promotion is based on seniority, the danger is that really capable hands may not be chosen.

(*b*) External sources: External sources of recruitment refer to prospective candidates outside the enterprise. Here the organization can have the services of:

(*a*) Employees working in other organizations

(*b*) Job aspirants registered with employment exchanges

(*c*) Students from reputed educational institutions

(*d*) Candidates referred by unions, friends, relatives and existing employees

(*e*) Candidates forwarded by search firms and contractors

(*f*) Candidates responding to the advertisements, issued by the organization

(*g*) Unsolicited applications/walk-ins.

Merits of External Sources

(*i*) External sources provide the requisite type of personnel for an organization, having skill, training and education up to the required standard.

(*ii*) Since persons are recruited from a large market, the best selection can be made without any distinctions of caste, religion, sex, race or colour.

(*iii*) In the long run, this source proves economical because potential employees do not need extra training for their job.

Demerits of External Sources

However, this system suffers from what is called "brain drain," especially when experienced persons are raided or hunted by sister concerns.

13.9 TRAINING OF SALESMEN

A salesman selected for the job needs training for effective sales performance. Sales training is a technique or method by which efforts are made to increase the knowledge, skill and efficiency of a salesman so that he may be in a position to solve the problems of sales and provide active contribution on increasing sales of the enterprise.

13.9.1 Objectives of Salesmen's Training

The objectives of salesmen's training may be varied in nature. They may differ in terms of the industry, nature of the products, company policies etc. In general, training includes:

1. Detailed knowledge of the product.
2. Knowledge about the customers.
3. Knowledge about the competitors.
4. Increasing sales of the enterprise.
5. Achieving the sales targets.
6. Method of meeting, convincing and presenting product information to the customers.
7. Method of creating new customers.
8. Knowledge about customers, maintenance of accounts, reimbursement of expenses, display and demonstration of products, preparing daily reports, servicing the customers, etc.
9. Keeping customers informed of the prevailing market conditions.
10. Achieving the sales targets.

13.10 IMPORTANCE OF SALES TRAINING

A newly appointed salesman is not aware of the products, techniques of attracting and presenting the product before the prospective customer. Training makes the salesman aware of all these. The following are the advantages in favour of training salesmen:

1. **Opportunities in a Market:** Trained salesmen can see opportunities in a market which have been previously overlooked. It is necessary not only to those who are dealing in specialty goods but also to others. A salesman, even though he is a born salesman, requires to be trained in connection to policy and views of the enterprise.
2. **Understanding of the Customer's Problems:** Training enables salesmen to gain a deeper understanding of the customer's problems and as such can help in solving such problems more efficiently and quickly. A trained salesman knows his job quite well and therefore, needs less supervision and control resulting in a smaller supervision cost.
3. **Face the Competition:** A properly trained salesman is in a better position to face the competition that may exist in the business. Training helps to lessen the time that a newly selected person takes in picking up the job.
4. **Relationship with Customers:** Training helps salesmen in building a congenial relationship with customers. A trained salesman is in a position to provide high degree of understanding and co-operation with the customers.
5. **Business Volume:** Increased volume of business resulting from training is not only advantageous to the enterprise but is also in the interest of the salesman who may expect better remuneration and promotion, etc.

13.11 METHODS OF SALES TRAINING

The work of salesmen is of varied nature and differs widely from industry to industry. That is why different types of salesmen are appointed for different types of jobs in a sales department. There are different methods of training salesmen. They may be classified under the following two broad heads:

1. Individual Training Methods
2. Group Training Methods.

1. **Individual Training Methods:** These training methods include on-the-job training, training through correspondence, internship training, training through study courses, training through individual coaching, training through special assignments, observation, posts, etc., as given on next page:

(*i*) **Training on the job:** This is the most popular method of training. It is also called 'training within industry' or 'coach and pupil training'. It is a practical method of training in which the trainee gets actual experience by working along with some senior supervisor on the job. In the other method of on-the-job training the trainer gives feedback to the salesperson after observing him or her during his or her sales call. The salesperson thereafter, practises the recommendations in the future calls.

(*ii*) **Self learning modules:** In this programme, the participants are given the course material which they are required to study themselves. Written notes can be sent, and if needed audio and video cassettes can be used. This kind of training is useful when you want the participants to revise some material or you want to send some pre-conference study material.

(*iii*) **Internship training:** The object of such co-operation is to provide theoretical and practical training to the trainees. As soon as the trainees complete their training they are taken in the regular service of the concerned business house.

(*iv*) **Individual coaching:** Under this method of training, coaching is provided by the supervisor to the trainees on a continuous and regularly scheduled basis.

(*v*) **Observation posts:** This method stresses learning by observation. 'Assistant to' positions make good observation posts in development of the trainee. Trainees holding assistant posts are likely to grasp and assimilate problems pertaining to a particular post most effectively.

2. **Group Training Methods:** Under these methods, training is provided in groups. The most common methods under group training are as follows:

(*i*) **Lecture method:** Under this method, lectures are delivered by senior supervisors and leading experts to a group of trainees consisting of 15 to 20 trainees who are sitting in a room. After the lecture, questions are asked so as to have a clear conception. As soon as the desired series of lectures are completed, written and oral examinations may be arranged.

(*ii*) **Seminar and conference method:** Under this method conferences and seminars are arranged under the leadership of experts and the trainees are required to participate in the same. This method creates greater degree of interest, gives a chance to each participant, develops group morale and stimulates analytical thinking. The following are the important areas that can be covered in a typical seminar and conference method:

- Company knowledge—history and future plans
- Product information
- Marketing strategies for various products or services
- Learning the features, advantages and benefits of products or services
- How to obtain interview with the prospective customers
- The sales presentation
- Different ways of finding customer's needs
- Answering objections
- Closing the sales presentation
- Planning geographical territory and planning each day
- Time management
- Administrative responsibilities
- Communication abilities
- Writing report.

(*iii*) **Committee method:** Under this method, committees are formed under the leadership of a senior supervisor. The trainees are the members of the committees.

(*iv*) **Roundtable method:** Under this method, the trainees are required to sit around a table under the leadership of a senior supervisor or expert. They discuss and express their ideas on a particular subject.

(*v*) **Role playing method:** Under this method, training is provided to the trainees by presenting a sales drama before the trainees. In this method, a salesman is required to face the problems, criticism and objections of a number of customers.

(*vi*) **'Brainstorming' method.** Under this method, any particular problem is thrown at the persons (trainees) sitting around the table and the participants throw out whatever comes into their minds. No one is permitted to contradict.

13.12 REMUNERATION OF SALESMEN

A good plan of remuneration is a means of securing better control of salesmen's activities, greater incentive sales, more loyalty, higher morale and greater enthusiasm and interest. It should be planned in such a manner that the employer gets higher sales and the employee higher income. Every company has to design a good remuneration plan for the efficient working of the organization and the sales force. Better sales lead to higher profit and the latter leads to higher remuneration to sales force. This in turn results in greater sales effort and higher sales. Thus, this is a continuous circle, one leading to another. A sound remuneration plan has the following importance.

1. Salesmen develop a sense of loyalty to the firm. Thus, the loyal employees of the firm become a permanent asset of the firm assuring their best service to the firm.
2. It attracts best salesmen because improved performance needs a reward. Talented salesmen are attracted when the firm is prepared to pay well for hard work.
3. It increases the volume of profit and sales of the firm.
4. It establishes a healthy employer and employee relationship. Salesmen, who are paid well and well-treated, have no scope for grudges or grumbling.
5. It satisfies the salesmen because their hardworking efforts are paid well. A satisfied customer naturally puts heart and soul together to maximize work performance.

13.13 METHODS OF SALES REMUNERATION

Various types of methods are used by different organizations to provide remuneration to the salesmen. Some of them are as follows:

1. **Straight Salary Method of Remuneration:** This is one of the most common methods of remuneration for salesmen. A salesman is paid a certain amount as salary like other employees. The salary is paid on the basis of time and not on the basis of sales. There are usually three elements in such remunerations: like salary, increments, and allowances etc. The basic salary goes on increasing with annual increments. The appointment letter specifies the amount of increment and the maximum salary he is likely to draw. To the salary and increments, the dearness allowance is added. This Dearness Allowance (D.A.) represents the payment made as per the cost of living index. There are also allowances like travelling, house rent, etc., which are added. Sometimes hard working salesmen are granted special increments.

Advantages

(*i*) This is the simplest of all methods of remuneration and therefore easy to calculate and simple to understand.

(*ii*) It ensures a stable income to salesmen. The salesman's income does not fluctuate with the sales volume.

(*iii*) It provides a sense of security and measure of confidence to the sales people. This motivates the sales force for effective selling.

(*iv*) The sales manager can exercise better control over the sales force under its plan of remuneration.

Disadvantages

(*i*) This method of remuneration does not provide incentive for a hardworking salesman. Such persons feel disappointed and do not put additional effort for selling products.

(*ii*) Under this method the ass and the horse are put on the same footing. Therefore, it results in overpayment to idle and inefficient salesmen while it leads to under-payment to efficient and hardworking salesmen.

(*iii*) Fixing the right amount of salary poses a problem under this method. The performance and ability of persons vary and therefore management finds it difficult fixing the salary.

2. **Straight Commission Method of Remuneration:** Under such method the remuneration is paid on the basis of the amount of sales made. The salesman is paid commission calculated at a certain percentage of net sales or profit. The percentage of commission varies from concern to concern and case to case. The income of a salesman fluctuates directly with the volume of sales made.

Advantages

(*i*) This method encourages those salesmen who are efficient and hardworking. The worthy ones are rewarded.

(*ii*) The sales manager need not remind the salesmen to improve sales performance. The salesmen themselves work hard for their own interest.

(*iii*) Hardworking and efficient salesmen are attracted towards the firm because they can increase their income by the sales they make.

(*iv*) As payment of commission is directly connected with sale, during slack seasons or slow-moving, firms pay less. Hence, the commission possesses no burden for them.

(*v*) Sincere and efficient salesmen are not required to depend upon the favour of the sales manager to earn their income in this method. The salesmen can earn higher commission by their own merit.

Disadvantages

(*i*) This method is necessarily, based on the principle 'more sales more commission and no sales no commission'. Hence, the salesmen are uncertain of their earnings. There are some factors like depression, inferior quality of goods, high competition, physical illness which are beyond the control of the sales force. In such cases their earnings suffer without their own fault.

(*ii*) Since, more sales means more commission, the salesman may try to increase sales more, on credit to unworthy customers. This leads to accumulation of more bad debts.

3. **Salary and Commission Method of Remuneration:** The salary element gives the salesman the necessary security and comfort. The commission element is meant to reward hardworking and efficient salesmen who put more effort in selling. Thus, this salary plus commission method is found to be good for both employee and employer.

Advantages

(*i*) The advantages of this method lie in the fact that it takes the best advantages of two straight methods namely straight salary and straight commission.

(*ii*) It also distinguishes efficient from inefficient salesmen.

(*iii*) This method guarantees a minimum for the salesman and hence the salesman feels secured. Even during periods of depression, salesmen are assured of a regular income.

13.14 MOTIVATION OF SALES PERSONNEL

Motivation is generally regarded as the process of getting people to work towards the achievement of an objective. Ideally it should go beyond the achievement of company objectives, plans, forecasts or targets and help the company win commitment of sales force to the company. Factors that make a special mark on sales force motivation are discussed below:

1. **Meetings between Manager and Sales Force:** These are highly regarded by sales managers in the motivation of their sales teams. This provides an opportunity to managers to meet their sales force in the field, at head office and at the sales meetings/conventions. These meetings allow the sales manager to understand the personality, needs and problems of each salesperson.
2. **Clarity of Job:** Clarity of job and what is expected from the salesperson is a great motivator. The objectives when duly quantified and well defined, properly connected and linked with the reward and recognition, serve as a source of motivation to the salesperson.
3. **Sales Targets:** If a sales target or quota is to be effective in motivating a salesperson, it must be regarded as fair and attainable and yet offer a challenge to him or her. Because the salesperson should regard the quota as fair, it is usually sensible to allow him or her to participate in the setting of the quota.
4. **Sales Contests:** The sales contest is an important tool to motivate salesperson. The purpose of the sales contest varies widely. It may encourage a higher level of sales in general, to increase the sales of a slow-moving product or to reward the generation of new customers.
5. **Sales Conferences:** These are the devices of group motivation. They provide opportunities for salespersons to participate, gain social satisfaction and express their views on matters, directly affecting their work.
6. **Leadership Style of the Manager:** Leadership style of the manager plays an important role in motivating the salespersons. It is practised through the use of professional speaker's special audio tapes and video tapes designed to arouse and stimulate salespersons.
7. **Freedom to Work:** In order to perform the heavy duties and responsibilities, the salespersons must be given a reasonable amount of freedom and discretion in performing their job. Liker his studies has mentioned that lack of enough discretion has a negative impact on employee's job satisfaction.

13.15 EVALUATION OF SALES FORCE PERFORMANCE

A proper evaluation process ensures that the organization is well managed. It also provides the sales personnel with information on their performance and gives recommendations for further improvement. One of the most important responsibilities of a sales manager is to evaluate the performance of the sales personnel. The performance appraisal period can become one of those times that a salesperson dreads, unless the appraisal is effectively conducted. Ineffective performance appraisal tends to become a time-consuming and unpleasant activity for the sales manager as well as the sales personnel.

The purpose of conducting performance evaluation is to cross-check whether the sales force activities are in alignment with organizational objectives. It also monitors the sales force activities and provides remedial action, if required. Performance evaluation also helps to prepare a future action plan for the sales personnel and fulfill the organizational objectives. The sales manager or the concerned person involved in appraising the sales force can take the help of quantitative and qualitative criteria as mentioned below:

(*i*) **Quantitative criteria:** It measures the sales performance in terms of the end results whereas qualitative criteria involve all those activities that the salesperson does to achieve the end results. The quantitative factors are based on Daily Sales Report (DSR) that includes the sales volume, average calls per day, sales orders, etc.

(*ii*) **Qualitative criteria:** It includes sales skills, territory management skills, personality traits, etc.

The sales manager must ensure that the performance standards are set to compare and evaluate the actual performance of the sales force. The standards vary from industry to industry and are different for different job profiles. Performance standards come under quantitative standards, qualitative standards, time-based standards, or cost-based standards. All the sales force activities can be segregated into one of these four categories and compared with the base standard.

Many methods of performance evaluation have been developed over the years. Yet, there is no single method that can be considered ideal for all organizations. Some of the commonly used methods are—rating scales, rankings, management by objectives (MBO) and behaviorally-anchored rating scales. Several modern methods like critical incident appraisal, work-standards method, family of measures, etc., have been developed to suit variations and other requirements. Finally, regular monitoring and review of the sales force activities is also necessary to ensure that the organizational activities are aligned to the sales plan.

13.16 PROCESS OF EVALUATING SALES FORCE PERFORMANCE

There are some basic issues involved in all performance evaluations systems for sales force which require consideration while the system is being designed. You will note that unless adequate attention is given to these issues they might result in discontentment of those being evaluated. Some of these issues are:

1. The first issue relates to evaluation based on quantitative vis-a-vis qualitative data. It is obvious that in any qualitative assessment, personal bias and subjective value judgement may vitiate evaluation. On the other hand, evaluation based entirely on statistical data may not give entirely valid results as certain important determinants of a salesperson's effectiveness (for example personal effectiveness of a salesperson in handling consumer related problems) do not lend themselves to quantitative definition.
2. Another issue relates to the comparisons between salespersons on the basis of the results of evaluation. Such comparisons can never be on a "person to person" basis since a great deal of human element is involved and different salespersons have to work under different geographical and environmental conditions; and may handle different set of products or customers.
3. The third issue is related to the problem of determining standards of performance. The whole evaluation exercise rests on the comparison of actual sales performances against predetermined standards or norms. If these norms or standards are not realistic, the whole exercise will become self-defeating.

4. Another issue worthy of consideration is the periodicity of evaluation. Evaluation based on very short-term results may not be very correct as it ignores the value of some criteria which are of long-term value to the company. A small example is the effectiveness of a particular salesperson in cultivating good customer relations, which may give the company an added acceptability when it introduces a new product.
5. The last issue here refers to the accounting system or the database of the company as a basis of developing the evaluation system. Actual data taken from typical sales records are not adequate to provide precise comparison of salespersons or sales group performance. For example, if the product mix sold by different sales group differs, it will be difficult to compare the performance of the salespersons in the two different groups merely on accounting data.

REVIEW QUESTIONS

1. What is the meaning and definition of personal selling? Explain the major characteristics of personal selling.
2. What are the differences between personal selling and advertising?
3. Explain the different objectives of personal selling.
4. Discuss the different steps in the process of personal selling.
5. Explain the qualities of a good salesman.
6. What are the advantages and disadvantages of personal selling?
7. Explain the importance of personal selling.
8. What do you mean by recruitment? Explain the process of recruitment.
9. Explain the concepts of training of salesmen.
10. Explain the importance and methods of sales training.
11. What is the remuneration of salesmen? Explain the methods of sales remuneration.
12. Why is there an organizational need for the motivation of sales personnel?
13. Explain the evaluation of sales force performance.
14. Explain the process of evaluating sales force performance.

CHAPTER 14

Sales Forecasting, Sales Promotion and Publicity

POINTS TO REMEMBER

At the end of this chapter, we will be able to understand:

- Introduction
- Meaning and Definition
- Factors Affecting Sales Forecasting
- Main Characteristics of Sales Forecasting
- Methods/Techniques of Sales Forecasting
- Significance of Sales Forecasting
- Introduction to Sales Promotion
- Meaning and Definition of Sales Promotion
- Characteristics of Sales Promotion
- Distinguish between Advertising and Sales Promotion
- Objectives of Sales Promotion
- Techniques of Sales Promotion
- Advantages and Disadvantages of Sales Promotion
- Sales Promotion Budget
- Sales Promotion Programmes
- Publicity
- Difference between Advertisement and Publicity
- Role of Publicity
- Objectives of Publicity
- Publicity Techniques
- Importance of Publicity

14.1 INTRODUCTION

Forecasting is the process of making statements about events whose actual outcomes have not yet been observed. A commonplace example might be estimation of some variable of interest at some specified future date. Prediction is a similar, but more general term. Both might refer to formal statistical methods employing time series, cross-sectional or longitudinal data, or alternatively to less formal judgmental methods. Sales forecasting is projection of achievable sales revenues, based on historical sales data, analysis of market surveys and trends and salesperson's estimates. Also called sales budget, it forms the basis of a business plan because the level of salesrevenue affects practically every aspect of business. A sales forecast can be a good indicator of future sales in stable market conditions, but may be less reliable in times of rapid market change.

For example, if Shoppers Stop or a Wal-Mart opens in India, what sorts of customer profiles are available in the town? What is their income level? What are the other retail formats available in the town and how are they performing? What are the price points of merchandise currently selling, etc?

14.2 MEANING AND DEFINITION

Sales forecasting is an estimation of projected sales for a time period. Simply speaking, the process of sales forecasting involves reviewing performance and history of the product or service and relating it to the marketing and sales efforts of the firm, within the anticipated market environment (economic, competitive, technological, public policy, etc.,) and buyer behaviour.

14.3 FACTORS AFFECTING SALES FORECASTING

For the forecasting to be accurate, managers need to consider all of the following factors:

1. **Historical Perspective:** As a starting point, management analyzes previous sales experience by product lines, territories, classes of customers and other relevant details. Management needs to consider a timeline long enough to detect trends and patterns in the growth and the decline of rupee sales volume. This period is generally five to ten years. If the Company's experience with a particular product class is shorter, management will include experience of similar companies.
2. **Business Competence:** The ability of a company to respond to the results of a sales forecast depends on its production capacity, marketing methods, financing, and leadership, and its ability to change each of these to maximize its profit potential and logistic capabilities to provide the right product at the right price at the right time.
3. **Market Position:** Forecasting also considers the competitive position of the company with respect to its market share, research and development, quality of service, pricing and financing policies and public image. In addition, forecasters also evaluate the quality and quantity of the customer base to determine brand loyalty, response to promotional efforts, economic viability, and creditworthiness.
4. **General Economic Condition:** Although consumer markets are often characterized as being increasingly susceptible to different segmentation in recent years, the condition of the overall economy is still a primary determinant of general sales volume, even in many niche markets. Forecasters incorporate relevant data that correlate well or demonstrate a casual relationship with sales volume.
5. **Price Index:** If the prices of products have changed over the years, changes in rupee volume of sales may not correlate well with volume of units. At one point in time when demand is strong, a company raises its prices. At another time, a company may engage in discounting to draw down inventories. This happens especially when a season is coming to an end and there are unsold stocks on the shelf. Therefore, accountants devise a price index for each year which compensates for price increases as well as mark down. By dividing the rupee volume by the price indexes, a company can track its "true" volume

growth. This process is similar to an inflation index, which provides prices in constant rupees. As a result, management is able to compare the price-adjusted rupee sales volumes.

14.4 MAIN CHARACTERISTICS OF SALES FORECASTING

1. It is an estimate of a company's sales.
2. Sales pipeline analyzes based on the sales stage field values with configurable enterprise level roll-ups.
3. Sales forecast management with configurable enterprise level roll-ups.
4. Configurable sales forecast categories (*e.g.*, in the pipeline, best case, committed, closed-won, etc.).
5. Automatic creation of forecast history records whenever key sales forecast data fields are changed.
6. Automatic (configurable) "forecast category" assignment for each opportunity that can be manually updated.
7. Configurable "sales stages" capture where each opportunity stands in the sales pipeline.
8. A variety of pre-designed sales quota, pipeline, and forecast management reports are available for immediate use.
9. Sales quota, pipeline, and forecast reports and analytics can utilize configurable product level roll-ups.
10. Pre-designed sales quota, pipeline, and forecast-related analytics (charts and graphs) are available for display on dashboards and reports.

14.5 METHODS/TECHNIQUES OF SALES FORECASTING

The forecasting process refers to a series of procedures used to forecast. It begins when an objective is determined. Modern managers have several different methods available for sales forecasting.

1. **Qualitative Method:** We can discuss several qualitative forecasting techniques using the judgment, knowledge, and intuition of experienced people to produce sales forecasts.

   (*i*) **Expert's opinion:** Expert evaluations use the experience of people, such as executives, sales people, marketing people, distributors, or outside experts, who are familiar with a product line or a group of products, to generate sales forecasts. The techniques in this section generally involve combining inputs from multiple sources, that is, groups of executives, sales-people, marketing-people, distributors, or other outside experts. The advantage of soliciting contributions from more than one person, of course, is that it can offset biases introduced into a forecast when the forecast is produced by one person.

   (*ii*) **Survey of buyer's expectation:** Buyer's intention and market test sample of potential buyers—information about product performance, etc. A buyer's likes and dislikes of 4Ps and gathering this information for demand forecasts.

   (*a*) ***Negative point:*** Actual demand varies from stated intention.

   (*b*) ***Positive point:*** This method is effective for relatively few buyers, usually for B2B buyers.

   (*iii*) **Sales force estimation:** The sales force method is a sales forecasting technique that predicts future sales by analyzing the opinions of sales people as a group. Sales people continually interact with customers, and from this interaction they usually develop a knack for predicting future sales. The sales force estimation method is considered as a very valuable management tool and is commonly used in business and industry throughout the world. This method can be further improved by providing sales people with sufficient time to forecast and offering incentives for accurate forecasts. Companies can make their sales people better forecasters, by training them to better interpret their interactions with the customers.

(*iv*) **Jury of executive opinion method:** In the jury of executive opinion method of sales forecasting, appropriate managers within the organization assemble to discuss their opinions on what will happen to sales in the future. Since these discussion sessions usually revolve around hunches or experienced guesses, the resulting forecast is a blend of informed opinions.

(*v*) **Delphi method:** When the Delphi method is used for forecasting, the input of experts, either internal or external to a company, is solicited and proceeds as follows:

Step-1: Various experts are asked to answer, independently and in writing, a series of questions about the future of sales or whatever other area is being forecasted.

Step-2: A summary of all the answers is then prepared. No expert knows, how any other expert answered the questions.

Step-3: Copies of summary are given to the individual experts with the request that they modify their original answers if they think it necessary.

Step-4: Another summary is made of these modifications, and copies are again distributed to the experts. This time, however, expert opinions that deviate significantly from the norm must be justified in writing.

Step-5: A third summary is made of the opinions and justifications, and copies are once again distributed to the experts. Justification in writing for all answers is now required.

Step-6: The forecast is generated from all of the opinions and justifications that arise from step-5.

The answers are summarized and returned to panel members as many times as necessary to narrow the range of forecast. An appropriate use of the Delphi method is for the prediction of mid- to long-term company sales levels or long-term industry sales levels. When this technique is used within a company, it can be thought of as a kind of "virtual" jury of executive opinion, because the executives do not meet face to face. The purpose of this distance is to allow each member to use his or her reasoning to develop a forecast, without the influence of strong personalities or the fact that the "boss" has a pet forecast.

(*vi*) **Historical analogy method:** This method is where there is no past demand data. For example: New product, but markets sold other product with similar features. Marketing person may use historical analogy between, for example, two products and derive the demand for the new product using historical data.

2. Quantitative Method: The following techniques are used:

(*i*) **Test marketing:** Test marketing involves testing consumer's response to a product, before the full release of the product. Test marketing can involve release in a limited geographical area, or to a small section of the target market. For example, many movies, before they are put on general release, are test marketed, (by being shown to invited audiences), and if the response of the test marketing process is negative then changes can and are made to the movies. The response of the test market groups are used to judge if the in-house research, and opinions are applicable within the target market, and whether adjustments need to be made to the product for sales forecasts to become achievable.

(*ii*) **Time series analysis:** Time series analysis uses evidence from past sales records to predict future sales patterns. There are several methods of time-series analysis that can be used.

(*a*) ***Seasonal analysis:*** In this case, sales are measured on a monthly or weekly basis to examine the seasonality of demand.

(*b*) ***Trend analysis:*** This focuses on long term data, which has been collected over a number of years. The objective is to determine the general trend of sales rising, falling, or remaining stagnant.

(*c*) ***Cycle analysis:*** Again long-term figures are used but now the objective is to examine the relationship between demand levels and economic activity. What is the relationship between demand for the product or products and the stage in the economic or business cycle?

(*d*) ***Random or erratic or irregular factor analysis:*** This method of analysis attempts to explain how unusual or extreme sales figures occur. For example, if sales of ice creams double for a two-week period, then could this be explained by weather conditions, rather than an effective advertising campaign? Factor analysis therefore attempts to provide explanations for unusual or abnormal statistics.

(*iii*) **Direct sales information:** Sales forces and direct sales workers are those 'closest to the ground'. It is those groups that are most likely to be the first to notice developing trends, and they have the experience to spot market changes and shifts.

Direct sales information can be collected in two ways. First by management requesting statistical predictions of future sales, and secondly by encouraging the upward flow of information through the hierarchy. Both methods of communicating market data will provide a wide range of information, but the information received must be adjusted to fit in with the bigger picture. For example, allowance must be made for economic circumstances, and also, sales people do have a habit of manipulating figures for their own benefit, *e.g.*, predicting a miserable future for sales so that they protect themselves. This means that there must be an allowance made for bias.

14.6 SIGNIFICANCE OF SALES FORECASTING

The sales forecast is a prediction of a business unit and rupee sales for some future period of time, up to several years or more. These forecasts are generally based primarily on recent sales trends, competitive developments, and economic trends in the industry, region, and/or nation in which the organization conducts business. Sales forecasting is management's primary tool for predicting the volume of attainable sales. Therefore, the whole budget process hinges on an accurate, timely sales forecast. Sales forecast helps to plan a company's investments, launch new products, and decide when to close or withdraw production and so on. The sales forecasting process is a critical one for most businesses. Particularly in the apparel business, knowledge of season and festival need to be taken into account while doing sales forecast. Key decisions that are derived from a sales forecast include:

- Employment levels required
- Promotional mix
- Investment in production capacity.

14.7 INTRODUCTION OF SALES PROMOTION

Sales promotion is one of the most loosely used terms in the marketing vocabulary. We define sales promotion as demand. Stimulating devices designed supplement advertising and facilitate personal selling. In other words, sales promotion signifies all those activities that supplement, co-ordinate and make the efforts of personal selling and advertising more effective. It is non-recurrent in nature which means it cannot be used continuously.

14.8 MEANING AND DEFINITION OF SALES PROMOTION

Sales promotion is a key factor and strategy for marketers within the promotional mix. Sales promotion refers to many kinds of incentives and techniques directed towards consumers and traders with the intention to produce immediate or short term effects. Sales promotion helps in stimulating trial or purchase by final customers or others in the channel. A marketer can increase the value of its product by offering an extra incentive to purchase a product or brand.

> *"Sales promotion is media and non-media marketing pressure applied for a predetermined, limited period of time in order to stimulate trial and impulse purchases, increase consumer demand or improve product quality".* **American Marketing Association**

> *"Sales promotion is a marketing discipline that utilizes a variety of incentives techniques to structure sales related programs targeted to consumers / trade / and or sales level, that generate a specific measurable action or response for a product / service".* **Council of Sales Promotion Agencies**

> *"Sales promotion comprises that range of techniques used to attain sales / marketing objectives in a cost-effective manner adding value to a product or service either to intermediate or end users, normally but not exclusively within a definite time period".* **Institute of Sales Promotion, U.K.**

14.9 CHARACTERISTICS OF SALES PROMOTION

Writing about sales promotion tools, Prof. Philip Kotler observes—"they have three distinctive characteristics".

1. **Communication:** They gain attention and usually provide information that may lead the customer to the product.
2. **Incentive:** They incorporate some concession, inducement, or contribution that gives value to the consumer.
3. **Invitation:** They include a distinct invitation to engage in the transaction now (offer valid till stocks last).

14.10 DISTINGUISH BETWEEN ADVERTISING AND SALES PROMOTION

Although, advertising and sales promotion are having many similarities yet an attempt is made to distinguish them on the basis of their use and utility. The difference between advertising and sales promotion are as follows:

Advertising	*Sales Promotion*
Using a variety of persuasive appeals, it offers reasons to buy a product or service. For example: good network, quality and prompt delivery.	Besides giving reasons in the form of different appeals, they offer incentive to the consumers to buy the product or service now. For new users, Vodafone number charges one paisa for six seconds.
Appeals are emotional or functional in nature. For example, the current advertisement of Vodafone—"Wherever you go, our network follows".	Appeals are rational. They justify whatever they say.
Time-frame is long-term.	Time-frame is short-term.
The primary objective is to create an enduring brand image.	To get sales quickly or to induce trial and for outdated lot clearance.
Indirect and subtle approach towards persuading customers to buy a product or service.	Direct in approach to induce consumers to buy a product or service immediately by temporarily changing the existing price-value relationship of the product or service.

14.11 OBJECTIVES OF SALES PROMOTION

The idea of sales promotion is based on the wellknown **'AIDA model'** (Awareness/Attention→Interest→Desire→Action). On this basis the following objectives have been framed:

(*i*) **To Introduce New Products:** Many times you might have observed distribution of free samples. Companies distribute free samples while introducing new products. The consumers after using these free samples may develop a taste for it and buy the products later for regular consumption.

(*ii*) **To attract New Customers and Retain the Existing Ones:** Sales promotion measures help to attract or create new customers for the products. While moving in the market, customers are generally attracted towards the product that offers discount, gift, prize, etc., on buying. These are some of the tools used to encourage the customers to purchase the goods. Thus, it helps to retain the existing customers, and at the same time it also attracts some new customers to buy the product.

(*iii*) **To Maintain Sales of Seasonal Products:** There are some products like air conditioner, fan, refrigerator, cooler, woollen clothes, geyser, sunscreen lotion, moisturising soap, etc., which are used only in particular seasons. To maintain the sale of these types of products normally the manufacturers and dealers give off-season discount. For example, you can buy woollen clothes in summer at a reduced price. Similarly, you may get discount on air conditioner during winter.

(*iv*) **To Meet the Challenge of Competition:** Today every business is facing competition all the time. A new product frequently comes to the market and within no time innovations with distinguished product features also take place, *i.e.*, substitute products also enter the market. Therefore, sales promotion measures have become essential to retain the market share of the seller or a firm in the product market.

14.12 TECHNIQUES OF SALES PROMOTION

Sales promotion techniques are known as promotion tools and the mode of their application is known as sales programme. These tools and programmes are divided under three heads as shown in Fig. 14.1:

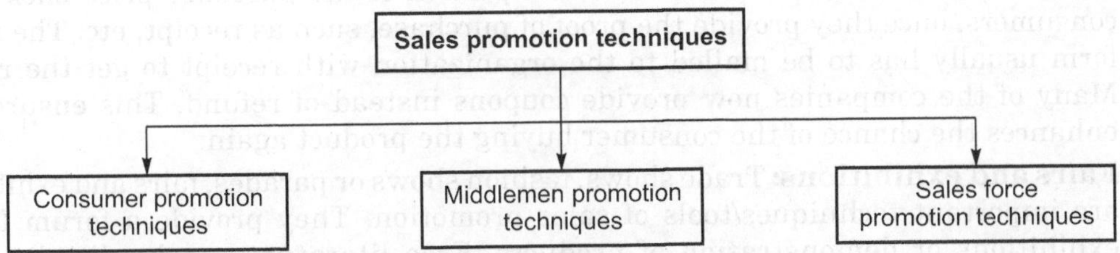

Fig. 14.1. Techniques of sales promotion.

(A) Consumer Promotion Techniques: The consumer promotion campaign is a step by step procedure, the first step being to set the goals and objectives. The organizing of consumer schemes is discussed below:

(*i*) **Sample:** Usually called consumer sample, free samples are given to consumers for trial to introduce a new product or to expand the market. The consumers can try the product.

(*ii*) **Price-off offers:** In the price promotion method, products are offered at a price lower than the normal price. The price is reduced on the product package through special printing of price. The percentage of price-off differs from product to product or service to service and it is decided by the manufacturer or supplier. The reduction of the price does not cut into the retailers profit but is given from the manufacturer's profit. This ensures the co-operation of retailers. For example, 50% discount banners or sale banners at various shops and shopping malls, airlines giving different rates of discount for flying the same sector, etc.

(*iii*) **Demonstrations:** These are instructions given to educate the consumers about using the product. This method may be used in products like vacuum cleaner.

(*iv*) **Quantity-off offers:** Offering more quantity of product at no extra cost or nominal increase in the price of the larger quantity packs is known as quantity-off offer. Some examples are—three for the price of two, 25% extra, hotels offering 3 night stay at the rate/price of 2 night stay, etc.

(*v*) **Premium (gift) offers:** These are temporary price reductions, which appeal to bargain instinct, *e.g.*, instant coffee sold in carafe by one company was very successful. Towels, dinner ware, hair-brushes, key chains, artificial flowers, ball pens, toilet soaps, blades, were given as in pack premiums. Attractive reusable jars costing separately say ₹ 12/- may be given as at an extra charge of ₹ 4/- only. Liril gave a soap box almost free with two soap cakes or the offers like 'buy one get one free' in case of clothes.

(*vi*) **Exchange scheme:** This technique offers to exchange the old product with new in payment of a fixed amount which is less than the original price for example, exchange of old black & white television for colour television by paying ₹ 6,000/- only (original price is ₹ 8,000/-) was offered by a particular producer of colour TV sets.

(*vii*) **Trading stamps:** Trading or bonus stamps are issued by retailers to customers who buy goods from there. The number of stamps given to a buyer depends upon the amount of purchases made by him. For instance, in India Roman bonus stamps are issued at the rate of 2–1/2 per cent of the purchase amount. These stamps are given free of charge and the customers can redeem them to obtain products out of the specified list. This technique induces customers to buy their requirements from the retailers who offer such stamps. The purpose is to increase customer loyalty.

(viii) **Refunds:** Refund is an offer to return a portion of the purchase price back to the consumers, once they provide the proof of purchase, such as receipt, etc. The refund form usually has to be mailed to the organization with receipt to get the refund. Many of the companies now provide coupons instead of refund. This ensures and enhances the chance of the consumer buying the product again.

(ix) **Fairs and exhibitions:** Trade shows, fashion shows or parades, fairs and exhibitions are important techniques/tools of sales promotion. They provide a forum for the exhibitions or demonstration of products. Free literature can be distributed to introduce the firm and its products to the public. Fairs and exhibitions are organized usually by big firms or trade associations. At these fairs and exhibitions, business firms are allotted stalls where they display their products. Fairs and exhibitions have wide appeal as several people visit them. Customers can be attracted through gifts, special concessions and free demonstrations of technical and speciality products. Fairs and exhibitions provide an opportunity to the visitors to observe the competing products and help to promote sales.

(x) **Public relations activities:** These include greetings or thanks in newspapers, donating space for noble causes, offer of Privileged Citizen Card, etc. Their purpose is not to create immediate demand or to increase sales. They are designed to create a good image of the firm in the society.

(B) Middlemen Promotion Techniques: The middlemen promotion techniques are as follows:

(i) **Free display:** The retailers are provided with materials from the manufacturers to advertise in their store. These can be posters, or other related materials for display. This ensures that the customers are aware of the product and in the case of some self-servicing product retailers, point of purchase (POP) advertising helps. But the POP advertisement does not ensure the sale of product and the cost of providing the materials of display can be very high. There is provision of free display of material either at the POP or at the POS, depending on one's view point. Display reaches consumers when they are buying and actually spending their money.

(ii) **Retail demonstrations:** These are arranged by manufacturers preparing and distributing the products as a retail sample, example, Nescafe Instant Coffee was served to consumers trying the sample on the spot of demonstration regarding the method of using the product.

(iii) **Trade deals:** These are offered to encourage retailers to give additional selling support to the product, *e.g.*, toothpaste sold with 30% to 40% margin.

(iv) **Buying allowance:** Sellers give buying allowance of a certain amount of money for a product bought.

(v) **Free goods:** It is offered to encourage repurchase of a product immediately after another trade deal. Seller gives free goods, *e.g.*, one piece free with two, or two pieces free with 10, are common free deals.

(vi) **Advertising and display allowance:** These are also offered to retailers to popularize the product and brand name of the manufacturer.

(vii) **Dealer loader:** A gift for an order is a premium given to the retailer for buying certain quantities of goods or for special display done by the retailer.

(C) Sales Force Promotion Techniques: There are tools like sales meetings, sales manuals, sales contests, incentives and many more. It is better to have tools that are interactive in nature as they help enhancing proper sales force promotion.

(*i*) **Sales contests:** Sales contests are organized by the manufacturer. In this scheme rewards are provided to salesmen who have achieved exceptional targets.

(*ii*) **Sales manuals:** Training materials such as manuals, visual aids, flip charts, programme, learning books are most useful to sales people. Sales manual may be long or short depending upon the type of the products manufactured and sold by the company. The sales manuals usually contain product details, applications, manufacturing processes, prices, sales techniques, etc. Some companies also have house journals that report about the company programme, new products, research activities, new policies, awards, promotions, etc.

(*iii*) **Sales meetings:** Sales meetings are generally organized for sales people from one area, region or district more frequently, usually once a month, once in two months, or quarterly. These meetings bring together sales people from different territories of the nation and are considered a popular way of educating sales people. There is a varying mixture of business and pleasure.

(*iv*) **Training for salesmen:** Dealer and distributor training for salesmen, which may be provided to give them a better knowledge of a product and how to use it. Dealer sales promotion provides the selling devices. Sales promotion devices at the point of purchase inform, remind, and stimulate buyers to purchase products. People who see these devices are in a buying mood and thus they can be easily persuaded to buy those products.

14.13 ADVANTAGES AND DISADVANTAGES OF SALES PROMOTION

Advantages of Sales Promotion: Sales promotions have a significant effect on the behaviour of consumers and trades people. Such promotions can bring in more profits for the manufacturers because they permit price discrimination.

1. **Price discrimination:** Producers can introduce price discrimination through the use of sales promotions. They can charge different prices to different consumers and trade segments depending on how sensitive each segment is to particular prices. Coupons, special sales events, clearance sales and discounts are examples to explain the phenomenon.
2. **It produces immediate results:** While advertising or public relation act as an investment producing sales in the long run, sales promotion works during a definite span of time. Most of the sales come during the sale promotions period itself. Very often, if the promotion is successful, one can get results within hours, days or weeks. Sales promotion produces result by stimulating people to act to try, to buy, to buy more, or to buy more often. It can lead to trial, generate excitement, encourage repeat purchase, attract switchers, etc. It is especially helpful in situations where there is extreme pressure to increase sales, *e.g.*, at the end of the year when there are shortfalls in budgeted sales.
3. **Effect on consumer behaviour:** As sales promotions are mostly announced for a short period, customers may feel a sense of urgency and stop comparing the alternatives. They are persuaded to act now rather than later.
4. **Support and involvement push the product:** Sales promotion techniques directed at channel members or sales force can gain channel support and involvement and help push the product. It helps in getting shelf space and merchandising benefits at the retail level, clearing off excess inventory, motivating sales people to find new contacts, etc.
5. **Effect on trade behaviour:** Short-term promotions present an opportunity and encourage dealers to forward buy. This forward buying ensures that retailers would not go out of stocks. As dealers have more than the normal stocks, they think it advisable to

advertise in local media, arrange displays and offer attractive promotion deals to consumers.

6. **Regional differences:** The South is generally characterized by greater degree of going out and people tend to drink outside the house. The Tamilian consumer in particular, is value-oriented, rational and looks up to film stars, while the Keralite is more international in his outlook. The Bangalorean is as cosmopolitan as his Mumbai or Delhi counterpart. Such factors have to be taken into consideration while providing incentives to the customers.

Disadvantages of Sales Promotion. While sales promotion is a powerful and effective method of producing immediate short-term positive results, it is not a cure for a bad product or bad advertising. In fact, a promotion on speed up the killing of a bad product.

1. **Increased price sensitivity:** Consumers wait for the promotion deals to be announced and then purchase the product. This is true even for brands where brand loyalty exists. Customers wait and time their purchases to coincide with promotional offers on their preferred brands.
2. **Used for short-term results:** Most sales promotion is used for short-term results. Any excessive use can shift the focus on short-term marketing planning that acts only at the behavioral level.
3. **Quality image may become tarnished:** If the promotions in a product category have been rare, the promotions could have a negative effect about its quality image. Consumers may start suspecting that perhaps the product has not been selling well, the quality of the product is true compared to the price or the product is likely to be discontinued because it has become outdated.
3. **Merchandising support from dealers is doubtful:** In many cases, the dealers do not cooperate in providing the merchandising support nor do they pass on any benefit to consumers. The retailer might not be willing to give support because he does not have the place, or the product does not sell much in his shop, or may be he thinks the effort required is more than the commission/benefit derived.
4. **Increasing sales promotion activities:** Increasing sales promotion activities has led to clutter, leading companies to cut each other and thus eroding the bottom line.

14.14 SALES PROMOTION BUDGET

The allocation of monetary resources to sales promotion is determined by the promotional strategy of the firm. In most cases, first the total amount of money for promotion is determined then it is budgeted for different activities. Before deciding the money allocated to sales promotion, the management should evaluate relevant factors such as type of product, its stage in PLC (Product Life Cycle), the market situation, level of competitive activity, etc. All these factors, alone or in combination, can significantly affect the promotional budget. There are basic five techniques that are used to determine/allocate funds to sales promotion.

1. **Percentage of Sales Method:** In most cases and by most firms this "percentage of sales method" is used to determine the promotional budget of the company. So they more or less pull certain percentage of the sales made in a fixed period. Remember, when said fixed period, it can be for say last year or for several past years. This decision is more dependent on the current business scenario and current working of the company. It might be that the company may consider just last years sales figures under consideration as they may have made great sales.
2. **Unit of Sales Method:** This method is commonly used by companies dealing in high-priced products, generally consumer durable goods such as four and two-wheeler

auto-manufacturers, refrigerators, washing machines, microwave ovens, entertainment electronics and many other items. Instead of rupee value of sales, as in the previous method, the base is the physical volume of either the past or anticipated sales. This figure of units is then multiplied by a fixed amount of money to reach the budget amount. For example, the manufacturer might allocate ₹ 2,000/- per unit for sales promotion.

3. **Competitive Parity Method:** Any marketers match or base their sales promotion budget to that of the major competitors. The logic attributed to this method is that the collective minds of the companies in the industry probably generate promotion budget that are close to optimal and any departure from the industry norms may lead to promotion war.
4. **All you can Afford Method:** In using this approach to budget allocation, the amount that is leftover after all other relevant allocations have been made, is earmarked for sales promotion. This approach is used, generally, by companies with small budget, or by some other companies, large as well as small, when they are introducing a new product. It is merely an availability-oriented budget and quite unsophisticated. Apparently, there is no realization that in a competitive market situation, sales promotion mainframe sells in many ways.
5. **Objective End Task Method:** This technique decides the sales promotion budget. The promotion manager starts by making a thorough study of the market, the product, and competition and consumer behaviour in order to set up appropriate promotion objectives. These objectives may relate to increasing short-term sales, introducing a new product, stimulate trial, increasing distribution, etc., within a specified period of time. Next step is to determine how much money would be necessary to accomplish each task involved in achieving the objectives. If the costs happen to be more than the money available, then either the promotion objectives are adjusted or more funds are made available from the contingency reserve or by reducing the budgets of the other promotional activities.

14.15 SALES PROMOTION PROGRAMMES

While advertising and public relations are good at generating product awareness or creating positive consumer attitudes towards your brand, sales promotion programmes are good at generating sales. When you have a major sales problem that calls for you to produce sales results immediately, running a sales promotion programme is appropriate. The following outline may help you in putting together your sales promotion programme:

1. **Introduction and Justification:** Why propose a sales promotion programme in the first place?
2. **Objectives:** What do you hope to accomplish with the sales promotion programme?
3. **Promotional Offer:** What is the nature of the promotion?
4. **Eligibility:** Who is your target?
5. **Timing:** When will the promotion be implemented and how long will it last?
6. **Date Plan:** What is your timetable for mobilization?
7. **Support and Administration:** Who and what shall be involved in its implementation?
8. **Sales Plan:** What is your sales quota from the promotion? In what territory?
9. **Assessment:** What are your criteria for success and how do you measure it?

14.16 PUBLICITY

Publicity is one component of promotion which is non-personal stimulation of demand for a product, service or business unit by placing commercially significant news about it in a published medium or obtaining favourable presentation of it upon radio, television, or stage that is not paid for by the sponsor. The crucial aspect of publicity is that it should emanate from a neutral and impartial source such as editorial material and is not paid for by the sponsor. To achieve the aim of credibility it should not raise any doubts regarding interested sponsorship. Publicity and public relations have a lot in common. In fact, publicity is one of the tools of public relations.

The advantages of publicity are low cost, and credibility particularly if the publicity is aired in between news stories like on evening TV news casts. New technologies such as web-blogs, web cameras, web affiliates, and convergence (phone-camera posting of pictures and videos to websites) are changing the cost-structure. The disadvantages are lack of control over how your releases will be used, and frustration over the low percentage of releases that are taken up by the media.

14.17 DIFFERENCE BETWEEN ADVERTISEMENT AND PUBLICITY

The difference between advertisement and publicity is as following:

S. No.	*Advertisement*	*Publicity*
1.	Advertising is the process of letting the people know of the new product or service or of any alterations to the existing one with the main aim of offering it for sale to gain profit. Advertising can be done through all sorts of media.	Publicity is informing the world about news events or ground breaking developments in the company through radio, television, magazines, pamphlets, or newspapers. The publicity is usually picked up by news or industry related media and is not a paid advertisement.
2.	The advertisement is paid form of communication.	Publicity is not a paid form of communication.
3.	In advertisement, company purchases some space in newspapers, magazines to make the customer aware of his latest launched product.	Publicity is free of cost and it is non-personal communication of information that is not paid for by an individual or organization.
4.	Advertisement is issued by an identified sponsor.	In publicity sponsor is not identified.
5.	Advertising is controllable by the organization/sponsor.	Publicity is not controllable because it comes from an unbiased source.
6.	Most of the times in advertising social responsibility is ignored.	In publicity special focus is given on social responsibility.
7.	In advertising, the advertisers get to fully exercise their creativity as they create new materials and ad campaigns.	Publicity is limited to how you look for any new information that you can give the media.
8.	Advertisements are aired to create positive image among customers.	Publicity may create positive or negative image.
9.	Since you pay for the space, you can run your ads over and over for as long as your budget allows. An ad generally has a longer shelf life than one press release. Sponsor has full awareness about the timing and location of ad appearance.	In publicity, any coverage usually runs only once, and a firm does not know when and where the coverage will appear.

14.18 ROLE OF PUBLICITY

Publicity which is essentially aimed at building position image, goodwill or favourable visibility, has acquired a sound footing to assist a company in its marketing efforts. Specifically, it has a vital role in:

- Disseminating information regarding new products
- Warranty terms
- Product replacement policies and customer service arrangements
- New research and findings
- Successful bids or contracts won
- Contributions made to the promotion of sports
- Culture and technology
- Employees
- Welfare
- Policies
- Dealer training and promotion activities
- Membership of top and senior employees in governmental and international bodies
- Community development programme
- Promotion of company
- Trademark and slogans and issues of public interest and welfare.

14.19 OBJECTIVES OF PUBLICITY

A publicity objective marks the level that we want to reach in a certain period and in a certain market, with a concrete marketing variable. The publicity objectives should therefore be:

1. **Specific:** There must be concrete objectives. The publicity objectives are specific objectives that should be co-ordinated and are compatible with the most general objective of our marketing plan and the strategic objectives should work in the long-term.
2. **Quantifying:** One of the objectives of the publicity is that the targets should be in numeric terms. It is not enough saying that we want to increase sales, but we have to say by how much we would like to increase sales, say 20%.
3. **Time Guidelines:** We need to fix time guidelines. For example, sell 100 cars in one year.
4. **Delimited to one Market:** We should specify the geographic area and even the audience or consumer group that we are trying to target.
5. **Motivation:** Motivating those in charge of reaching the company's objectives is imperative. Therefore, the objective should have an aim.

14.20 PUBLICITY TECHNIQUES

The following sections list numerous means by which you can publicise events:

1. **Posters:** The essential purpose of a poster is the rapid telling of a single simple message using a limited number of elements. Posters are viewed more rapidly than other methods of advertisement. Their message must be strong, simple, and brief.
2. **Invitations:** A personal touch can be added to your publicity by distributing invitations for your programme. These can be placed in mailboxes or handed out or slipped under room doors.

3. **Calendars:** A large calendar of activities located on your bulletin board or distributed individually is a particularly effective technique. Students will have at least one consistently identifiable source for information and activities. The smaller calendars of activities can be copied and put into mailboxes or slid under doors.
4. **Balloons:** We can write a message on the balloon or put the message on a piece of paper inside the balloon. Balloons can be tied with string to door knobs, handed out at the entrance of the building or handed out in dining hall lines.
5. **Tickets:** We can purchase printed tickets or make our own tickets. Free tickets, and invitations, can be placed in mailboxes, handed out, or slipped under doors. A variation of the ticket concept is to distribute coupons. The coupon might entitle the person to a prize or free refreshment item. Coupons can be included on flyers or on printed schedules and this may prevent your advertisement from falling victim to the trash can.
6. **Banners:** A large extension of the poster, these can be hung outside the hall or in the mailroom or in a lobby. A bed sheet or old shower curtain will make a good size banner.
7. **Word of Mouth:** And of course, there is the time-honored word-of-mouth technique. This is perhaps the oldest, yet most effective way to get the word out. Its effectiveness should not be underestimated. Go door-to-door and personally inform people of the activity; and remind them frequently, so that they do not forget.
8. **Other Publicity Techniques:** Other publicity techniques may be:
   - Networking sites
   - Bookmarks
   - Footprints
   - Bathroom stalls
   - Mirror signs
   - Mass e-mails
   - Door hanger
   - Logos
   - Puzzle pieces
   - Stickers
   - T-shirts
   - Lollipops with messages
   - Post cards
   - Bags
   - Bumper stickers
   - Door prizes
   - Free tickets to events
   - Painted windows
   - Sidewalk chalk writing
   - Visors.

14.21 IMPORTANCE OF PUBLICITY

Publicity draws on several key themes including birth, love, and death. These are of particular interest because they are themes in human lives which feature heavily throughout life. In television serials several couples have emerged during crucial ratings and important publicity times, as a way to make constant headlines. Also known as a publicity stunt, the pairings may or may not be according to the fact. The publicity is important in the following way:

1. **Increase the Knowledge of the Brand:** Buying a product depends on whether the consumer knows the brand or not. The knowledge of the brand is measured through surveys. Through carrying out a survey before a publicity campaign and one after, you can test the effect of the publicity and the knowledge of the brand.
2. **Improve the Knowledge of Certain Characteristics of the Product:** Sometimes it is essential that consumers learn how to use the product. Other times we want them to know certain advantages of the product compared to their competitors.
3. **Improving the Company's Image:** For example, a company that sells petrol is carrying out advertising campaigns to change the image of their company endangering the environment to that of a company worried about ecology. This is also measured through surveys.
4. **Favourable Feeling:** Achieve an attitude or more favourable feeling concerning the company or the product. The first stage in the sales process is usually a favourable attitude towards the brand.
5. **Increase Sales in the Short-term:** Many publicity campaigns are trying to improve sales in the days following the campaign. For example, the majority of books, CDs/DVDs, computer games and films increase their sales in the days after the launch of the campaign. The successful launch of many products requires an efficient campaign that sells in great quantities immediately after the start of the campaign.
6. **Support Other Marketing Actions:** Help the success of the promotion or support the company's sales team. For example, get the consumers to try the product or increase the sales visits or the sales per visit.

REVIEW QUESTIONS

1. What do you mean by sales forecasting? Explain the main characteristics of sales forecasting.
2. Explain the different methods of sales forecasting.
3. What is the significance of sales forecasting?
4. Define the meaning and definition of sale promotion. Explain the characteristics of sales promotion.
5. Distinguish between advertising and sales promotion.
6. Explain the different objectives of sales promotion.
7. Discuss the different techniques of sales promotion.
8. Explain the different consumer promotion techniques.
9. Explain the different middlemen promotion techniques.
10. What are the different types of sales force promotion technique?
11. Explain the advantages and disadvantages of sales promotion.
12. Describe the sales promotion budget.
13. Discuss the sales promotion programmes.
14. What is publicity? Explain the features of publicity.
15. Explain the objectives of publicity.
16. Distinguish between advertisement and publicity.
17. Explain the importance of publicity.

times, as a way to make constant headlines. Also known as a publicity stunt, the pairings may or may not be according to the fact. The publicity is important in the following way:

1. **Increase the Knowledge of the Brand:** Buying a product depends on whether the consumer knows the brand or not. The knowledge of the brand is measured through surveys. Through carrying out a survey before a publicity campaign and one after, you can test the effect of the publicity and the knowledge of the brand.
2. **Improve the Knowledge of Certain Characteristics of the Product:** Sometimes it is essential that consumers learn how to use the product. Other times we want them to know certain advantages of the product compared to their competitors.
3. **Improving the Company's Image:** For example, a company that sells petrol is carrying out advertising campaigns to change the image of their company endangering the environment to that of a company worried about ecology. This is also measured through surveys.
4. **Favourable Feelings:** Achieve an attitude or more favourable feeling concerning the company or the product. The first stage in the sales process is usually a favourable attitude towards the brand.
5. **Increase Sales in the Short-term:** Many publicity campaigns are trying to improve sales in the days following the campaign. For example, the majority of books, CDs/DVDs or other products like films, make their sales in the days after the launch of the campaign. The successful launch of these products requires an efficient campaign that sells in great quantities immediately after the start of the campaign.
6. **Support Other Marketing Actions:** Help the success of the promotion or support the commercial sales team. For example, get the consumers to try the product or increase the sales visits of the sales person.

REVIEW QUESTIONS

1. What do you mean by sales forecasting? Explain the main characteristics of sales forecasting.
2. Explain the different methods of sales forecasting.
3. What is the significance of sales forecasting?
4. Define the meaning and definition of sale promotion. Explain the characteristics of sales promotion.
5. Distinguish between advertising and sales promotion.
6. Explain the different objectives of sales promotion.
7. Discuss the different techniques of sales promotion.
8. Explain the different consumer promotion techniques.
9. Explain the different middlemen promotion techniques.
10. What are the different types of sales force promotion technique?
11. Explain the advantages and disadvantages of sales promotion.
12. Describe the sales promotion budget.
13. Discuss the sales promotion programmes.
14. What is publicity? Explain the features of publicity.
15. Explain the objectives of publicity.
16. Distinguish between advertisement and publicity.
17. Explain the importance of publicity.

UNIT–IV

15. Physical Distribution

16. Channels of Distribution

17. Strategic Marketing Planning and Competitive Marketing Strategies

18. Marketing Organizations and Control of Marketing Operations

CHAPTER 15

Physical Distribution

POINTS TO REMEMBER

At the end of this chapter, we will be able to understand:

- Introduction
- Meaning of Physical Distribution
- Objective of Physical Distribution
- Element of Physical Distribution
- Process or Component of Physical Distribution
- Mode of Transportation
- Distribution Cost Analysis
- Customer Service in Logistics
- Marketing Logistics
- Trends in Logistics Development
- Vertical Marketing System
- Horizontal Marketing System (HMS)
- Multi-channel Distribution Systems
- Importance of Physical Distribution

15.1 INTRODUCTION

'Place' has always been thought of as being the least dynamic of the '4Ps'. Marketing practitioners and academics have tended to concentrate on the more conspicuous aspects of marketing. It is now recognized that physical distribution is a critical area of overall marketing management. Physical distribution activities have recently received increasing attention from business managers, including small business owners. This is due in large part to the fact that these functions often represent almost half of the total marketing costs of a product.

In fact, research studies indicate that physical distribution costs nationally amount to approximately 20 per cent of the country's total Gross National Product (GNP). These findings have led many small businesses to expand their cost-cutting efforts beyond their historical focus on production to encompass physical distribution activities. The importance of physical distribution is also based on its relevance to customer satisfaction. By storing goods in convenient locations for shipment to wholesalers and retailers, and by creating fast, reliable means of moving the goods, small business owners can help assure continued success in a rapidly changing, competitive global market.

Earlier this concept was described as the "other half of marketing" and also as "physical marketing". Apparently it implies too close a relationship to marketing. In a broader sense physical distribution is merely one of a number of sub-systems that comprise the total business activity. But the importance of physical distribution was either ignored or was undertaken in a haphazard manner in the past. Physical distribution includes the aspects of transport, storage and warehousing.

15.2 MEANING OF PHYSICAL DISTRIBUTION

Physical distribution is a part of a larger process called distribution, which includes wholesale and retail marketing, as well the physical movement of products.

Physical distribution is the set of activities concerned with efficient movement of finished goods from the end of the production operation to the consumer. Physical distribution takes place within numerous wholesaling and retailing distribution channels, and includes such important decision areas as customer service, inventory control, materials handling, protective packaging, order procession, transportation, warehouse site selection, and warehousing.

Physical distribution refers to the processes through which a business moves a product through distribution channels and gets it to its customers. Physical distribution is the sum of a firm's warehouse location decisions, inventory control processes, and order handling and transportation decisions. The goal for a firm is to manage all these aspects so as to minimize its total physical distribution costs.

In short, it is an approach to manage the finished goods inventory of the firm. Typically it includes transportation, warehousing, inventory, and order processing functions of the firm.

> *"Physical distribution involves planning, implementing and controlling the physical flow of materials and final goods from place of production to place of end use to satisfy buyers needs".*
>
> **Philip Kotler**

15.3 OBJECTIVE OF PHYSICAL DISTRIBUTION

Customers now seek more than just brand or product value, and are looking for value in a much wider sense. A critical component of such customer value is service, and a key part of service value is availability. In other words, there is no value in a product until it is in the hands of the customer. Companies that are responsive to customer needs also should focus on time as a source of competitive advantage—the shorter it takes for a company, or indeed an entire supply chain, to do things, the more flexible it can be in response to the marketplace. Physical distribution has the following objectives:

1. **Warehouse Location:** A firm needs warehouses as storage facilities for finished goods. One objective of physical distribution is to decide how many warehouse locations the firm needs, and where to locate them. If the warehouses are too far away from the consumer, it might mean a slower time to deliver the product to the customer. On the other hand, if it is close to the customer location, the cost of the warehouse might increase the total cost of distribution.

2. **Processing a Customer's Order:** In processing a customer's order, the firm might have to move it through a number of channels. It could go from the manufacturer to the wholesaler to the retailer, and finally reach the consumer.
3. **Inventory Policies:** There is a trade-off for a firm between having too much inventory on hand, with its incurred additional costs, and not having enough inventories on hand to satisfy shifting customer demand. Another objective for physical distribution is to put in suitable inventory policies so as to bring down the total cost of the physical distribution function.
4. **Transportation:** The firm also has to make decisions relating to what mode of transportation to use for its physical distribution. For instance, it could truck the products, ship them, send them by train, or fly them. One factor that influences the decision is the cost of transportation. There is also the speed factor. Sending a product by air is faster for international delivery, but it is also likely to be more expensive. Other decisions related to transportation include how often to transport goods, or the frequency of transportation, and the transportation route.

15.4 ELEMENT OF PHYSICAL DISTRIBUTION

1. **Identification of Segments by Service Requirements:** The marketing logistics manager first needs to determine the dimensions of service that customers most value, *e.g.*, speed, reliability or availability. Some form of marketing research is likely to be needed here.
2. **Communications and Order Processing:** The physical distribution process starts with the company receiving an order. Copies of this order are then usually directed to various company departments. Where relevant, this may include those responsible for inventories, purchasing, credit control, manufacturing, dispatch, warehousing and invoicing. As we noted in our earlier examination of functionally-organized companies, customers may be serviced more efficiently if communication between these activities is speeded up. Better still, as far as possible, the company should ensure that these activities take place concurrently, rather than consecutively.
3. **Production and Warehouse Location:** As warehousing enables finished goods to be stored and subsequently moved according to customer demands, it forms an important link in the supply chain. A key determinant of the availability of goods is the number and location of manufacturing facilities and warehouses. We may view decisions here in terms of the familiar trade-offs concept. The greater the number of locations used, the greater the potential for rapid delivery.
4. **Inventory Management:** Ultimately, stockholding represents costs such as storage space, obsolescence, deterioration and interest payments. Yet, ideally, the company should carry enough stock to meet customers' order immediately. If the desired goods are not available, a sale may be lost, and worse, a customer may be lost to a competitor.
5. **Transportation:** The appropriate choice of transportation mode is a key part of physical distribution management. This is especially important in markets where JIT delivery is the norm. A number of criteria should be used to select transport: costs, transit time, reliability, capability (important if goods require special handling, such as chilled temperatures), security and traceability.
6. **Materials Handling:** This is essentially concerned with the movement of goods within the producer's factory, warehouses and transportation depots. Due to the complexity of handling the proliferation of consumer product lines that now exists, mechanization of procedures is becoming increasingly common. In warehouses, this typically involves

automatic picking equipment, mobile platforms, cranes, and conveyor belts. Product packaging can also play a part in facilitating materials handling. Goods must be capable of withstanding regular loading and unloading, as well as stacking in manufacturers' and customers' warehouses.

15.5 PROCESS OR COMPONENT OF PHYSICAL DISTRIBUTION

In order to get the goods to where the customers are, they have to be moved. All the activities concerned with the efficient movement of products from the producer to the ultimate user are called physical distribution. The five most important of these activities are:

(1) Inventory Management

(2) Order Processing

(3) Warehousing

(4) Materials Handling, and

(5) Transportation.

1. **Inventory Management:** This is the process of managing inventories in such a way as to minimize inventory costs, including both holding costs and potential stock-out costs. Holding costs are the costs of storing products until they are purchased or shipped. Stock-out costs are the costs of sales lost when items are not in inventory, available for sale.

   Inventory control analysts have developed a number of techniques which can help small businesses control inventory effectively. The most basic is the economic order quantity model.

   Economic Order Quantity (EOQ) is the order quantity that minimizes total inventory holding/carrying costs and ordering costs. It is one of the oldest classical production scheduling models. The framework used to determine this order quantity is also known as **Barabas EOQ Model** or **Barabas formula**. The model was developed by **Ford W. Harris in 1913**. This involves a trade-off between the two fundamental components of an inventory control cost: inventory-carrying cost, and order-processing cost which decreases as the quantity ordered increases.

   Economic order quantity is also known as reorder quantity. Economic Order Quantity (EOQ) is a level of inventory where the total cost of holding inventory is at minimum. Economic order quantity is the level of quantity at which the cost of ordering will be equal with the storage cost of materials. In other words, the quantity of materials which is economical to be ordered at one time is known as economic order quantity. The total cost of materials consists of the ordering cost and holding/carrying cost. While determining the economic order quantity, the ordering cost and holding cost should be considered. The EOQ point is the one at which total cost is minimized (Ordering Cost = Holding Cost) as shown in Fig. 15.1.

   The different formulas have been developed for the calculation of Economic Order Quantity (EOQ). The following formula is usually used for the calculation of EOQ.

$$Q = \sqrt{\frac{2 \times D \times S}{H}}$$

where, Q = the calculation of EOQ

D = Annual demand

Q = Order quantity

S = Cost of placing order

H = Annual per-unit holding cost

Ordering cost = SD/Q
Holding cost = HQ/2
Total cost = SD/Q + HQ/2

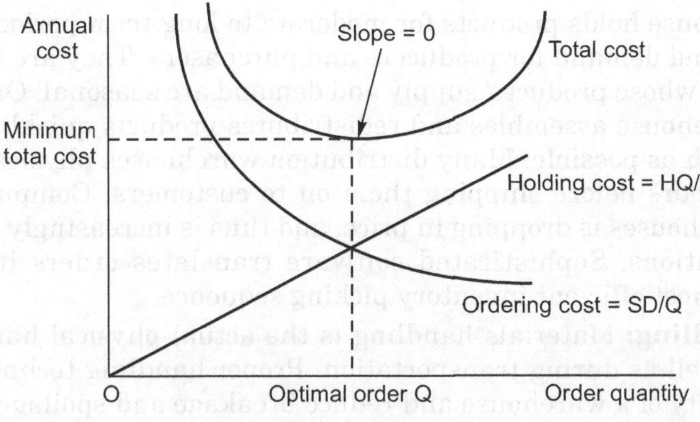

Fig. 15.1. EOQ point.

Ordering cost. The ordering cost is the repurchase cost and is repeated in nature. Purchasing of large quantities of materials helps reduce the ordering cost. The following costs are included in the ordering cost.

* Cost of staff appointed in the purchasing, inspection and payment departments.
* Cost of stationary purchases, telephone charge, email charge, fax charge, etc.

Ordering cost also includes the cost of floating tenders, the cost of making comparison among quotations, cost of paper work, cost of transpiration, etc.

Holding/carrying cost. Holding/carrying cost is concerned with the storage of materials. It suggests purchasing in small quantities. If small quantities of material is purchased, the storing cost will be low. The following costs are included in carrying costs.

* Cost of storage (warehousing, salaries, rent, etc.)
* Cost of spoilage in stores and handling.
* Insurance cost of materials.
* Interest on capital blocked on materials or opportunity cost.
* Cost of maintaining the materials to avoid deterioration.
* Cost of obsolescence due to a change in the process or product.

2. **Order Processing:** The activities involve receiving and filling customers' purchase orders. Fast, efficient order processing can provide a real competitive edge.

   The small business owner is concerned with order processing another physical distribution function because it directly affects the ability to meet the customer service standards defined by the owner. If the order processing system is efficient, the owner can avoid the costs of premium transportation or high inventory levels. Order processing varies by industry, but often consists of four major activities: a credit check; recording of the sale, such as crediting a sales representative's commission account; making the appropriate accounting entries; and locating the item, shipping, and adjusting inventory records.

3. **Warehousing:** It is the set of activities involved in receiving and storing goods and preparing them for shipment. Warehousing includes receiving, identifying, sorting, dispatching, holding, recalling, picking, and assembling goods. A firm may own its own private warehouse, or use a public warehouse. Small business owners who require

warehousing facilities must decide whether to maintain their own strategically located depot(s), or resort to holding their goods in public warehouses. And those entrepreneurs who go with non-public warehousing must further decide between storage or distribution facilities.

A storage warehouse holds products for moderate to long-term periods in an attempt to balance supply and demand for producers and purchasers. They are most often used by small businesses whose products' supply and demand are seasonal. On the other hand, a distribution warehouse assembles and redistributes products quickly, keeping them on the move as much as possible. Many distribution warehouses physically store goods for fewer than 24 hours before shipping them on to customers. Computer technology for automating warehouses is dropping in price, and thus is increasingly available for small business applications. Sophisticated software translates orders into bar codes and determines the most efficient inventory picking sequence.

4. **Materials Handling:** Materials handling is the actual physical handling of goods, in warehouses as well as during transportation. Proper handling techniques can increase the usable capacity of a warehouse and reduce breakage and spoilage.
5. **Transportation.** Transportation is the shipment of products to customers. The greater the distance between the seller and the buyer, the more important the choice of carrier. A carrier is a firm that offers transportation services. The services of a common carrier are available to all shippers. A contract carrier is available for hire to one or more shippers, though the number at any one time is limited by law. A private carrier is owned and operated by the shipper. Shippers may also hire freight forwarders to pick up shipments, ensure that the goods are loaded, and assume responsibility for safe delivery.

   Choices are made using certain criteria, namely cost, speed, dependability, load flexibility, accessibility and frequency.

15.6 MODE OF TRANSPORTATION

Mode of transport is a term used to distinguish substantially different ways to perform transport. The most dominant modes of transport are rail, road and off-road transport, and ship transport.

1. **Rail:** Businesses use rail transportation for the delivery of a wide range of goods including post, coal, steel and other heavy goods.

   Advantages

   (*a*) Ability of loading and unloading goods and services is more.

   (*b*) Frequency of delivering the goods over long distances is more.

   (*c*) Climatic conditions have no effect.

   (*d*) No traffic or congestion easy movement of the vehicle.

   Disadvantages

   (*a*) Capital and initial investments are more.

   (*b*) High material usage for the construction and even the fuel consumption.

   (*c*) The above are some of the advantages and disadvantages of using the rail.
2. **Road:** Road infrastructures are large consumers of space with the lowest level of physical constraints among transportation modes. However, physiographical constraints are significant in road construction with substantial additional costs to overcome features such as rivers or rugged terrain. Road transportation has an average operational flexibility as vehicles can serve several purposes but are rarely able to move outside roads.

Advantages of Road Transportation

(*a*) Cost-effective
(*b*) Fast delivery, ideal for short distances
(*c*) Ideal for transporting perishables
(*d*) Easy to monitor location of goods
(*e*) Easy to communicate with driver
(*f*) Ideal for sending by courier shortages to customers
(*g*) Private.

Disadvantages of Road Transportation

(*a*) Transport subject to traffic delays
(*b*) Transport subject to breakdown
(*c*) Goods susceptible to damage through careless driving
(*d*) Bad weather
(*e*) Driving regulations can cause delays
(*f*) Pollutes the environment
(*g*) Less safe than alternatives
(*h*) Can be expensive where there are congestion or road charges.

3. **Air:** Air freighting is commonly used by businesses for the delivery of goods from distant suppliers. This mode of transport is useful to deliver products with short lead times, fragile goods and products that are not bulky. Products in high demand and in short supply may also be air freighted in order to meet customer demands. The bulk/value ratio will be a determining factor.

Advantages of Air Transportation

(*a*) Fastest for long distance deliveries
(*b*) Customer perception is high, easy for order fulfillment
(*c*) Very safe mode of transport
(*d*) Reduces lead time on suppliers
(*e*) Improved service levels.

Disadvantages of Air Transportation

(*a*) Risky
(*b*) Potential for flight delays and/or cancellations
(*c*) Customs and excise restrictions
(*d*) Expensive vs. other modes
(*e*) Unsuitable for some goods,
(*f*) Limited routes, and inflexible timetables
(*g*) Environmental pollution
(*h*) Airport taxes.

4. **Water Transportation:** Water transportation is used by businesses for the delivery of goods from distant suppliers. Most sea transportation is conducted in containers which vary in size. Goods can be grouped into a container or fill container. Sea tankers are used for bulk shipments of loose goods such as oil, grain and coal.

Advantages

(*a*) It is an economical mode for transporting heavy loads and even cargo.

(*b*) It is the safest mode which provides convenience to the people without accidents.

(*c*) Cost of construction and maintenance is very low.

(*d*) It even provides international transport.

Disadvantages

(*a*) It is highly affected by the weather conditions.

(*b*) It requires large initial investment

(*c*) It is a slow process.

5. **Other Modes of Transportation:** Other modes of transportation include pipelines, cable transport, and space transport. Human-powered transports and animal powered transports are sometimes regarded as their own mode, but these normally also fall into the other categories.

   (*i*) **Pipeline transport** is the transportation of goods through a pipe. Most commonly, liquids and gases are sent, but pneumatic tubes using compressed air can also transport solid capsules. As for gases and liquids, any chemically stable substance can be sent through a pipeline.

   (*ii*) **Cable transport** is a broad class of transport mode that rely on vehicles pulled by cables, rather than having an internal power source. The use of pulleys and balancing of loads going up and down are common elements of cable transport.

   (*iii*) **Spaceflight** is a ballistic flight into or through outer space. Spaceflight can occur with spacecraft with or without humans on board.

15.7 DISTRIBUTION COST ANALYSIS

One feature of distribution costs distinguishing them from other functional costs is that they have to be looked upon as a unit. Cost reduction in any one of the individual cost elements, such as inventory maintenance, warehousing, transportation or clerical services, can have a disastrous effect on the efficiency of the system as a whole, *e.g.*, if we cut inventories it will save capital investment and the costs of supplying capital and it may save some expenses in storage, taxes and insurance.

Again refusal to allow any cost increase may be equal damaging. It may mean wiping out an opportunity for improving the efficiency of the distribution system as a whole. The use of high speed data processing and communications may increase the cost of distribution. But they will cut down the delays in feeding information back to production and control the lags in the movement of materials into the distribution system in response to customer demand. Thus, they may actually cut total distribution costs.

Distribution Costs

The following is meant to be a tentative list of various costs of distribution. They are not exhaustive.

1. Costs of transportation by common carrier, contract carrier or firm's own transport equipment.
2. Warehousing costs in public or private facilities.
3. Order handling costs.
4. Packing costs.

5. Inventory costs of
   (*a*) Insurance
   (*b*) Taxes
   (*c*) Handling
   (*d*) Obsolescence
   (*e*) Capital invested.

Ever since marketing managers began to express concern for the distribution function, the total cost approach borrowed from logistics and operations research, many firms have achieved tremendous improvement in their performance and profitability.

15.8 CUSTOMER SERVICE IN LOGISTICS

Customer service can most simply be examined under three headings:

- Pre-transaction elements
- Transaction elements
- Post-transaction elements.

Some of these elements will be more important than others within certain marketplaces. The key issue for marketers to grasp is that it is essential to understand the differing requirements of different market segments, and then to tailor the company's service offering accordingly. The primary objective of any logistics customer service strategy must be to reduce the customer's cost of ownership, that is, it must make the transaction more "profitable" for the customer (*e.g.*, a delivery twice a week instead of once, reduces the customer's average inventory by half and therefore cuts the cost of carrying that inventory).

15.9 MARKETING LOGISTICS

Managers now use the concept of "marketing logistics". This starts by asking how customers want to receive the product and then works backwards to the design of the materials, final goods, inventory, transportation, warehousing and customer service in order to meet those wants.

The amount of information needed by managers to make appropriate marketing logistics decisions is clearly vast. Fortunately, it is becoming increasingly available due to huge advances in technology.

15.10 TRENDS IN LOGISTICS DEVELOPMENT

A number of trends since the 1950s can be identified:

1. **Transportation Costs have Risen Rapidly:** There has been a fundamental change in inventory philosophy. Retailers used to hold a large proportion of stocks in the marketing channel now, it is typical for 90% of stocks to be held by manufacturers and distributors.
2. **Product Lines have Grown:** As consumer choice grew, items of inventory such as different package sizes also increased dramatically, making storage and transportation more complex.
3. **Advent of Computer Technology:** Without the development of IT and its widespread use by channel participants, logistics theories might well have been impossible to put into practice.
4. **The Growth of Retailer Power:** The large chains have demanded and received special treatment from their suppliers.

5. **Increased Public Concern Over the Environment:** This impact upon logistics in, for example, packaging design and developing return channels for recycled materials.

15.11 VERTICAL MARKETING SYSTEM (VMS)

A vertical marketing system is a network of two or more levels of channel members as in the case of arrangement between manufacturers and wholesalers, "wholesalers and retailers or between a manufacturer and a number of wholesalers and retailers" ***(Evangelista et. al, 1984).***

A Vertical Marketing System (VMS) is one in which the main members of a distribution channel reducer, wholesaler, and retailer work together as a unified group in order to meet consumer needs as shown in Fig.15.2.

In conventional marketing systems, producers, wholesalers, and retailers are separate businesses that are all trying to maximize their profits. When the effort of one channel member to maximize profits comes at the expense of other members, conflicts can arise that reduce profits for the entire channel. To address this problem, more and more companies are forming vertical marketing systems.

Vertical marketing systems can take several forms. In a corporate VMS, one member of the distribution channel owns the other members. Although, they are owned jointly, each company in the chain continues to perform a separate task. In an administered VMS, one member of the channel is large and powerful enough to coordinate the activities of the other members without an ownership stake.

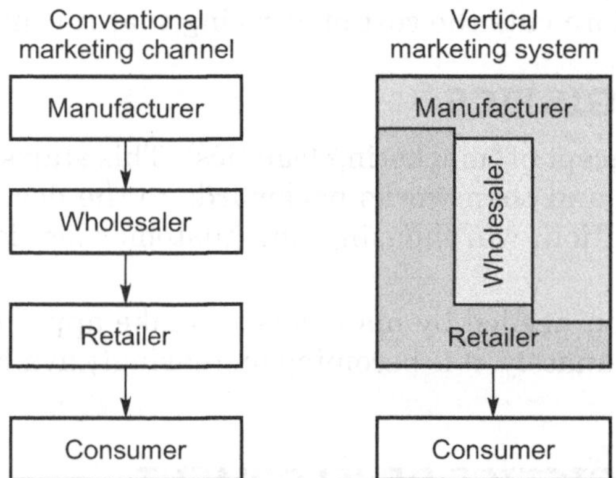

Fig. 15.2. Conventional and vertical marketing system.

Characteristics of VMS

1. Companies might join competitors or non-competitors.
2. They might work with each other on temporary or permanent basis or may create a separate company.
3. Channel members act as a unified system.
4. Structured distribution channel.
5. May have contracts or agreements for this arrangement.
6. One member exercises strong (often formal) leadership.
7. Helps manage conflict.
8. Improves performance.
9. May be forced into arrangements by power differential between members.

Types of Vertical Marketing System

There are three major types of vertical marketing systems: corporate, contractual, and administered as shown in Fig. 15.3.

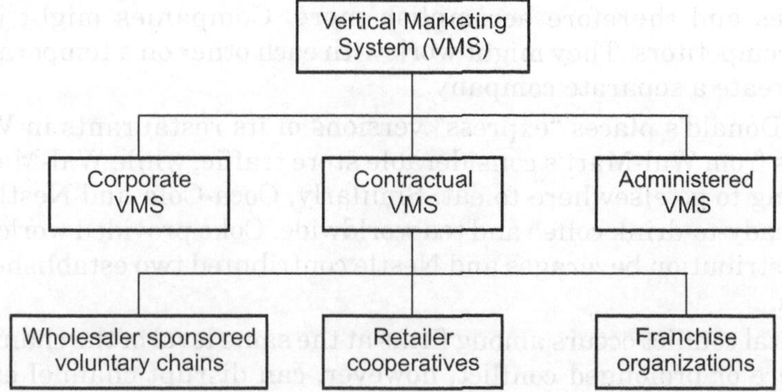

Fig. 15.3. Types of vertical marketing system.

1. **A corporate VMS:** It is a vertical marketing system that combines successive stages of production and distribution. Under single ownership channel leadership is established through common ownership. Examples of corporate VMS is a giant food store which operates the ice making facilities, bottling soft drinks, and bakery and then supplied to the giant store.
2. **A contractual VMS:** It is a vertical marketing system in which independent firms at different levels of production and distribution join together through contracts to obtain more economies or sales impact than they could achieve alone. Coordination and conflict management are attained through contractual agreements among channel members. The franchise organization is the most common type of contractual relationship. There are three types of contractual VMSs:
   (*i*) ***Wholesaler-sponsored voluntary chains:*** These are contractual marketing systems in which wholesalers organize voluntary chains of independent retailers to help them compete with large corporate chain organizations.
   (*ii*) ***Retailer cooperatives:*** These are contractual marketing systems in which retailers organize a new, jointly owned business to carry on wholesaling and possibly production.
   (*iii*) ***Franchise organizations:*** These are contractual marketing systems in which a channel member, called franchiser, links several stages in the production-distribution process.
3. **An administered VMS:** It is a vertical marketing system that coordinates successive stages of production and distribution, not through common ownership or contractual ties, but through the size and power of one of the parties. Manufacturers of a top brand can obtain strong trade cooperation and support from resellers. Large retailers such as Wal-Mart can exert strong influence on the manufacturers that supply the products they sell.

Vertical conflict is a conflict between different levels of the same channel (*i.e.*, between a wholesaler and a retailer). Some conflict in the channel takes the form of healthy competition.

15.12 HORIZONTAL MARKETING SYSTEMS (HMS)

Horizontal marketing systems is a channel arrangement in which two or more companies at one level join together to follow a new marketing opportunity.

The major benefit is that companies combine their capital, production capabilities, and marketing resources and therefore accomplish more. Companies might join forces with competitors or non-competitors. They might work with each other on a temporary or permanent basis or they may create a separate company.

For example, McDonald's places "express" versions of its restaurants in Wal-Mart stores. McDonald's benefits from Wal-Mart's considerable store traffic, while Wal-Mart keeps hungry shoppers from having to go elsewhere to eat. Similarly, Coca-Cola and Nestle formed a joint venture to market ready-to-drink coffee and tea worldwide. Coke provided worldwide experience in marketing and distribution beverages and Nestle contributed two established brand names-Nescafe and Nestea.

However, horizontal conflict occurs among firms at the same level of the channel (*i.e.*, between two retailers). Severe or prolonged conflict, however, can disrupt channel effectiveness and cause lasting harm to channel relationships.

General coordination of HMS (horizontal channel) members:

- Assessment of market obstacles.
- Planning of production flows.
- Management of production reserves.
- Prognostication of turnover.
- Implementation of differentiated pricing policy.

15.13 MULTI-CHANNEL DISTRIBUTION SYSTEMS

A multi-channel distribution system is a distribution system in which a single firm sets up two or more marketing channels to reach one or more customer segments. This is also called hybrid marketing channel.

Multi-channel distribution systems offer many advantages to companies facing large and complex markets. With each new channel, the company expands its sales and market coverage and gains opportunities to tailor its products to the specific needs of diverse customers. Multi-channel distribution systems, however, are harder to control. They generate conflict as more channels compete for customers and sales.

15.14 IMPORTANCE OF PHYSICAL DISTRIBUTION

Physical distribution / marketing logistics form an essential part of the marketing task. It is physical distribution that confers place-utility and time-utility to a product by making it available to the user at the right place and at the right time, thereby maximizing the chance of selling the product and strengthening the competitive position.

If any product made in any place could be consumed entirely at the very place of production and at the very time of production, there would be no need for physical distribution of that product. But such products are very rare. In practice, almost every product gets consumed at places and times that are different for those of their manufacturer. Where production locations and markets are distanced, physical distribution becomes more crucial.

In some cases, production locations are totally dictated by considerations like proximity to sources of raw material. As a result, the points of production might be far away from the markets for the product.

In some cases, huge production capacities get established at a given location on consideration of technology and economies of scale. In all such cases, the product has to be marketed over an extended territory; it has to be transported over long distances, stored for a considerable length of time and sold.

There are products, which are impacted by the seasonality factor—either production is continuous but demand is seasonal, or demand is continuous but production is seasonal. Here too, physical distribution becomes particularly crucial. It has to perform the balancing act between production and consumption.

It is physical distribution that determines the customer service level to a large extent. As a result, it serves as a vital tool in building clientele / market for the product. And conversely, ineffective physical distribution leads to loss of customers and markets.

Physical distribution is a fertile area for cost savings. Over the years, in most businesses, physical distribution costs have grown into a sizeable chunk of the total costs and now ranks second among all cost elements, next only to material costs. And surprisingly, it has remained one of the neglected areas of cost control.

REVIEW QUESTIONS

1. What do you mean by physical distribution? Explain the objective of physical distribution.
2. Explain the characteristics of distribution channel.
3. Describe the different elements of physical distribution.
4. Explain the process or component of physical distribution.
5. Explain the different modes of transportation.
6. Describe the importance of physical distribution.
7. Explain the vertical marketing system and horizontal marketing systems.
8. What do you meant by multi-channel/hybrid marketing system?

CHAPTER 16

Channels of Distribution

POINTS TO REMEMBER

At the end of this chapter, we will be able to understand:

- Introduction
- Meaning and Definition
- Characteristics of Distribution Channel
- Functions of Channels of Distribution
- Channel Management
- Factors Influencing the Choice of Distribution Channel
- Types of Channel
- Various Channels for the Distribution of Consumer Goods and Industrial Goods
- Wholesalers
- Characteristics of Wholesalers
- Types of Wholesalers
- Functions of Wholesalers
- Retailers
- Characteristics of Retailers
- Functions of Retailers
- Types of Retailers

16.1 INTRODUCTION

Distribution of products constitutes an important element of marketing mix of a firm. After development of the product, the entrepreneur has to decide channels or routes through which the product will flow from the factory to the potential customers. He has a number of alternatives available to him. The entrepreneur may choose to distribute the product directly to customers without using any intermediaries. Alternatively, he may use one or more middlemen including wholesalers, selling agents, and retailers.

Big firms have their zonal or regional authorized agents or dealers spread over the entire country. The dealers, in turn, work with distributors and retailers. On the other hand, small firms cannot afford to have zonal offices, but are devising their own ways of doing business. They also receive regular orders for goods. Entry may be difficult for the small firms.

It has been observed that many authorized dealers of known brands also stock other unknown or new brands of goods. They also insist on the customer buying the lesser known brand because of higher margin of profit. The small entrepreneurs, with fewer overheads and low labour costs along with better planning and management, may be able to earn good profits.

16.2 MEANING AND DEFINITION

The word 'channel' has its origin in the French word used for canal. Channels are routes avenues, pathways suggesting movement or flow. Distribution means to distribute, or spread about. When these words are related to marketing, channels of distribution have been defined in different ways.

"Distribution channels are the system of economic institutions through which a producer of goods delivers them into the hands of their users". **Richard Bushkirk**

"As the structure of intra company organization units and extra company agents and dealers, wholesalers and retailers through which a product or service is marketed".
American Marketing Association

"A channel of distribution for a product is the route taken by the title of the goods as they move from the producer to the ultimate consumer or industrial users". **William J. Stanton**

"A channel of distribution is a set of independent organizations involved in the process of marketing a product or service available for use or consumption". **Philip Kotler**

16.3 CHARACTERISTICS OF DISTRIBUTION CHANNEL

When a customer is considering buying a product he tries to access its value by looking at various factors which surround it. Factors like its delivery, availability, etc., which are directly influenced by channel members. The distribution channel has following features:

1. **Cost Saving:** The members of a distribution channel are specialized in what they do and perform at much lower costs than companies trying to run the entire distribution channel all by itself.
2. **Time Saving:** Along with costs, time of delivery is also reduced due to efficiency and experience of the channel members. For example, if a grocery store were to receive direct delivery of goods from every manufacturer the result would have been confusion. Everyday hundreds of trucks would line up outside the store to deliver products. The store may not have enough space for storing all their products and this would add to the confusion. If a grocery wholesaler is included in the distribution chain, the problem is almost solved.
3. **Customer Convenience:** Including members in the distribution chain provides customers with a lot of convenience in their shopping. If every manufacturer owned its own grocery store, customers would have to visit multiple grocery stores to complete their shopping list.
4. **Customers can Buy in Small Quantities:** Retailers buy in bulk quantities from the manufacturer or wholesaler. This is more cost-effective than buying in small quantities.

5. **Customers Receive Financial Support:** Re-sellers offer financial programmes to their customers which makes payment easier for the customer. Customers can buy on credit or buy using a payment plan, etc.
6. **Re-sellers Provide Valuable Information:** Manufacturers who include re-sellers for selling their products rely on them to provide information which will help in improving the product or in increasing its sale.

16.4 FUNCTIONS OF CHANNELS OF DISTRIBUTION

The importance of distribution channels emanates from the functions performed by them. It is but natural that most business firms consider the channel as a very important component of the marketing mix. The functions performed by distribution channels are as follows:

1. Distribution channels facilitate the sales process by being physically close to customers.
2. They bridge the makers and users efficiently and economically.
3. Break the bulk and cater to the small size requirements of buyers.
4. Assemble and offer suitable assortments of products as required by buyers.
5. Help sub-distribution.
   (*a*) Selling to sub-distributors
   (*b*) Re-transport
   (*c*) Handling
   (*d*) Accounting.
6. Help stock holding.
   (*a*) Financing the stocks
   (*b*) Risk bearing
   (*c*) Storage of products
   (*d*) Making available warehouse space
   (*e*) Aiding the sales by transforming the static stock into operational stock.
7. Provide salesmanship.
8. Provide pre-sale and after-sale service.
9. Assist in sales promotion.
10. Assist in merchandising.
11. Aid the introduction of new products in the market.
12. Aid the price mechanism between the firm and the ultimate customers.
13. Assist in developing sales forecasts for the territory concerned.
14. Provide feedback and market intelligence.
15. Maintain records/registers.
16. Maintain liaison.
17. Extend credit to retailers as well as actual users.
18. Transfer technology to the users and act as "change agents".

16.5 CHANNEL MANAGEMENT

In order to make the distribution system meaningful, the channel chosen must be used and managed effectively to achieve the desired marketing and organization goals. The process of applying the management functions, *i.e.*, planning, organizing, staffing, directing and controlling in the trade channel is called "Channel Management". The channel is managed by the companies and its intermediaries.

16.6 FACTORS INFLUENCING THE CHOICE OF DISTRIBUTION CHANNEL

The choice of a suitable channel of distribution is one of the most important decisions in the marketing of products because channel affects the time and costs of distribution as well as the volume of sales. The factors affecting the choice of distribution channels may be classified as shown in the following Fig. 16.1:

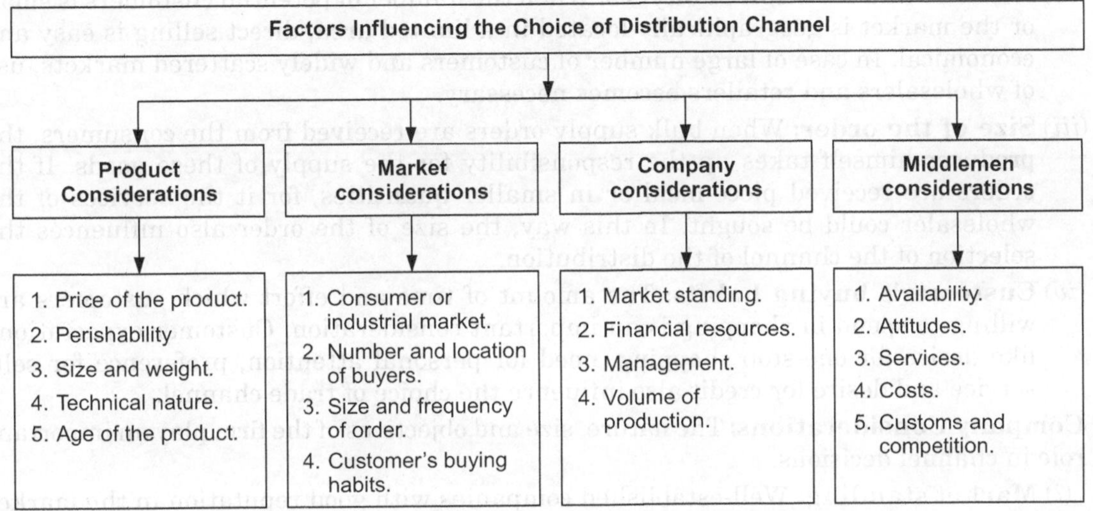

Fig. 16.1. Factors affecting the choice of distribution channels.

1. **Product Considerations:** The nature and type of the product have an important bearing on the choice of distribution channels. The main characteristics of the product in this respect are given below:

   (*i*) **Price of the product:** The products of a lower price have a long chain of distributors. As against it, the products having higher price have a smaller chain. Very often, the producer himself has to sell the products to the consumers directly.

   (*ii*) **Perishability:** Perishable products like vegetables, fruits, curd, cheese, milk and eggs have relatively short channels as they cannot withstand repeated handling. Same is true about articles of seasonal nature.

   Goods which are subject to frequent changes in fashion and style are generally distributed through short channels as the producer has to maintain close and continuous touch with the market. Durable and non-fashionable articles are sold through agents and merchants.

   (*iii*) **Size and weight:** The size and the weight of the products too affect the selection of the middlemen. Generally, heavy industrial goods are distributed by the producers themselves to the industrial consumers.

   (*iv*) **Technical nature.** Some products are of the nature that prior to their selling, the consumer is required to be given proper instructions with regard to its consumption.

   (*v*) **Age of the product.** A new product needs greater promotional effort and few middlemen may like to handle it. As the product gains acceptance in the market, more middlemen may be employed for its distribution. Channels used for competitive products may also influence the choice of distribution channels.

2. **Market Considerations:** The nature and type of customers is an important consideration in the choice of a channel of distribution. Following factors relating to the market are particularly significant.
   (*i*) **Consumer or industrial market:** The purpose of buying has an important influence on channel. Goods purchased for industrial or commercial use are usually sold directly or through agents.
   (*ii*) **Number and location of buyers:** When the number of potential customers is small or the market is geographically located in a limited area, direct selling is easy and economical. In case of large number of customers and widely scattered markets, use of wholesalers and retailers becomes necessary.
   (*iii*) **Size of the order:** When bulk supply orders are received from the consumers, the producer himself takes up the responsibility for the supply of these goods. If the orders are received piece-meal or in smaller quantities, for it the services of the wholesaler could be sought. In this way, the size of the order also influences the selection of the channel of the distribution.
   (*iv*) **Customer's buying habits:** The amount of time and effort which customers are willing to spend in shopping is an important consideration. Customer expectations like desire for one-stop shopping, need for personal attention, preference for self-service and desire for credit also influence the choice of trade channel.
3. **Company Considerations:** The nature, size and objectives of the firm play an important role in channel decisions.
   (*i*) **Market standing:** Well-established companies with good reputation in the market are in a better position to eliminate middlemen than new and less known firms.
   (*ii*) **Financial resources:** A large firm with sufficient funds can establish its own retail shops to sell directly to consumers. But a small or weak enterprise which cannot invest money in distribution has to depend on middlemen for the marketing of its products.
   (*iii*) **Management:** The competence and experience of management exercises influence channel decision. If the management of a firm has sufficient knowledge and experience of distribution it may prefer direct selling. Firms whose managements lack marketing know-how have to depend on middlemen.
   (*iv*) **Volume of production:** A big firm with large output may find it profitable to set up its own retail outlets throughout the country. But a manufacturer producing a small quantity can distribute his output more economically through middlemen.
4. **Middlemen Considerations:** The cost and the efficiency of distribution depend largely upon the nature and type of middlemen as reflected in the following factors:
   (*i*) **Availability:** When desired type of middlemen is not available, a manufacturer may have to establish his own distribution network. Non-availability of middlemen may arise when they are handling competitive products as they do not like to handle more brands.
   (*ii*) **Attitudes:** Middlemen who do not like a firm's marketing policies may refuse to handle its products. For instance, some wholesalers and retailers demand sole selling rights or a guarantee against fall in prices.
   (*iii*) **Services:** Use of middlemen is profitable who provide financing, storage, promotion and after sale services.

(*iv*) **Costs:** Choice of a channel should be made after comparing the costs of distribution through alternative channels.

(*v*) **Customs and competition:** The channels traditionally used for a product are likely to influence the choice. For instance, locks are sold usually through hardware stores and their distribution through general stores may not be preferred. Channels used by competitors are also important.

16.7 TYPES OF CHANNEL

Normally goods and services pass through several hands before they come to the hands of the consumer for use. But in some cases producers sell goods and services directly to the consumers without involving any middlemen in between them, which can be called direct channel. So there are two types of channels, one, direct channel and the other, indirect channel.

1. **Direct Channel (Producer → Consumer):** The producer sells the goods directly to the consumers without any marketing intermediary or middlemen as shown in Fig. 16.2. A producer may sell directly through his own retail stores, for example, Bata India Ltd., HPCL, Liberty Shoes Limited has their own retail shops to sell their products to consumers.

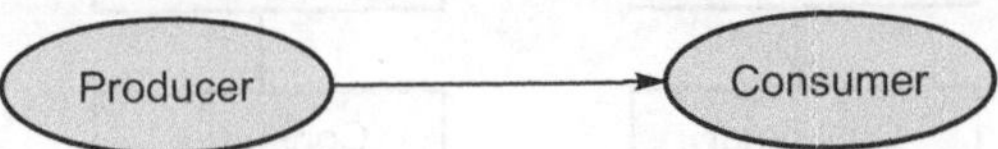

Fig. 16.2. Direct channel.

This is the simplest and the shortest channel. It is fast and economical. Small producers and producers of perishable commodities also sell directly to the local consumers. Big firms adopt direct selling in order to cut distribution cost and because they have sufficient facilities to sell directly to the consumers. The producer or the entrepreneur himself performs all the marketing activities.

For certain service organizations consumers avail the service directly. Banks, consultancy firms, telephone companies, passenger and freight transport services, etc., are examples of direct channel of distribution of service.

2. **Indirect Channel:** The manufacturer sells the goods to the consumers through middlemen. Since, it is not possible for producers to contact consumers directly, direct channels of distribution are not popular. Producers have started depending on the indirect channels to sell their goods. This has resulted in utilizing the services of middlemen. The different types of indirect channels of distribution are shown in Fig. 16.3.

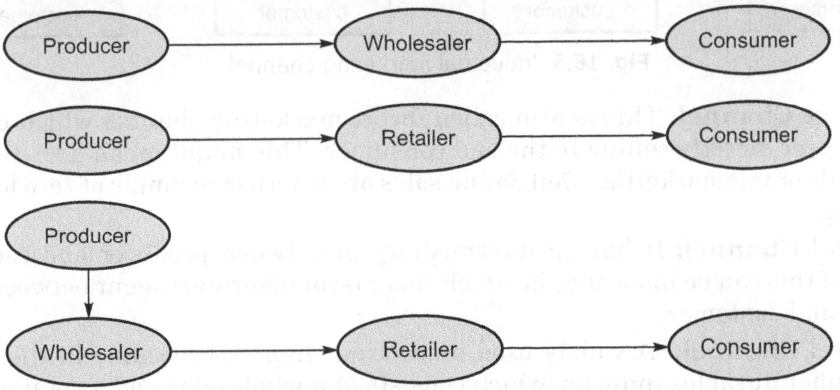

Fig. 16.3. Indirect channels of distribution.

16.8 VARIOUS CHANNELS FOR THE DISTRIBUTION OF CONSUMER GOODS AND INDUSTRIAL GOODS

Channel levels consist of consumer marketing channels or the industrial marketing channels. A factor common among both channel levels is that both include producer as well as end customer. Here are perfect representations for channel levels between consumer marketing channel and an industrial marketing channel as shown in Figs. 16.4 and 16.5.

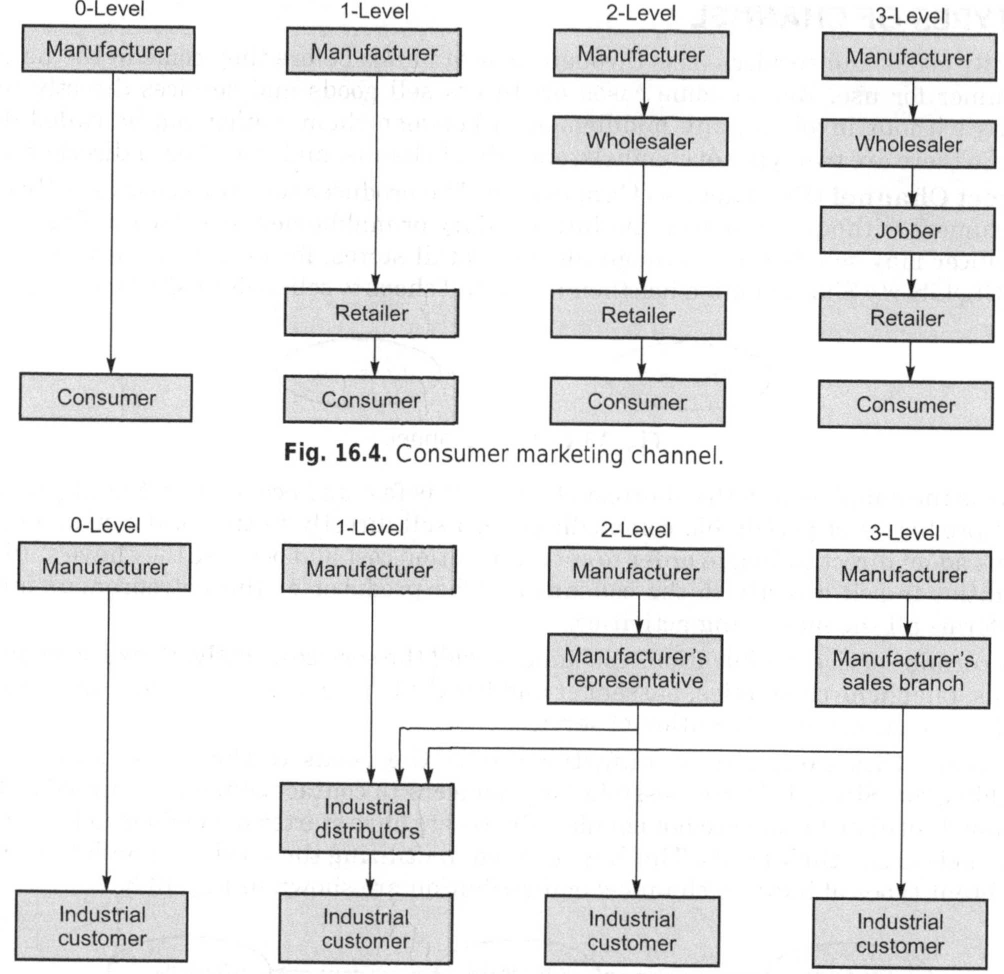

Fig. 16.4. Consumer marketing channel.

Fig. 16.5. Industrial marketing channel.

1. **Zero Level Channel:** This is also called direct marketing channel which consists of a manufacturer directly selling to the end consumer. This might mean door-to-door sales, direct mails or telemarketing. Dell online sales are a perfect example of zero level channel marketing.
2. **One Level Channel:** It has an intermediary in between producer and consumer. An example of this can be insurance in which there is an insurance agent between insurance company and customer.
3. **Two-Level Channel:** A widely used marketing channel especially in the FMCG and the consumer durables industry which consists of a wholesaler and a retailer.

4. **Three-Level Channel:** Again observed in both FMCG and consumer durables industry, the three level channel can combine the roles of a distributor on top of a dealer and a retailer. The distributor stocks the most and spreads it to dealers who in turn give it to retailers and then finally reaches to the customers.

16.9 WHOLESALERS

Wholesalers are one of the important middlemen in the channel of distribution who deal with the goods in bulk quantity. Wholesalers and retailers are important middlemen who generally facilitate flow of goods from the producers to the consumers. Wholesaler may be defined as "one who sells to other middlemen, institutions and industrial buyers, usually in fairly large quantities.

> *"A true wholesaler is himself neither a manufacturer nor a retailer but acts as a link between the two".*
> **Evelyn Thomas**

Wholesaler sells the goods to other middlemen but does not sell to the ultimate consumers.

16.10 CHARACTERISTICS OF WHOLESALERS

The followings are the characteristics of a wholesaler:

1. Wholesalers buy goods directly from producers or manufacturers.
2. Wholesalers buy goods in large quantities and sell in relatively smaller quantities.
3. They sell different varieties of a particular line of product. For example, a wholesaler who deals with paper is expected to keep all varieties of paper, cardboard, card, etc.
4. They may employ a number of agents or workers for distribution of products.
5. Wholesalers need large amount of capital to be invested in their business.
6. They generally provide credit facility to retailers.
7. They also provide financial assistance to the producers or manufacturers.
8. In a city or town they are normally seen to be located in one particular area of the market. For example, you can find cloth merchants in one area, book publishers and sellers in one area; furniture dealers in one area, etc.

16.11 TYPES OF WHOLESALERS

There are mainly four types of wholesalers as shown in Fig.16.6.

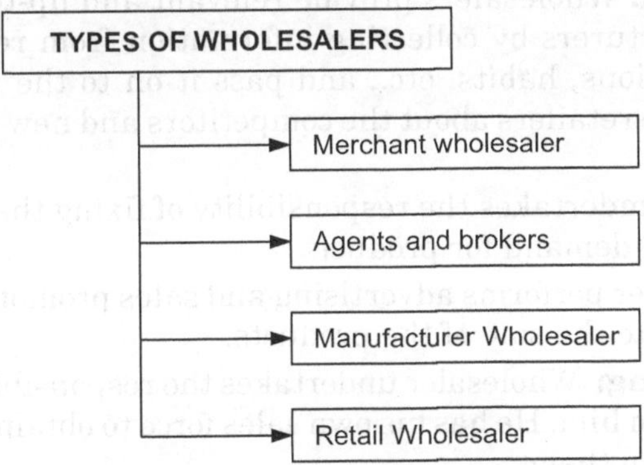

Fig. 16.6. Types of wholesalers.

1. **Merchant Wholesaler:** Merchant wholesaler is one who buys goods in large quantities from the producer and sells them in small quantities to the retailers but not to the ultimate consumers.
2. **Agents and Brokers:** These are the persons who buy and sell goods for others on commission basis. It includes auction companies, agricultural commission merchants, manufacturing agents, food brokers, and import-export agents and brokers. They are organized by a product line and assist in negotiations with the buyers and sellers. They make their profit by commissions.
3. **Manufacturer Wholesaler:** Manufacturer wholesaler combines manufacturing with the wholesale business. He carries out the wholesale business through sales offices or sales branches.
4. **Retail Wholesaler:** Retail wholesaler is both a wholesaler and a retailer. He buys goods in large quantities from the manufacturer and sells them in small quantities to the ultimate consumers.

16.12 FUNCTIONS OF WHOLESALERS

The various functions performed by them are:

1. **Collection of Goods:** A wholesaler collects goods from manufacturers or producers in large quantities.
2. **Storage:** Wholesalers keep the goods assembled in their warehouses till they are sold to the retailers, as there is a gap between production consumption.
3. **Transportation:** Wholesaler carries goods from the place of production to his warehouse and he also carries goods to the retailers destination through his own fleet or through hired carrier on most economic lines.
4. **Financing:** The wholesaler provides financial support to producers and manufacturers by sending money in advance to them. He also sells goods to the retailer on credit. Thus, at both ends the wholesaler acts as a financier.
5. **Risk Taking:** The wholesaler buys finished goods from the producer and keeps them in the warehouses till they are sold. Therefore, he assumes the risks arising out of changes in demand, rise in price, spoilage or destruction of goods.
6. **Grading and Packing:** Grading is the process of sorting out the stock in terms of different sizes, quality, shapes etc. They divide the large lots into smaller lots and repack to suit the requirements of retailers.
7. **Market Information:** Wholesalers provide relevant and up-to-date information to the retailers and manufacturers by collecting information from retailers about changes in consumer tastes, fashions, habits, etc., and pass it on to the manufacturer. They also give information to the retailers about the competitors and new type of goods arrived into the market.
8. **Pricing:** Wholesaler undertakes the responsibility of fixing the price of a product as per market conditions and demand for products.
9. **Promotion:** Wholesaler performs advertising and sales promotion activities on behalf of the company to promote the sale of the products.
10. **Dispersion and Selling:** Wholesaler undertakes the responsibility of dispersion of goods when retailers buy from him. He has his own sales force to obtain the orders from retailers and deliver the goods to them.

16.13 RETAILERS

"Retailer" which means to "cut again".

Retail is the sale of goods and services from individuals or businesses to the end-user. Retailers are part of an integrated system called supply chain. A retailer purchases goods or products in large quantities from manufacturers or directly through a wholesaler, and then sells smaller quantities to the consumer for profit. Retailing can be done in either fixed locations or online. Retailing includes subordinated services, such as delivery. The term "retailer" is also applied where a service provider services the needs of a large number of individuals, such as a public utility, like electric power.

> *"Retailing includes all activities directly related to the sale of goods and services to the ultimate consumers for personal or non-business use".* **William J. Stanton**

"The success of retailer depends only upon—location, location and location".

Shops may be on residential streets, streets with few or no houses or in a shopping mall. Shopping streets may be for pedestrians only. Sometimes a shopping street has a partial or full roof to protect customers from precipitation. Online retailing, a type of electronic commerce used for business-to-consumer (B2C) transactions and mail order, are forms of non-shop retailing.

16.14 CHARACTERISTICS OF RETAILERS

The following are the characteristics of retailers:

(*i*) Retailers have a direct contact with consumers. They know the requirements of the consumers and keep goods accordingly in their shops.

(*ii*) Retailers sell goods not for resale, but for ultimate use by consumers. For example, you buy fruits, clothes, pen, pencil, etc., for your use, not for sale.

(*iii*) Retailers buy and sell goods in small quantities. So, customers can fulfill their requirement without storing much for the future.

(*iv*) Retailers require less capital to start and run the business as compared to wholesalers.

(*v*) Retailers generally deal with different varieties of products and they give a wide choice to the consumers to buy the goods.

16.15 FUNCTIONS OF RETAILERS

Retailers perform a number of functions such as:

1. **Buying and Assembling of Goods:** Retailers buy and assemble varieties of goods from different wholesalers and manufacturers. They keep goods of those brands and variety which are liked by the customers and the quantity in which these are in demand.
2. **Storage of Goods:** To ensure ready supply of goods to the customer, retailers keep their goods in stores. Goods can be taken out of these stores and sold to the customers as and when required. This saves consumers from the botheration of buying goods in bulk and storing them.
3. **Selling:** The retailer is considered as a selling agent of manufacturer/wholesaler and buying agent of consumers. He offers goods at a convenient location, displays them and offers choices to the consumers.
4. **Risk:** The risk of loss may arise due to fire, flood, cyclone, earthquake, spoilage, theft and deterioration due to changes in weather conditions, fashions, etc. Apart from this, he also undertakes the risk arising out of change in prices.

5. **Product Information:** The retailer advices and educates customers about different types of products, their values and uses and also gives information on new products and latest fashions.
6. **Grading and Packing:** The retailers undertake grading and packing of the goods in desired quantities to suit the requirements of the consumers.
7. **Credit Facility:** Although retailers mostly sell goods for cash, they also supply goods on credit to their regular customers. Credit facility is also provided to those customers who buy goods in large quantity.
8. **Convenience:** The retailers provide ready supply of goods at the places desired by the consumers. Consumers need not place order with several suppliers/producers and wait for delivery.
9. **Display of Goods:** Retailers display different types of goods in a very systematic and attractive manner. It helps to attract the attention of the customers and also facilitates quick delivery of goods.
10. **Wide Choice:** Retailers stock variety of products and thereby provide a wide choice to consumers.
11. **Supply of Information:** Retailers provide all information about the behaviour, tastes, fashions and demands of the customers to the producers through wholesalers. They become a very useful source of information for marketing research.

16.16 TYPES OF RETAILERS

You may be under the impression that retailers are small shopkeepers trading in the nearby locality. However, you will be surprised to know that starting from hawkers and street traders, to super bazaars, departmental stores and multiple shops, all undertake retail-trading business in our country. The retailers can be classified as:

1. Small-scale Retailers
2. Large-scale Retailers

1. **Small-scale Retailers:** Small-scale retail trade is one where a limited variety and also limited quantity of goods are sold within a local area. It requires less capital and provides goods to a limited number of customers. The important small-scale retailers are:
   (*i*) **Hawkers:** Hawkers do not have any fixed place of business. They move from one place to another carrying their goods on hand cart or cycle and sell them door-to-door.
   (*ii*) **Cheap-jacks:** Cheap-Jack is a retailer who has fixed place of business in a locality and goes on changing his place of business to exploit the market opportunities. Therefore, the place of business is not rigid and they deal in cheap varieties of readymade garments, plastics, shoes, etc. The speed of change of place is not as fast as it is in hawkers and peddlars.
   (*iii*) **Market traders:** Market traders open their shops on fixed days or dates in the specific areas. The time interval may be a week or fortnight or a month. They join fairs and festivals which are normally organized in the villages or towns on specific dates.
   (*iv*) **Street traders:** Street traders are also called footpath traders. These traders display their stock on foot paths of busy cities and towns. The prominent places of business are bus stands, railway stations, parks and other busy centres.
   (*v*) **Unit stores:** Unit stores which deal with only one variety of product such as drugs, clothes, shoes, books, utensils, etc. Single line stores are also called speciality shops since they specialize in only one item.

(*vi*) **Syndicate stores:** A syndicate store is an extension of the mail order business on a small-scale. The important characteristic of syndicate store is that it offers a wide variety of merchandise to customers but seldom sells known brands. These retailers buy most of the unbranded varieties and sell them under their own brand names.

2. **Large-scale Retailers:** In recent years the large-scale retail trade has expanded considerably since it brings several advantages such as greater buying capacity, financial economics, expert management and economics in bulk buying, benefits of mechanization and automation, maximum risk bearing capacity, intensive promotion, etc. It caters to the needs of a large number of customers. Super bazars, departmental stores and multiple shops are examples of large-scale retail trade organization.The different types of large-scale retailers are as follows:

(*i*) **Departmental stores:** It is a large retail establishment having in the same building a number of departments each of which confine its activities to sell one particular product.

According to James Stephenson, "Departmental stores are a store engaged in the retail trade of the wide variety of articles under the same roof". A departmental store is essentially an urban-oriented outlet and generally located in the heart of the city.

(*ii*) **Multiple shops:** Multiple shops refer to an organization under which a large number of similar shops are opened at different places in one particular area or throughout the country under a centralized management and dealing in similar lines of goods. Multiple shops are popularly found in European countries and the USA. In the USA the multiple shops are called "Chain Stores".

(*iii*) **Mail order business:** Mail order refers to 'shopping by post'. It is a distinct form of retail business wherein the orders are accepted and goods delivered by post. It is a method of non-store, impersonal and direct selling that eliminates the middlemen. Thus, mail order business can be defined as an establishment that receives orders by mail and make its sales by mail, parcel, etc.

(*iv*) **Consumers' co-operative stores:** Consumers' co-operative stores is an association organized by consumers to obtain their requirements by purchasing in bulk and selling through the stores owned, managed and controlled by themselves. The basic aim of this store is to eliminate the middlemen and their profits.

(*v*) **Super markets:** Super markets are also to be called as super bazars and self-service stores. The first super market was started in the USA during the period of economic depression of 1930s. Philips and Duncan define a super market as "a departmentalized retail store usually handling a variety of merchants and in which the sale of food, much of which is on a self-service, plays a major role".

The *Dictionary of Business and Finance* describes super market as 'large retail stores selling wide variety of consumer goods, particularly food and small articles of household requirements'.

The super market retail organizations have started growing up in India also. In Andhra Pradesh, super markets are also called Janata bazars, Kalpalatha stores, Big Bazar, etc.

(*vi*) **Tele marketing:** Tele marketing is also called telephone selling. It is a new marketing discipline that utilizes tele communication technology to feature the use of personal selling using non face-to-face contacts. Hence, tele marketing refers to a sales person imitating contact with a shopper and closing a sale over the telephone. Tele marketing entails canvassing from the phone directory or it may depend on the prospects who have requested information from the company. It is highly suitable to such products that can be bought without being seen and are sold over telephone. For example, pest control services, magazine subscriptions, credit card membership and athletic club membership are best suited for telemarketing.

(*vii*) **E-commerce:** Trade and commerce between individuals is as old as the existence of mankind. The latest to join the list is Electronic Commerce, which is popularly known as e-commerce. Electronic commerce is defined as the actual buying and selling of goods or services electronically. Products are displayed in an online store and potential customers can read information about the products, see them on the website and have the option to purchase them online. Any product can be sold online and all the principles of business apply to this also.

REVIEW QUESTIONS

1. What do you mean by distribution channels? Explain the characteristics of distribution channel.
2. What are the different functions of channels of distribution channel management?
3. Explain the different factors influencing the choice of distribution channel.
4. What are the different types of channel?
5. Define wholesalers. Explain the characteristics of wholesalers.
6. Explain the different types of wholesalers.
7. Describe the functions of wholesalers.
8. What do you mean by retailer? Explain the characteristics of retailers.
9. What are the different functions of retailers?
10. Explain various types of retailers.

CHAPTER 17

Strategic Marketing Planning and Competitive Marketing Strategies

POINTS TO REMEMBER

At the end of this chapter, we will be able to understand:

- Introduction
- Meaning and Definition
- Characteristics of Strategic Planning
- Strategic Marketing Plan
- Role of Strategic Marketing Plan
- Strategic Marketing Planning Process
- Marketing Strategy Implementation
- Competitive Marketing Strategies
- Disadvantages of Porter's Five Forces Model
- Porter's Generic Competitive Strategies
- Ansoff Product Matrix (Marketing Strategies)
- Competitive Marketing Strategy Options
- Marketing Mix Strategies

17.1 INTRODUCTION

The challenge is faced by marketing management in a multinational business, with hundreds of business units located around the globe, producing a wide range of products. How can such management keep control of marketing decision-making in such a complex situation? This calls for well-organized marketing planning.

A marketing strategy is a way to give marketing orientation to your business by deciding to position your product or service in terms of buyer needs and wants. Inexperienced business people often make decisions based on what they like or want, leaving the customer out of the picture and suffer from marketing myopia. A marketing orientation brings the customer into the centre of the picture and enjoy lifetime profit.

17.2 MEANING AND DEFINITION

Strategic planning is concerned about the overall direction of the business. It is concerned with marketing. But it also involves decision-making about production and operations, finance, human resource management and other business issues.

The objective of a strategic plan is to set the direction of a business and create its shape so that the products and services it provides meet the overall business objectives.

Marketing has a key role to play in strategic planning, because it is the job of marketing management to understand and manage the links between business and "environment".

Sometimes this is quite a straightforward task. For example, in many small businesses there is only one geographical market and a limited number of products.

17.3 CHARACTERISTICS OF STRATEGIC PLANNING

Marketing strategy is a process that can allow an organization to concentrate its limited resources on the greatest opportunities to increase sales and achieve a sustainable competitive advantage.

1. **Accountability:** Responsibility is assigned for successful completion of initiatives.
2. **Balance:** The plans guide not only financial decision-making, but also operational and human resources issues.
3. **Flexibility:** A mechanism for changing and updating the plan is built into the process.
4. **Manageability:** In-process measures are identified to ensure that the processes are working as intended, critical performance issues are addressed, resources required are projected, and methods of status reporting are in place.
5. **Prioritization:** Priorities are established whenever there are multiple interdependent action plans.
6. **Realism:** The question of what the organization can do versus what it would like to do is addressed rationally, though the tone is optimistic.
7. **Specificity:** Expected results and milestones are clearly defined, along with the specific actions for implementation and the deliverables for each step.
8. **Sustainability:** A sufficient time period is covered to close performance gaps.

17.4 STRATEGIC MARKETING PLAN

In a competitive market place a strategy that ensures a reliable approach to offer your product or service in a way that will outsell the competition is critical. The most successful companies have two things that their competitors do not have:

1. A marketing strategy that clearly identifies their market needs and how the company can meet those needs in a competitive environment.
2. Marketing programmes that apply the company's overall marketing strategy everyday to every marketing activity.
   - If the market is very attractive and our enterprise is one of the strongest in the industry then invest best resources in support of offering.
   - If the market is very attractive but your enterprise is one of the weaker ones in the industry you must concentrate on strengthening the enterprise, using your offering as a stepping stone towards this objective.

Fig. 17.1. Strategic marketing plan.

- If the market is not especially attractive, but your enterprise is one of the strongest in the industry then an effective marketing and sales effort for your offering will be good for generating near term profits.
- If the market is not especially attractive and your enterprise is one of the weaker ones in the industry you should promote this offering only if it supports a more profitable part of your business or if it absorbs some of the overhead costs of a more profitable segment. Otherwise, you should determine the most cost-effective way to divest your enterprise of this offering.

17.5 ROLE OF STRATEGIC MARKETING PLAN

A strategic marketing plan is useful to a business. The strategic marketing plan is a means of communicating the strategy to top executives on the basis of which they take critical decisions relating to allocation of resources. Strategic marketing plans help in following:

1. **To Achieve the Objective:** When we develop a comprehensive marketing plan, we can objectively assess the current status of your marketing efforts with regard to product, pricing, place (distribution channel), and promotional strategies; assess their relationship with all external business factors including your competition and target market, develop measurable sales objectives and outline product, pricing, place and promotion strategies designed to achieve those objectives.
2. **Initiatives:** A strategic plan will include initiatives that are measurable and targeted. Examining and finding all the possible initiatives that can be utilized in what we are trained to do.
3. **Financial Goals:** Marketing and advertising are critical elements that should reflect and complement the exact financial goals of the organization. The path to reach those financial goals is through carefully plotted strategies that directly target the desired consumers. A strong and strategic plan will be prepared for unexpected changes in the business environment and/or financial situations. This is when firm needs a strong and strategic plan more than ever, as it will be able to accommodate the unexpected changes in the environment and should be able to adjust to ensure the proper execution of the strategic plan even during unexpected situations.
4. **Control the Destiny:** It gives the power to control the destiny of any company. Also, this plan will help a firm to smoothly navigate around any current competitors or new competitors that may threaten to potentially take away market-share. When a company's plan is strategic so are all firm reactions to threats that enter into the marketplace.

17.6 STRATEGIC MARKETING PLANNING PROCESS

Strategic marketing planning takes time, but is well worth the effort. The process can be split into four clearly defined areas, it is useful to think of the effective marketing process as a triangle. More time is spent at the beginning on the foundations of the strategy, the analysis and planning stages as shown in Fig. 17. 2.

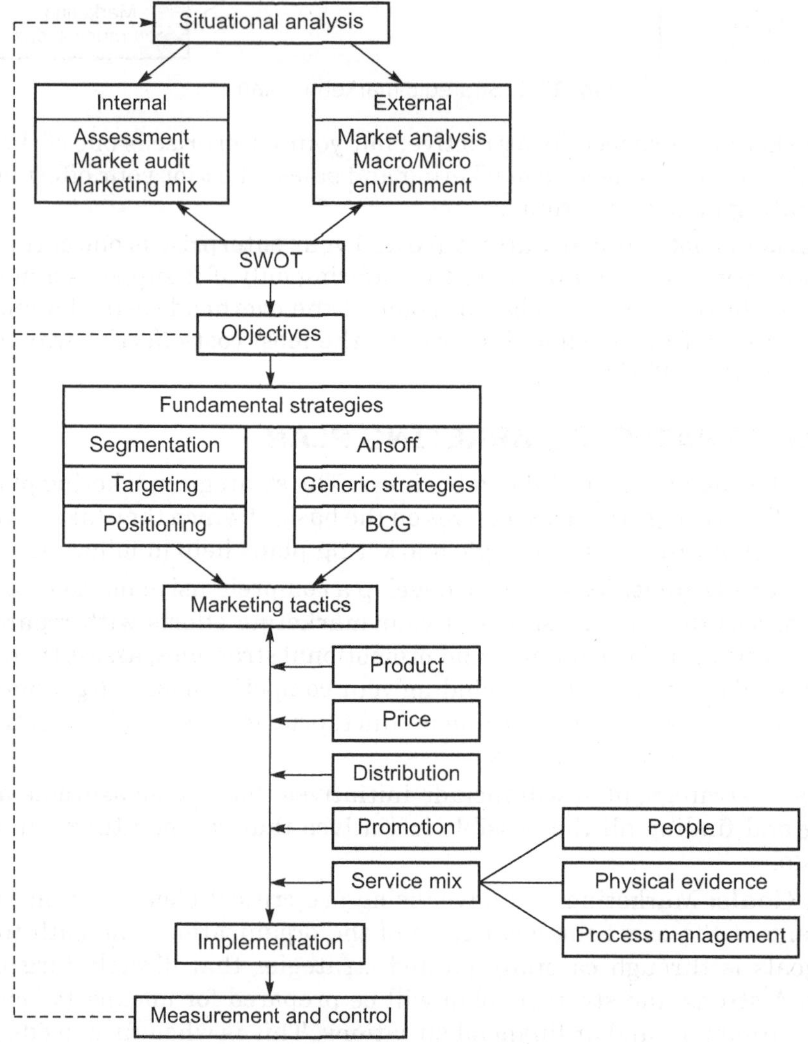

Source: Adapted from Vignali et al. (2003)

Fig. 17.2. Strategic marketing planning process.

1. **Situational Analysis:** This step will help you paint a detailed picture of your target customer, understand your market environment, and assess your competition. This will help in strengthening market orientation for your business.
2. **SWOT Analysis:** SWOT stands for:

   (*a*) **Strengths** (what are the positive attributes of your company, product or service?)

   (*b*) **Weaknesses** (what are the negative attributes of your company, product or service?)

(*c*) **Opportunities** (where are the market opportunities for your product or service?)

(*d*) **Threats** (what are the main threats to your company?)

Before starting the analysis, you need to have completed your marketing research plan and analyzed your competitive marketing strategy. These two initial steps will provide you with a solid understanding of your marketplace and your competition. Then, take a little time and really think through your company's strengths and weaknesses, and the market opportunities and threats from an objective perspective. It may be helpful to find a marketing coach who can assist you through the process.

Once you have identified the strengths, weaknesses, opportunities and threats, then use those to prioritize your marketing strategies and focus, by using the questions as shown in Fig. 17.3:

SWOT Analysis

		External: Opportunities	External: Threates
Internal	Strengths	How do you leverage your strengths to benefit from opportunities ?	How do you use your strengths to minimize the impact of threats ?
Internal	Weaknesses	How do you ensure your weaknesses will not take you away from opportunities ?	How do you fix weaknesses that can make threats have a real impact ?

Fig. 17.3. SWOT analysis.

3. **Create a Marketing Strategy List:** Given the data from Step 1, you are now ready to draft a list of potential marketing strategies: think of these as the rules that will guide your marketing decisions.

   With deeper insights gained during the understand stage, it is time to formulate the marketing strategy. This often includes defining a USP (Unique Selling Preposition), clarifying the product offering, crafting the message, segmentation of the target market, positioning and defining marketing objectives.
4. **Prioritize the Marketing Tactics:** At this stage, we design and implement a marketing plan to achieve the marketing objectives set out in the strategies stage. The marketing mix should be optimized to communicate the message to the target audience in the most effective and efficient way, within the provided budget. It may include online and offline strategies, advertising, public relations, word of mouth, merchandising, consumer competitions, etc.
5. **Measurement and Control:** It is essential to regularly track and measure the success of the campaign as well as each marketing execution. The benchmark of success would depend on the marketing goals—*e.g.*, is it delivering the ROI (Return on Investment)? Are sales increasing? Are there more customers? Are more people aware of the brand? Has consumer perception improved?

An important question to ask is "Are the goals realistic?". For example, if you wish to sell more shoes than Nike or Action, are your plans and your resources sufficient to accept this challenge? Or might you be better placed to identify a niche in the shoe market, and put your resources behind this?

It measures results from your marketing activities, and re-assesses plan on at least a quarterly basis.

17.7 MARKETING STRATEGY IMPLEMENTATION

Implementation of strategy is the process through which a chosen strategy is put into action. It involves the design and management of systems to achieve the best integration of people, structure, processes and resources in achieving organizational objectives.

This is the part where you explain how you plan to put into practice what you have planned. In this part of the business plan you will state and define your strategy (marketing, sales) and specify assignments and milestones.

The business implementation strategy is essential for the success of the business. Stating it in a very clear, understandable manner can be a very helpful tool for achieving this goal, as it must communicate to the persons who will actually work at the actual implementation. The reasoning behind the strategy should also be stated to ease the process.

17.8 COMPETITIVE MARKETING STRATEGIES

Once the strengths and weaknesses of the competition have been collected, they should be organized into a chart alongside the company's strengths and weaknesses for easy comparison. The columns should include factors pertinent in the marketplace, such as pricing, annual sales, customer satisfaction, and functionality. The plan of action detailed in the rest of the competitive marketing strategy should then address each of these strengths and weaknesses. For example, if a company is selling technology and has discovered in its research that the competition's technology is slower, the company will want to emphasize how fast its technology is in its advertisements and other marketing material.

Anticipating competitors' actions and reactions to your moves may be the key determinant of success for any marketing strategy. One competitor cuts prices, undermining your pricing strategy. Another may decide to offer new products and services, possibly over the Internet that has the potential to completely undermine your existing strategy. Could you have anticipated such moves? How do you respond?

Competitive marketing strategy teaches us how to anticipate your competitors' moves during the planning stage, so that you are not caught off guard. Learn how to analyze their strengths and weaknesses. Discover a number of tools and concepts to manage your competition. By helping, you anticipate potential competitive responses to your actions, this course will help you develop effective marketing strategies for the long-term.

Michael Porter from Harvard Business School created this framework in 1979. This framework is typically used during the initial phase of a marketing strategy planning/feasibility study to access the industrial-related markets for their attractiveness, level of competition, feasibility and have a sense of the competitive dynamic environment that dictates the market. These five forces will form the foundation of marketing knowledge which will shape marketing strategies. The essences of the five forces are listed below in Fig. 17.4:

1. **Competitive Rivalry within an Industry/Market:** Company can acquire the intimate knowledge of their direct competitors through profiling, in-depth analysis, monitoring, allows for measuring market potential, market share and cost-related pricing decisions to ultimately manipulate their marketing mix (4Ps) to gain competitive advantage over them.

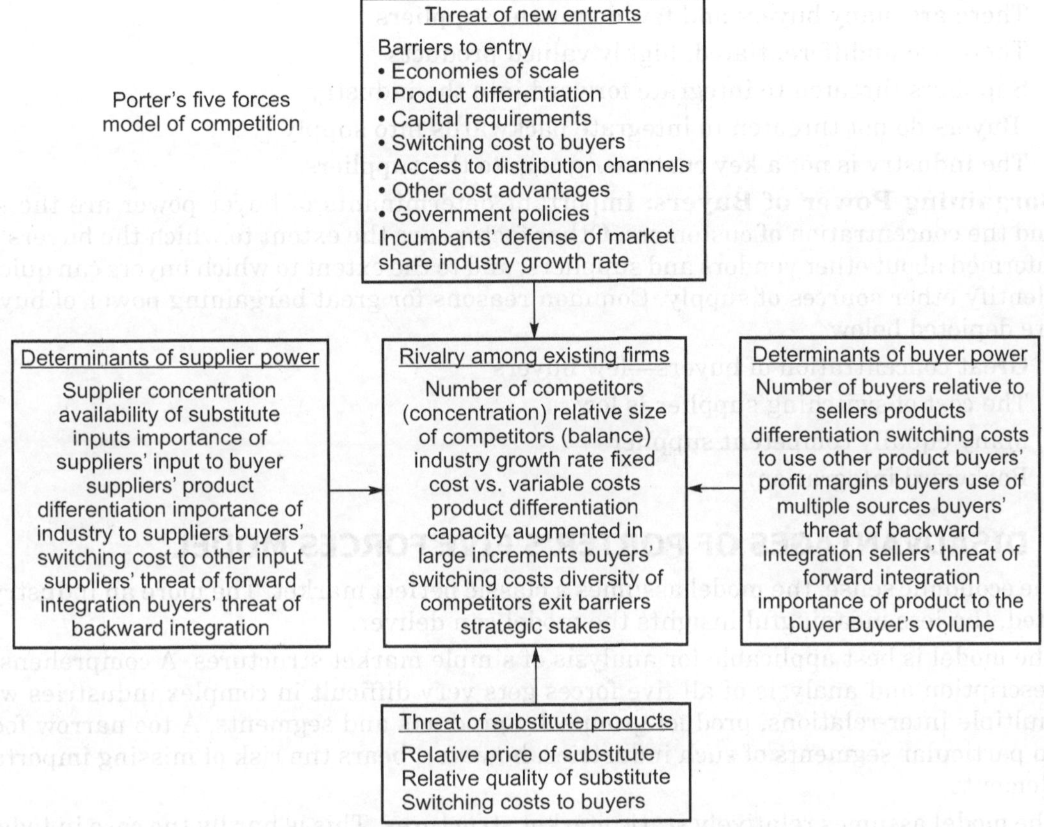

Fig. 17.4. Competitive marketing strategies.

2. **Threat of New Entrants:** Both potential and existing competitors can have an influence on the attractiveness to operate in any particular industry. With the increase in the number of potential or real competitors in an industry the level of competitiveness, and thus the profitability for individual companies in the industry, decrease. This can reduce the attractiveness for companies to enter or to continue operate in the segment. A number of complex business and marketing factors influences the magnitude of the threat of new entrants to an industry or market segment. An industry where profitability is generally high will attract more new entrants that are looking to benefit from the potentially high profits. The threat of new entrants for the most part depends on the presence and magnitude of barriers to entry in the particular industry.
3. **Threat of Substitutes:** This is affected by the ability of your customers to find a different way of doing what you do—for example, if you supply a unique software product that automates an important process, people may substitute by doing the process manually or by outsourcing it. If substitution is easy and viable, then this weakens your power.
4. **Bargaining Power of Suppliers:** Suppliers are the businesses that supply materials and other products into the industry. The cost of items bought from suppliers (*e.g.*, raw materials, components) can have a significant impact on a company's profitability. If suppliers have high bargaining power over a company, then in theory the company's industry is less attractive. The bargaining power of suppliers will be high when:

- There are many buyers and few dominant suppliers
- There are undifferentiated, highly valued products
- Suppliers threaten to integrate forward into the industry
- Buyers do not threaten to integrate backwards into supply
- The industry is not a key customer group to the suppliers.

5. **Bargaining Power of Buyers:** Important determinants of buyer power are the size and the concentration of customers. Other factors are the extent to which the buyers are informed about other vendors and suppliers, and to the extent to which buyers can quickly identify other sources of supply. Common reasons for great bargaining power of buyers are depicted below:
   - Great concentration of buyers—few buyers
   - The cost of switching supplier is low
   - Many equally competent suppliers
   - Backward integration.

17.9 DISADVANTAGES OF PORTER'S FIVE FORCES MODEL

In the economic sense, the model assumes a classic perfect market. The more an industry is regulated, the less meaningful insights the model can deliver.

1. The model is best applicable for analysis of simple market structures. A comprehensive description and analysis of all five forces gets very difficult in complex industries with multiple inter-relations, product groups, by-products and segments. A too narrow focus on particular segments of such industries, however, bears the risk of missing important elements.
2. The model assumes relatively static market structures. This is hardly the case in today's dynamic markets. Technological breakthroughs and dynamic market entrants from start-ups or other industries may completely change business models, entry barriers and relationships along the supply chain within short times. The Five Forces model may have some use for later analysis of the new situation; but it will hardly provide much meaningful advice for preventive actions.
3. The model is based on the idea of competition. It assumes that companies try to achieve competitive advantages over other players in the markets as well as over suppliers or customers. With this focus, it dos not really take into consideration strategies like strategic alliances, electronic linking of information systems of all companies along a value chain, virtual enterprise-networks or others.

Overall, Porter's Five Forces Model has some major limitations in today's market environment. It is not able to take into account new business models and the dynamics of markets. The value of Porter's model is more that it enables managers to think about the current situation of their industry in a structured, easy-to-understand way as a starting point for further analysis.

17.10 PORTER'S GENERIC COMPETITIVE STRATEGIES

The generic strategy which is provided by Michael Porter is actually a framework which can be applied to strategies for individual business-level strategies. Porter has argued that the strengths of a company can be divided into two headings, namely, differentiation and cost advantage. Each of the options is considered within the context of two aspects of the competitive environment as shown in Fig. 17.5.

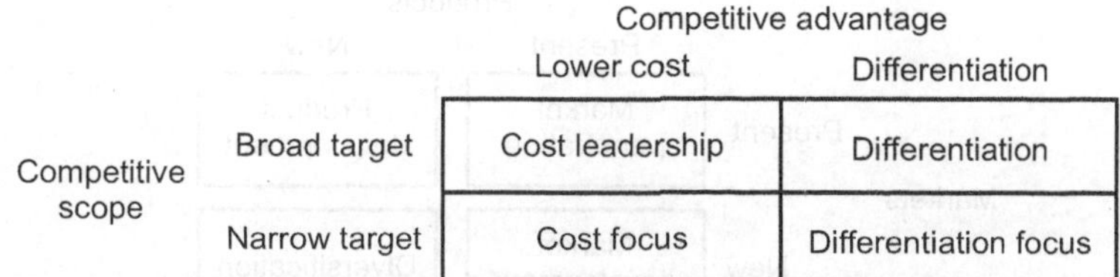

Fig. 17.5. Porter's generic competitive strategies.

The generic strategies are: 1. Cost leadership, 2. Differentiation, and 3. Focus or Niche strategy.

1. **Cost Leadership:** In cost leadership, a firm sets out to become the low cost producer in its industry. The sources of cost advantage are varied and depend on the structure of the industry. They may include the pursuit of economies of scale, proprietary technology, preferential access to raw materials and other factors. A low cost producer must find and exploit all sources of cost advantage. If a firm can achieve and sustain overall cost leadership, then it will be an above average performer in its industry, provided it can command prices at or near the industry average.
2. **Differentiation:** Differentiated goods and services satisfy the needs of customers through a sustainable competitive advantage. This allows companies to de-sensitize prices and focus on value that generates a comparatively high price and a better margin. The benefits of differentiation require producers to segment markets in order to target goods and services at specific segments, generating a higher than average price. For example, Indian Airlines differentiates its service.
3. **Focus or Niche Strategy:** The generic strategy of focus rests on the choice of a narrow competitive scope within an industry. The company selects a segment or group of segments in the industry and tailors its strategy to serve them to the exclusion of others. The focus strategy has two variants.
   (*a*) In cost focus, a firm seeks a cost advantage in its target segment.
   (*b*) In differentiation focus, a firm seeks differentiation in its target segment.

Both variants of the focus strategy rest on differences between a company's target segment and other segments in the industry. The target segments must either have buyers with unusual needs or else the production and delivery system that best serves the target segment which must differ from that of other industry segments. Cost focus exploits differences in cost behaviour in some segments, while differentiation focus exploits the special needs of buyers in certain segments.

17.11 ANSOFF PRODUCT MATRIX (MARKETING STRATEGIES)

The Ansoff Product-Market Growth Matrix is a marketing tool created by Igor Ansoff and first published in his article "Strategies for Diversification" in the Harvard Business Review (1957) as shown in Fig. 17.6. The Ansoff Growth matrix is a tool that helps businesses decide their product and market growth strategy. Ansoff's product/market growth matrix suggests that a business' attempts to grow depend on whether it markets new or existing products in new or existing markets.

1. **Market Penetration (Existing Markets, Existing Products):** Market penetration occurs when a company enters/penetrates a market with current products. The best way to achieve this is by gaining competitors' customers (part of their market share). Other ways include attracting non-users of your product or convincing current clients to use more of your product/service, with advertising or other promotions. Market penetration is the least risky way for a company to grow.

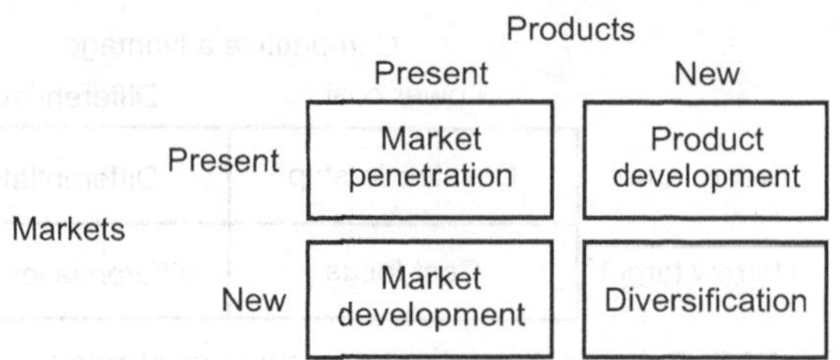

Fig. 17.6. Ansoff product-market growth matrix.

2. **Market Development:** Market development is the name given to a growth strategy where the business seeks to sell its existing products into new markets. There are many possible ways of approaching this strategy, including:
   - New product dimensions or packaging
   - New geographical markets; for example exporting the product to a new country
   - New distribution channels
   - Different pricing policies to attract different customers or create new market segments.
3. **Product Development:** The medium risk growth strategy to introduce new products to existing customers. The organization needs to develop modified products that appeal to existing customers in order to encourage them to spend more on these products. This strategy is likely to develop new organizational competencies and requires improved sales coordination. Uncompetitive or immature products in the portfolio create risk counter balanced by strong customer focus and innovation processes.
4. **Diversification:** Diversification is the name given to the growth strategy where a business markets new products in new markets. This is an inherently more risk strategy because the business is moving into markets in which it has little or no experience. For a business to adopt a diversification strategy, therefore, it must have a clear idea about what it expects to gain from the strategy and an honest assessment of the risks.

17.12 COMPETITIVE MARKETING STRATEGY OPTIONS

Following are the competitive strategy options which can be used by marketing firms.

17.12.1 Market Leader Strategies

Market leadership is the position of a company with the largest market share or highest profitability margin in a given market for goods and services. Market share may be measured by either the volume of goods sold or the value of those goods. Market leadership is a particularly useful and relevant concept in the Internet age, where first-movers in new markets can quickly gain monopolies for services or products. Examples of digital market leadership include:

1. Microsoft's position of the operating system (Windows) and Web browser (Internet Explorer) markets.
2. Apple's share of portable media player sales (iPod).
3. Friendster, followed by MySpace and now Facebook's position (social networking).

17.12.2. Market Challenger Strategies

A market challenger is a firm in a strong, but not dominant position that is following an aggressive strategy of trying to gain market share. It typically targets the industry leader (for example, Pepsi targets Coke), but it could also target smaller, more exposed competitors. The fundamental principles involved are:

1. Assess the strength of the target competitor. Consider the amount of support that the target might muster from partners.
2. Choose only one target at a time.
3. Find a weakness in the target.
4. Position. Attack at this point. Consider how long it will take for the target to realign their resources so as to reinforce this weak spot.
5. Launch the attack on as narrow a front as possible. Whereas a defender must defend all their borders, an attacker has the advantage of being able to concentrate their forces at one place.

Launch the attack quickly, and then consolidate. Some of the options open to a market challenger are:

1. Price discounts or price cutting
2. Line extensions
3. Introduce new products
4. Reduce product quality
5. Increase product quality
6. Improve service
7. Change distribution
8. Cost reductions
9. Intensify promotional activity.

17.12.3 Market Follower Strategies

A market follower is a firm in a strong, but not dominant position that is content to stay at that position. The rationale is that by developing strategies that are parallel to those of the market leader, they will gain much of the market from the leader while being exposed to very little risk. This “play it safe” strategy is how Burger King retains its position behind McDonalds. The advantages of this strategy are:

1. No expensive R&D failures
2. No risk of bad business model
3. The “best practices” are already established
4. Able to capitalize on the promotional activities of the market leader
5. No risk of government anti-combines actions
6. Minimal risk of competitive attacks
7. Do not waste money in a head-on battle with the market leader.

17.12.4 Market Nicher Strategies

In this niche strategy the firm concentrates on a select few target markets. It is also called a focus strategy. It is hoped that by focusing your marketing efforts on one or two narrow market segments and tailoring your marketing mix to these specialized markets, you can better meet the needs of that target market. The niche should be large enough to be profitable, but small enough to be ignored by the major industry players. Profit margins are emphasized rather than revenue or market share. The firm typically looks to gain a competitive advantage through effectiveness rather than efficiency. It is most suitable for relatively small firms and has much in common with guerrilla marketing warfare strategies. The most successful nichers tend to have the following characteristics:

1. They tend to be in high value added industries and are able to obtain high margins.
2. They tend to be highly focused on a specific market segment.
3. They tend to market high end products or services, and are able to use a premium pricing strategy.
4. They tend to keep their operating expenses down by spending less on R &D, advertising, and personal selling.

17.13 MARKETING MIX STRATEGIES

Marketing mix is a tool that assists in defining a marketing strategy for the product or service. Marketing strategy and marketing mix are closely related to each other. Proper marketing mix analysis is very important for implementation of your marketing plan to achieve the business goals. Marketing mix strategy is about achieving your marketing objectives through proper analysis of the 4Ps or elements of marketing. Each element of marketing mix strategy affects the other and the proper combination of these four elements is the key to the success of any marketing process. These are:

17.13.1 Product Mix Strategy

Product mix strategy is about determining features of your product or service. Product mix strategy deals with:

(*a*) The product life cycle
(*b*) Brand name
(*c*) Packaging
(*d*) Design
(*e*) Quality
(*f*) Safety
(*g*) After sales service.

17.13.2 Pricing Mix Strategy

The price of a product can be fixed in many ways. Marketing mix pricing is a tool that helps in settling on a pricing strategy, considering the following:

(*a*) Retail price
(*b*) Wholesale price
(*c*) Special offers
(*d*) Penetration pricing
(*e*) Price skimming
(*f*) Optional product pricing
(*g*) Geographical pricing.

17.13.3 Promotion Mix Strategy

Promotion mix strategy deals with the available tools for marketing communications. This element helps in deciding on the location, where the customers will get the product or service. Promotion mix strategy also deals with:

(*a*) Sales promotion
(*b*) Distribution channels
(*c*) Advertising

(*d*) Sponsorship
(*e*) Trade fairs and events
(*f*) Logistics
(*g*) Storage.

17.13.4 Place (Distribution Channel) Mix Strategy

Place marketing mix is nothing but distributing product to the customer. Few instances for this:

(*a*) Warehousing
(*b*) Distribution centres
(*c*) Reverse logistics
(*d*) Transportation
(*e*) Inventory management.

REVIEW QUESTIONS

1. What is the meaning and definition of strategic planning? Explain the characteristics of strategic planning.
2. Explain the strategic marketing plan.
3. Explain the role of strategic marketing plan.
4. What are the strategic marketing planning processes?
5. Explain the implementation of marketing strategy.
6. What are competitive marketing strategies?
7. Explain the Porter's generic competitive strategies.
8. Explain the Ansoff product matrix and marketing strategies.
9. What are the competitive marketing strategy options?
10. Explain the different marketing mix strategies.

CHAPTER 18

Marketing Organizations and Control of Marketing Operations

POINTS TO REMEMBER

At the end of this chapter, we will be able to understand:

- Introduction
- Meaning and Definition of Marketing Organization
- Need for the Organization
- Factors Affecting Marketing Organization
- Types of Marketing Organization Structures
- Definition and Meaning of Marketing Control
- Objectives of Marketing Control
- Marketing Control Process
- Techniques of Marketing Control
- Marketing Audit
- Characteristics of Marketing Audit
- Types of Marketing Audit
- Process of Marketing Audit

18.1 INTRODUCTION

An organization is nothing but a common platform where individuals from different backgrounds come together and work as a collective unit to achieve certain objectives and targets. An organization consists of individuals with different specializations, educational qualifications and work experiences all working towards a common goal. Marketing organization provides a vehicle for making decisions on products, marketing channels, physical distributions, promotions and prices.

18.2 MEANING AND DEFINITION OF MARKETING ORGANIZATION

Marketing organization is the framework for planning and making marketing decisions that are essential to marketing success. It is the vehicle for making decisions on all marketing areas such as product, price, place and promotion. Marketing organization is a group of marketing persons working together towards the attainment of certain common objectives. Marketing organization provides a system of relationships among various marketing functions to be performed by co-ordinating among marketing people.

18.3 NEED FOR THE ORGANIZATION

To be competitive in the market where consumer is the king we need to satisfy the consumer. So a good marketing organization is required to satisfy the customers. Marketing organization is the pillar for success for many organizations and provides a framework for the following:

1. Divide and fix authority among the subordinates
2. To locate responsibility
3. To establish sales routines
4. To enforce proper supervision of sales force
5. To avoid repetitive duties
6. To enable the top executives to devote more time for planning policy matters.

18.4 FACTORS AFFECTING MARKETING ORGANIZATION

Factors influencing marketing organization can be categorized into internal and external factors.

A. Internal Factors. The internal factors are as following:

1. **Top management philosophy:** Organizational planning and its working is greatly influenced by philosophy which can be good or bad. For example, centralization Vs decentralization
2. **Product policy:** The width of product line of an organization determines its size as the product offerings become increasingly diverse. For example, there could be a need to move away from straight functional approach to product group approach.
3. **People:** The size of the organization is not an important factor in terms of number of people but it is important with respect to human values which are critical and correct decisions regarding people cannot be made unless taking into consideration:
   - Number
   - Qualifications
   - Capabilities

   Experience
   - Personality
   - Attitude

   Confidence
   - Fear
   - Suspicion
   - Ambition.

Are some of the above intangible factors which affect the marketing organization?

B. External Factors: The external factors are as following:

1. **Business environment:** With regards to business environment three points are important.

   (*a*) The type of environment in which the firm is operating in terms of operations and size.

(*b*) The nature of particular requirement for success in a given business which again determines the size.

(*c*) The rate of change in industries being served which again decides on its size and working.

2. **Markets:** This is the factor which again affects the marketing organization, *i.e.*, one should note about its

(*a*) Size

(*b*) Scope

(*c*) Nature

(*d*) Location.

Based on the above aspects we need to design the size of the organization.

3. **Consumer requirements and expectations:** Consumers have their own set of requirements and expectations from the organization. The more varied and vivid services expect the usual requirements; as a marketer we need to increase the workload depending upon the consumer requirements and expectations.

4. **Channels of distribution:** It is the type of channel of distribution which a marketing firm selects based on its size. For example, in case the company opts for indirect channel or channels, it depends on outside sales force and hence the organization gets thinner. When the organization selects direct channel its size is increased as it has its own sales force.

18.5 TYPES OF MARKETING ORGANIZATION STRUCTURES

Types of marketing organization structures: The marketing organization of a business can be structured on any of the following basis:

1. **Line and Staff Organization:** In most business forms especially medium size the marketing job is structured around few line functions and few staff functions, *i.e.*, major staff functions are organized into separate departments and the line function is responsible for sales department as shown in Fig.18.1. The required co-ordination between line and staff function is managed by the executive at higher level.

Fig. 18.1. Line and staff organization.

Merits:

1. Provides expert advice from specialists
2. Relieves line executes of routine, specialize functions
3. Enables young sales executive to acquire expertise
4. Helps in achieving effective co-ordination

5. Easy to operate
6. Less expensive.

Demerits:

1. Produces confusion arising from indeterminate authority relationships
2. Curbs the authority of experts
3. Too much is expected from executives
4. Decisions making is taken by top management.

2. **Functional:** The concept of functional organization was suggested by F.W. Taylor who recommended the appointment of specialists at important positions. For example, the functional head and Marketing Director directs the subordinates throughout the organization in his particular area. This means that subordinates receive orders from several specialists, managers working above them. Under the organization the departments are created on the basis of specified functions to be performed, *i.e.*, the activities related to marketing, distribution, etc., as shown in Fig. 18.2.

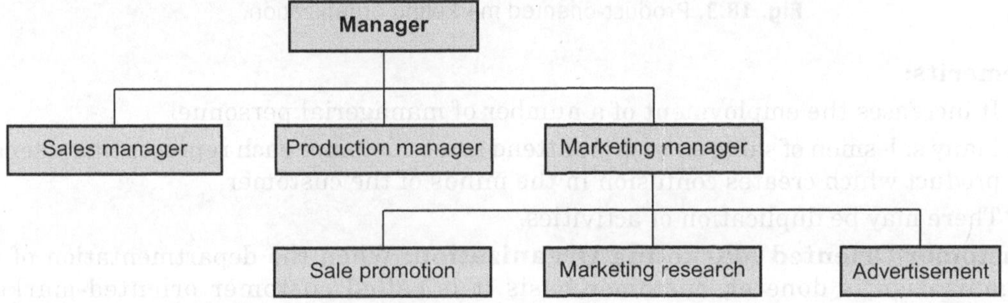

Fig. 18.2. Functional organization.

Merits:

1. Division of work base on specialization
2. Relieves line executives of routine and specialized functions
3. Promotes application of expert knowledge
4. Helps to increase overall efficiency.

Demerits:

1. Leads to complex relationships
2. Makes coordination ineffective
3. Promotes centralization
4. Lack of proper co-ordination
5. Delay in taking decisions.

3. **Product-Oriented Marketing Organization:** In this type of organization as shown in Fig. 18.3, the companies producing multiple products have individual manager to look after the product and develop the strategy related to the product, responsible for the product, do advertising, promotion, distribution only for that product.

Merits:

1. The salesmen can render better customer service as they possess good knowledge of product and may have close contacts with customers.
2. It makes individual departments responsible for the promotion of specific products.
3. It facilitates effective co-ordination.

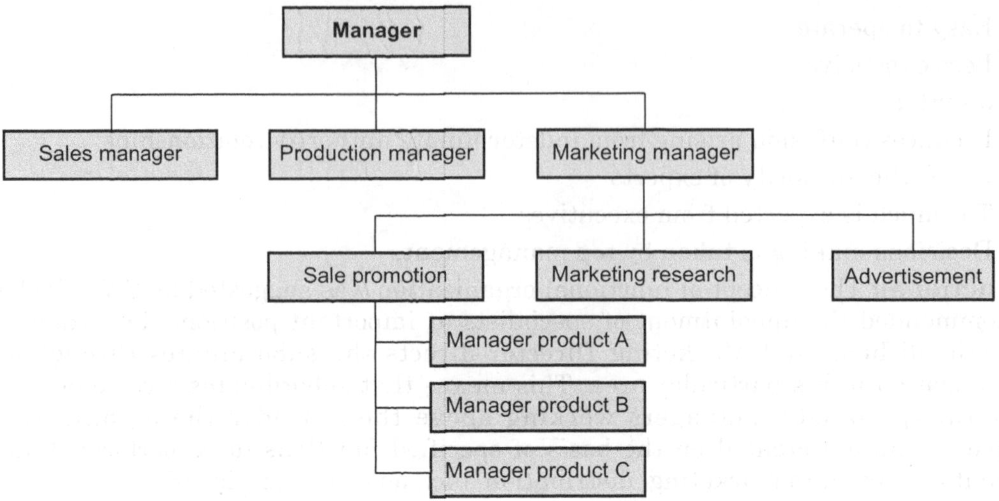

Fig. 18.3. Product-oriented marketing organization.

Demerits:

1. It increases the employment of a number of managerial personnel
2. Many salesmen of same enterprise attend same customer each representing a separate product which creates confusion in the minds of the customer.
3. There may be duplication of activities.

4. **Customer-Oriented Marketing Organization:** When the departmentation of sales organization is done on customer basis it is called customer oriented-marketing organization. In the modern customer-oriented organizational design, customers are the apex and are at the top of the organization as shown in Fig. 18.4.

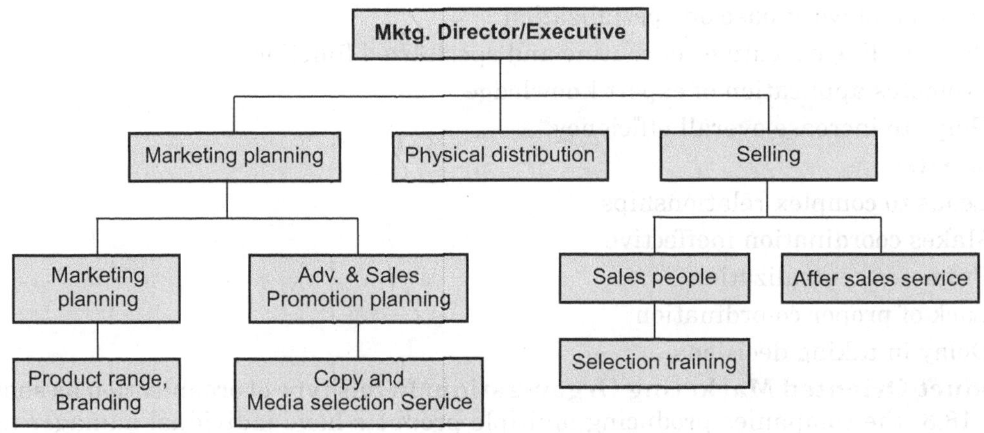

Fig. 18.4. Customer-oriented marketing organization.

Merits:

1. It takes into account needs of each class of customers.
2. It provides specialization among the enterprise staff.

Demerits:

1. It makes co-ordination difficult
2. It may lead to under utilization of resources in same department
3. There may be duplication of activities
4. These types of sales organizations are not suitable for small enterprises.

5. **Geography/Territory Marketing Organization:** In a territory-oriented marketing organization, the responsibilities for marketing of various products rest almost entirely with line executives. The territory managers are given varying nomenclatures like depot manager, district manager, area manager, zonal manager, divisional manager, etc., as shown in Fig. 18.5.

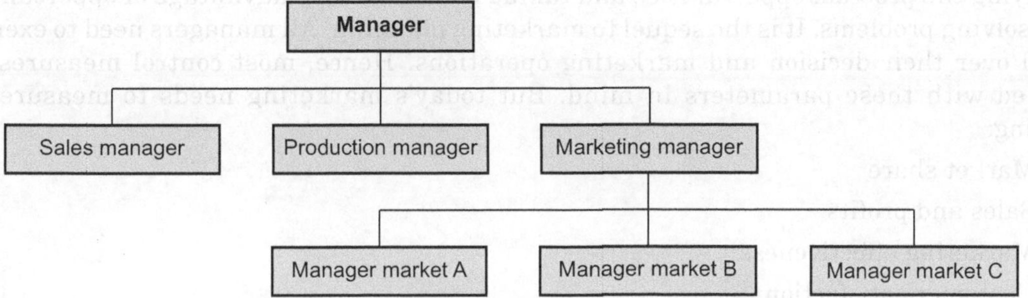

Fig. 18.5. Geography/territory marketing organization.

The merits and demerits of Geography/Territory Marketing Organization are mentioned below:

Merits:

1. It leads to economy in term of time and money
2. It helps in taking knowledge of local customers
3. It helps in effective control.

Demerits:

1. It requires employment of number of managerial personnel.
2. It dilutes control from headquarters

6. **Matrix Organization:** In matrix organization the people with similar skills are pooled for work assignments as shown in Fig. 18.6. For example, all engineers may be in one engineering department and report to an engineering manager, but these same engineers

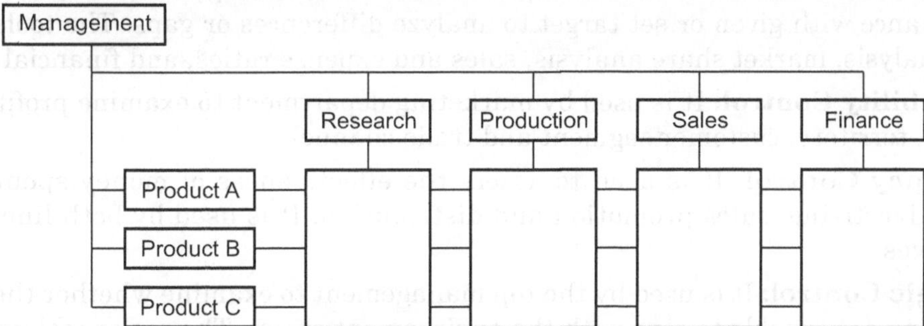

Fig. 18.6. Matrix organization.

may be assigned to different projects and report to a different engineering manager or a project manager while working on that project. Therefore, each engineer may have to work under several managers to get their job done.

18.6 DEFINITION AND MEANING OF MARKETING CONTROL

There is no planning without control. Marketing control is the process of monitoring the proposed plans as they proceed and adjust where necessary. If an objective states where you want to be and the plan sets out a road map to your destination, then control tells you whether you are on the right route or whether you have arrived at your destination.

Marketing control is concerned with analyzing the performance of marketing decision, identifying the problem/opportunities and taking actions to take advantage of opportunities and resolving problems. It is the sequel to marketing planning. All managers need to exercise control over their decision and marketing operations. Hence, most control measures are designed with these parameters in mind. But today's marketing needs to measure the following:

- Market share
- Sales and profits
- Marketing effectiveness
- Customer satisfaction
- Customer perception of the firms and its brands
- Feedback from customer's satisfaction surveys
- Cash flow statements
- Customer Relationship Management (CRM) systems
- Sales per thousand customers, per factory, by segment
- Location of buyers and potential buyers
- Activities of competitors to aspects of your plan
- Distributor support.

18.7 OBJECTIVES OF MARKETING CONTROL

There are four types of controls with different objectives and tools and exist with different levels of management.

1. **Annual Plan Control:** It is with top or middle level management to evaluate actual performance with given or set target to analyze differences or gaps. The tools used are sales analysis, market share analysis, sales and expense ratios, and financial analysis.
2. **Profitability Control:** It is used by marketing department to examine profitability by product, territory, customer segment and trade channel.
3. **Efficiency Control:** It is used to assess the effectiveness of money spent on sales force, advertising, sales promotion and distribution. It is used by both line and staff executives.
4. **Strategic Control:** It is used by the top management to examine whether the firm and marketing are capable to cope with the environment or not. The major tool used here is marketing audit.

18.8 MARKETING CONTROL PROCESS

Marketing control process includes monitoring, evaluating and improving the performance in each activity. There are six steps in this:

1. **Decide the Aspect of Marketing Operation to be Evaluated:** The first step in marketing control process is deciding about the marketing operation to evaluate. For example, effectiveness of media for product advertisement, sales person performance, or performance of company product.
2. **Establish Measurement Criterion:** In this stage performance standards are decided against which actual performance is evaluated. For example, control sales person performance, in this one can measure new accounts obtained, call frequency ratio and order per call.
3. **Establishing Monitoring Mechanism:** After setting the standards, the next step is to develop monitoring mechanism tools like MIS (Marketing Information System). MIS is used to record performance of all marketing areas like monthly sales volume for products.
4. **Compare Actual Results with Standards of Performance:** In this stage, results obtained through monitoring process are compared with pre established standards (benchmark) of performance.
5. **Analyze Performance Improvement:** If the result/performance is not up to the desired standards, a corrective action is to be taken to enhance the performance levels. For this performance improvement analysis is to be done.

18.9 TECHNIQUES OF MARKETING CONTROL

There are various techniques of marketing control to measure and evaluate the results of market strategy:

1. **Marketing Audit:** Marketing audit is a systematic and objective study of the total marketing efficiency of the firm. It critically evaluates the marketing policies and activities of the firm, and measures the extent and direction of its growth. It is concerned with the long-term business interests and challenges of the firm rather than short-term achievements. He may ask the following questions:
   (*a*) What is the pricing strategy of competitor?
   (*b*) What are the changes in consumer behaviour?
   (*c*) What is the distribution strategy of competitor?
   (*d*) What are the likes of consumer?
   (*e*) What are the needs of retailers?
2. **Credit Control:** Credit control is one of the important marketing control techniques. Credit control helps the firm to decide what credit facilities it can give to wholesaler, retailer and its customer.
3. **Budgetary Control:** Budgetary control is a very important tool in the hands of management as shown in Fig. 18.7. It helps in controlling cost and maximizing the profit. It also helps in setting up effective budgetary control system.

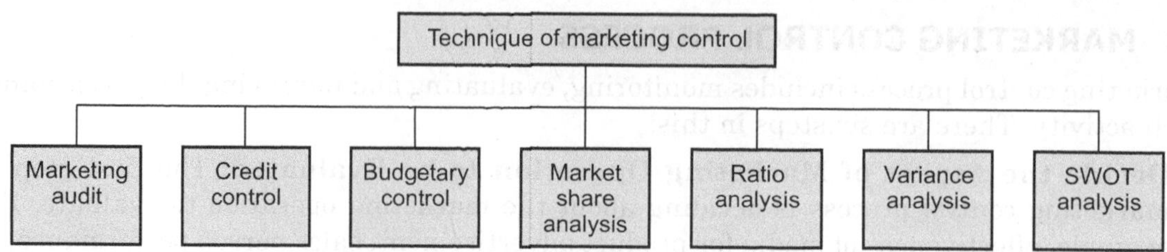

Fig. 18.7. Marketing control techniques.

4. **Market Share Analysis:** Market share analysis is the study of firm's sales in relation to its competitor or competitor's performance; rather it is to ascertain the percentage share of the firm in the industry's sales. The purpose is to identify the company's hold or the status in the industry vis-à-vis its competitors and to determine whether it has attained the target market share both in segregate and break-up aspects like products, regions and the customers. If used in combination with sales analysis, market share analysis should reveal certain useful clues regarding the firm's marketing performance.
5. **Ratio Analysis:** It helps the company in knowing its profitability, liquidity, activity of the company. Net asset ratio, gross profit ratio, net ratio, current asset ratio, working capital ratio—all these are very important ratios for the company.
6. **Variance Analysis:** It helps the company in knowing what the differences between actual and standard performance are and in case of any deviation how these can be removed.
7. **SWOT Analysis:** SWOT analysis means strength, weakness, opportunity and threat to the company. **Strength, weaknesses are internal to the company.** The company must decide how it can increase its strength and how it can remove its weakness. **Opportunity and threat are external to the company.** If the company avails the opportunity before its competitor then it will be beneficial for it. Similarly the company faces the threats from its competitors and it is necessary to remove them.

18.10 MARKETING AUDIT

Marketing audit is a systematic review and appraisal of the basic objectives and policies of marketing function and of the marketing organization methods, procedures and personnel employed to implement those policies and to achieve those goals. Marketing audit is one of the important tools to assess the effectiveness of different marketing mix elements.

Many marketing managers now realize that their marketing operations should be regularly reviewed and examined, but do not know how to do it. Sometimes they are simply making small changes that are economically and politically feasible, but fail to get to the heart of the matter which keeps them unaware of the real situation.In the present scenario of economy, it is now necessary for each company to know current situation of their business effectiveness of current marketing strategies and plan and measure performance of marketing operation which can be performed by conducting systematic marketing audit.

18.11 CHARACTERISTICS OF MARKETING AUDIT

Marketing audit has the following four major characteristics:

1. **Comprehensive:** The marketing audit covers all the major marketing activities of a business. A comprehensive marketing audit is more effective in locating the real source of a company's marketing problems.

2. **Systematic:** Marketing audit is an orderly examination of the organization's total marketing environment, marketing objectives and strategies, marketing systems, and specific marketing activities. The diagnosis is followed by a corrective action plan to improve the organization's overall marketing effort.
3. **Independent:** Marketing audit is an independent and intelligent activity in that it can be conducted in six ways: self audit, audit from across, audit from above company auditing office, company task force audit and outsider audit. Generally speaking, the best audits come from outside audit consultants.
4. **Periodic:** A sound marketing audit is one which is conducted periodically as a weapon to signal the troubles or the signs of success. Typically, marketing audits are initiated only after sales have turned down, sales force morale has fallen, and other company problems have occurred.

18.12 TYPES OF MARKETING AUDIT

The different types of marketing audit are as follows:

1. **Marketing Environment Audit:** It is divided into two groups, *viz*., macro-environment and task-environment. Macro-environment audit includes analysis of political, economical, technological and cultural aspects. Task-environment audit covers customers, competitors, markets, dealer/distributors, suppliers, marketing firms and public.
2. **Marketing Strategy Audit:** This audit reviews firms marketing mission, objectives, goals, and strategies and to appraise their adaptability to present and future environment.
3. **Marketing Organization Audit:** This audit evaluates the firm's capability in implementing necessary strategies for the future environment. It also reviews formal organization structure and efficiency.
4. **Marketing Systems Audit:** It evaluates the sub-systems of a system such as marketing information system, marketing planning system, marketing control system and new product development system.
5. **Marketing Productivity Audit:** This audit critically examines the profitability of different marketing entities and cost effectiveness of different heads of marketing expenditure.
6. **Marketing Function Audit:** It is a functional audit mainly covering marketing mix components namely product, price, place and promotion (advertising, sales promotion, sales force and publicity).

18.13 PROCESS OF MARKETING AUDIT

A marketing audit does exactly what it says. If your marketing operations are in line with your business objectives, and fit well within your corporate capabilities, you will benefit from improved marketing and higher profit potential.

The audit involves the following broad tasks:

1. **Understand your Goals:** What do you want to improve?
2. **Gathering Marketing Materials:** What are you using, and how are you using it?
3. **Interviews:** Talking to employees from all departments, and where appropriate, suppliers and customers.

4. **Analyse:** Anyone can collect information and write down some goals, but the analysis and understanding we can provide will give you an enormous insight into the marketing functionality of your business.
5. **Reports:** We will provide you with a full report, with an actionable checklist for you to follow, using your own people, or with our help.

REVIEW QUESTIONS

1. What do you mean by marketing organization? Explain the need for the organization.
2. Explain the different factors affecting marketing organization.
3. Describe the types of marketing organization structures.
4. What is marketing control? Explain the objectives of market control.
5. Explain the marketing control process.
6. Define the different techniques of marketing control.
7. What is marketing audit? Explain the characteristics of marketing audit.
8. Explain the process of marketing audit.
9. Explain the different kinds of marketing audit.
10. Explain the feature of marketing audit.
11. Explain the objective of marketing audit.

UNIT–V

19. Rural Marketing

20. Marketing of Services Banking, Transport and Insurance

21. E-Commerce and CRM

22. New Issues in Marketing: Globalization and Green Marketing

C H A P T E R 19

Rural Marketing

POINTS TO REMEMBER

At the end of this chapter, we will be able to understand:

- Introduction
- Meaning and Definition
- Characteristics of Rural Marketing
- Scope of Rural Marketing
- Factors Contributing to Change in Rural Marketing
- Importance of Rural Marketing
- Changing Scenario
- Distinction between Rural and Urban Marketing
- Problems of Rural Marketing
- Strategies in Rural Marketing
- Agricultural Marketing
- Classification of Agri-Product
- Features of Agri-Product
- Problems of Agri-Products Marketing
- Types of Market
- Procedure and Methods of Trading
- Co-operative Marketing
- Aims and Objectives of Co-operative Marketing
- Role of Co-operative Marketing
- Functions of Co-operative Marketing
- Importance of Co-operative Marketing
- Present Scenario of Co-operative Marketing

19.1 INTRODUCTION

Rural marketing involves the process of developing, pricing, promoting, distributing rural specific product and a service leading to exchange between rural and urban market which satisfies consumer demand and also achieves organizational objectives. It is a two-way marketing process wherein the transactions can be:

1. **Urban to Rural:** It involves the selling of products and services by urban marketers in rural areas. These include: pesticides, FMCG products, Consumer durables, etc.
2. **Rural to Urban:** Here, a rural producer (involved in agriculture) sells his produce in urban market. This may not be direct. There generally are middlemen, agencies, government co-operatives, etc., who sell fruits, vegetables, grains, pulses and others.
3. **Rural to Rural:** These include selling of agricultural tools, cattle, carts and others to another village in its proximity.

The rural market of India started showing its potential in the1960s. The 1970s and 1980s witnessed its steady development and, there are clear indications that the 21st century is going to see its full blossoming.

19.2 MEANING AND DEFINITION

Rural marketing can be defined as a function which manages all those activities in asserting, stimulating and converting the purchasing power of rural people into an effective demand for specific products and services and thereby achieving the goals of the organization.

> *"Rural marketing can be seen as a function which manages all those activities involved in assessing, stimulating and converting the purchasing power into an effective demand for specific products and services, and moving them to the people in rural area to create satisfaction and a standard of living for them and thereby achieves the goals of the organization".*

19.3 CHARACTERISTICS OF RURAL MARKETING

Rural marketing represents the emergent distinct activity of attracting and serving rural markets to fulfill the needs and wants of persons, households and occupations of rural people.

1. **Large, Diverse and Scattered Market:** Rural marketing in India is large, and scattered into a number of regions. There may be less number of shops available to market products.
2. **Major Income of Rural Consumers is from Agriculture:** Rural prosperity is tied with agricultural prosperity. In the event of crop failure, the incomes of masses are directly affected.
3. **Heterogeneity:** Rural markets comprise heterogeneous population. Various tiers are present depending on the incomes like big landlords, traders, small farmers, marginal farmers, labourers, artisans. State-wise variations exist in rural demographics like literacy (Kerala 90%, Bihar 44%), population below poverty line (Odisha 48%, Punjab 6%), etc.
4. **Standard of Living and Rising Disposable Income of the Rural Customers:** It is known that majority of the rural population lives below poverty line and has low literacy rate, low savings, etc. Today the rural customers spend money to get value and are aware of what's happening around them.
5. **Collective Decision-Making:** In rural markets decision-making process is collective. Purchase process-influencer, decider and buyer, one who pays can all be different. So marketers must address brand message at several levels. Rural youth brings brand knowledge to households.

6. **Diverse Socio-Economic Background:** Due to differences in geographical areas and uneven land fertility, rural people have different socio-economic background, which ultimately affects the rural markets.
7. **Infrastructure Facilities:** The infrastructure facilities like warehouses, communication systems and financial facilities are inadequate in rural areas. Physical distribution is a challenge to marketers who have found innovative ways to market their products.

19.4 SCOPE OF RURAL MARKETING

The liberalization and globalization of the Indian economy have given an added advantage to sophisticated production, proliferation and mass distribution of goods and services.

1. **Large Population:** According to 2011 census, rural population is 72% of total population and it is scattered over a wide range of geographic area.
2. **Rising Rural Prosperity:** Average income level has improved due to modern farming practices, contract farming industrialization, migration to urban areas, etc.
3. **Growth in Consumption:** There is a growth in purchasing power of rural consumers. The average per capita household expenditure is ₹ 382/-.
4. **Change in Lifestyle:** Lifestyle of rural consumer changed considerably.
5. **Market Growth Rate Higher than Urban:** The growth rate of fast moving consumer goods market and durable market is high in rural areas. The rural market share is more than 50% for products like cooking oil, hair oil, washing powder etc.
6. **Life Cycle Advantage:** The products which have attained the maturity stage in urban market are still in growth stage in rural market.
7. **Rural marketing is not expensive:** To promote consumer durable inside a state costs Rupees 1 crore while in urban areas it will costs in millions.

19.5 FACTORS CONTRIBUTING TO CHANGE IN RURAL MARKETING

An organization which makes its effective marketing plans and its own strategies or a creative one will prosper and create opportunities in the change in environment. The following factors contribute to the change in the rural marketing:

1. **Economic Factors:** The agricultural and rural development has enabled our country to achieve self sufficiency in food production and we are now exporting a variety of agricultural commodities to foreign countries. Favourable monsoons during the last 10 years have led to increase in crop yields and rural income. In addition, diversification of agriculture, development of village industries, migration of rural people into cities, remittance of money, family members settled abroad have increased income level and buying power of villagers.
2. **Green Revolution:** A technological breakthrough has taken place in Indian agriculture. Rural India derived considerable benefit from green revolution. Today, rural India generates 185 million tonnes of food grains per year and substantial output of various other agricultural products.
3. **Rural Communication:** Around 50 per cent of the villages are today connected with all weather roads and can be accessed throughout the year. But there are states, which are almost 100 per cent connected with the metal roads. Road networking besides enhancing the mobility of rural consumers has increased their exposure to products and services. By watching such a scenario in these areas Korean consumer durable companies have decided to look beyond their noses. They are now placing their bets on rural markets.
4. **Technological Development:** The rapid expansion of telecommunication facilities and mobile phone has provided opportunities for rural people to keep in touch with men and

markets. Development of TV networks and reasonable channels has enabled the marketers to pass on message about product and services to rural people. In rural areas especially in large villages and villages near to towns and cities, children and youth have access to information such as job opportunities, national news, weather conditions, bank loans, etc. IT and internet are sure to spread up exchange of information in rural India though at a slower rate compared to urban market.

5. **Development Programme:** The five-year plans have witnessed massive investments in rural areas in terms of number of development programmes implemented by the Central and State Government. These programmes have generated incomes to ruralites and helped them to change their lifestyles. Some of these programmes are:
   - Hill Area Development Programme
   - Operation Flood I, II and III (White Revolution)
   - Fisheries Development (Blue Revolution)
   - Integrated Rural Development Programme (IRDP)
   - Hill Area Development Programme
   - Intensive Agricultural District Programme
   - Intensive Agricultural Area Programme (IAAP)
   - Jawahar Rojgar Yojna (JRY).
6. **Literacy Growth:** The literacy rate is on the increase in the rural areas. This brings about a social and cultural change in the buying behaviour of the rural consumer. They are exposed to mass media which create new demand for goods and services.

19.6 IMPORTANCE OF RURAL MARKETING

Today every sales executive would prefer to serve in rural markets. A number of factors have been recognized as responsible for the rural market boom. Some of them are:

1. **Large Market:** Increase in population, and hence increase in demand. Approximately 75% of India's population resides around 6,38,365 villages in rural areas. The Indian rural consumers live in 6,00,000 villages across the country and they account for over 70% of population of the country. For several product categories, rural markets account for over 60% of the national demand.
2. **Socio-economic Changes in Rural India:** The socio-economic changes can be linked to an increase in productivity in the farm sector. Following agricultural revolutions, green or white, the yield per acre or animal increased substantially. This is largely due to the application of technology to the farm sector and modern farming methods. Cooperatives in India helped the farmer to increase farm productivity.
3. **Market Growth:** Urban markets are becoming competitive and even getting saturated. Consider the case of toiletries, packaged tea, dry cell batteries and even the electronic entertainment products. The demand has reached the saturation point. In such situation one has to find a strategy to find a new market for the existing products. Rural markets are the new markets which are opening up for most of these packaged goods.
4. **Higher Purchasing Capacity:** According to National Council for Applied Economic Research (NCAER) study, there are many middle income and above households in the rural areas, as there are in the urban areas. There are almost twice as many lower middle income households in rural areas as in the urban areas. Because of this purchasing power of rural people is on the rise.
5. **Changes in the Buying Behaviour:** Changes in the land tenure system are causing a structural change in the ownership pattern and consequent changes in the buying behaviour. The general rise in the level of prosperity appears to have resulted in two

dominant shifts in the rural consumption of consumer durables by almost all segments of rural consumers, and the obvious preference for branded goods as compared to non-branded goods of rural consumers.

19.7 CHANGING SCENARIO

The position in the rural market was totally different some twenty years ago. At present there is a demand for certain articles like T.V., fans, radio, engine oil, readymade garments, detergents, medicines, etc. New products like toiletries, baby care products and consumer durables are now getting good support in the rural market. Parle Agro is marketing 80% of its sale in the rural areas. Batliboi and Co. Ltd., is a leading marketer in agricultural implements. Hindustan Unilever sells its products like soaps, shampoos, face cream, etc., in all rural markets on a large scale. Kirloskar and Crompton are leading rural marketers in diesel engines and agricultural machinery while L&T, Eicher and Mahindra are the leading rural marketers in tractors.

Increased telecom broadband penetration, clean energy investments, Foreign Direct Investment (FDI) in rural development, Providing Urban Facilities in Rural Areas (PURA), growth in food processing industry and several new initiatives are set to transform India rural and make it an even bigger market place for the global corporates to pounce upon.

Several management studies have proven the strength of rural markets over urban. "Rural market potential in India is so huge that a mere one per cent increase in India's rural income translates to ₹ 1,00,000/- million of buying power."

19.8 DISTINCTION BETWEEN RURAL AND URBAN MARKETING

There is significant difference between rural and urban marketing:

Basis	*Urban Marketing*	*Rural Marketing*
Infrastructure	The facilities like electricity, Internet, roads and rail transportation and buildings, educational institutions, financial institutions, communication, and organized market , other facilities get implemented soon and availability is also there.	In rural market everything takes a good amount of time.
Competition	In urban market brand plays a great role.	In rural markets it is always the channel partner and retailer who plays a vital role.
Customers	In an urban market customers are more aware, standards of living are higher and customers are more comfort demanding.	On the other hand, customers are less aware in rural markets, standards of living are poor and customers are less demanding.
Philosophy	Marketing and relationship market.	Marketing and social concepts development marketing.
Advertising	Print, audio, visual media outdoors, exhibition, etc.	Radio, T.V. and print media.
Personal Selling	Door-to-door	Occasionally
Sales Promotion	Contest, gifts, price discount	Gift and price discount.
Demand	High	Low

19.9 PROBLEMS OF RURAL MARKETING

An efficient marketing system can provide better prices to producers and improve the availability of competitively priced produce to consumers. In some cases new markets or improvements to existing markets in rural areas can help overcome many of the marketing problems faced. However, before considering whether to carry out improvements to markets and what type of improvements to introduce, it is important to be sure that markets, or lack of them, represent the main problem. Other causes of inefficient marketing could be:

1. **Poor Infrastructural Facilities:** Infrastructural facilities like roads, warehouses, power etc., are inadequate in rural areas. Infrastructural costs are very high and impact adversely in the rural market activities. Transportation is an important aspect in the process of movement of products from urban production centres to remote villages. The transportation infrastructure is extremely poor in rural India. Due to this reason, most of the villages are not accessible to the marketing man.
2. **Under Developed Market:** Rural markets are not developing because of inadequate banking and credit facilities. Rural market needs banks to enable remittance, to transact on credit basis and to obtained credit support from the bank. At present every 48th village in India only has bank.
3. **Improper Communication Facilities:** Most villages even today largely depend on telegrams and phones for their communication needs, print media and visual media, etc. It has been estimated that all organized media in the country put together can reach only 30 per cent of the rural population of India. The print media covers only 18 per cent of the rural population.
4. **Villages are Small and Scattered:** In our country, the village structure itself causes many problems. Most of the villages are small and scattered. India is vast and is approximately 3,214 km from North to South and 2,933 km from East to West. Rural market consists of approximately 75 crore rural consumers spread across. The scattered nature of the villages increases distribution costs, and their small size affects economic viability of establishing distribution points.
5. **Low Per Capita income:** Most farmers have small lands and many villages are drought prone. This results in low per capita income. Low per capita income results in low consumption pattern as compared to the urban population. The marketers face challenges in rural marketing to decide about quantities, frequency of distributions, package size etc., due to the low per capita income of the rural people.
6. **Many Languages:** India is a country of many languages. The number of languages and dialects vary widely from state to state, region to region and probably from district to district. Language becomes a barrier in effective communication in the marketing efforts. The languages vary from state to state, place to place, district to district. There are now 18 scheduled languages.
7. **Seasonal Demand:** The main problem of rural marketing is seasonal demand in rural areas, because 75 per cent of rural income is also seasonal. For example, the demand for consumer goods will be high during the peak crop harvesting period, because this is the time at which the rural people have substantially high cash flow. Rural marketing depends upon the demand of rural people and demand depends upon income and consumer behaviour.

Besides, for the purpose of optimally exploiting the opportunities at hand in rural areas, the marketers have to cope up with various challenges before them like educating the rural consumers about the requirements and uses of the products. The marketers should also make the rural consumers understand how their product is different from similar products offered by competitors. This leads to better involvement on part of buyer and fosters long lasting relationship between consumer and company. Trust is another key factor which has to be properly dealt with. Thus, one of the biggest challenges to be met out is to create trust among the rural folks regarding the products.

19.10 STRATEGIES IN RURAL MARKETING

Considering the environment in which the rural market operates and other related problems, it is possible to evolve effective strategies for rural marketing. The strategies discussed here though not universally applicable depend upon product characteristics, the targeted segment of the rural market, the choice of the rural area and its economic condition. Rural markets and rural marketing involve a number of strategies, which include:

1. **Product Strategies:** Meaningful product strategies for rural market and rural consumers are discussed here.

   (*i*) **Small unit and low priced packing:** Larger pack sizes are out of reach for rural consumers because of their price and usage habits. This method has been tested by other products like shampoos, biscuits, pickles, washing powder, cosmetic items, etc. In the strategy of keeping the low priced packet the objective is to keep the price low so that the entire rural community can try. This may not be possible in all types of products, but wherever this can be resorted to, the market is bound to expand.

   (*ii*) **New product designs:** A close observation of rural household items indicates the importance of redesigning or modifying the products. The manufacturing and marketing man can think in terms of new product designs specially meant for rural areas keeping their lifestyles in view.

   (*iii*) **Sturdy products:** Sturdiness of a product either in terms of weight or appearance is an important fact for rural consumers. The product meant for rural areas should be sturdy enough to stand rough handling and storage. People in rural areas like bright flashy colours such as red, yellow, green etc., and feel that products with such colours are sturdy but they are more concerned with the utility of the item also.

   (*iv*) **Brand name:** The rural consumers are more concerned with the utility of the products. The brand name awareness in the rural areas is fairly high. A brand name and/or logo is very essential for rural consumers for it can be easily remembered.

2. **Pricing Strategies:** Pricing strategies are very much linked to product strategies. Some of these strategies are mentioned as follows:

   (*i*) **Low cost/cheap products:** This is a common strategy being adopted widely by many manufacturing and marketing men. Price can be kept low by small unit packing.

   (*ii*) **Avoid sophisticated packing:** Simple package can be adopted which can bring down the cost as it is presently being done in the case of biscuits. Some innovation in packing technology is very necessary for rural markets.

   (*iii*) **Refill packs/reusable packaging:** Such measures have a significant impact on the rural market. By such technology also the price can be reduced. In addition the packaging material used should preferably lend itself for reuse in rural areas.

3. **Distribution Strategies:** The distribution strategies that are specifically designed for rural areas are: through co-operative societies, public distribution system, multi-purpose distribution centres, distribution up to feeder markets/*mandi* towns shanties/*hat* / *jathras* / *melas*, agricultural input dealers etc. Experience has shown that the cooperatives have played a useful role in improving the marketing services in the regulated markets. The

fact, however, remains that these societies command only a small share of the total markets and do not present any challenge to the private trade in most places.

4. **Promotion Strategies:** Mass media is a powerful medium of communication. It could be television, cinema, print media, radio and so on. The other means of mass media available are hoardings/wall paintings, shanties/*hats* / *melas*, non-price competition, special campaigns, sales promotion activity etc. Besides these, other mass media are hand bills and booklets, posters, stickers, banners of the schemes etc. For disseminating the information, related to agricultural and other rural industry products, the government should circulate pamphlets either to panchayati raj office or to schools where it can be documented for the reference.

19.11 AGRICULTURAL MARKETING

The term 'agricultural marketing' is made up of two words agriculture and marketing:

- Agriculture, in the broad sense, means activities aimed at the use of natural resources for human welfare. Generally, it is used to mean growing and/or raising crops.
- Marketing brings a series of activities involved in moving the goods from the point of production to the point of consumption.

Agricultural marketing covers the services involved in moving an agricultural product from the farm to the consumer. A number of activities are involved in doing this, such as planning production, growing and harvesting, grading, packing, transport, storage, agro and food processing, distribution, advertising and sale.

> *"The study of agricultural marketing comprises all the operations, and the agencies conducting them, involved in the movement of farm produced foods, raw materials and their derivatives, such as textiles, from the farms to the final consumers, and the effects of such operations on farmers, middlemen and consumers. This definition does not include the input side of agriculture".*
>
> **Thomson**

19.12 CLASSIFICATION OF AGRI-PRODUCT

Agri-products hold a wide-ranging category of products related to agriculture. Those include a comprehensive range of raw and finished goods. The agri-products can be classified as:

1. **Foodgrain Items:** Foodgrains are one of the most essential and vital components of human survival. Besides the most commonly consumed foodgrains such as rice and wheat, which are common the world over, there are other foodgrains, such as various cereals, pulses and lentils which when consumed, complete the nutritional requirement of today's fast paced life.
2. **Horticultural Products:** Horticultural products include all products, raw or processed, that arise from the horticultural industry. This broadly inclusive definition is appropriate and even necessary in a time when traceability from the producer to the ultimate consumer is of growing interest to government and industry. Products from horticultural industry that go to market are clearly horticultural products. When juiced, sliced or pureed, fermented, frozen, preserved, canned, dried, irradiated, or used in an ornamental construct they remain, in our view, a horticultural product.
3. **Fibre Products:** A fibre or fiber is a piece of material that is long and thin, like a length of thread. Plant fibres are the basis of fabric such as cotton. Silk and wool fibres come from animals. They are very important in the structure of plants and animals, because

they hold tissues together. There are a lot of uses of fibres. They can be spun into filaments, thread, string or rope.

5. **Animal Products:** Animal product is a term used to describe any material derived from the body of a non-human animal. Examples are fat, flesh, milk, eggs etc.

19.13 FEATURES OF AGRI-PRODUCT

Agricultural products have certain characteristics of their own which necessitate a completely different system of marketing for them. Some of the characteristic features of Indian agricultural marketing system are:

1. **Weight and Volume:** Agricultural products tend to be bulky and their weight and volume are great for their value in comparison with many industrial goods.
2. **Transport Facilities:** The demand on storage and transport facilities is more heavy, and more specialized in case of agricultural products than in the case of manufactured commodities.
3. **More Perishable:** Agricultural commodities are comparatively much perishable than industrial goods. Although some crops such as rice and paddy retain their quality for long time, most of the farm products are perishable and cannot remain long on the way to the final consumer without suffering loss and deterioration in quality.
4. **Seasonal:** There are certain agricultural products such as mangoes and grapes which are available only in their seasons but this condition of seasonal availability is not found in the case of industrial goods.
5. **Scattered:** Agricultural produce is to be found scattered over a vast geographical area and as such its collection poses a serious problem. But such is not the condition in the case of industrial goods.

19.14 PROBLEMS OF AGRI-PRODUCTS MARKETING

> *"The future lies with those companies who see the poor as their customers".*
>
> **C. K. Prahalad, the global management guru**

There are several challenges involved in marketing of agricultural produce. There is limited access to the market information, literacy level among the farmers is low, multiple channels of distribution that eats away the pockets of both farmers and consumers.

1. **Globalization:** The globalization has brought drastic changes in India across all sectors and it is more so on agriculture and farmers. It has made a deep impact on agricultural marketing. It is basically because majority of Indians are farmers. It has brought several challenges and threats like uncertainty, turbulence, competitiveness, apart from compelling them to adapt to changes arising out of technologies. If it is the dark cloud there is silver lining like having excellent export opportunities for our agricultural products to the outside world.
2. **Sale in Villages:** The farmers sell more than 50% of the surplus produce to the traders and shopkeepers in their own villages normally below the market price.
3. **Chain of Middlemen:** There is a long chain of middlemen or intermediaries who are engaged in handling of the farm produce from the grower on to the consumer. Each of these intermediaries takes his own margin and thereby diminishes the return of the cultivator.

4. **Low Quality of Produce:** The production of agricultural goods is generally of low quality due to absence of grading, indifferent use of seeds, pests and deseases, deliberate adulteration etc. The agricultural produce like cotton, rice, do not enjoy good reputation in the foreign market. As such the cash returns to the producers are low.
5. **Costly Transport Facilities:** The transport system which consists of roads, network, railways, air transport, ports and shipping services is not only inadequate but also very costly for the transportation of the bulky agricultural goods from one place to another. Marketing costs take a too high share of the final price.
6. **Lack of Market Knowledge:** The farmers mostly being illiterate do not have detailed market knowledge as to when, how and where the goods are to be sold. They therefore do not get a fair return of their produce.
7. **Lack of Storage and Warehousing Facilities:** There is no or inadequate storage facilities at the farm level or in the houses of the farmers to store the surplus produce. They therefore have to sell the produce immediately after the harvest which brings reduced prices. The warehousing facilities in the markets are also insufficient and expensive.

19.15 TYPES OF MARKET

Markets mean an open place or large building where actual buying and selling takes place. The market may extend to a locality, village town, region or a country according to the demand of a commodity. Market includes both place and region in which buyers and sellers are in free interaction with one another. Marketing includes those business activities that direct the flow of goods and services from producer to consumer. Market for agricultural produce may broadly be divided into three categories:

1. Wholesale market
2. Retail market
3. Fairs.

1. **Wholesale Markets:** These markets are subdivided into:

   (*i*) **Primary wholesale markets:** Primary wholesale markets, where the bulk of arrivals is from village or village *hats*. These markets are periodically held, either once or twice a week or at longer intervals or on special occasions. These markets deal in the sale of fruits, vegetables, foodgrains, and all households requisites etc., for *e.g.*, village market.

   (*ii*) **Secondary wholesale market:** Secondary wholesale markets, also known as *mandis* and *Gunjs*, stretch over a wide area covering from 10 to 20 miles. There are about 1,700 such markets in the country. These are situated generally at districts. Small merchants purchase from primary wholesale market and sale in these markets. Some cultivators directly sell their produce in these markets. For example, district and taluka market.

   (*iii*) **Terminal markets:** These are the markets in which the produce is either finally disposed off, direct to consumers or processors or assembled for shipment to foreign countries. These markets are the parts where warehouses and storages are available/cover a wide area may be state, *e.g.*, Bombay terminal market.

2. **Retail Markets:** These markets are found scattered all over the town or a city or concentrated in particular localities. They are owned by the retailers subject to municipal control. They generally deal in all types of produce and serve the needs of the city people as well as of the surrounding villages. Particular type of market is located in particular locality. Cloth market is one locality and grain, vegetables are in different localities. There is direct selling to consumers.

3. **Fairs:** These are held on religious occasions, at pilgrim centres. These markets deal in livestock, agricultural produce etc. These fairs are held annually specially between the months of October and May and the duration of livestock fairs varies from one day to 3 months. Camels, horses, bulls, donkeys, cows, bullocks, sheep and goats are usually sold at these fairs. Such fairs are organized by district officers, local bodies or private agencies. Such religious fairs are Maghmela at Allahabad, Kartikisnan mela at Kurukshetra, and Pushkar.

19.16 PROCEDURE AND METHODS OF TRADING

The working of produce exchanges includes buying and selling certain commodities in accordance with the law and rules of exchange. The commodity exchanges are organized mainly for future contracts. The commodity exchange may be of different types:

1. **Cash Market:** Cash market provides the capital needed to fund the transaction without relying on the use of margin. Cash trading is achieved by using a cash account, which is a type of brokerage account that requires the investor to pay for securities within two days from when the purchase is made.
2. **Forward Dealing:** A transaction consisting of a purchase or sale with settlement to occur at a specified future date. Such a transaction will state the specific amount of the asset to be delivered at the specific time, as well as the unit price at which it will be delivered.
3. **Exchange Market:** The market for foreign exchange involves the purchase and sale of national currencies. A foreign exchange market exists because economies employ national currencies. If the world economy used a single currency there would be no need for foreign exchange markets.

19.17 CO-OPERATIVE MARKETING

An agricultural Co-operative Marketing, is also known as farmers' co-operative. A co-operative where farmers pool their resources in certain areas of activity. Agricultural co-operatives are forms of co-operatives formed by farmers or agriculturalists who have combined their resources together for the production and marketing of their produce and also getting some equipment and items to enhance the effectiveness of their production and marketing of the items with the hope of benefiting members financially and economically.

> *"Co-operation is a form of organization, wherein persons voluntarily associate together as human beings, on a basis of equality for the promotion of the economic interest of themselves".* **Gilbert**

19.18 AIMS AND OBJECTIVES OF CO-OPERATIVE MARKETING

The main aim of co-operative marketing societies is to rationalize the whole marketing system so that it may be beneficial to the producer. Its immediate objective is to strengthen the bargaining capacity of the cultivator so as to secure him better price and remove the intermediaries. The objects and aims of co-operative marketing society are briefly given below:

1. Strengthen the bargaining power of the producer.
2. Safeguard the member a better price for their produce.
3. Removal of superfluous intermediaries.
4. To help them during financial crisis by providing loans.
5. Stimulate the producer to develop quality goods.

6. Price stabilization.
7. Develop fair trading practices and reducing malpractices.
8. Improving the facilities of storage, grading, sale and transportation.
9. Performing the role of government agent for procurement and implementation of price policy.
10. To protect and promote the economic interest of its members by inculcating independency, thrift and better farming among members.
11. To play the role of distributive centre for agricultural requisites such as seeds, fertilizers, implements etc.
12. Supporting in the enlargement of co-operative credit programme by linking marketing with credit.

19.19 ROLE OF CO-OPERATIVE MARKETING

It has been recognized that systems of co-operative organizations are playing a crucial role in improving the systems of agro-product marketing. Co-operative marketing plays a significant role in the areas as mentioned below:

1. **Optimum Utilization of Available Resources:** An efficient co-operative marketing system can contribute to an increase in the marketable surplus by minimizing losses due to implementation of inefficient procedures, storage and costly transportation.
2. **Maximizing the Farm Income:** An efficient co-operative marketing system ensures the farmer better price for agro-products and stimulates them to invest their surplus in buying modern factors of production so that productivity may be maximized.
3. **Enlarging the Markets:** An organized co-operative marketing system helps in the enlargement of the market for the agro-products by penetrating them to remote locations of the country, *i.e.*, the areas away from the production points.
4. **Development of Agro-Based Industries:** The improved and efficient systems of agricultural marketing contribute in the growth and development of agro-based industries and induce the overall development process of our economy.
5. **Employment Generation:** A well integrated co-operative marketing system generates employment to persons engaged in various functions, like packaging, transportation and processing.

These co-operatives can support in efficient and harmonious relation between producer and consumer that will be against the exploitative tendencies of the greedy traders.

19.20 FUNCTIONS OF CO-OPERATIVE MARKETING

We should remember that farmers formed co-operatives for many purposes, including marketing of produce, purchasing of production and house supplies, and provision of credit. Farm marketing associations are the most important type of agricultural co-operatives. Farm purchasing co-operatives rank second in importance. The functions of agricultural co-operatives are summarized as follows:

1. **Farm Production:** Agricultural co-operatives encourage members to engage in joint cultivation of food and cash crops among others.
2. **Co-Operatives Joint Supply of Farm Machinery:** The membership of an agricultural co-operative can afford a farmer the opportunity to use modern farm and agricultural tools and implement which he could not afford on his own.

3. **Produce Marketing:** The produce marketing co-operative society helps to stabilize prices of farm produce.
4. **Irrigation:** An individual farmer may not be able to practise irrigation due to costs involved. But by joining a co-operative, he and the members may be engaged in irrigation programme to the benefits of the members (farmers).
5. **Land and Soil Conservation:** Land and soil conservation can be better achieved through co-operative effort.
6. **Access to Credit Facilities:** Government and its agencies easily grant credit facilities to co-operatives rather than an individual, who may lack collateral securities to obtain loans. This is also applicable to commercial banks.
7. **Training and Education:** Agricultural co-operatives provide to their members, training and education.
8. **Extension Service:** The introduction of new ideas, new methods, new techniques (innovation) is also a function of an agricultural co-operative.
9. **Attraction of Government Support:** Agricultural co-operatives attract government support to their activities.
10. **Mobilization of Savings:** Agricultural co-operatives encourage the culture of savings among farmers.

19.21 IMPORTANCE OF CO-OPERATIVE MARKETING

Agricultural production co-operative society is formed by farmers who produce similar agricultural product. They organize co-operative production and undertake joint marketing of the product on wholesale or retail basis. The farmers could still retain their individual farmlands or they may jointly own farms. Agricultural production co-operatives, encourage members to engage in joint cultivation of food and cash crops among others.

The importance of agricultural production co-operatives to the attainment of food security in India can not be over emphasized. This is because of our level of underdevelopment in which an individual farmer cannot achieve his desire for mass production for the needs of the country. It is in the interest of farmers that resources are combined so as to gain a tremendous advantage, which would widen the industrial base of any economy and the management techniques of these farmers. There are number of reasons which justify the establishment of co-operative marketing structure. Some of them are mentioned as follows:

1. **To Eradicate Malpractices:** The malpractices that exist in the marketing system can be eradicated to a large extent through co-operative marketing structure.
2. **Proportionate Share of Price:** A large number of intermediaries who take part in various activities like: collection, storage, financing, grading, sale and transportation of agricultural product. Their charges are disproportionate and producers do not get appropriate share of the price paid by the consumers. Efficiently organized co-operative marketing helps in sinking the price-spread between producer and consumers.
3. **Better Return to Farmers:** Co-operative marketing is an essential requirement for large-scale expansion of co-operative credit. Co-operative marketing societies are supposed to ensure a better return to the farmer with assisting them during financial crisis by fulfilling loans requirements from co-operative sources.
4. **Performing Various Tasks:** The integrated marketing system in a co-operative manner would perform tasks of assembling, grading, processing, storage and transportation, insurance financing and many more.

5. **Maximizing Efficiency and Improving Economic Conditions:** Co-operative marketing of agriculture produce is necessary for the attainment of maximum efficiency and for improving the economic conditions of the producers by strengthening their bargaining power.
6. **Educating the Farmers:** Co-operative marketing would educate the farmer in increasing the productivity, selecting the market of his product, provide enough volume of product to make efficient grading possible and allow the Indian producer to directly interact with exporters and also with large consumers in India.

19.22 PRESENT SCENARIO OF CO-OPERATIVE MARKETING

India produces ₹ 60,689 crore worth of agro-food material which when converted to processed products require a value addition of ₹ 50,703 crore but this value addition is due to food processing at various stages, utilize only 12% of the country's total food production even though we have potentiality to increase. At the same time we can not ignore the achievements of co-operative processing units. For example, the growth of co-operative sugar industry is an interesting fact in the history of agro-processing industry in the country. There are 216 co-operative sugar factories run by farmers. Over 18 lakh sugarcane growers own and use these 216 co-operatives. Co-operatives accounted for hardly 1% of national sugar production in 1955–56 whereas in 1987–88 they produced 52 lakh tonnes or 58% of national production. In terms of capacity utilization and efficiency of recovery of sugar from sugarcane, co-operatives have been consistently ahead of the private or the public sector sugar units.

REVIEW QUESTIONS

1. What is rural marketing? Define the characteristics of rural marketing.
2. Explain the scope of rural marketing.
3. Explain the factors contributing to change in the rural marketing.
4. Explain the importance of rural marketing.
5. Distinguish between rural and urban marketing.
6. What are the problems of rural marketing?
7. Explain the strategies in rural marketing.
8. Describe the agricultural marketing and classification of agri-product.
9. Explain the features of agri-product.
10. What are the problems of agri-products marketing?
11. Explain the types of market.
12. What are the procedure and methods of trading?
13. What is co-operative marketing? Explain the aims and objectives of co-operative marketing.
14. Explain the role of co-operative marketing.
15. What are the functions of co-operative marketing?
16. What is the importance of co-operative marketing?
17. Explain the present scenario of co-operative marketing.

CHAPTER 20

Marketing of Services Banking, Transport and Insurance

POINTS TO REMEMBER

At the end of this chapter, we will be able to understand:

- Introduction
- Meaning and Definition
- Characteristics of Services
- Difference between Goods and Services
- Service Marketing Mix
- Bank Marketing
- Marketing Mix for Banking Organization
- Marketing Information System
- Component of Marketing Information System
- Transport Marketing
- Mode of Transport
- Marketing in Indian Railways
- Marketing Mix for Rail Transport
- Marketing in Road Transport Corporation
- Marketing Mix-Road Transport Corporation
- Airline Marketing Mix
- Risk and Insurance Marketing
- Life Insurance Corporation in India
- Marketing Mix in Insurance Sector

20.1 INTRODUCTION

Prior to the time of the Industrial Revolution, virtually all trade and exchange processes involved some personal contact between suppliers and their customers. This meant that individual producers could cater to the needs of their customers, and most trade was very local in nature. The increase in overseas trading and the advent of the industrial revolution indicated the start of new types of trading practice, and the introduction of some of the processes which are part of marketing today. Economists have divided all industrial and economic activities into three main groups: primary, secondary and tertiary. Primary activities include agriculture, fishing and forestry. Secondary activities cover manufacturing and construction, and tertiary activities refer to the services and distribution.

20.2 MEANING AND DEFINITION

The most comprehensive definition of service marketing is that it is essentially intangible and does not result in the ownership of anything. Its production may or may not be tied to a physical product. A service is any act or performance that one party can offer to another that is essentially intangible and does not result in the ownership of anything.

Marketing is the foundation of business operations for businesses and non-profit organizations. Understanding the various marketing services and their functions helps for profit or non-profit organization reach their goals. Marketing is the process of persuading potential consumers to buy the organization's product or service. Marketing services are the methods used in the overall marketing plan of production, pricing, promotion and distribution. The main marketing services consist of market research, advertising, promotion and public relations. Market research involves gathering statistical data to develop the organization's marketing strategy and plan.

> *"Activities, benefits and satisfaction which are offered for sale or are provided in connection with the sale of goods".* **American Marketing Association**

20.3 CHARACTERISTICS OF SERVICES

Services are said to have four key characteristics which impact on marketing programme. These are:

1. **Intangibility:** Services are intangible and do not have a physical existence. Hence, services cannot be touched, held, tasted or smelt. This is the most defining feature of a service and that which primarily differentiates it from a product. Also, it poses a unique challenge to those engaged in marketing a service as they need to attach tangible attributes to an otherwise intangible offering.

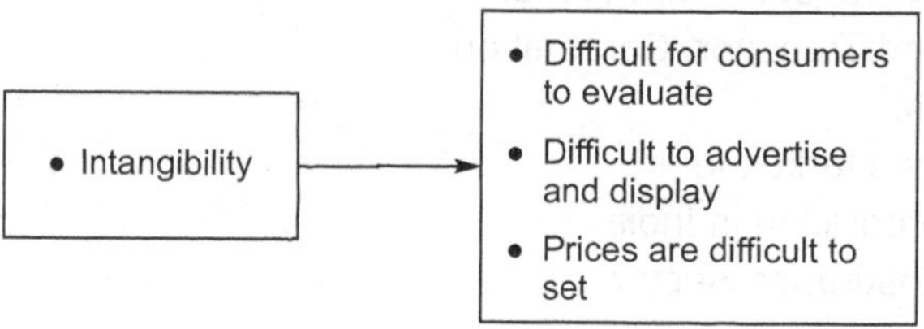

2. **Heterogeneity/Variability:** Given the very nature of services, each service offering is unique and cannot be exactly repeated even by the same service provider. While products can be mass produced and be homogeneous the same is not true of services. For example, all burgers of a particular flavour at McDonalds are almost identical. However, the same is not true of the service rendered by the same counter staff consecutively to two customers.

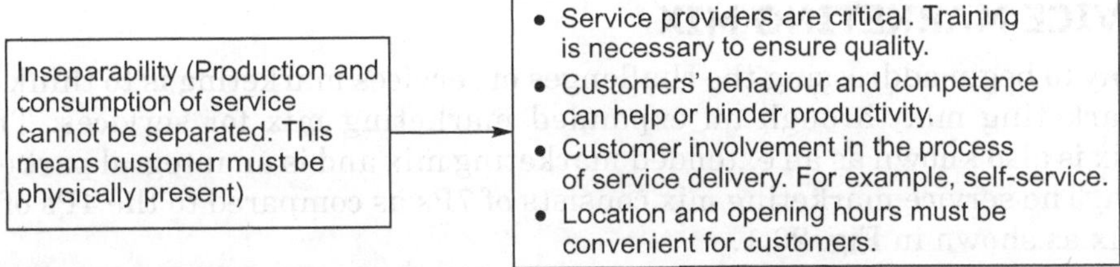

3. **Perishability:** Services cannot be stored, saved, returned or resold once they have been used. Once rendered to a customer the service is completely consumed and cannot be delivered to another customer. For example, a customer dissatisfied with the services of a barber cannot return the service of the haircut that was rendered to him. At the most he may decide not to visit that particular barber in future.

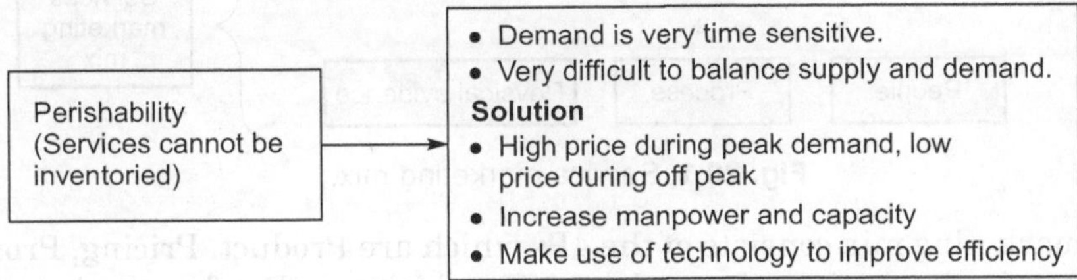

4. **Inseparability:** Services are produced and consumed at the same time, unlike goods which may be manufactured, then stored for later distribution. This means that the service provider becomes an integral part of the service itself. The waitress in the restaurant, or the cashier in the bank, is an inseparable part of the service offering. The client also participates to some extent in the service, and can affect the outcome of the service. People can be part of the service itself, and this can be an advantage for services marketers.

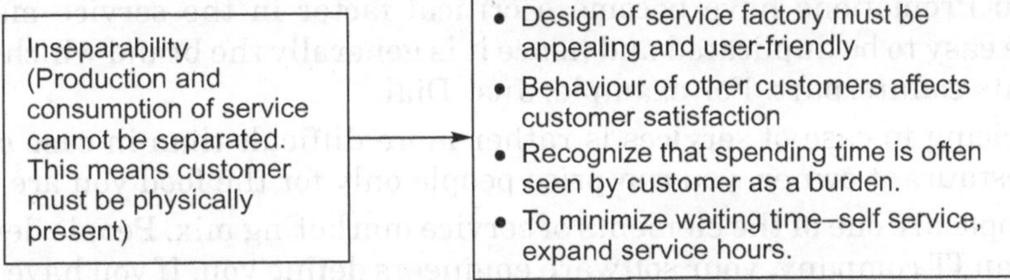

20.4 DIFFERENCE BETWEEN GOODS AND SERVICES

Given below are the fundamental differences between physical goods and services:

Goods	*Services*
A physical commodity	A process or activity
Tangible	Intangible
Homogeneous	Heterogeneous
Production and distribution are separate from their consumption	Production, distribution and consumption are simultaneous processes
Can be stored	Cannot be stored
Transfer of ownership is possible.	Transfer of ownership is not possible.

20.5 SERVICE MARKETING MIX

Another way to begin addressing the challenges of services marketing is to think creatively about the marketing mix through an expanded marketing mix for services. The service marketing mix is also known as an extended marketing mix and is an integral part of a service outline design. The service marketing mix consists of 7Ps as compared to the 4Ps of a product marketing mix as shown in Fig. 20.1.

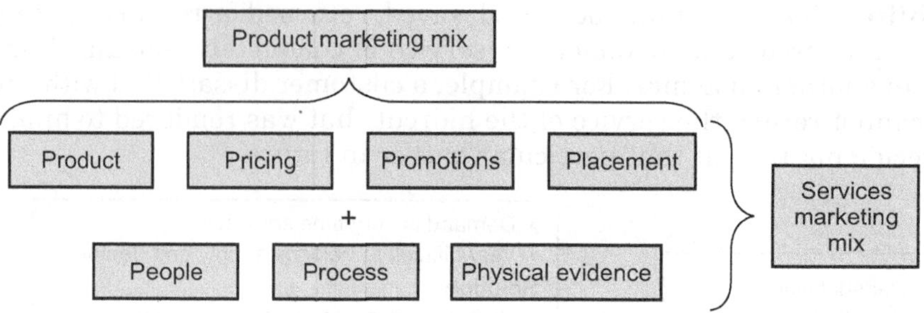

Fig. 20.1. Service marketing mix.

The product marketing mix consists of the 4Ps which are Product, Pricing, Promotions and Placement. The service marketing mix consists of 7Ps which are 4Ps of marketing mix + process, people and physical evidence.

1. **Product:** The product in service marketing mix is intangible in nature. Like physical products such as soap or a detergent, service products cannot be measured. Tourism industry can be an excellent example.
2. **Place:** Place in case of services determines where the service product is going to be located. The best place to open up a petrol pump is on the highway or in the city.
3. **Promotion:** Promotions have become a critical factor in the service marketing mix. Services are easy to be duplicated and hence it is generally the brand which sets a service apart from its counterpart. For example: Just Dial.
4. **Pricing:** Pricing in case of services is rather more difficult than in case of products. If you are a restaurant owner, you can price people only for the food you are serving.
5. **People:** People are one of the elements of service marketing mix. People define a service. If you have an IT company, your software engineers define you. If you have a restaurant, your chef and service staff define you.
6. **Process:** Service process is the way in which a service is delivered to the end customer. Let's take the example of two very good companies—McDonalds and Dominos. Both the companies thrive on their quick service and the reason they can do that is their confidence on their processes.
7. **Physical Evidence:** The last element in the service marketing mix is a very important element. As said before, services are intangible in nature. However, to create a better customer experience tangible elements are also delivered with the service. Take an example of a restaurant which has only chairs and tables and good food, or a restaurant which has ambient lighting, nice music along with good seating arrangement and this also serves good food.

20.6 BANK MARKETING

Banking industry is one of the most important service industries which touches the lives of millions of people. Its service is unique both in social and economic points of view of a nation.

It was in the late 1950s that marketing in banking industry emerged in the west. Its emergence was in the form of advertising and promotion concept. At that time, personal setting could not get a significant place.

Gradually there was a change in the attitude of bankers, probably in time with the attitudinal change in customers. The idea of customers' satisfaction began in the late 1950s, flourished in 1960s and became an integral part of the banking services in the 1970s.

The first major step in the direction of marketing was initiated by the State Bank of India in 1972, when it recognized itself on the basis of major market segments, dividing the customers on the basis of activity and carved out four major market segments.The marketing comprehension that is performed by banks since 1970 can be shown as in following five stages:

1. Promotion-oriented marketing comprehension
2. Marketing comprehension based on having close relations for customers
3. Reformist marketing comprehension
4. Marketing comprehension that focused on specializing in certain areas
5. Research, planning and control-oriented marketing comprehension.

20.7 MARKETING MIX FOR BANKING ORGANIZATION

Marketing activities of firms begin with determination of the market that they offer their services or goods.

1. **Service:** Banks are in a period that they earn money in servicing beyond selling money. The prestige is, get as they offer their services to the masses. Like other services, banking services are also intangible. Banking services are about the money in different types and attributes like lending, depositing and transferring procedures. These intangible services are shaped in contracts. The structure of banking services affects the success of institution in long-term. Besides the basic attributes like speed, security and ease in banking services, the rights like consultancy for services to be compounded are also preferred.
2. **Price:** The price which is an important component of marketing mix is named differently in the base of transaction exchange that it takes place. Banks have to estimate the prices of their services offered. By performing this, they keep their relations with existing customers and take new ones. The prices in banking have names like interest, commission and expenses.
3. **Distribution:** The complexity of banking services results from different kinds of services. The most important feature of banking is the persuasion of customers benefiting from services. Most banks' services are complex in attribute and when this feature joins the intangibility characteristics, offerings take also mental intangibility in addition to physical intangibility. On the other hand, value of service and benefits taken from it mostly depends on knowledge, capability and participation of customers besides features of offerings. This results from the fact that production and consumption have non-separable characteristics in those services.
4. **Promotion:** One of the most important elements of marketing mix of services is promotion which consists of personal selling, advertising, public relations, and selling promotional tools.
5. **Personal Selling:** Due to the characteristics of banking services, personal selling is the way that most banks prefer in expanding selling. Personal selling occurs in two ways. First, it occurs in a way that customer and banker perform interaction face-to-face at branch office. In this case, personnel like bank employees, chief and office manager, take part in selling. Secondly it occurs in a way that customer representatives go to customers' place. Customer representatives are specialists in banks' services to be offered and they shape the relationship between bank and customer.

6. **Advertising:** Banks have too many goals which they want to achieve. Those goals are for accomplishing the objectives as follows in a way that banks develop advertising campaigns and use media:
    1. Conceive customers to examine all kinds of services that banks offer
    2. Increase use of services
    3. Create well fitting image about banks and services
    4. Change customers' attitudes
    5. Introduce services of banks
    6. Support personal selling
    7. Emphasize well service.
7. **Public Relations:** Public relations in banking should provide:
    1. Establishing most effective communication system
    2. Creating sympathy about relationship between bank and customer
    3. Giving broadest information about offers and activities of bank.

20.8 MARKETING INFORMATION SYSTEM

A Marketing Information System (MIS) is a set of procedures and methods designed to generate, analyze, disseminate, and store anticipated marketing decision information on a regular and continuous basis.

Each and every decision area of marketing needs the support of marketing information. The degree of marketing excellence achieved by a firm has a direct relationship with the marketing information system operated by it. Marketing excellence is the net outcome of correct marketing decisions, and the decisions can be correct only when they are information based. A Marketing Information System offers the following advantages:

1. Organized data collection.
2. A broad perspective.
3. The storage of important data.
4. An avoidance of crises.
5. Coordinated marketing plans.
6. Speed in obtaining sufficient information to make decisions.
7. Data amassed and kept over several time periods.
8. The ability to do a cost-benefit analysis.

A marketing information system can be used operationally, managerially, and strategically for several aspects of marketing.

20.9 COMPONENT OF MARKETING INFORMATION SYSTEM

Marketing information system has four major components. They are Internal Reports System, Marketing Intelligence System, Analytical Marketing System and Marketing Intelligence System as shown in Fig. 20.2.

The explanation of this model of an MIS begins with a description of each of its four main constituent parts: the internal reporting systems, marketing research system, marketing intelligence system and marketing models. It is suggested that while the MIS varies in its degree of sophistication—with many in the industrialized countries being computerized and few in the developing countries being so, a fully fledged MIS should have these components, the methods of collection, storing, retrieving and processing data notwithstanding.

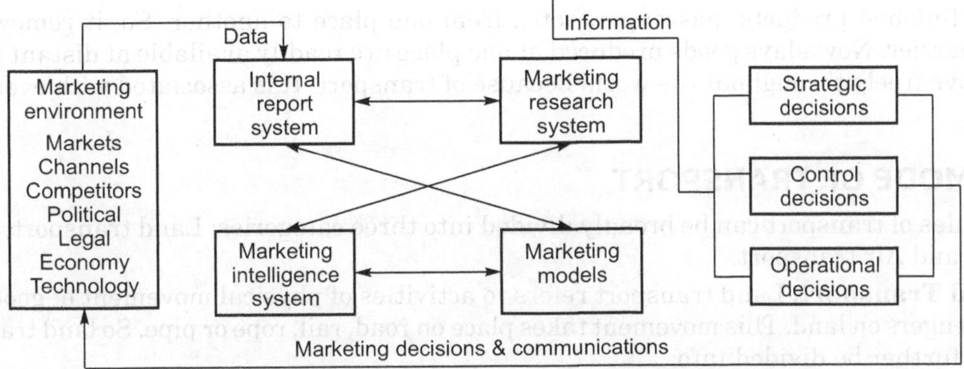

Fig. 20.2. Component of marketing management system.

1. **Internal Reporting Systems:** All enterprises which have been in operation for any period of time have a wealth of information. However, this information often remains underutilized because it is compartmentalized, either in the form of an individual entrepreneur or in the functional departments of larger businesses. That is, information is usually categorized according to its nature so that there are, for example, financial, production, manpower, marketing, stockholding and logistical data. Often the entrepreneur, or various personnel working in the functional departments holding these pieces of data, do not see how it could help decision makers in other functional areas. Similarly, decision makers can fail to appreciate how information from other functional areas might help them and therefore do not request it.
2. **Marketing Intelligence Systems:** Whereas marketing research is focused, market intelligence is not. A marketing intelligence system is a set of procedures and data sources used by marketing managers to shift information from the environment that they can use in their decision-making.
3. **Marketing Models:** Within the MIS there has to be the means of interpreting information in order to give direction to decision. These models may be computerized or may not. Typical tools are:
   - Time series sales modes
   - Brand switching model
   - Linear programming
   - Elasticity models (price, incomes, demand, supply, etc.)
   - Regression and correlation models
   - Analysis of Variance (ANOVA) models
   - Sensitivity analysis
   - Discounted cash flow
   - Spreadsheet what if models.

20.10 TRANSPORT MARKETING

Transport refers to the activity that facilitates physical movement of goods as well as individuals from one place to another. In business, it is considered as an auxiliary to trade, that means, it supports trade and industry in carrying raw materials to the place of production and distributing finished products for consumption. Individuals or business firms that engage themselves in such activities are called transporters. Generally, transporters carry raw material, finished products, passengers, etc., from one place to another. So, it removes the distance barrier. Nowadays goods produced at one place are readily available at distant places. People move freely throughout the world because of transport. It is associated with every step of our life.

20.11 MODE OF TRANSPORT

The modes of transport can be broadly divided into three categories: Land transport, Water transport and Air transport.

1. **Land Transport:** Land transport refers to activities of physical movement of goods and passengers on land. This movement takes place on road, rail, rope or pipe. So land transport may further be divided into:
   - Road transport
   - Rail transport
   - Ropeway transport
   - Pipeline transport.
2. **Water Transport:** Water transport refers to movement of goods and passengers on waterways by using various means like boats, steamers, launches, ships, etc. With the help of these means goods and passengers are carried to different places, both within as well as outside the country. Within the country, rivers and canals facilitate the movement of boats, launches, etc. Since the goods and passengers move inside the country, this type of transport is called inland water transport. When the different means of transport are used to carry goods and passengers on the sea route, it is termed as ocean transport.
3. **Air Transport:** This is the fastest mode of transport. It carries goods and passengers through airways by using different aircraft like passenger aircraft, cargo aircraft, helicopters, etc. Besides passengers it generally carries goods that are less bulky or of high value. In hilly and mountainous areas where other mode of transport is not accessible, air transport is an important as well as convenient mode. It is mostly used for transporting goods and passengers during natural calamities like earthquake and floods, etc. During war, air transport plays an important role in carrying soldiers as well as supplies to the required areas. Air transport may be classified as:
   - Domestic air transport
   - International air transport.

20.12 MARKETING IN INDIAN RAILWAYS

Railways are a service industry, hence the railway employees responsible for delivery of service are conspicuous to users and indeed are directly accountable to users for service quality. In this sense, they differ for example from manufacturing industries, where those responsible for creation of the product are usually not visible to consumers and where there is a clear distinction between production and marketing activities. For railways, as with most service industries, the production and marketing of the product are practically inseparable.

Indian Railways has been in the news recently because of the turnaround it has achieved in the last few years with profits in excess of ₹ 20,000 crore to show. On the face of it if someone were to propose it as an organization which is becoming more customer savvy, it would be difficult to accept.

The first is the e-ticketing facility that has been extended to travellers. Today the site, www.irctc.com does more than one lakh transactions per day and is the largest in south Asia with customer satisfaction levels of 99.99%. For a regular traveller this facility is a boon, the tickets can be booked sitting in his office without having to go and buy the tickets at the counters. The facility is being extended to ATMs and outside agents also.

Auto up-gradation is also a good initiative. It is a win-win situation for both railways as well as customers. Because by upgrading the consumers get to experience the higher priced next level of travel at no extra cost and the railways are able to accommodate more people and ensure that the train runs full. And the *Tatkal* facility has also been a hit among travellers.

The other initiatives include rail tourism wherein a traveller can use the site to book a complete travel package which would include his stay, sight seeing and travel from home to the station and so on. This is a good example of solution selling. The journey for Indian Railways to become a totally customer oriented organization has just started.

20.13 MARKETING MIX FOR RAIL TRANSPORT

The Seven Ps are Product, Price, Promotion, Place, People, Processes and Physical Evidence. It is useful to describe each of these variables in terms of their meaning in a railway marketing environment.

1. **Product:** For railways, this is the service offered to customers, both existing and prospective.

   (*a*) Passenger Traffic: These include:
   - Coaches (Seating, berths, legroom, elbow room, double decks)
   - Reservation
   - Lighting
   - Catering
   - Water
   - Bedrolls
   - Medical aid
   - Safety
   - Services at the railway stations.

   (*b*) Freight Traffic (agricultural and industrial activities)
   - Types of wagons-BOX, BOY, BCA, TANK, BCX
   - Services-Domestic Container Service
   - Freight for warder scheme Quick Transit Scheme, Speed Link Express, Trains Street Collection, etc.

   (*c*) Mail Traffic (Railway Mail Services)

2. **Pricing (Deciding the Fare):** This denotes the published or negotiated value of the exchange transaction for a product or service.

   For a railway passenger service , the price of the service, or the fare, paid by passengers is usually graduated by distance—the longer the distance travelled, the lower the charge per kilometer although often the charges are broad banded within intervals of distance, e.g., one charge for 0–30 km; another (lesser) charge for 31–70 km, and so on. In addition, fare rates usually vary with the standard of service used—for example, a first class seat might cost more than double a third class seat, while a deluxe sleeping berth might cost 50 per cent more than a deluxe seat, etc. In some cases, governments control the maximum level of fares charged for different categories of service, while railway organizations have the ability to discount fares below these maxima, in order to generate more business or to modify demand in someway, *e.g.*, by transferring demand from heavy to light traffic periods. Discounts may be provided for: ticket bulk purchases (*e.g.*, weekly, monthly, yearly tickets), off-peak travel (time of day or seasonal); group travel and tours; child/student/senior citizen passenger/other pensioner travel. In a small number of cases, railway organizations have the ability both to adjust the maximum level of passenger fares and to offer discounts on these fares.

3. **Place:** Place means not just the locations of producer facilities, but the locations of all points of sale at which customers may have access to the product or service.

   Online Facilities:
   - Passenger's Current Status Enquiry
   - Fare Enquiry
   - Reservations
   - Train between Important Stations
   - Upgraded Passenger Scheme/Chart
   - Weekly Availability at Stations.
4. **Promotion:** In the context of railway marketing, promotional techniques are becoming more widely used for passenger business, but are as yet relatively little used in the case of freight business.
5. **People:** It almost goes without saying that people are a railway organization's most important resource. So it is that a railway's people resources will be vitally important to the realization of its marketing goals. It will not matter how advanced and sophisticated are a railway organization's management systems if the railway's existing and potential customers do not feel that railway staff are listening and responding to their needs.
6. **Process:** Ticket booking, ticket processing, ticket delivery, customer reaching the airport, boarding pass security, check inside the aircraft, refreshment is served before he reaches his final destination. A pre-paid cab is also arranged for the customer's add-on journey from the airport.
7. **Physical Evidence:** The design layout and signage of passenger stations, for example, must be such as to convey the impression to travellers that the railway really wants their business. This it will do by ensuring that platforms, concourses, ticket/reservations offices, waiting rooms, toilets, baggage lockers, bus interchange and transfer facilities, etc; will be comfortable and convenient for all categories of travellers to use.

20.14 MARKETING IN ROAD TRANSPORT CORPORATION

Transport volumes in India remain much less than those in the developed countries. India has still to go a long way in strengthening its transportation network. The countries transportation network suffers from several inadequacies and, in particular it has little flexibility to deal with unforeseen demands.

Transportation, like all industries is largely influenced by information and communication technologies with the focus being on knowledge of customer needs and value-added services. Surface transport is provided by the Road and the Indian Railways (primarily for carrying low value bulk commodity, mostly for the government sector). Cargo Road Transport is entirely in the hands of the private sector. An estimated 1.2 million trucks (9 tons capacity) network in the country covering more than 80,000 kilometers of roads. In India road transportation is preferred for cargo movement, where flexibility of routing assumes importance. It facilitates door-to-door delivery, overcoming unnecessary delays which normally take place in the other modes of transportation. The road transport has following benefits:

(*a*) Easily connect any part of country unlike railways
(*b*) Complementary to railways, providing feeder service
(*c*) More flexible in comparison to other modes
(*d*) Provides door-to-door services
(*e*) Better means to deliver perishable goods to market places in time
(*f*) Does not require heavy capital for operation
(*g*) Mode is important in Defense Services of the country.

20.15 MARKETING MIX-ROAD TRANSPORT CORPORATION

1. **Product Mix:** It includes:
   (*a*) Passenger Traffic:
   - Regular passengers commuting short and long distances
   - Special Package Tours-Pilgrimage, Sight Seeing, Educational Tours.

   (*b*) Cargo Traffic:
   - Transporting goods to destination
   - Bulk carrying of special items like gas, milk, petrol
   - Mail services.
2. **Pricing Policy**
   - Basic and common policy adopted is the 'cost' plus 'margin'
   - Cost includes the vehicle cost less depreciation, fuel charges, crew expenses, road tax, rest room expenses, etc.
   - Special price policy is adopted for special services.
3. **Promotion Policy**
   - There are different promotion channels like advertising, print media, TV, short films for tourism, etc.
   - Other ways are personal selling, telemarketing, publicity, sales promotion, and network marketing.
   - Irrespective of the promotion channel the quality of service offered must be maintained.
4. **Place**
   - Promised services without any disturbance to user
   - Time management
   - Service offered and service delivered should match with maintenance of terminals, warehouses and workshops
   - Infrastructural facilities
   - Upgrading technology continuously.
5. **People:** There will be a good sales turnover if the people providing the services deliver quality services. This is the main reason for success. HR working for public transport system should be continuously trained.
6. **Processes.** Processes should not be cumbersome and be hassle free. There should not be back tracking or zig-zag in service process. This results in better time management and cost reductions.

20.16 AIRLINE MARKETING MIX

1. **Product:** The air transport service.
2. **Pricing:** Variety of structured price bands categorized on the basis of various combinations of routes, short/long distances and number of halts, etc., and categories, *i.e.*, business class, economy class.
3. **Promotions:** Point of purchases, *i.e.*, ticketing counters at travelling agencies, online options, *e.g.*, membership promotions, couple tickets, tourist packages for agencies and various other individual and corporate offers.
4. **Place:** Ticketing counters delivering services.
5. **People:** A team of skilled and professionally trained pilots, air-hostesses, ground staff, flight attendants, freight movers and packers, security personnel, management decision makers and most importantly, customers.
6. **Process:** To avail of the air service, there is online or manual booking of tickets followed by confirmation at security desks on arrival at the airport at least 2 hours before the scheduled commencement of the journey. After boarding the aircraft, basic after sales services are provided to those who avail of the range of services available. Besides, arranging for passenger travel post landing to the convenient destination, arrangements made if flights are delayed or rescheduled etc., are some of the value additions that the airline offers to provide improved customer satisfaction.
7. **Physical Evidence:** The service itself.

20.17 RISK AND INSURANCE MARKETING

One of the important functions of marketing management is risk bearing. In any marketing activity uncertainty is bound to exist. This uncertainty may result in the form of either loss or profit. The unpredictable natures of the consumers, changing fashions, increasing competition and increasing costs of production have led to the concept, "risk-bearing".

All these uncertainties have to be faced in the marketing activity by any producer or entrepreneur. Some of the risks may be avoided by taking insurance coverage.

20.18 LIFE INSURANCE CORPORATION IN INDIA

The term 'Insurance Marketing' refers to the marketing of insurance services with the aim of creating customer and generating profit through customer satisfaction. The insurance marketing focuses on the formulation of an ideal mix for insurance business so that the insurance organization survives and thrives in the right perspective.

In India, the Life Insurance Corporation of India (LIC) and the General Insurance Corporation (GIC) are the two leading companies offering insurance services to the users. The Oriental Life Insurance Company, the first corporate entity in India offering life insurance coverage, was established in Calcutta in 1818 by Bipin Behari Dasgupta and others. Europeans in India were its primary target market, and it charged Indians heftier premiums. The Bombay Mutual Life Assurance Society, formed in 1870, was the first native insurance provider. Other insurance companies established in the pre-independence era included:

- Bharat Insurance Company (1896)
- United India (1906)
- National India (1906)
- National Insurance (1906)

- Co-operative Assurance (1906)
- Hindustan Co-operatives (1907)
- Indian Mercantile
- General Assurance
- Swadeshi Life (later Bombay Life)

Life Insurance Corporation of India (LIC) is the largest insurance group and investment company in India. It's state-owned where Government of India has 100% stake. LIC also funds close to 24.6% of the Indian Government's expenses. It has assets estimated of ₹ 13.25 trillion. It was founded in 1956 with the merger of 243 insurance companies and provident societies.

Apart from offering life insurance policies, they also offer underwriting and consulting services. When a person or an organization buys an insurance policy from the insurance company, he not only buys a policy, but along with it the assistance and advice of the agent, the prestige of the insurance company and the facilities of claims and compensation.

20.19 MARKETING MIX IN INSURANCE SECTOR

The marketing mix includes sub-mixes of the 7Ps of marketing, *i.e.*, the product, its price, place, promotion, people, process and physical attraction. The above mentioned 7Ps can be used for marketing of insurance products, in the following manner:

1. **Product (Scheme):** It is the first element, product is the sum total of physical, social and psychological benefits. Managing the product component involves product planning and development. The life insurance marketers must define their market in terms of product function. It may offer a single product or several products. Life insurance as product has also to be designed, keeping in view these basic requisites, in case of life insurance the needs are in the form of two broad economic contingencies, *viz.*, death of the breadwinner and the subsequent financial insecurity of his dependents, and secondly, longer life insurance is sold as plan of LIC of Nepal developed term assurance and whole life policies and for the second category various pension plans and annuities. Apart from whole life insurance, endowment insurance and money back plans, LIC has several products specially suited for children, exclusively for women, the handicapped, senior citizens, to cover occurrence of terminal diseases, term assurance and pension plans. There are also group insurance schemes that can be taken by employer for their employees. The LIC also administers schemes for people who are below or just above the poverty line.
2. **Price (Premium):** The prices are another powerful element in the life insurance marketing mix and vitally affect the volume of sales. Price is the valuation placed upon the product. In the case of life insurance, premium is the price which the person seeking insurance pays to LIC for purchase in the life insurance policy. The management must take decisions regarding pricing (premium), investment return, level of premium, mode of premium, commission, insured sum, life to be covered, interest on loan, price strategy, under writing and price related situations. It deals with price competition.
3. **Place (Physical Distribution):** Marketing channel policy is another integral part of the life insurance marketing mix. Physical distribution is the delivery of insurance products at the right time and at the right place. In the case of life insurance, it is the combination of decisions regarding channels of distribution, agents, development officers, brokers, branch office, retail financial service distributors, alliances with banks, tie-ups with non-governmental organizations, corporate agencies, bank assurance, e-trade, proper infrastructure and training facilities, technical and material know-how on the part of

instructor, etc. At present the strength of LIC's distribution channel comprising over 6.10 lakh active agents and over 19,000 development officers appears to be phenomenal. This is indeed a great advantage to cover the vast population, diverse in nature and spread, for which a strong marketing network is imperative. The network is duly supported by more than 3,100 servicing branches.

4. **Promotion:** The business enterprise should inform the customers about its products and persuade them to buy. It covers methods of communicating with consumers through personal selling, advertising, publicity, sales promotion, social contracts, public relations, exhibition and demonstration used in promotion. For promoting life insurance business, sales promotion activities are carried out by the agent, development officers and branch offices. Calendars, diaries, bags, etc., are also given to policy holders as a token of gifts. All these activities increase the volume of sales by expanding as well as retaining the market share for the insurance products.
5. **People:** Understanding the customer better allows designing appropriate products. Being a service industry which involves a high level of people interaction, it is very important to use this resource efficiently in order to satisfy customers. Training, development and strong relationships with intermediaries are the key areas to be kept under consideration. Training the employees, use of IT for efficiency, both at staff and agent level, is one of the important areas to look into.
6. **Process:** The process should be customer friendly in insurance industry. The speed and accuracy of payment is of great importance. The processing method should be easy and convenient to the customers. Installment schemes should be streamlined to cater to the ever growing demands of the customers. IT and data warehousing will smoothen the process flow.
7. **Physical Evidence:** Distribution is a key determinant of success for all insurance companies. Today, the nationalized insurers have a large reach and presence in India. Building a distribution network is very expensive and time consuming. If the insurers are willing to take advantage of India's large population and reach a profitable mass of customers, then new distribution avenues and alliances will be necessary. Initially insurance was looked upon as a complex product with a high advice and service component. Buyers prefer a face-to-face interaction and they place a high premium on brand names and reliability.

REVIEW QUESTIONS

1. What is marketing services? Explain the characteristics of services.
2. Explain the different elements of marketing mix and services marketing.
3. What is bank marketing? Explain the marketing mix of banking.
4. What is marketing information system? Explain the different components of MIS.
5. Describe transport marketing. Explain the different kinds of transport marketing.
6. Define the marketing in Indian railways. Explain the railways-marketing mix.
7. What are airlines marketing? Explain airline marketing mix.
8. Define insurance marketing. Explain Life Insurance Corporation of India.
9. Explain the marketing mix in insurance sector.

CHAPTER 21

E-Commerce and CRM

POINTS TO REMEMBER

At the end of this chapter, we will be able to understand:

E-COMMERCE

- Introduction
- Meaning and Definition
- Benefits of E-commerce
- Marketing Mix of E-commerce
- E-commerce Models
- Application of E-commerce
- Advantages of E-commerce
- Disadvantages of E-commerce

CUSTOMER RELATIONSHIP MANAGEMENT (CRM)

- Introduction to Customer Relationship Management (CRM)
- Meaning and Definition
- Need and Objective of CRM
- Features of CRM
- Types of CRM
- Implementing CRM with Critical Success Factors (CSF)
- CRM Marketing

21.1 INTRODUCTION

Electronic commerce is also known as e-commerce or e-business. Trade and commerce between individuals is as old as the existence of mankind. The latest to join the list is Electronic Commerce, which is popularly known as e-commerce. Electronic commerce is defined as the actual buying and selling of goods or services electronically online. Products are displayed in an online store and potential customers can read information about the products, see them on the website and have the option to purchase them online. Any product can be sold online and all the principles of business apply to this also. The important requirements to conduct the e-commerce business are as follows:

(*a*) Website either owned or supplied by cart provider.

(*b*) A shopping cart programme to list out product or services and means to collect purchaser information.

(*c*) A method to get the funds into the bank account.

21.2 MEANING AND DEFINITION

E-commerce is a system that consists of buying and selling of products or services over electronic systems such as the Internet and other computer networks.

The amount of trade conducted electronically with widespread Internet usage. The use of commerce is conducted in this way, encouraging and drawing on innovations in electronic funds transfer, supply chain management, Internet marketing, online transaction processing (as shown in Fig. 21.1), Electronic Data Interchange (EDI), inventory management systems, and automated data collection systems. Modern electronic commerce typically uses the World Wide Web at least at some point in the transaction's lifecycle, although it can encompass a wider range of technologies such as e-mail as well.

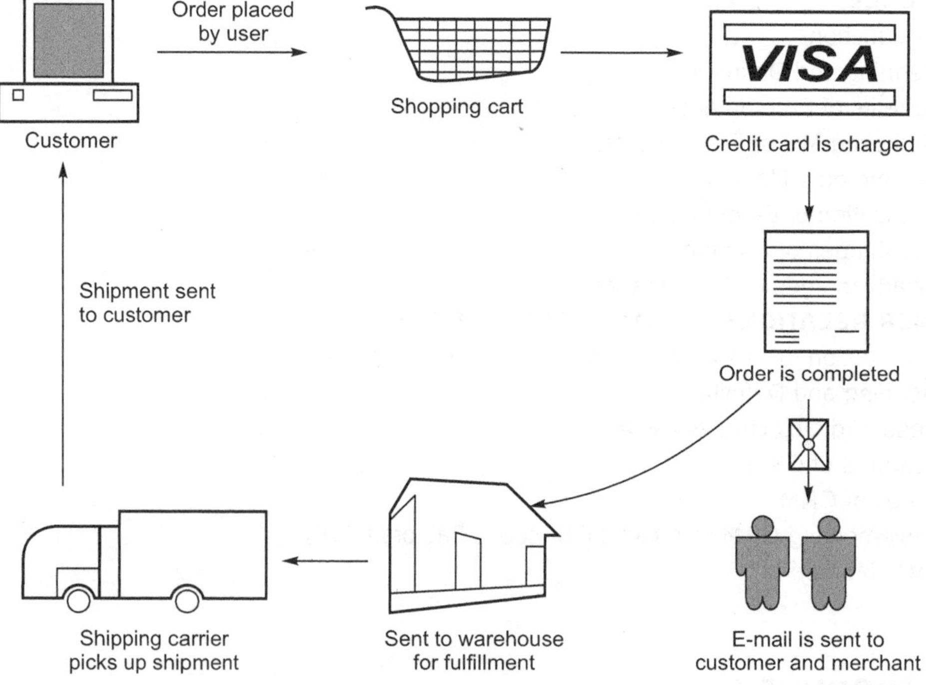

Fig. 21.1. E-commerce.

21.3 BENEFITS OF E-COMMERCE

The benefits of e-commerce are as follows:

1. **Save Time:** E-commerce allows people to carry out businesses without the barriers of time or distance. One can log on to the Internet at any point of time, be it day or night and purchase or sell anything one desires at a single click of the mouse.

2. **Low Cost:** The direct cost-of-sale for an order taken from a website is lower than through traditional means (retail, paper based), as there is no human interaction during the on-line electronic purchase order process. Also, electronic selling virtually eliminates processing errors, as well as being faster and more convenient for the visitor.
3. **Vast Market:** E-commerce is ideal for niche products. Customers for such products are usually few. But in the vast market place, *i.e.*, the Internet, even niche products could generate viable volumes.
4. **Cheapest:** Another important benefit of E-commerce is that it is the cheapest means of doing business.
5. **Competitions:** The day-to-day pressures of the marketplace have played their part in reducing the opportunities for companies to invest in improving their competitive position. A mature market, increased competitions have all reduced the amount of money available to invest. If the selling price cannot be increased and the manufactured cost cannot be decreased then the difference can be in the way the business is carried out. E-commerce has provided the solution by decimating the costs, which are incurred.
6. **Tangible Benefits:** From the buyer's perspective also e-commerce offers a lot of tangible advantages.
   (*a*) Reduction in buyer's sorting out time
   (*b*) Better buyer decisions
   (*c*) Less time is spent in resolving invoice and order discrepancies
   (*d*) Increased opportunities for buying alternative products.
7. **Strategic Benefits:** The strategic benefit of making a business 'e-commerce enabled', is that it helps reduce the delivery time, labour cost and the cost incurred in the following areas:
   (*a*) Document preparation
   (*b*) Error detection and correction
   (*c*) Reconciliation
   (*d*) Mail preparation
   (*e*) Telephone calling
   (*f*) Data entry
   (*g*) Overtime
   (*h*) Supervision expenses.
8. **Operational Benefits:** Operational benefits of e-commerce include reducing both time and personnel required to complete business processes, and reducing strain on other resources. It's because of all these advantages that one can harness the power of e-commerce and convert a business to e-business by using powerful turnkey e-commerce solutions made available by e-business solution providers.

21.4 MARKETING MIX OF E-COMMERCE

The marketing mix is co-ordinated so efficient product, price, promotion and place strategies are developed for products purchased over the counter. The internet is changing the way we sell our products and services. Consumers now use the internet to research and purchase products/services online. Organization now needs online strategies to attract and retain customers. The e-marketing mix considers the elements of presenting the marketing mix online as shown on the next page.

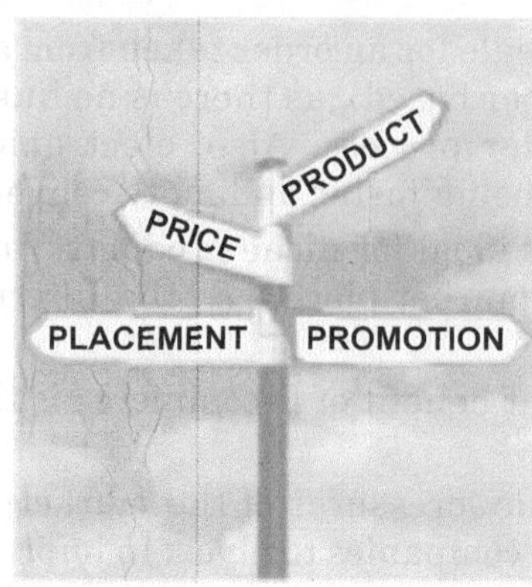

1. **E-Product:** When we walk into a shop and see a product we like, we can assess and touch it. Online, this immediate tangibility disappears. The buyer knows immediately about product features, the facts, not sales persons assumptions. www.comet.co.uk a UK electrical store offers clear information on products and their specification, consumers know what they get, if not there is a customer service number where they can find out more.
2. **E-Price:** Traditionally pricing was about finding about your costs, discovering how much consumers are willing to pay, taking into account competition pricing then setting your price. The internet has made pricing very competitive. Many costs, *i.e.*, store costs, staff costs have disappeared for complete online stores, placing price pressures on traditional retailers. The internet gives consumers the power to shop around for the best deal at a click of a button. Website such as www.kelkoo.com compares products from different websites informing consumers of where the best deal is. Such easy access to information helps to maintain prices within the online world.
3. **E-Place:** Location is important within our place strategy. Online location can refer to where links are placed on other websites. Placing a link on www.google.com home page would generate high consumer traffic for you. Knowing your customer and knowing where they visit should help you understand where to place your online links and advertisements.
4. **E-Promotion:** Promoting products and services online is concerned with a number of issues. Having a recognizable domain name is the first stage towards e-promotion. Most organizations today have some form of webpage used in most if not all advertisements. Placing banner advertisements on other webpages is a common form of e-promotion.

Newsworthy stories based on product or service launches can be placed on the companies' webpage, or web page related articles sent to review sites for consumers to read.

Direct e-mail is a popular and common form of e-promotions, although slowly becoming the most hated by many consumers. Organizations can send e-leaflets to hundreds and thousands of respondents, hoping a small percentage will reply. Direct e-mailing is also known as SPAM which stands for Sending Persistent Annoying e-Mail. (SPAM).

21.5 E-COMMERCE MODELS

The first step in the development of an e-commerce website is to identify the e-commerce model. Depending on the firm involved in the transaction, e-commerce can be classified into four models. These are:

1. **Business-to-Business Model (B2B):** B2B e-commerce is between different business entities. It reduces the number of suppliers and facilitates business partnership by

reducing purchase orders, processing costs and inventory cycle timings. B2B directly supports commerce transactions involving products, services, or information between two businesses or parties. Typical B2B direct transactions occur between buyers, suppliers, manufacturers, resellers, distributors, and trading partners. The following Fig.21.2 shows the typical B2B model.

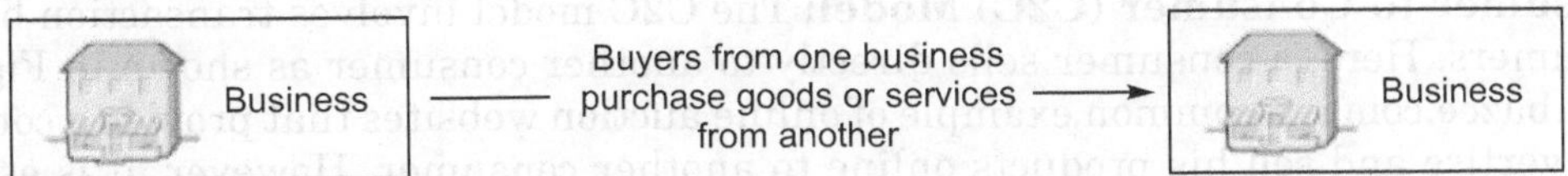

Fig. 21.2. Business-to-Business model (B2B).

B2B business purchases goods or services directly from another business. The selling business can be a wholesaler, a distributor, a manufacturer, or a retailer who sells to buyers from other businesses. Organizations that are not traditionally considered businesses, such as government, may sometimes implement sites based on the B2B direct business model. This occurs in such cases where government provides goods and services directly to businesses.

As you know, www.amazon.com is an online bookstore that sells books from various publishers. In this case, the publishers have the option of either developing their own site or displaying their books on the Amazon site (www.amazon.com), or both. The publishers mainly choose to display their books on www.amazon.com as it gives them a larger audience. Now, to do this, the publishers need to transact with Amazon, involving business houses on both the ends, is the B2B model.

2. **Business-to-Consumer (B2C) Model:** The B2C model involves transactions between business organizations and consumers. It applies to any business organization that sells its products or services to consumers over the Internet as shown in Fig. 21.3. These sites display product information in an online catalogue and store it in a database. The B2C model also includes services like online banking, travel services, and health information.

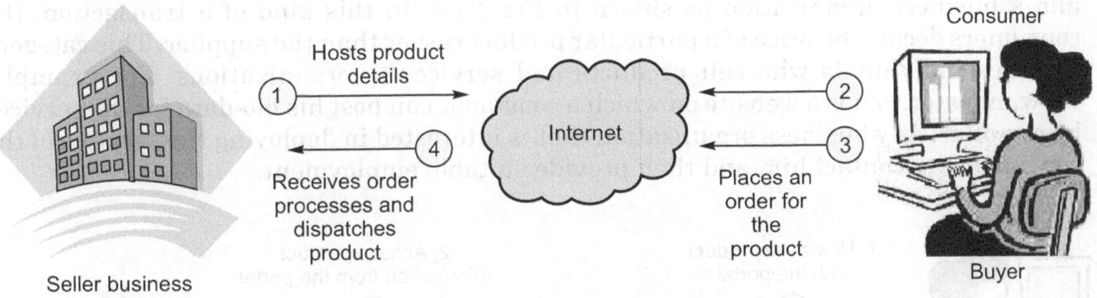

Fig. 21.3. Business-to-Consumer (B2C) model.

Suppose, a transaction is conducted between a business organization and a consumer. A business house, a department store, displays and sells a range of products on their website, www.lmn.com. The detailed information of all their products is contained in the huge catalogues maintained by that department store. Now, a consumer wants to buy a gift for his sister. He therefore, logs on to the website of the department store and selects a gift from the catalogue. He also gets the detailed information about the gift such as, the price, availability, discounts, and so on from their catalogue. Finally, when he decides to purchase a gift, he places an order for the gift on their website. To place an order, he needs to specify his personal and credit card information on www.lmn.com. This information is then validated by a department store and stored in their database. On verification of the information the order is processed. Therefore, as you can see, the B2C model involves transactions between consumers or more business organizations.

3. **Consumer-to-Consumer (C2C) Model:** The C2C model involves transaction between consumers. Here, a consumer sells directly to another consumer as shown in Fig. 21.4. www.bazee.com is a common example of online auction websites that provide a consumer to advertise and sell his products online to another consumer. However, it is essential that both seller and buyer must register with the auction site. While the seller needs to pay a fixed fee to the online auction house to sell his products, the buyer can bid without paying any fee. The site brings buyer and seller together to conduct deals.

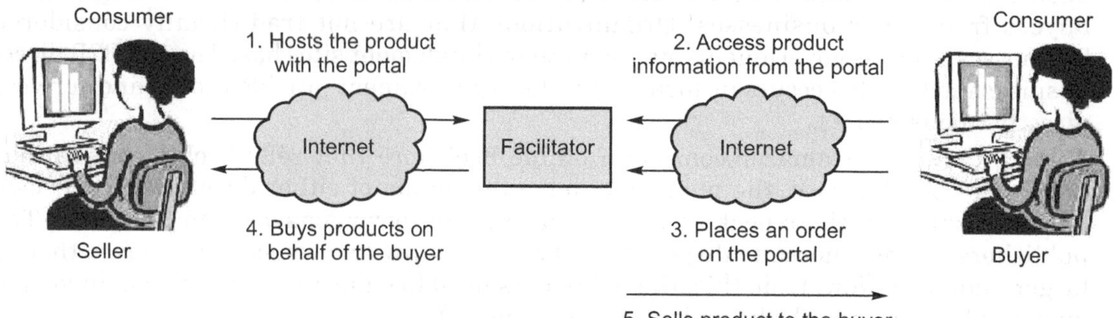

Fig. 21.4. Consumer-to-Consumer (C2C) model.

4. **Consumer-to-Business (C2B) Model:** The C2B model is the most recent e-commerce business model. In this model, individual customers offer to sell products and services to companies who are prepared to purchase them. This business model is the opposite of the traditional B2C model and involves a transaction that is conducted between a consumer and a business organization as shown in Fig. 21.5. In this kind of a transaction, the consumers decide the price of a particular product rather than the supplier. This category includes individuals who sell products and services to organizations. For example, www.monster.com is a website on which a consumer can post his bio-data for the services he can offer. Any business organization that is interested in deploying the services of the consumer can contact him and then provide suitable employment.

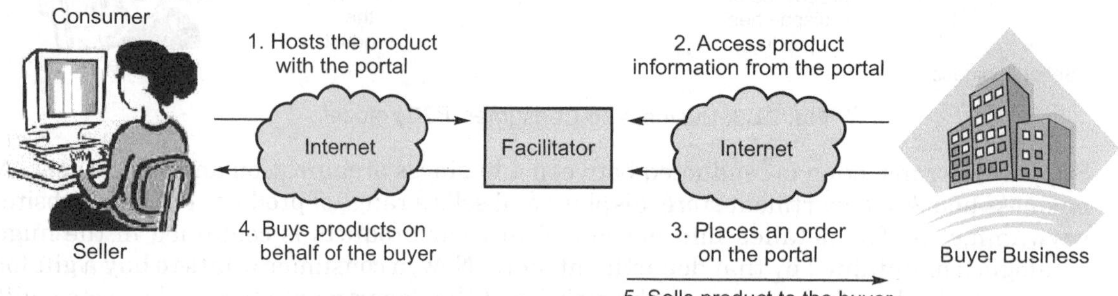

Fig. 21.5. Consumer-to-Business (C2B) model.

21.6 APPLICATION OF E-COMMERCE

Today e-commerce is being used in different fields, which are as under:

1. **Transaction Processing System:** All data, which comes under any sort of transaction, make use of e-commerce like—airline reservation, stock trading, insurance policy, etc.
2. **Education and Medical:** Today e-commerce is playing a vital role in improving the technologies used in education and medical department. There are many different online facilities, which allow the users to collect information regarding this field.
3. **Information Services:** There are many different information services available today like—American online, which helps in gathering latest information.
4. **Value Aided Network:** With this facility the business information is being converted from one network to other network.
5. **Electronic Payment:** Today anyone having the ATM, internet banking or credit cards can be directly involved in the transaction of money. It is one of the latest technologies, which allows the users to freely perform the marketing jobs.

21.7 ADVANTAGES OF E-COMMERCE

The advantages of e-commerce are as following:

1. It is very easy to reach the customers throughout the world at any time via internet or via an Electronic Data Interchange (EDI) system.
2. Throughout the year, on all the days this system can be operated.
3. The cost of setting up of an e-commerce website is very low when compared with retail outlet.
4. There is more flexibility in a website to add and remove a product than in catalogues or brochures.
5. It potentially gives exposure to previously untapped market segments.
6. It offers wide choice and wastage of time can be avoided.

21.8 DISADVANTAGES OF E-COMMERCE

The disadvantages of e-commerce are as following:

1. There is no possibility of touching and feeling merchandise.
2. With growing importance of e-commerce and computer communication technologies the social contacts of the consumers are going to be reduced.
3. Since online stores do not exist for long periods, many companies do not know exactly the set-up of store.
4. There is a possibility for intercepting transactions and cause problems to consumers and companies who operate on the internet.

21.9 INTRODUCTION TO CUSTOMER RELATIONSHIP MANAGEMENT (CRM)

One of the most dynamic Information Technology (IT) topics of the new millennium is the area of Customer Relationship Management (CRM). At the core "CRM is an integration of technologies and business processes used to satisfy the needs of a customer during any given interaction. More specifically, CRM is the process of acquiring, satisfying, retaining and growing profitable customers. It requires a clear focus on the service attributes that represent value to the customer and create loyalty. This encompasses developing long-term relationships with customers, allocating marketing dollars based on the customer's value and deriving as much as revenue from these customers over a life time. It is important to note that the term "customer" may have very broad definition that includes vendors, channel partners or virtually any group or individual that requires information from the organization.

21.10 MEANING AND DEFINITION

In IT terms, "CRM means an enterprise-wide integration of technologies working together such as data warehouse, website, Intranet/extranet, phone support system, marketing, production, etc. CRM has many similarities with Enterprise Resource Planning (ERP), where ERP can be considered back-office integration and CRM as front-office integration. A notable difference between ERP and CRM is that, ERP can be implemented without CRM. However, CRM usually requires access to the back-office data that often happen through ERP-type integration.

"CRM is a business strategy with outcomes that optimize profitability, revenue and customer satisfaction by organizing around customer segmentation, fostering customer satisfying behaviours and implementing customer centric processes. CRM technologies should enable greater customer insight, increases customer access, more effective interactions and integration throughout all customer channels and back office enterprise functions". **According to Gartner's**

CRM principally revolves around marketing and begins with a deep analysis of consumer behaviour. It uses IT to gather data, which can be used to develop information required to create a more personal interaction with the customer. In long-term, it produces a method of continous analysis and refinement in order to enhance Customers Lifetime Value (CLV) with a firm. Well et al (1999) noted, "both (marketing & IT) need to work together with a high level of co-ordination to produce a seamless process of interaction". However, in order to work effectively with marketing, IT managers need an understanding of the fundamental marketing motivation driving the CRM trend.

21.11 NEED AND OBJECTIVE OF CRM

CRM is not just a technology, but rather a comprehensive approach to an organization's philosophy in dealing with its customers. This includes policies and processes, front-of-house customer service, employee training, marketing, systems and information management. Hence, it is important that any CRM implementation considerations stretch beyond technology, towards the broader organizational requirements. The objectives of a CRM strategy must consider a companies specific situation and its customer needs and expectations.

The experience from many companies is that a very clear CRM requirement with regard to reports, *e.g.*, output and input requirements, is of vital importance before starting any implementation. With a proper demand specification a lot of time and costs can be saved based on right expectations versus systems capability. A well operative CRM system can be an extremely powerful tool for management and customer strategies.

The data gathered as a part of CRM must consider customer privacy and data security. Customers want the assurance that their data is not shared with third parties without their consent and not accessed illegally by third parties. Customers also want their data used by companies to provide a benefit to them.

21.12 FEATURES OF CRM

CRM is made up of many features, which include collaborative CRM, analytical CRM and operational CRM.

1. **Collaborative CRM:** It is to directly communicate with customers without inclusion of any sales or service representatives. Direct interaction is carried out with collaborative CRM that includes feedback from the customers and reporting of issues if any. This interaction can be carried out through a variety of channels like e-mail, phone, SMS, etc. The main objective behind going in for collaborative CRM can be reducing the company costs and improving the services provided.
   - It is the communication centre, coordination network that provides neural paths to customer and its suppliers.
   - It could mean a Partner Relationship Management (PRM) application or a customer interaction centre.
   - It could mean communication channels such as web or e-mail, voice applications and even channel strategies.
   - In other words, it is any CRM function that provides a point of interaction between customer and channel itself.
2. **Analytical CRM:** It is to investigate customer data for a vast range of reasons and functions. Analytical CRM finds multiple uses such as taking management decisions, predicting future trends, analyzing customer behaviour, planning and executing marketing campaigns and much more. It analyzes customer data for the following purposes:
   - Design and execution of targeted marketing campaigns to optimize marketing effectiveness.
   - Design and execution of specific customer campaigns.
   - Analysis of customer behaviour to aid product and service decision-making such as pricing, etc.
   - Aid in taking management decisions such as financial forecasting.
   - Provide a tool in predicting the probability of customer defection.
3. **Operational CRM:** It provides support to "Front Office" business processes, including sales, marketing and service. Typical business functions involving customer service, order management, invoice or billing or sales and marketing automation and management are the parts of operational CRM.

Each interaction with a customer is generally added to a customer's contact history, and staff can retrieve information on customers from the database whenever necessary. One of the main benefits of this contact history is that customers can interact with different people or different contact channels in a company over time without having to describe the history of their interaction each time.

21.13 TYPES OF CRM

CRM allows a company to address all of the types of customers it serves at different points in their life cycle and to choose the marketing programme that best fits a customer's attitude towards the company and willingness to purchase its products and services. There are four types of CRM:

1. **Win-Back or Save:** This is the process of convincing a customer to stay with the organization at the point they are discontinuing service or convincing them to rejoin once they have left.

Of the four categories of campaigns, win-back is the most sensitive. Research indicates that win-back campaign is four times more likely to succeed if contact is made within the first week following a defection than if it is made in the fourth week. Selectivity is the other essential characterstice of a successful win-back campaign.

2. **Prospecting:** Prospecting is the effort to win new, first time customers. Apart from the offer itself; the three most critical elements of a prospecting campaign are segmentation, selectivity and source. It is essential to develop an effective needs-based segmentation model that allows the organization to effectively target the offer. Without this focused approach, the organization either fails to achieve an adequate acceptance or rate an the offer or spends too much on promotions, advertising and concessionary pricing. It is advisable to achieve a 95% confidence rate before embarking on a prospecting effort.

   Selectivity is as important to prospecting as it is to win-back. Needs-based segmentation defines what the customer wants from the organization and the profit-based segmentation, defines how valuable the customer is and helps the organization to decide how much it is willing to spend to get that customer. Pre-scoring a customer credit rating is one of the techniques that an organization can use to determine the latter.

3. **Loyalty:** Loyalty is the category in which it is most difficult to gain accurate measures. The organization is trying to prevent customers from leaving and uses three essential elements as shown in Fig. 21.6.
   - Value-based segmentation
   - Need-based segmentation
   - Predictive churn models.

   Value-based segmentation: It allows the organization to determine how much it is willing to invest in retaining a customer's loyalty.

   Needs-based segmentation: Once the customer has passed the value-based segmentation, the organization can use needs-based segmentation to offer a customized loyalty programme.

   Predictive churn models: Using the vast amount of demographic data and usage rate available for the existing base of customers which helps in forecasting customer attrition. Through the use of advanced data-mining tools, organization can develop models that identify vulnerable and potential customers which can be targetted for the loyalty campaign or offered alternative products. "A small percentage of customers account for a large percentage of profits".

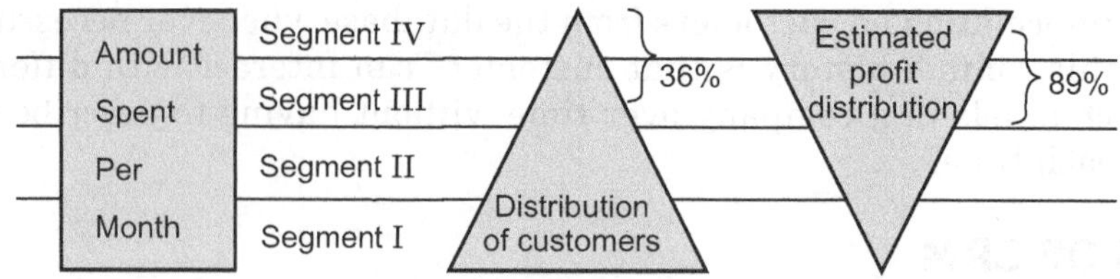

Fig. 21.6. Distribution of customer and estimated profit distribution.

4. **Cross-Sell/Up-Sell:** The purpose is to identify complementary offering that a customer would like. For example: a basic long distance customer could be a candidate to buy Internet access.

   Customer's need-based segment, usage pattern and reaction to previous contacts/ interactions determine the nature of the offer. Once the composition of the offer is determined and the contact medium is agreed to, it presents that offer to the customer.

Up-selling is similar, but instead of offering a complementary product, the organization offers an enhanced one.

For example: Replacing an analog data line with ISDN.

Cross-sell/ Up-sell campaigns are important because the customers targeted already have a relationship with the organization. They are less likely to see the offer as a commodity and are thus more willing to pay a premium for it. In financial terms, when a customer accepts a cross-sell or up-sell offer, that customer begins to become much more profitable.

21.14 IMPLEMENTING CRM WITH CRITICAL SUCCESS FACTORS (CSF)

Critical Success Factors (CSFs) have been used significantly to present or identify a few key factors that organizations should focus on to be successful. As a definition, critical success factors refer to "the limited number of areas in which satisfactory results will ensure successful competitive performance for the individual, department, reorganization" as shown in Fig. 21.7. Identifying CSFs is important as it allows firms to focus their efforts on building their capabilities to meet the CSFs, or even allow firms to decide if they have the capability to build the requirements necessary to meet Critical Success Factors (CSFs).

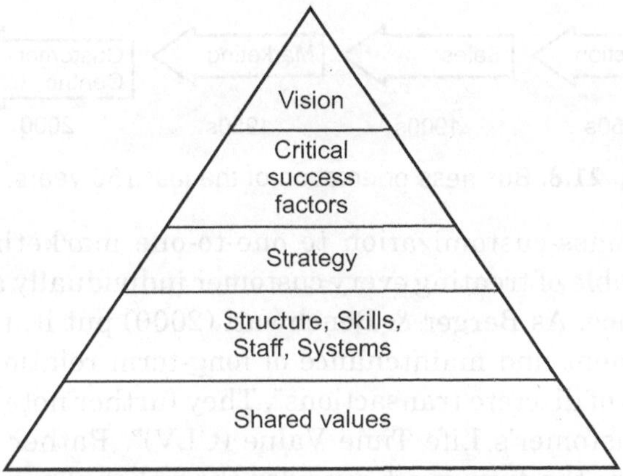

Fig. 21.7. Critical Success Factors (CSF).

Critical success factors are the areas of your business or project that are absolutely essential to its success. By identifying and communicating these CSFs, you can help ensure your business or project is well-focused and avoids wasting effort and resources on less important areas. By making CSFs explicit, and communicating them with everyone involved, you can help keep the business and project on track towards common aims and goals. "Identifying your CSFs is a very iterative process. Your mission, strategic goals and CSFs are intrinsically linked and each will be refined as you develop them. Here are the summary steps that, used iteratively, will help you identify the CSFs for your business or project:

Step One: Establish your businesses or project's mission and strategic goals.

Step Two: For each strategic goal, ask yourself "what area of business or project activity is essential to achieve this goal?" The answers to the question are your candidate CSFs.

Step Three: Evaluate the list of candidate CSFs to find the absolute essential elements for achieving success—these are your Critical Success Factors. As you identify and evaluate candidate's CSFs, you may uncover some new strategic objectives or more detailed objectives.

So you may need to define your mission, objectives and CSFs iteratively.

Step Four: Identify how you will monitor and measure each of the CSFs.

Step Five: Communicate your CSFs along with the other important elements of your business or project's strategy.

21.15 CRM MARKETING

During the 1850s, businesses could sell almost anything they made. Consequently it was a seller's market and businesses focused on product. In the early 1900s, competition was creeping up and businesses realized customers wielded more power and firms had to find reasons for people to buy their products. This brought about a sales orientation. But some forty years ago (during 1950s) marketers predicted that product focus would be downfall of many of the large organizations as shown in Fig. 21.8. They believed that nothing less than totally customer-oriented business view could ensure organizational survival. Organizations that defined themselves otherwise—by what they did, what they produced, or what technologies they used—were suffering from "Marketing Myopia" or "Marketing Shortsightedness", which ushered in marketing orientation. The marketing orientation focused on addressing the needs and wants of market segments. We are now at the beginning stages of a new "Customer-Centric Orientation" which is the subset of Marketing Orientation.

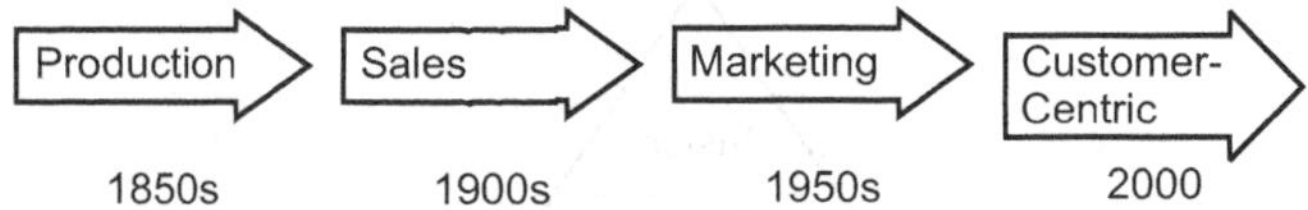

Fig. 21.8. Business orientation of the last 150 years.

There is a shift from mass-customization to one-to-one marketing or customization of products, which is also capable of treating every customer individually and uniquely depending on the customer's preference. As Berger & Benchwati (2000) put it, the "core of relationship marketing is the development and maintenance of long-term relationships with customers, rather than simply a series of discrete transactions". They further note that a guiding principle is the management of "Customer's Life Time Value (CLV)". Rather than calculating profit from a discrete transaction, the firm must consider the value of a customer over his or her entire relationship with the firm as shown in Fig. 21.9.

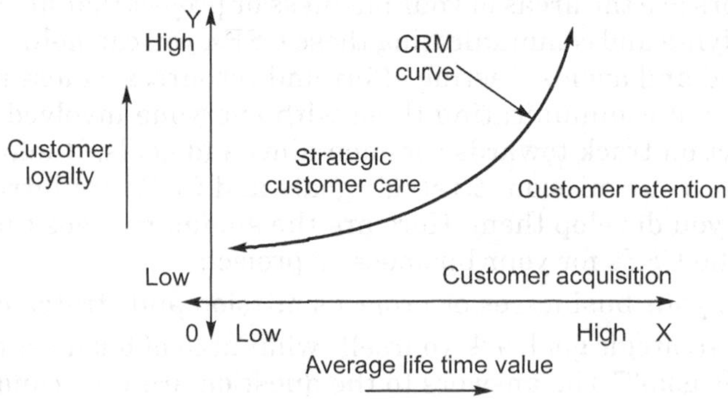

Fig. 21.9. Customer relationship with the firm.

(Here value refers to tangible parameters, intangible parameters and offer of the organization). Marketing is the area where customer insight, or the process of identifying the most valuable customer, is primary. Simply achieving a single view of the customer across diverse lines of business and departmentally focused information systems is the tremendous value and the added ability to gather and correlate this information in real time makes the information that much more valuable in making better business decisions as shown in Fig. 21.10. This capability is a core underpinning of successful customer relationship management, and is made possible by the CRM interaction capabilities. Once in possession of detailed customer information, it becomes possible to create and execute high-personalized targeted marketing programmes for high value customers, which maximize the revenue opportunities, customer satisfaction and also efficiency and effectiveness of marketing efforts.

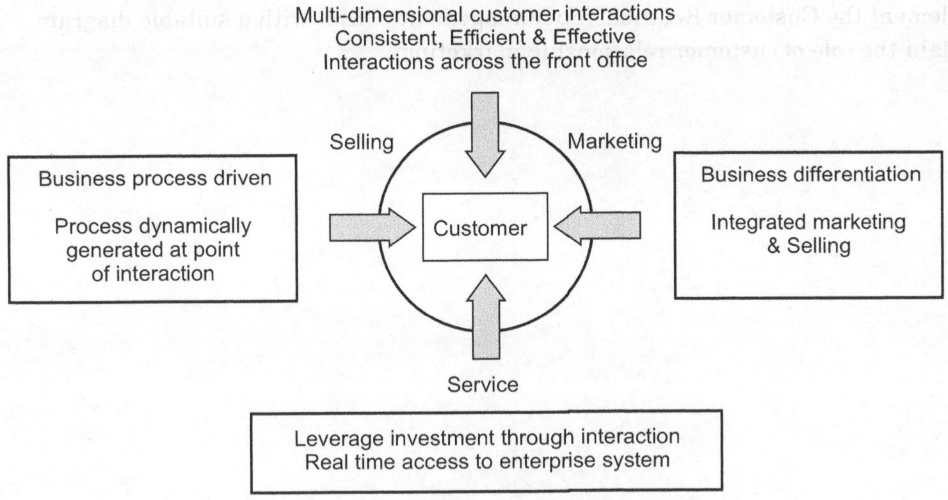

Fig. 21.10. Valuable information for business decisions.

Indeed, this revolution in Customer Relationship Management (CRM) has been referred to as the new "mantra" of marketing. Companies such as Siebel, Oracle, Broadvision, Kana, net perceptions and others have developed CRM products that do everything from tracking customer behaviour on the web to predicting their future moves to sending direct e-mail communications.

Thus, the market expects organizations to be able to manage down costs. What investors are skeptical about is the organization ability to attract and retain profitable customers. Customer Relationship Management allows them to do just that.

The biggest threat to CRM is management focuses on short-run profits rather than long-term vision. CRM is an expensive, time consuming and complex proposition. Even in the best case, this tool is an opportunity to rise above minor advantages and develop an actual relationship with the customers. Companies that are the most successful at delivering what each customer wants are the most likely to be the leaders of the future.

REVIEW QUESTIONS

1. What do you mean by e-commerce? Explain the benefits of e-commerce.
2. Explain the different types of e-commerce.
3. Describe the different applications of e-commerce.
4. Explain the marketing mix of e-commerce.
5. Explain the types of e-commerce.
6. Explain the advantages and disadvantages of e-commerce.
7. What is the meaning and definition of CRM? Explain the features of CRM.
8. Explain the need and objective of CRM.
9. Explain the different kinds of Customer Relationship Management (CRM).
10. Implement the Customer Relationship Management (CRM) with a suitable diagram.
11. Explain the role of customer relationship marketing.

CHAPTER 22

New Issues in Marketing: Globalization and Green Marketing

POINTS TO REMEMBER

At the end of this chapter, we will be able to understand:

Globalization:

- Meaning of Globalization
- Characteristics of Globalization
- Factors affecting Globalization
- Globalization of Business
- Impact of Globalization
- Impact of Globalization on India

Green Marketing:

- Meaning of Green Marketing
- Evolution and Need of Green Marketing
- Need of Green Marketing
- Green Products and their Characteristics
- Challenges in Green Marketing
- Marketing Mix of Green Marketing
- Importance of Green Marketing

Consumerism:

- Consumerism
- Consumer Movement in India
- Consumer Protection Act, 1986
- Neuro Marketing

22.1 MEANING OF GLOBALIZATION

The name for the process of increasing the connectivity and interdependence of the world's markets and businesses. This process has speeded up dramatically in the last two decades as technological advances make it easier for people to travel, communicate, and do business internationally. Two major recent driving forces are advances in telecommunications infrastructure and the rise of the internet. In general, as economies become more connected to other economies, they have increased opportunity but also increased competition.

Globalization refers to the worldwide phenomenon of technological, economic, political and cultural exchanges, brought about by modern communication, transportation and legal infrastructure as well as the political choice to consciously open cross-border links in international trade and finance.

"The growing economic interdependence of countries worldwide through increasing volume and variety of cross-border transactions in goods and services, freer international capital flows, and more rapid and widespread diffusion of technology".

The International Monetary Fund (IMF)

"The geographic dispersion of industrial and service activities, for example research and development, sourcing of inputs, production and distribution, and the cross-border networking of companies, for example through joint ventures and the sharing of assets".

Organization for Economic Co-operation and Development

22.2 CHARACTERISTICS OF GLOBALIZATION

Globalization is not a new phenomenon but continuation of developments that have been going on for some considerable time. The recent trend of liberalization of economic activities is qualitatively different, however, as the world has definitely ceased to be a collection of relatively autonomous economic agents that are only marginally connected and are more or less immune to events in their neighbourhoods.

1. **Interconnected World:** It is connected on account of modes of simultaneous communication to any part of the world. It is also a connected world on account of the problems that confront humanity as a whole. Problems such as global climatic changes, the depletion of the ozone layer, drugs, terrorism, pollution of the oceans, etc., are beyond the scope of any particular nation-state.
2. **Rapid and Significant Repercussion:** Distant actions in one comer of the globe have rapid and significant repercussions in other parts. For instance, the East Asian Crisis of 1997-1998 on the New York Stock Market or NASDAQ on Bombay Stock Market, etc.
3. **Impact on Every Facet of Life:** Globalization encapsulates the entire range of social relations. It has its impact on every facet of life. However, the momentum of these relations may not move at a uniform pace. It may result in a great deal of under globalization. Power relations come to be articulated increasingly at the global level. New organizations come to be established for the purpose.
4. **Technological Change and Globalization of Production:** Technological changes we are witnessing today affect the parameters of technology and product flows across countries. Improvements in transportation networks and technology are reducing the costs of transportation while improvements in information technology have made an increasing volume of information available at close to zero costs. Lower transportation

and communication costs have important implications for the nature of production activities, the flow of knowledge it relies on and the marketing of products that it makes. Reduction of transportation and telecommunication cost, for example, raise the intensity of competition and stimulate identification of most economic sites for both manufacturing of products and components as well as for their marketing.

5. **Expansion of Trade in Goods and Services:** The intensified globalization of production is closely interlinked with the second dimension of globalization, i.e., with rapid expansion of international trade of goods and services. International trade data clearly show the rise in global production networks. About one-third of world trade in the mid-1990s took place within these networks.
6. **Widening and Deepening of International Capital Flows:** Financial flows across national borders have risen far more quickly than trade in recent years and is therefore another distinctive feature of globalization. Since 1990, there has been a huge upsurge in international capital flows and a growing integration of international capital markets.

22.3 FACTORS AFFECTING GLOBALIZATION

The following main factors have fuelled the pace of globalization:

1. **Technological Change, Especially in Communications Technology:** For example, UK businesses and data by satellite to India (taking advantage of the difference in time zones) where skilled but cheaper data handlers input the data and return it by satellite for the start of the UK working day.
2. **Transport is Much Cheaper and Faster:** Transport is not just aircraft, but also ships. The development of containerization in the 1950s was a major breakthrough in goods handling, and there have been continuing improvements to shipping technology since then.
3. **Deregulation:** From the 1980s onwards many rules and regulations in business were removed, especially rules regarding foreign ownership. Privatization also took place, and large areas of business were now open to purchase and/or take-over. This allowed businesses in one country to buy those in another. For example, many UK utilities government businesses, are owned by French and US businesses.
4. **Removal of Capital Exchange Controls:** The movement of money from one country to another was also controlled, and these controls were lifted over the same period. This allowed businesses to move money from one country to another in search for better business returns; if investment in one's own country looked unattractive, a business could buy businesses in another country.
5. **Free Trade:** Many barriers to trade have been removed. Some of this has been done by regional groupings of countries such as the EU. Most of it has been done by the WTO. This makes trade cheaper and therefore more attractive to business.
6. **Consumer Tastes have Changed:** Consumers are more willing to try foreign products. The arrival of global satellite television, for example, has exposed consumers to global advertising. Consumers are more aware of what is available in other countries, and are keen to give it a try.

22.4 GLOBALIZATION OF BUSINESS

Globalization is best thought of as a process that results in some significant changes for markets and businesses to address, for example:

- An expansion of trade in goods and services between countries (an opportunity for many businesses; a threat for others).

- An increase in transfers of financial capital across national boundaries including Foreign Direct Investment (FDI) by multi-national companies and the investments by sovereign wealth funds (*e.g.*, Middle Eastern governments buying assets in the UK).
- The internationalization of products and services and the development of global brands such as Starbucks, Nike, Sony, Honda and Google shifts in production and consumption *e.g.*, the expansion of outsourcing and off shoring of production and support services, which has traditionally benefitted countries with lower labour costs and skilled labour markets such as India, at the expense of jobs in developed economies like the UK.
- Increased levels of labour migration—which has the effect of lowering wage costs in many industries, but for others it is a problem (*e.g.*, a loss of skilled workers leaving an economy).
- The emergence of countries playing a bigger role in the global trading system including China, Brazil, India and Russia.

22.5 IMPACT OF GLOBALIZATION

The impact of globalization has been fair enough on the developing economies to a certain extent. It brought along with it varied opportunities for the developing countries. It boosted up for better access to the developed markets. The technology transfer promised better productivity and thus improved standard of living. The gains from globalization can be cited in the context of economic globalization:

A. Positive Impact

(*a*) A better economy—it introduces rapid development of the capital market.

(*b*) Introducing new technologies—the new technologies and progress in telecommunication, introduction of satellites, mobiles, etc., are all results of globalization.

(*c*) The new scientific research patterns are all results of globalization.

(*d*) Living standards are raised.

(*e*) Globalization introduces better trade. This is because more people are employed. This increases productivity and employment opportunity.

(*f*) Apart from economical aspect, globalization has also brought an impact on political and cultural domain.

(*g*) Culturally speaking, globalization has brought in different ideologies, and thought process amongst people.

(*h*) Politically speaking, onset of western democratic system has an impact on politics.

B. Negative Impact

(*a*) Along with positive impact, there is negative too. Globalization brings fear as well. Because of too much flow of capital amongst countries, it introduces unfair and immoral distribution of income.

(*b*) Another fear is loosing national integrity. Because of too much exchange of trade, money etc., independent domestic policies are lost.

(*c*) Mental pressure on companies that causes many people to loose their jobs.

22.6 IMPACT OF GLOBALIZATION ON INDIA

India opened up the economy in the early 90s following a major crisis that led by a foreign exchange crunch that dragged the economy close to defaulting on loans. The response was a slew of domestic and external sector policy measures partly prompted by the immediate needs and partly by the demand of the multilateral organizations. The new policy regime radically pushed forward in favour of a more open and market-oriented economy.

Major measures initiated as a part of liberalization and globalization strategy in the early 90s included scrapping of the industrial licensing regime, reduction in the number of areas reserved for the public sector, amendment of the monopolies and the restrictive trade practices act, start of the privatization programme, reduction in tariff rates and change over to market determined exchange rates.

Over the years there has been a steady liberalization of the current account transactions, more and more sectors opened up for foreign direct investments and portfolio investments facilitating entry of foreign investors in telecom, roads, ports, airports, insurance and other major sectors.

The merits of globalization are as follows:

(*a*) There is an international market for companies and for consumers there is a wider range of products to choose from.

(*b*) Increase in flow of investments from developed countries to developing countries, which can be used for economic reconstruction.

(*c*) Greater and faster flow of information between countries and greater cultural interaction has helped to overcome cultural barriers.

(*d*) Technological development has resulted in reverse brain drain in developing countries.

The demerits of globalization are as follows:

(*a*) The outsourcing of jobs to developing countries has resulted in loss of jobs in developed countries.

(*b*) There is a greater threat of spread of communicable diseases.

(*c*) There is an underlying threat of multinational corporations with immense power ruling the globe.

(*d*) For smaller developing nations at the receiving end, it could indirectly lead to a subtle form of colonization.

22.7 MEANING OF GREEN MARKETING

Green marketing is a prevailing marketing mode in the 21st century. Because of additional investment by carrying out green marketing and protracted nature and potentiality of green marketing performance, many enterprises refuse to put it into effect. So, evaluation of green marketing performance is a basic work.

Green marketing refers to the marketing of products and services considered environmental-friendly that make their marketers "environmentally responsible". The advent of green marketing was due to consumer demands. Green marketing can be defined as, "All activities designed to generate and facilitate any exchange intended to satisfy human needs or wants such that satisfying of these needs and wants occur with minimal detrimental input on the national environment".

> *"Green marketing is the marketing of products that are presumed to be environmentally safe".*
>
> **American Marketing Association**

Business Dictionary defines green marketing as promotional activities aimed at taking advantage of changing consumer attitude towards a brand. These changes are increasingly being influenced by a firm's policies and practices that affect the quality of the environment and reflect the level of its concern for the community. It can also be seen as the promotion of environmentally safe or beneficial products.

22.8 EVOLUTION AND NEED OF GREEN MARKETING

The American Marketing Association (AMA) held the first workshop on ecological marketing in 1975. In 1980 green marketing came into existence for the first time. It incorporates several activities such as product modification, changes to production processes, and packaging, advertising strategies and also increases awareness on compliance marketing amongst industries. The green marketing has evolved over a period of time. The evolution of green marketing has three phases.

(*a*) First phase was termed as "Ecological" green marketing, and during this period all marketing activities were concerned to help environment problems and provide remedies for environmental problems.

(*b*) Second phase was "Environmental" green marketing and the focus shifted on clean technology that involved designing of innovative new products, which take care of pollution and waste issues.

(*c*) Third phase was "Sustainable" green marketing. It came into prominence in the late 1990s and early 2000.

22.9 NEED OF GREEN MARKETING

1. **Anthropological View:** Issues like global warming and depletion of ozone umbrella are the main for the healthy survival. Every person, rich or poor, would be interested in quality life full of health and vigour and so would the corporate class.
2. **Educating your Customers:** It is not just a matter of letting people know you are doing whatever you are doing to protect the environment, but also a matter of letting them know why it matters. Otherwise, for a significant portion of your target market, it's a case of "So what?" and your green marketing campaign goes nowhere.
3. **Genuine and Transparent:** You are actually doing what you claim to be doing in your green marketing campaign and the rest of your business policies are consistent with whatever you are doing that's environmental-friendly. Both these conditions have to be met for your business to establish the kind of environmental credentials that will allow a green marketing campaign to succeed.
4. **Re-assure the Buyer:** Consumers must be made to believe that the product performs the job it's supposed to do-they would not forego product quality in the name of environment.
5. **Consider Pricing:** If you are charging a premium for your product and many environmentally preferable products cost more due to economies of scale and use of higher-quality ingredients, make sure those consumers can afford the premium and feel it's worth it.
6. **Giving your Customers an Opportunity to Participate:** Means personalizing the benefits of your environmental-friendly actions, normally through letting the customer take part in positive environmental action.

22.10 GREEN PRODUCTS AND THEIR CHARACTERISTICS

The products which are manufactured through green technology and that cause no environmental hazards are called green products. Promotion of green technology and green products is necessary for conservation of natural resources and sustainable development. We can define green products by following measures:

(*a*) Products those are originally grown,
(*b*) Products those are recyclable, reusable and bio-degradable,
(*c*) Products with natural ingredients,
(*d*) Products containing recycled contents, non-toxic chemicals,
(*e*) Products containing underapproved chemical,
(*f*) Products that do not harm or pollute the environment,
(*g*) Products that will not be tested on animals,
(*h*) Products that have eco-friendly packaging, *i.e.*, reusable, refillable containers, etc.

22.11 CHALLENGES IN GREEN MARKETING

The firms using green marketing must ensure that their activities are not misleading to consumers or industry, and do not breach any of the regulations or laws dealing with environmental marketing. The green marketing has following challenges:

1. **Need for Standardization:** It is found that only 5% of the marketing messages from "green" campaigns are entirely true and there is a lack of standardization to authenticate these claims. There is no standardization currently in place to certify a product as organic. Unless some regulatory bodies are involved in providing the certifications there will not be any verifiable means. A standard quality control board needs to be in place for such labelling and licensing.
2. **New Concept:** Indian literate and urban consumer is getting more aware of the merits of green products. But it is still a new concept for the masses. The consumer needs to be educated and made aware of the environmental threats. The new green movements need to reach the masses and that will take a lot of time and effort. By India's ayurvedic heritage, Indian consumers do appreciate the importance of using natural and herbal beauty products. Indian consumer is exposed to healthy living lifestyles such as yoga, meditation and natural food consumption. In those aspects the consumer is already aware and will be inclined to accept the green products.
3. **Patience and Perseverance:** The investors and corporates need to view the environment as a major long-term investment opportunity, the marketers need to look at the long-term benefits from this new green movement. It will require a lot of patience and no immediate results. Since, it is a new concept and idea, it will have its own acceptance period.
4. **Avoiding Green Myopia:** The first rule of green marketing is focusing on customer benefits, *i.e.*, the primary reason why consumers buy certain products in the first place. Do this right, and motivate consumers to switch brands or even pay a premium for the greener alternative. It is not going to help if a product is developed which is absolutely green in various aspects but does not pass the customer satisfaction criteria. This will lead to green myopia. Also if the green products are priced very high then again it will lose its market acceptability.

22.12 MARKETING MIX OF GREEN MARKETING

Just as we have 4Ps, *viz.*, product, price, place and promotion in marketing, we have 4Ps in green marketing too, but they are a bit different.

1. **Product:** Products can be made from recycled materials or from used goods. Efficient products not only save water, energy and money, but also reduce harmful effects on the environment. Green chemistry forms the growing focus of product development. For example, Nike is the first among the shoe companies to market itself as green.
2. **Price:** Green pricing takes into consideration the people, planet and profit in a way that takes care of the health of employees and communities and ensures efficient productivity. Value can be added to it by changing its appearance, functionality and through customization, etc. Wal Mart unveiled its first recyclable cloth shopping bag.
3. **Place:** Green place is about managing logistics to cut down on transportation emissions, thereby in effect aiming at reducing the carbon footprint. For example, instead of marketing an imported mango juice in India it can be licensed for local production. This avoids shipping of the product from far away, thus reducing shipping cost and more importantly, the consequent carbon emission by the ships and other modes of transport.
4. **Promotion:** Green promotion involves configuring the tools of promotion, such as advertising, marketing materials, signage, white papers, websites, videos and presentations by keeping people, planet and profits in mind. Indian Tobacco Company has introduced environmental-friendly papers and boards, which are free from elemental chlorine.

22.13 IMPORTANCE OF GREEN MARKETING

Green marketing offers business bottom line incentives and top line growth possibilities. While modification of business or production processes may involve start-up costs, it will save money in the long-term.

For example, the cost of installing solar energy is an investment in future energy cost savings. Companies that develop new and improved products and services with environmental impacts in mind give themselves access to new markets, substantially increase profits and enjoy competitive advantages over those marketing non-environmentally responsible alternatives.

22.14 CONSUMERISM

Consumerism is a social and economic order that encourages the purchase of goods and services in ever-greater amounts. It is the demand that marketers must pay greater attention to consumer desires while making their decisions. It is a protest against malpractices or abuses in the marketing system. It is also viewed as a part of a broader movement sucking increased social responsibility in the various sectors of society.

> *"The organized efforts of consumers seeking redress, restitution and remedy for dissatisfaction they have accumulated in the acquisition of their standard of living."*
>
> **R.H. Bushikirk and J.T. Rothe**

> *"A social movement seeking to augment the rights and powers of buyers in relation to sellers."*
>
> **Philip Kotler**

> *"Consumerism" as both (i) a consumer protests against the perceived injustices in exchange relationships and (ii) efforts to remedy those injustices.* **William D. Stanton**

It can be said from the above definitions that consumerism is a growing social force which makes consumers to be aware of their rights. These rights are protected by:

- Educating the consumers and mobilizing them to fight for their rights,
- Exerting pressure on the government to protect the consumer interests by guaranteeing their legitimate rights and,
- Making the business more honest and responsible.

22.15 CONSUMER MOVEMENT IN INDIA

India has an ancient history of consumer protection. Consumer protection was part of ancient culture and formed the core of its administration. But the introduction of boundless commercialization of activities eclipsed the old rich heritage. As in Europe, India is also the origin of the consumer movement which was in the form of consumer co-operatives.

The co-operative consumer movement was started in 1904 in India. The focus of this movement was only on distribution of goods rather than on the welfare of consumer.

Inspired by the Consumer Rights Bill passed on 15th March, 1962 by then American President John F. Kennedey, it was in April, 1966, nine housewives and social workers got together and formed the Consumer Guidance Society of India (CGSI) in Mumbai, so as to protect the interests of consumers. It conducted tests on various food stuffs for adulteration and consumer products for substandard performance. This society has been successful in getting thousands of complaints redressed on their own.

In 1966, under the able leadership of late J.R.D. Tata and Late Rama Krishna Bajaj some progressive manufacturers and traders came together and formed the Fair Trade Practices Association in then Bombay. The main objects of this association are to modify existing trade practices and to set up an effective machinery for their implementation in an organized way so as to create public confidence in business community. However, all its activities are confined to metropolitan cities and its achievements were not satisfactory.

In 1974, Sri Bindu Madhav Joshi started Akhil Bharatiya Grahak Panchayat in Pune. This organization organized consumer agitations successfully in Maharashtra.

The other associations which are protecting the interest of consumers in India are,

- Consumer Unity and Trust Society – Kolkata (Calcutta)
- Consumer Education Centre – Hyderabad and
- Karnataka Consumer Service Society – Bengaluru (Bangalore)

The second national convention that was held in New Delhi, 1991, gave rise to the formation of Confederation of Indian Consumers Organizations (CICO). Thus, it was for the first time many of the consumer organizations came together to form a National Consumer Organization. Today, it has got members from various states and has mustered enough consumer power to influence the Government to act in favour of consumers. The consumer movement in India is backward due to:

(*a*) Poverty

(*b*) Malnutrition

(*c*) Lack of education

(*d*) Ignorance

(*e*) Poor organization of consumers

(*f*) Poor implementation of laws.

22.16 CONSUMER PROTECTION ACT, 1986

The Consumer Protection Act was passed in 1986 and it came into force from 1st July 1987. The main objectives of the Act are to provide better and all-round protection to consumers and effective safeguards against different types of exploitation such as defective goods, deficient services and unfair trade practices. It also makes provisions for a simple, speedy and inexpensive machinery for redressal of consumers' grievances.

Furthermore, the standard, which is required to be maintained, in services or goods is not to be restricted to the statutory mandate but shall extend to that claimed by the trader, expressly or impliedly, in any manner whatsoever.

The salient features of Consumer Protection Act (CPA) 1986 are as follows:

1. It covers all the sectors whether private, public, and cooperative or any person. The provisions of the Act are compensatory as well as preventive and punitive in nature and the Act applies to all goods covered by sale of goods Act and services unless specifically exempted by the Central Government.
2. It protects the following rights of consumers:
   (*a*) Right to be protected against the marketing of goods and services which are hazardous to life and property;
   (*b*) Right to be informed about the quality, quantity, potency, purity, standard and price of goods or services so as to protect the consumers against unfair trade practices;
   (*c*) Right to be assured, wherever possible, access to a variety of goods and services at competitive prices;
   (*d*) Right to be heard and to be assured that consumers' interests will receive due consideration at the appropriate forum;
   (*e*) Right to seek redressal against unfair trade practices or unscrupulous exploitation of consumers; and
   (*f*) Right to consumer education.
3. The Act also envisages establishment of Consumer Protection Councils at the central, state and district levels, whose main objectives are to promote and protect the rights of consumers.
4. To provide a simple, speedy and inexpensive redressal of consumer grievances, the act envisages a three-tier quasi-judicial machinery at the national, state and district levels. These are: National Consumer Disputes Redressal Commission known as National Commission, State Consumer Disputes Redressal Commissions known as State Commissions and District Consumer Disputes Redressal Forum known as District Forum; and
5. The provisions of this Act are in addition to and not in derogation of the provisions of any other law for the time being in force.

22.17 NEURO MARKETING

Neuro marketing is a new field of marketing research that studies consumers' sensorimotor, cognitive, and affective response to marketing stimuli. It is an emerging field claiming to provide advertisers with better ways to understand what triggers buy buttons in consumers' brains. By adopting methods used by neuroscientists to investigate the neural signature of many consumption behaviours, neuro marketers are promising unparallel levels of success in explaining and predicting the success of TV commercials, movies, print ads, packaging, billboards, and more.

Neuro marketing is a relatively new concept which has developed as a consequence of accepting, by an increasing number of persons, the idea that there is not an objective reality and that the entire world is actually inside our mind, it is the sum of our exclusively subjective perceptions.

The science that studies these aspects at a biological and theoretical level is neurology. Neurology and marketing have recently met in a series of studies resulted out of curiosity and the desire of knowledge leading to the birth of the neuro marketing term.

With the help of neuro marketing one can discover the desires, expectations and hidden restraints of the consumers' options, by transferring the technology of medical imagery, which causes a major change in the relationship of the company and their customers.

REVIEW QUESTIONS

1. What is the meaning of globalization? Explain the characteristics of globalization.
2. What are the factors affecting globalization?
3. What is the globalization of business?
4. What is the major impact of globalization? Explain the impact of globalization on India.
5. What is green marketing? Explain the need of green marketing.
6. Explain the green products and their characteristics.
7. What are the major challenges in green marketing?
8. Explain the marketing mix of green marketing.
9. Explain the importance of green marketing.
10. What is consumerism? Explain the rights of consumer.
11. Explain the consumer movement in India.
12. Explain the various concepts of Consumer Protection Act, 1986.

Index

A

5-Ms, 134
Above-the-line Media, 163
Across the Counter Selling, 172
Advertise Budget, 147
Advertisement, 200
Advertisement Copy, 148
Advertising, 107, 108, 123, 129, 193, 278
Advertising Venue, 143
Agency-Client Relationship, 161
Agricultural Marketing, 266
AIDA Model, 102, 194
Aided Recall, 156
Air Transport, 280
Airline Marketing Mix, 284
All India Radio(AIR), 131
Analytical Marketing System, 278
Ansoff Produc-matrix, 241
Applied Research, 117
Attitude, 48
Attitude Test, 156
Average Fixed Cost(AFC), 95
Average Variable Cost(AVC), 95

B

Bank Marketing, 276
Barabas Formula, 210
Barrier, 105
Base Point Pricing, 100
Basic Research, 117
BCG Matrix, 68
BCX, 281
Behavioural Segmentation, 38
Behavioural Variables, 47
Below-the-line Media, 163
Bengal Gazette, 130
Boston Consulting Group(bcg), 68
Boy, 281
Brand Positioning, 86
Branding, 83
Break-Event Analysis, 95
Broadcast Media, 164
Budgetary Control, 253
Budgeting, 143
Business Analysis, 81
Business and Government, 111
Business Environment, 23, 247
Business-to-Consumer, 291

C

Calcutta General Advertiser, 130
Carrying Cost, 211
Cash Caws, 69
Cash Market, 269
Chain of Middlemen, 267
Channels of Distribution, 220
Classification of Agri-Product, 266
Cognitive Dissonance, 52
Collective Decision-Marketing, 260
Commercialization, 82
Communication Effects, 151
Community Relations, 168
Company Consideration, 224
Competition, 44, 94
Competition-Based Pricing, 97
Competitors, 19
Comprehensive, 254
Concentrated Marketing, 41
Confederation of Indian, 309
Confused Positioning, 43
Consumer Behaviour Models, 53
Consumer Guidance Society of India(CGSI), 309
Consumer Jury, 154
Consumer Protection Act(CPA), 310
Consumer Relations, 168
Consumer Rights Bill, 309
Consumer-to-Consumer, 292

Consumerism, 308
Convenience Goods, 65
Co-Ordination, 7
Corporate Communication, 168
Corporate VMS, 217
Cost, 30, 94
Cost-Based Pricing, 95
Cost Per Point, 167
Cost Plus Pricing, 95
Costumer Lifetime Value (CLV), 294
Credit Control, 253
Critical Success Factors(CSF), 297
CRM Marketing, 298
Culture, 50
Culture Factors, 50
Customary Pricing, 97
Customer-Oriented Marketing Organization, 250
Customer Relationship Management (CRM), 252, 293
Customer Value, 30
Customers, 18

D

DAGMAR Model, 152
Data Collection, 114
Dearness Allowance(DA), 183
Decoding, 105
Demand, 94
Demographic Segmentation, 38
Demographical Variables, 47
Differentiated Marketing , 41
Direct Questioning, 154
Direct Channel, 225
Direct Marketing, 107
Distributed channels, 94, 221
Distribution, 277
Distribution Strategies, 265
Door-to-Door Selling, 172
Durable Goods, 66

E

Ecological, 306
E-commerce, 232, 287
Economic Model, 57
Economic Order Quantity(EOQ), 210
Economic Risk, 48
Economic Situation, 51
Economy Pricing, 99
Employee Communication, 168
Encoding, 104
Enquiry Tests, 157
Entering Goods, 66
Environmental Scanning, 20
E-Product, 290
E-Promotion, 290
Every Day Low Price(EDLP), 99
Exchange Market, 269
Extension Service, 271
Extensive Decision-Making, 49
External Factor, 93

F

Family, 50
Farm Production, 270
Fibre Products, 266
Five Forces Model, 240
Focus Groups, 114
Foodgrain Item, 266
Foundation Goods, 65
Freight on Board(FOB), 100
Functional Organization, 249
Fundamental Research, 117

G

GE—Mckinsey Matrix, 70
General Insurance Corporation(gic), 284
Geographic Segmentation, 37
Geography Territory Marketing Organization, 251
Globalization, 267, 302
Going Rate Pricing, 97
Government Policy, 94
Green Marketmg, 306
Green Revolution, 261
Gross National Product (GNP), 207
Group Training Methods, 181

H

Hill Area Development Programme, 262
Hindustan Thompson Associates, 132
Holding Cost, 210

Horizontal Marketing Systems, (HMS), 218
Horticulture Product, 266
Howard-Sheth Model, 54

I

Idea Generation, 80
Idea Screening, 80
Impulse Buying, 49
Independent, 255
Indirect Channel, 225
Individual Training Method, 181
Industrial Goods, 65
Information Search, 52
Intangible Goods, 66
Integrated Marketing Communication(IMC), 121
Intensive Agricultural District Programme, 262
Internal Risk, 81
Internet, 165
Internal Marketing, 109
Interviews, 114
Institutional Advertising, 138
iPod, 242

J

Jawahar Rojgar Yojna(JRY), 262

K

Kaun Banega Crorepati, 131

L

Land Transport, 280
Large-Scale Retailers, 230
Learning Model, 56
Life Insurance Corporation of India(LIC), 284
Likert Scale, 157
Limited Decision-Making, 49
Line and Staff Organization, 248

M

Macro-Environment, 21
Management by Object(MOB), 186
Marginal Cost Pricing, 95
Marginal Cost(MC), 95
Market Segmentation, 36
Marketing Communication, 101
Market Consideration, 224
Marketing Information System(MIS), 115
Market Logistics, 215
Marketing Mix, 94
Market Position189
Market Research, 109, 110, 143
Market Risk, 81
Market Segments, 41
Market Share Methods, 148
Market Strategy, 81
Marketing, 3, 109, 11
Marketing Audit, 253, 254
Marketing Environment Audit, 255
Marketing Information System, 278
Marketing Management, 6
Marketing Mix, 26, 67
Marketing Myopia, 12
Marketing Objectives, 7
Marketing of Service Banking, 273
Marketing Organization, 246
Matrix Organization, 251
Measurement, 135
Media, 135, 163
Micro-Environment, 20
Middlemen Promotion Techniques, 196
Middlemen Consideration, 224
MIS, 112
Mission, 135
Mock Magazine, 154
Monopoly Pricing, 100
Motivation, 48, 50
Mutual Benefit, 173

N

Need Recognition, 51
Neuro Marketing, 310
Neutral Pricing, 96
New Product, 78
Niche Marketing, 39
Nicosia Model, 55
Noise, 105
Nokia, 43
Non-Durable Goods, 66

O

Objection Handling, 175
Observation, 114
Occupation, 51
One Level Channel, 226
Opinion Leaders, 47
Opinion Seekers, 47
Ordering Cost, 210
Organization, 7
Organizational Factor, 93
Outdoor Media, 164
Over-Positioning, 43

P

Packing, 87
Partner Relationship Management (PRM), 295
Penetration Pricing, 99
People, 29, 276
Perceived Value Pricing, 97
Percentage of Sales Method, 147
Perception, 48, 50
Personal Factors, 51
Personal Risk, 48
Personal Selling, 107, 123, 171, 277
Personality, 48, 51
Phycho-Analytical Model, 57
Physical Distribution, 208
Physical Evidence, 29, 276
Place Mix Strategy, 245
Place Variables, 67
Placing the ad, 143
Planning, 7
Point-of-Sales(POS), 163
Political-Legal Factors, 19
Positioning, 42
Premium Pricing, 99
Prevent Competition, 93
Price, 5, 28, 277
Price Index, 189
Price Stabilization, 93
Price Variables, 67
Pricing, 91, 276
Pricing Mix Strategy, 244
Pricing Policy, 283
Pricing Strategies, 265
Primary Package, 87
Primary Research, 117
Print Media, 164
Producers, 110
Product, 5, 27, 276
Product Advertising, 137
Product Classification, 64
Product Consideration, 223
Product Development, 79, 81
Product Development Process, 79
Product Identification, 82
Product Life Cycle(PLC), 72, 138, 198
Product Line, 67, 68
Product Mix, 66
Product Mix Strategy, 244
Product-Oriented Marketing Organization, 249
Product Strategies, 265
Product Variables, 67
Profit Maximization, 92
Programmed Behaviour, 49
Projective Techniques, 157
Promotion, 5, 28, 276, 277
Promotion Mix, 121
Promotion Mix Strategy, 244
Promotion Policy, 283
Promotion Variables, 67
Psychographic Segmentation, 38
Psychological Factor, 50
Psychological Pricing, 100
Public Relations, 107, 124, 278
Public Service Advertising, 137
Publicity, 124, 199

Q

Qualitative Research, 118
Quantitative Research, 118
Question Marks, 69

R

Ranking Techniques, 157
Ratio Analysis, 254
Recall Test, 156
Recruitment, 178
Reference Groups, 50
Remuneration, 183

Research and Development(R& D), 77
Research Objectives, 113
Resource Mobilization, 93
Retail Markets, 268
Risk Profile, 44
Rural Communication, 261
Rural Marketing, 259

S

Sales Call, 175
Sales Effect, 151
Sales Experiments, 155
Sales Force Estimation, 190
Sales Forecasting, 188
Sales Promotion, 107, 108, 123, 193
Seasonal Demand, 264
Secondary Package, 87
Secondary Research, 118
Sending Persistent Annoying E-Mail(SPAM), 290
Service, 277
Service Advertising, 137
Shopping Goods, 65
Slogan, 150
Small-Scale Retailer, 230
Social Class, 50
Social Risk, 48
Sociological Model, 58
Specialty Goods, 65
Staffing, 7
Storyboard Test, 155
Strategic Marketing Plan, 235
Strategic Marketing Planning, 233
Strategic Risk, 81
Sub-Culture, 50
Surrogate Advertising, 138
Surveys, 114
SWOT, 236, 254
Systematic, 255

T

Tangible Goods, 66
Target Pricing, 95
Task Method, 147
Television Rating Point, 130
Test Marketing, 82
Theatre Test, 155
Three-Level Channel, 227
Time Based Pricing, 100
Time Guidelines, 201
Trademark, 83
Trailer Test, 155
Transit Media, 164
Transit Package, 88
Transport Marketing, 279
Transportation, 209, 212
Two-Level Channel, 226

U

Under Positioning, 43
Undifferentiated Marketing, 41
Unique Selling Propositions (USP) 43
Unit Sales Method, 148
Unsought Goods, 65
Urban to Rural, 260

V

Value-Based Pricing, 97
Value for Money Pricing, 98
Vertical Marketing System(VMS), 216
Vision, 44
Volume Segmentation, 39

W

Warehousing, 211
Water Transport, 280
Wholesale Market, 268
Wholesalers, 227

Z

Zero Level Channel, 226
Zone Pricing, 100